D0800433

*Dialogues
in
Public Art*

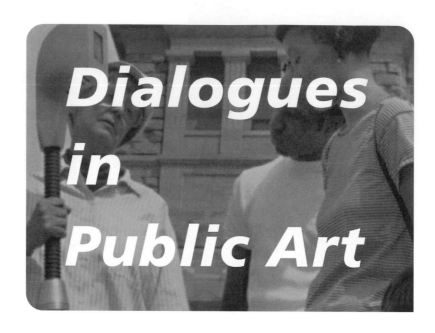

Dialogues in Public Art

The MIT Press · Cambridge, Massachusetts · London, England

Tom Finkelpearl

Interviews with:

Vito Acconci
John Ahearn
David Avalos
Rufus L. Chaney
Mel Chin
Douglas Crimp
Paulo Freire

Andrew Ginzel
Linnea Glatt
Louis Hock
Ron Jensen
Kristin Jones
Maya Lin
Rick Lowe
Jackie McLean
Frank Moore

Jagoda Przybylak
Denise Scott Brown
Assata Shakur
Michael Singer
Elizabeth Sisco
Arthur Symes
Mierle Laderman Ukeles
Robert Venturi
Krzysztof Wodiczko

First MIT Press paperback edition, 2001
©2000 Massachusetts Institute of Technology
All rights reserved. No part of this book may be reproduced in any form by any electronic or
mechanical means (including photocopying, recording, or information storage and retrieval)
without permission in writing from the publisher.

This book was set in Frutiger by Graphic Composition, Inc.

Printed and bound in the United States of America.

Library of Congress Cataloging-in-Publication Data
Finkelpearl, Tom.
  Dialogues in public art : interviews with Vito Acconci, John Ahearn ... / Tom Finkelpearl.
    p. cm.
  Includes bibliographical references and index.
  ISBN 978-0-262-06209-1 (hc. : alk. paper) — 978-0-262-56148-8 (pb. : alk. paper)
  1. Public art—United States. 2. Art, Modern—20th century—United States. 3. Art—
Commissioning—United States. 4. Community art projects—United States. 5. Artists—
United States—Interviews. I. Acconci, Vito, 1940– II. Title.

N8835 .F56 2000
701'.03—dc21
                                                                        99-050079
10 9 8 7 6

This book is dedicated to my immediate family:
Eugenie, Jukie, Mom, Dad, and Ellen
—T.F.

Preface

Dialogues in Public Art tells the story of a selected group of public art projects through interviews with a range of artists, architects, bureaucrats, and others whose lives have been affected by these projects. This book does not set out to be an authoritative text on public art, but raises a set of critical issues from an unusually broad set of perspectives. The book is meant for anyone interested in art outside the walls of the museum: beginners in the field of public art, students, artists, and scholars alike. The book includes the most extensive information yet published on many projects, and these are interesting stories. It is my opinion that public art is the most dynamic field in contemporary artistic practice, but also the most frustrating. My conflicted relationship with public art was the impetus to publish this book. When I was director of the Percent for Art Program in New York City (1990–1996), I felt that very few people outside the immediate communities we were working in knew about most of the projects we completed, and I wanted to get the word out. At the same time, working on this project gave me a bit of a buffer from the disasters. When something went wrong, I could comfort myself by thinking how interesting it might be to include in this book.

Through selected firsthand accounts, *Dialogues in Public Art* chronicles a period in which artists, administrators, and communities have reinvented the field of public art. Since modernism effectively segregated art to the museum context, there was no recent tradition to draw upon when hundreds of Percent for Art laws were enacted across the United States in the 1970s and 1980s. Suddenly, there was a funding source for contemporary art at practically every firehouse, park, library, and government office building in the country, interest in large-scale projects at corporate headquarters, and a number of nonprofit organizations dedicated to sponsoring public art projects. For better or worse, a new professional category had emerged. Quiet successes and well-publicized disasters ensued.

After an introduction that creates an historical context for the current state of affairs, *Dialogues in Public Art* is divided into four sets of interviews: I: Four Controversies in Public Art; II: Four Experiments in Public Art as Architecture and Urban Planning; III: Five Dialogues on Dialogue-based Public Art Projects; and IV: Two Efforts in Public Art for Public Health. Each section includes voices from within and outside the art world.

The interviews in the first part focus on four projects that met with significant controversy: Richard Serra's *Tilted Arc,* John Ahearn's three bronzes in the South Bronx, Maya Lin's *Vietnam Veterans Memorial,* and *Welcome to America's Finest Tourist Plantation* by David Avalos, Louis Hock, and Elizabeth Sisco. Controversies led to the removal of Serra's *Tilted Arc* and Ahearn's bronzes, while bureaucratic intervention threatened the installation of Lin's memorial and led to the installation of a second, realist sculpture on the site. Avalos, Hock, and Sisco, on the other hand, planned for and welcomed controversy as a part of their project. Although these projects have been extensively documented, this book adds new perspectives to each, in a series of five interviews. Douglas Crimp, one of Richard Serra's greatest supporters at the time, reflects upon the *Tilted Arc* controversy and what has changed in the decade since the *Arc*'s removal. John Ahearn describes the process that led him to request that his Bronzes be removed from their site in the South Bronx, while Arthur Symes, a vocal opponent of the sculptures, discusses why he found the work so offensive. Maya Lin discusses her memorial in the context of her practice as an artist, and her insistence upon placing it in the context of her landscape projects sheds new light on the nature of the project and its relationship with its audience. Avalos, Hock, and Sisco describe how they used the bus poster they designed as a catalyst for public discussion of the role of undocumented workers in San Diego's tourist economy.

The second series of interviews, Four Experiments in Public Art as Architecture and Urban Planning, discusses one of the directions that public art took in the wake of the controversies like that encountered by Serra—use-oriented work that moves away from traditional definitions of art and toward landscape design, architecture, and planning. The section begins with an interview with architects Denise Scott Brown and Robert Venturi, in which they discuss their uneasiness with the imposition of art in the public design process. Sculptor Vito Acconci speaks of how he has managed to infiltrate architectural design in his artistic practice. Michael Singer and Linnea Glatt discuss their design of the Solid Waste Management Facility in Phoenix, Arizona, while Ron Jensen, the former Director of Public Works for Phoenix, discusses the process that led to hiring two artists with little architectural background to be the lead designers on a multimillion dollar facility. The Solid Waste Management Facility is one of the few instances where the design and planning decisions in a public building were made by artists. Finally, Rick Lowe and Assata Shakur tell the story of Project Row Houses, an art project that transformed twenty-two derelict shotgun-style houses into a contemporary art exhibition space, housing for single mothers, and a community center. Rick Lowe is an artist whose work moved from the realm of architectural sculpture to urban design, while Assata Shakur is a former resident in Project Row Houses' Young Mothers Residential Program, and currently a graduate student in sociology at Penn State University.

The third series of interviews, Five Dialogues on Dialogue-based Public Art Projects, focuses on public art that makes dialogue an essential element of the work itself. Although it is clear that artworks like *Tilted Arc* created a tremendous amount of public discussion, and the bus poster project in San Diego was designed to provoke dialogue, the projects in this section were created through a deliberate process of collaboration and dialogue. The first interview is with Paulo Freire, the late philosopher, activist, and educational theorist from São Paulo, Brazil. Freire talks about the structure of dialogue and the uses of art to promote critical consciousness. Mierle Ukeles discusses her longstanding collaboration with the New York City Department of Sanitation. Jagoda Przybylak and Krzysztof Wodiczko separately discuss the *Alien Staff,* an instrument for the presentation of issues related to immigration and alienation in the city. Kristin Jones and Andrew Ginzel discuss their work *Mnemonics* (literally a memory device) in which they invited hundreds of people from Stuyvesant High School in New York City to donate personal mementos to be built into a new school building.

The final section, "Two Efforts in Public Art and Public Health," focuses on *Revival Fields* and the AIDS Ribbon. Artist Mel Chin and Dr. Rufus Chaney of the United States Department of Agriculture separately discuss *Revival Field,* an art and science collaboration that seeks to cleanse toxic waste sites using "green remediation." The book concludes with two interviews about the AIDS Ribbon: Artist Frank Moore discusses how he helped initiate the ribbon, and Jackie McLean describes how she worked on the production of the ribbon at a women's shelter while a member of the Artist and Homeless Collaborative.

In this book, when I use the term "public art," I am relying on an understanding of common usage. Public art is often sponsored by public agencies, usually exists outside museums and galleries, and addresses audiences outside the confines of the art world. But I do not want to define the words or the field. I will say that the word "public" is associated with the lower classes (public school, public transportation, public housing, public park, public assistance, public defender) as opposed to the word "private," which is associated with privilege (private school, private car, private home, private country club, private fortune, private attorney). Art is generally associated with the upper classes, at least in terms of those who consume it—collectors and museum audiences. Many of the projects in this book explicitly or implicitly address the class contradictions inherent in the term "public art" by bringing different sorts of people into contact in creative ways. Art is a potent tool for communication, and the communication can cross all sorts of boundaries. Another problematic word used throughout the book is "community." While community literally means a group of people who live in the same locale or share a common interest, it too has class overtones. For example, a typical usage appeared in an article on developing new audiences in which the author contrasted the Walker Art Center's "elitist" past with its new interest in "community partnering."[1] What was meant by "community" in this context was people of color, the new ethnic communities in the Minneapolis/St. Paul area that the museum wished to include in its audience. The category of well-heeled art lovers does not qualify as a "community" in this sense—art created for insiders in the art world is never referred to as community art. So, when one refers to community-oriented public art, the terms are loaded, but the usage is fairly clear: it is art that includes people from the lower classes in its creation, consumption, or both. This does not mean that the upper classes are excluded from participating in the projects as well, only that they are not the exclusive audience.

The participants in these interviews have had a fair degree of control over the final product. After each interview was transcribed and a draft prepared, the participants had an opportunity to make changes. Sometimes this was a quick and simple process. In others cases it required four or five more drafts, and additional interview sessions. In an effort to be faithful to the content of the discussion that took place, I have resisted the temptation to edit the interviews too radically. There are sections of interviews in this book that may not seem immediately relevant to the question at hand, but they are included because they are important to the person who was interviewed, and relevant to his or her work as an artist, administrator, collaborator, or consumer of public art.

In general, I have sought to use photographs that include people, to suggest the sorts of interactions that the projects created and for scale. However, even in the case of public art projects it is difficult to find populated photographs. It is my feeling that this reflects the modernist notion of the autonomy of the art object (which I will discuss in the introduction). Even the captions point out differences between public and museum art. A typical caption for a painting includes the artist, date, dimensions, materials, and the collection that owns it. As with other public art books, I have included artist, date, location, and commissioning agency. How a public artwork comes into existence is a very important part of its meaning. In researching this book, I have visited sites in Arizona, California, Connecticut, Georgia, Massachusetts, Minnesota, Missouri, Ohio, Oregon, Pennsylvania, Texas, Washington, D.C., and Washington State. However, for public art, it is not really sufficient to visit the site of a completed project. Understanding the broader context is essential—from the origins of the project, to its commissioning process, to the ongoing public response. For this reason, the projects featured in this book are by artists whose work I have been following closely for the last ten to fifteen years. This has limited my scope to artists in the United States, with a slant toward artists from the East Coast, particularly New York. I have also tried to steer clear of projects that have been discussed at length in other books on public art (with the almost unavoidable exception of the works in the section on public art controversies). I regret there are so many important projects that I have not addressed, particularly in California and in the northwest, but I must write about what I know best.

Note

1. Phil Anderson, "Developing New Audiences with Community Collaborators," in *1998 Field Guide,* National Association of Artists Organizations, Washington, D.C., 1998, p. 30.

Acknowledgments

First and foremost, I want to thank Eugenie Tsai, my wife, for her patience and support as I spent an inordinate amount of time over several years getting this project together. Second, I want to thank all of the interviewees in this book. In many cases, the interviews that appear here were the result of a tremendous amount of work on their part. Thanks to Roger Conover at the MIT Press for his encouragement throughout the lengthy process of completing this project. We have been discussing this book for years. It has been a pleasure working with everyone at MIT Press. Julie Grimaldi was always encouraging and responsive. Melissa Vaughn had very helpful editorial suggestions. Mary Jane Higgins did wonders copyediting the manuscript. Ori Kometani's design is in perfect harmony with the content of the book. Angela Kramer Murphy assisted greatly, from her thorough and intelligent research, to obtaining photographs, to helping urge the interviewees to hand in their final edits. Elizabeth Lenas and Rachel Schuder did great work transcribing the sometimes lengthy taped interviews. Their understanding of the topics discussed made my editing job much easier. Parts of the introduction were originally published in the catalogue of "Uncommon Sense" at the Museum of Contemporary Art, Los Angeles. Thanks to the museum for permitting the material to be reprinted here. Finally, I would like to thank my employers during the course of the project: The New York City Department of Cultural Affairs, and the Skowhegan School of Painting and Sculpture. Without their flexibility, this book would not have come about.

**Dialogues
in
Public Art**

Introduction: *The City as Site*

I have a very clear memory of a warm night late in the summer of 1985. Having come to "Art on the Beach," an outdoor venue on a landfill in Lower Manhattan, I sat with a couple of hundred other people on the sand listening to Sun Ra and his Solar Arkestra. The concert was set before an architectural environment called *Delta Spirit House* created by David Hammons, Jerry Barr, and Angela Valerio. The backdrop was perfect for Sun Ra: a beautifully designed shack painstakingly constructed with materials scavenged from the streets of New York. And the audience was the sort of mixture one hopes for in New York—people from the downtown art world, friends of Hammons, Barr, and Valerio from the Lower East Side, Brooklyn, and Harlem, and jazz enthusiasts from all over the city. The racial and economic mix was significant, but everyone was casual and relaxed. As the sun set, Sun Ra revealed to us that he was from the moon, chanting, "Space is the place." We were transported, but content in the very immediate surroundings of the Hudson River, the traffic on the West Side, the grandiose scale of the Lower Manhattan business district, and the intense artistic and musical invention before us. But this was one of the last moments of "Art on the Beach," and the place where we sat listening that evening is now a part of Battery Park City, a luxury neighborhood synonymous with the 1980s' version of urban development and public art in the United States. In a review in *Artforum,* critic Patricia Phillips lamented the end of "Art on the Beach" and the encroachment of the developers' bulldozers:

In the final installation of Creative Time's "Art on the Beach," there was a significant sense of timely conclusion; the situation was not unlike that of a professional athlete or musician who, in deciding when to retire, must balance personal goals—perhaps unfulfilled—with the desire to go out on top, with dignity. . . . The condition of the landfill site was the most poignant indication of the finale. Bulldozers had shaped a large plateau in the center of the site, leaving a depressed corridor around the edge where most of the installations were built. A cyclone fence had been erected along the southern and western edges, obstructing access to the Hudson River. The encroachment of Battery Park City Authority development was imminent.[1]

At the time, the transformations that were about to take place on the site still seemed unreal to me. After all, Creative Time[2] had been presenting "Art on the Beach" for exactly the six years I had been in New York, and it was an art world institution. The World Financial Center had just opened, and its polished brass and granite seemed

Left: Sun Ra concert in front of Delta Spirit House by David Hammons, Jerry Barr, and Angela Valerio, 1985, Creative Time's "Art on the Beach," New York, New York. Photograph: Lawrence I. Lesman, courtesy of Creative Time.

Right: Battery Park City (on right), New York, New York, as seen from the World Trade Center in 1998.

like a vision of everything the 1980s stood for, but it was not until "they" closed down "Art on the Beach" that I began to think more seriously about the relationship of art to the city, and who "they" were. When I had built an installation on the landfill in the summer of 1985, I was, perhaps, in a partnership with the developers who were in a holding pattern as they got their money together to build on the site. As an artist, I had helped keep the site active, helped attract people to the landfill. When the Authority was ready to build, out went "Art on the Beach" and its temporary experimental feel, and in came a set of luxurious apartments and suitably high-priced permanent art installations spread throughout the development. I began to consider the role that art was asked to play in the development of the city. When I walk through Battery Park City today, I still think of the evening when I heard Sun Ra. I think of the modesty and originality of the architecture of *Delta Spirit House,* as well as the social and racial diversity of the crowd who had come to the concert. And I wish that the Battery Park City Authority could have seen the potential in that moment. In fact, as Rosalyn Deutsche has pointed out, they did everything they could to ensure a lack of economic diversity among the residents of their development. On the insistence of the Authority (with the acceptance of the state), *all* of the subsidized housing units were eliminated from the site. In 1999, Battery Park City's Web site proudly proclaims this victory with the following timeline entry, "1986: New York Legislature passed, and Governor signed, legislation which allowed Battery Park City's excess revenue to be used for low- and moderate-income housing in the Bronx and Harlem."[3] After "Art on the Beach" ended, Sun Ra's audience was not invited to live together on the site. This course of events places Battery Park City squarely within the mainstream postwar urban development in the United States.

The history of public art is most often told with an emphasis on the word "art," and very little consideration of the public context. Writers discuss the sequence of artistic development, usually paying no more than lip service to the development of the twentieth-century city, or modern art's relationship with those developments. To contextualize the projects discussed in this book, it is necessary to look back to the transformations in the American city after World War II. This essay is not meant to be an exhaustive analysis of postwar urbanism. Rather, I want to set up a very basic dialectic between top-down, "pro-growth" development initiated by or for business elites, and grassroots, "community-oriented" development initiated by or for people outside the traditional mainstream of power in the United States. In one way or another, the art projects discussed in the interviews (with the possible exception of Richard Serra's *Tilted Arc*) relate more closely to the second sort of urban development—toward sharing power rather than imposing solutions, toward healing wounds inflicted by the fragmentation and social segregation of contemporary public space.

When World War II ended, veterans returned to a new American Dream. The good life required owning a car and a home of one's own. "Moving up" meant moving out of the city. Expressways were built at a feverish rate as population in the suburbs increased by 45 percent in the 1950s.[4] Between 1945 and 1965, the registration of automobiles nearly tripled.[5] Highways became a new focus for Americans. Where mass transit had accounted for more than one-third of passenger miles in 1945, its share had dwindled to 5 percent by 1965. The white middle class got off the subway, into their cars, and out of the cities.[6] The space people sought in postwar America was increasingly private, from their homes to their mode of transport. In abandoning the street for the highway, the subway for the car, and the city for the suburbs, Americans lost everyday sites for social interaction. Where a street is a confusing melange of activities—a social scene, a place for commerce, a site for transit—the highway has a single use, the transportation of people from one place to another. The individual driver in a private car, on the way to a private home, is independent and isolated.

And highways are not only lines of transit; they can also create lines of division. It is well documented how highways tore the heart out of neighborhoods during this period of reckless construction. In his book *The Power Broker,* Robert Caro relates how Robert Moses brazenly plowed highways through neighborhoods. One of the most egregious examples was the Cross Bronx Expressway that was constructed without the least concern for the lives of the thousands of people it would displace. At one famous juncture, a well-organized community group suggested a slight alteration of the route of the highway that would have saved 1,530 apartments from demolition, tearing down 6 instead of 159 buildings over the stretch of a mile. Starting when they received eviction notices in 1952, a neighborhood group led by a housewife named Lillian Edelstein fought the demolition of their homes along this stretch. After a fierce battle, Moses prevailed and the highway went through as originally planned. Many people trace the downward spiral of the Tremont section of the Bronx to the construction of the Cross Bronx Expressway.[7] The "success" of this highway was repeated in cities across the United States, displacing millions of low-income tenants with little thought of where they might move. The narrative of urban renewal often seems to have pitted women like Edelstein against male master planners like Moses.

The goal of highways like the Cross Bronx Expressway may have been to make the city more efficient, but the result was a quicker exit; the cities' loss was the suburbs' gain. Of course, highways did not completely empty the cities. They simply created an escape route for those who were allowed to use it. Systematically excluded from many suburbs, African Americans found themselves in cities of diminishing resources.

Among the most famous developers during the postwar period were the Levitt brothers, who built "Levittowns" on Long Island and outside of Philadelphia. Rows of nearly identical homes on identical lots were differentiated only by variations in exterior trim. As fast as these houses were built, they were inhabited, largely by veterans and their families. While Jews, Irish people, and Italians were welcome in these instant suburbs, African Americans were not. In fact, the contract signed by each new homeowner in Long Island's Levittown included a clause that read: "No dwelling shall be used or occupied by members of other than the Caucasian race."[8] This was not exceptional. In his classic study of the suburbanization of the United States, Kenneth Jackson traces the roots of suburban segregation, and argues that the Federal Housing Administration (FHA) played a significant role. Not simply turning a blind eye to racial prejudice, this New Deal agency actually initiated the practice of "red lining" certain areas that would not qualify for federal loan guarantees, and racial division was an essential criterion in this practice.[9] The FHA, which was augmented by the Veterans Administration after the war, was a major contributor to the suburbanization of the United States. Jackson says:

FHA helped to turn the building industry against the minority and inner city housing market, and its policies supported the income and racial segregation of suburbia. For perhaps the first time, the federal government embraced discriminatory attitudes of the marketplace. Previously, prejudices were personalized and individualized; FHA exhorted segregation and enshrined it as public policy. Whole areas of cities were declared ineligible for loan guarantees.[10]

Developers, banks, real estate agents, the federal government, and community groups made sure that the suburbs remained white. And, as feminist critics have pointed out, the social and physical architecture of the suburbs created a prescribed role for women. Where the war effort had expanded the options of women in the workforce in the 1940s, the suburbs rigidified their domestic roles in the 1950s. No longer "Rosie the Riveter," the new American woman was a housewife in the 'burbs. As Dolores Hayden has argued, the national priority of employing veterans after the war meant removing women from the workforce.[11] There were several types of segregation in the suburbanization of the United States: The segregation of the increasingly black cities from the white suburbs, the segregation, for men, of the business day in the city and the domestic evening at home in suburbia, and the gender segregation of the breadwinning husband and the stay-at-home wife.

The banality of these suburbs was attacked vehemently by architects at the time. Of course, architects were effectively shut out of the design of these homes, and

Public Housing in lower Manhattan, New York, 1998.

their attacks were generally more aesthetic than social. After the war, architecture was dominated by High Modernist thought, particularly the design and theories of Le Corbusier, the Swiss-born Parisian. An essential force in the creation of Modernist architecture (a.k.a. the International Style), his radical vision had become commonplace by the 1950s. Since the 1930s, architecture and planning schools in the United States had been dominated by his followers. As Lewis Mumford said, the appeal of Le Corbusier was that he

. . . brought together the two architectural conceptions that separately dominated the modern movement: machine-made environment, standardized, bureaucratized, "processed," technically perfected to the last degree; and to offset this the natural environment, treated as so much visual open space, providing sunlight, pure air, green foliage, and views. [12]

The result of this synthesis was the vertical garden city—monolithic high-rise buildings with green areas between. Le Corbusier's notion was to bulldoze the old city in favor of a clean, logical, well-engineered vision of the future. Following Le Corbusier's exhortation, "WE MUST BUILD IN THE OPEN,"[13] architects sought to create open space around their buildings, be they high-rise office towers on plazas, or high-rise housing built off the street, surrounded by green space.

Le Corbusier's imagination was not limited to the drawing board, or even the design of specific buildings, but bore fruit in a new conception of urban life. His proposal for a city of 3 million people (1922) was the High Modernist utopia, and one outstanding aspect was a clear separation of elements—separation of buildings from one another, separation of housing and manufacturing, separation of pedestrian and motor vehicle traffic, and so on. For example, Le Corbusier argued that, in his ideal design, "The river flows far away from the city. The river is a kind of liquid railway, a goods station and sorting house. In a decent house the servants' stairs do not go through the drawing room—even if the maid is charming (or if the little boats delight the loiterer leaning on a bridge)."[14] Advocating the separation of the city from its traditional life blood, the river, Le Corbusier's condescending reference to the "little boats" reveals a tremendous arrogance, but he had no place for sentimentality. And, in an odd metaphor for a socialist, Le Corbusier points to the advantages of the separation of the classes, "even if the maid is charming."

In 1958, one of the most significant modernist buildings in America was completed. The Seagram Building, designed by Ludwig Mies van der Rohe and Philip Johnson, created a sensation in New York City. Stark and elegant, it was set back from the street on Park Avenue, providing a rare public plaza. From newspaper reports at the time, this space was well used by the office workers in the area. One reporter wrote:

A half-acre plaza in front of the new thirty-eight story Seagram Building on Park Avenue has become an oasis for office workers and passers-by. The plaza is 100 feet deep and a full blockfront wide, between Fifty-second and Fifty-third Streets. It was designed by Mies Van Der Rohe, principal architect of the bronze skyscraper, to provide a spacious setting for the building and give a little breathing space to pedestrians. He feels they are too often hemmed in by towering buildings. [15]

It is important to remember how unusual this plaza was at the time. If one walks up Park Avenue from Fiftieth to Sixtieth Street today, it is still possible to see how this modest plaza came as a relief, and in looking at photographs from the late 1950s, you can understand how exciting and modern the design must have felt. But from a con-

Ludwig Mies van der Rohe and Philip Johnson, Seagram Building, 1956–1958, New York, New York. Photograph: Ezra Stoller, © ESTO, courtesy of Joseph E. Seagram & Sons, Inc.

temporary perspective, it seems that the commentators in 1958 were suffering from urban claustrophobia. They consistently repeated terms of derision for the city like "hemmed in," "airless," and "dark"—hardly phrases that come to mind today in describing Park Avenue. Whatever one feels about the Seagram Building, its popular success led to the so-called Plaza Law of 1961, New York City's first incentive zoning device. The device was simple: Developers could build larger structures with a higher "floor area ratio" if they provided a plaza or arcade—to produce public spaces like those at the Seagram Building or Lever House across the street.[16] The 1961 changes in the zoning laws of New York City encouraged developers to construct high-rise buildings on small footprints, creating a series of open plazas. When it was passed, the *New York Times* called the plaza law a "tremendous victory in the cause of building a better city of the future."[17] It is interesting to note the terms in which the debate over the law took place. A *New York Times* article in 1959 hailing the proposed zoning law began thus:

There is an old New York story of an Irishman who returned to his former neighborhood and found no one he knew. "Where are the Irish?" he asked a Jewish man. The answer was another question, "Where are all the Indians?" The zoning resolution made public today won't bring back the Indians—not at today's prices. In time, though, it might open the way for a return to New York City of some of the nomads from the suburbs.[18]

This period piece (set at the time when Jews were replacing Irish people in New York neighborhoods) expresses a clear motivation of the zoning law: creating a city that is appealing to those who had left for the suburbs. The thirst for open space, away from crowding was a sign of the times, just as the move to the suburbs had been.

As crime grew in the 1960s, 1970s, and 1980s, the public spaces created by the Plaza Law became increasingly regulated—including the construction of illegal fences and spikes expressly intended to prevent sleeping or sitting.[19] By the 1980s, the value of these zoning laws was in question; the incentive was reduced in many areas and eliminated in others.[20] Laws of this nature have proven to be particularly problematic in historic districts where they are seen as precluding contextual design.[21]

By the early 1960s, modern architecture's hold on public design was such that there was little regard for historically significant buildings. An egregious example was the demolition of McKim, Mead, and White's Pennsylvania Station in New York in 1964, making way for a modern structure that is now universally despised. While the old Penn Station boasted a grand waiting room 800 feet long, with Corinthian columns and a 150-foot-high vaulted ceiling, the new version fit the term "men's room modern." The demolition of Penn Station led directly to the establishment of the Landmarks Preservation Commission in New York City, but the immediate result was an interest in saving the city's great landmarks, not the fabric of the city.[22] In fact, even in Le Corbusier's most extreme plans, he sought to preserve the gems of the past, while bulldozing the city as a whole. In a postmodern irony, thirty years after its demolition, the architecture of the old Penn Station has reappeared on the site in a permanent public artwork called *Ghost* (1993–1994) by Andrew Leicester. Now, as you walk to the Long Island Railroad trains, you pass by low-relief recreations of fallen columns from the grand classical building that once stood on the site. Plans are now under way to move Penn Station to the vast Post Office building across the street, to recapture the grandeur that was lost in the creation of the efficient Modernist building.

Though African Americans were excluded from many suburbs during the postwar period, they too were in transit. Millions of African Americans moved from the South to the North during the 1940s and 1950s. Escaping Jim Crow, they sought better-paying factory jobs in the northern industrial cities. For example, while the white population of Chicago declined 13 percent from 1950 to 1960, the black population increased by 65 percent. There were nine race riots in Chicago during this period—nervous whites reacting violently to the threat of black encroachment.[23]

In the 1950s, profound contradictions characterized urban policy in the United States. On the one hand, federal government-supported initiatives like massive highway projects contributed to the suburbanization of the United States, draining resources from the cities. On the other hand, "urban blight," and the abandonment of the city became a national concern. Planners and bureaucrats across the country embarked on vast "urban renewal" projects, which meant bulldozing the old city in favor of a cleaner replacement, with an emphasis on bulldozing. Between 1949 and 1968, 300,000 more units of low-income housing (mostly in minority communities) were demolished for redevelopment than were built.[24] It is hard to say whether it would have been better or worse if more units had been replaced. The low-income units constructed under urban renewal programs were generally gigantic high-rise projects designed in the stripped-down Modernist style of the day. These were what Colin Rowe and Fred Koetter call the cut-price, bureaucratic rendition of Le Corbusier's vision.[25]

The archetypal housing project, the urban mirror of suburban Levittown, was Pruitt-Igoe in St. Louis. When it was designed in the early 1950s, Pruitt-Igoe was meant to "save not only people but money."[26] In reality, it wasted both. At the time of its construction, *Architectural Forum* hailed it as a project that would "cut two big sections out of the collar of slums which is threatening to strangle the downtown business section."[27] One money-saving innovation was elevators that only stopped on every third floor. At each elevator lobby was a "gallery" where children could play while their mothers did the laundry. The notion was to create vertical "neighborhoods," because the tenants were coming from (razed) communities that were 90 percent single houses.[28] But these galleries were barren abstractions of the communities that were destroyed. People were transported from "blight" of the street into the geometry of the International Style. Because of the height of the buildings and the space-saving innovations at Pruitt-Igoe, there was a "river" of open space that made its way through the project, just the sort of green relief that Le Corbusier and his followers advocated.

In 1965, little more than a decade after the completion of Pruitt-Igoe, another article appeared in *Architectural Forum* under the headline, "The Case History of Failure."[29] The occasion of the new article was the renovation of the housing project. Even at a time in which St. Louis was suffering from a shortage of low-cost housing, people were avoiding Pruitt-Igoe; it was one-third empty.[30] By all accounts it was an unsafe and unpleasant place to live. The "galleries" were a convenient site for crime, referred to as "gauntlets" by the tenants. Children did play there, but their games were too loud and rough for the scale of the galleries—outdoor play in an indoor setting. Three children had fallen from the galleries. The open space, such a high priority in the project's early conception, that river of green, was strewn with broken glass and trash.[31] In the 1965 *Architectural Forum* article, there was some hand-wringing by the original architect from Hellmuth, Yamasaki, and Leinweber, but the Housing Authority had hired the same firm to oversee the project's renovation. It is interesting to note that when the project was being designed, the architects and critics had no reservations with the notion of "architectural determinism"—the idea that the physical space would create a social environment and "save lives" of slum dwellers. When the project failed, a whole spectrum of social problems, along with the architecture, was blamed.

But Pruitt-Igoe was no longer only a housing complex; it was a symbol. When a crime was committed in the part of St. Louis near the project, it was referred to by the newspapers as a "Pruitt-Igoe crime," which meant that the perpetrator was African American.[32] The projects, designed to clean up the city, were now a racist symbol of urban chaos. As early as 1957, Catherine Bauer, a great advocate of public housing for decades, argued that the monotonous standardization of the projects made them look harshly institutional, and demeaned the tenants with the stigma of charity.[33]

As Kenneth Jackson points out, the concentration of public housing in the inner city was not typical of the European or British postwar reconstruction. There, government housing projects were built where land was least expensive, often in the suburbs rather than in the city. This rarely happened in the United States for two reasons. First, to qualify for federal housing funds, a local municipality had to set up its own housing agencies—a step suburban communities invariably failed to take. Second, there was a requirement that one slum unit be eliminated for every unit of public housing that was built. Therefore, only areas that had slums were eligible for federal funding.[34] Jackson says:

However confused the situation appears, however much government officials argue that Washington programs have been consistently motivated by the desire to produce social benefit for all income groups, the basic direction of federal policies toward housing has been the concentration of the poor in the central city and the dispersal of the affluent to the suburbs. American housing policy was not only devoid of social objectives, but instead helped establish the basis for social inequities. Uncle Sam was not impartial, but instead contributed to the general disbenefit of the cities and to the general prosperity of the suburbs. [35]

As Pruitt-Igoe was built, abstract expressionism was becoming a high-end commodity item in the world of painting. Individually designed Modernist homes were also stylish, but in the world of real estate, Modernist *standardization* was strictly low-end. By 1968, The National Commission on Urban Problems concluded that housing projects of this sort were "anticommunity," and blamed the architects who advocated high-rise housing. Other late 1960s reports came to the same conclusion and advocated scattering small-scale contextual projects through the cities.[36] Pruitt-Igoe, born of the rubble of bulldozed neighborhoods, was imploded in 1972. I remember watching it on television. A great nightmare of bureaucratic Modernism was reduced to dust, and, as Kate Nesbitt has written, "The dramatic, intentional bombing of this work of modern architecture (which had been widely celebrated at its opening) was a clear wake-up call to the profession."[37]

And where were the artists while all of this was happening in the city? Just as High Modernism held sway in the architectural and planning community, it was dominant in the artistic community. And High Modernism segregated art to an "autonomous" aesthetic realm. In his famous essay, "Towards a Newer Laocoön" (1940), Clement Greenberg articulated his vision of Modernist art, arguing that painting, first and foremost, addresses issues that are inherent in painting. Greenberg's position has had tremendous influence either overtly or covertly on how most of us think about aesthetics. Greenberg wrote:

. . . the avant-garde arts have in the last fifty years achieved a purity and radical delimitation of their fields of activity for which there is no previous example in the history of culture. The arts lie safe now, each within its "legitimate" boundaries, and free trade has been replaced by autarchy [self-rule]. Purity in art consists in the acceptance, willing acceptance, of the limitations of the medium of the specific art . . . The arts, then have been hunted back to their mediums, and they have been isolated, concentrated, and defined. It is by virtue of its medium that each art is unique and strictly itself.[38]

As Thomas Crow points out, this early formulation of Greenberg's critical position sounds reluctant if not regretful[39]—it is only out of necessity that the arts have been "hunted back to their mediums." While conservative critics like Hilton Kramer are the most ardent protectors of this position today, it seems relevant to note that Greenberg was coming from a leftist, if not Marxist perspective,[40] and that the project of Modernism has generally been considered progressive; Le Corbusier was a socialist as well. But what is important is how these two influential men embraced the notion of purity and division.[41]

As time progressed, Greenberg became a champion of aesthetic purity, and his articulation has been tremendously influential. As a lecturer on public art, I have found that people are often exasperated with any discussion of art that is not "pure." How often have I heard some version of the complaint, "Why can't we just concentrate on the *art* of these projects instead of worrying about politics or history?" "Art" in this context means aesthetics divorced from social context. Of course, there are many "Modernisms," including a strain that has sought to "integrate art and life"— from Courbet, to Duchamp, to Pop art. Perhaps this strain could be called "low Modernism." In this essay, I am referring to the High Modernism of Clement Greenberg's later writings, Le Corbusier's urban planning, etc.

Whatever critical dialogue may have emerged, it seems clear that an institution has developed to protect the "purity" of the art object from those external forces that might pollute its autonomy: the modern art museum. In the long view, the history of art is the history of public art. Although the pyramids and cathedrals may seem like museums today, this was not the case at the time of their creation. There were no museums in the middle ages. What would have been in them? Art had a specific site and use. To remove the art from its site would have been a sacrilege—literally. The development of the museum is a symptom of the same sort of ideology that Greenberg articulated. In the last 100 years for the first time, artists have been making art for museums, places where art can be "strictly itself." In his essay, "Healing in Time," Michael Brenson argues that Modernist artists have consistently set out to heal the divisions of the modern world. He would certainly take issue with the notion that Greenbergian isolation has been the dominant concern of Modernist artists. However, Brenson concludes that despite their intention to address and counteract the traumas of the modern world, the fate of these artists' creations has been compromised by context:

The healing power of images now seems limited. Most of the responses of modernist painting and sculpture to dislocation, displacement, and injustice —and to the denial and defensiveness of institutional thinking—found their homes in living rooms, galleries, and museums. The museums with which modernist painting is identified are now establishment institutions whose curatorial decisions inevitably defend the social and economic interests of their well-heeled and mostly white corporate boards of trustees. The increasing isolation of modernist painting and sculpture from the texture of the world in which they were created has reinforced the view that Modernism is now itself both a symptom and a victim of the fragmentation and divisiveness many modernist artists tried, in their own way to heal.[42]

But High Modernism has also had potent critics even as it held sway as the dominant ideology. In 1961, Clement Greenberg confidently wrote "Modernist Painting," a concise reiteration of the ideas he had formed two decades earlier, now stated in terms of the triumph of Modernism. By this time his power in the art world was immense. That same year, however, an ambitious attack on Modernist urbanism was mounted by Jane Jacobs in *The Death and Life of Great American Cities.* Jacobs championed the interactions that take place on the traditional urban street. She wrote:

Le Corbusier was planning not only a physical environment. He was planning for a social Utopia too. Le Corbusier's Utopia was a condition of what he called maximum individual liberty, by which he seems to have meant not liberty to do anything much, but liberty from ordinary responsibility. In his Radiant City nobody, presumably, was going to have to be his brother's keeper any more. Nobody was going to have to struggle with plans of his own. Nobody was going to be tied down.[43]

Jacobs sees Le Corbusier's utopia as a hell of division and isolation; the freedom of Le Corbusier's Modernism is freedom *from* others. Jacobs contrasts this with the "freedom of the city" that she sees in more traditional urban spaces, a complex order of intricate interplay. It is an order composed of "movement and change"—what she calls the "art of the city." Outside the rigid geometric order of the Modernist city, individuals take part in an "urban ballet," in which each understands his or her part but is able to improvise in relation to the others.[44]

Jacobs also had some angry words to describe the sort of open space that Le Corbusier's followers championed, from Seagram's plaza to the river of green at Pruitt-Igoe:

In New York's East Harlem there is a housing project with a conspicuous rectangular lawn which became an object of hatred to the project tenants. A social worker frequently at the project was astonished by how often the subject of the lawn came up, usually gratuitously as far as she could see, and how much the tenants despised it and urged that it be done away with. When she asked why, the usual answer was, "What good is it?" Or "Who wants it?" Finally one day a tenant more articulate than the others made this pronouncement: "Nobody cared what we wanted when they built this place. They threw our houses down and pushed our friends somewhere else. We don't have a place around here to get a cup of coffee or a newspaper even, or borrow fifty cents. Nobody cared what we need. But the big men come and look at the grass and say, 'Isn't it wonderful! Now the poor have everything!'"

This tenant was saying what moralists have said for thousands of years: Handsome is as handsome does. All that glitters is not gold.

She was saying more: There is a quality even meaner than outright ugliness or dis-order, and this meaner quality is the dishonest mask of pretended order, achieved by ig-noring or suppressing the real order that is struggling to exist and be served.[45]

Jacobs attacked Modernist urbanism's oppressive order. Pitting the traditional street, as exemplified by her own Greenwich Village neighborhood, against the clean designs of the city-planning establishment, she extolled the value of the interconnection that develops through repeated casual interaction. She argued against the value of the precious green space and light-at-any-expense sought by Modernist designers, and this was profoundly anti-institutional at the time. Remember that *The Death and Life of Great American Cities* was written the same year that the Plaza Law was enacted in New York. Of course, Jacobs agreed with the tenant who said that the space could have better been used as a newsstand or a coffee shop. But this open space was worse than useless. It created a buffer zone, a disconnection that tended to pull people apart. Instead of low-rise, high-density streets like Greenwich Village, these projects were built tall and separate. Considering the fact that she started out as a community activist rather than an urban theoretician, it is not surprising that Jacobs called for a more democratic design process that included the voice of the user.

Jane Jacobs's Hudson Street, 1999.

Even though Jacobs seems to feel that every street should be like her own in Green-wich Village, her observations are astute and relevant almost forty years later, and her efforts helped save Greenwich Village from the sort of destructive "revitalization" it did not need.

Critics like Jane Jacobs had been sounding the alarm since the early 1960s, but it took disasters like Pruitt-Igoe to change the tide in the bureaucratic and aes-thetic establishment. Architects played a significant role in the transformation of the city, but it would be absurd to blame them altogether. Blaming Le Corbusier for Pruitt-Igoe is like blaming Marx for the design of the Soviet State—not irrelevant, but reductivist and incomplete. The "blighted" areas that were bulldozed did, by and large, have significant social problems, which were transported to the projects, and amplified. And it was not architects who created the desire to abandon the city and seek suburbia. Rather, the architects and the people moving to Levittown were sub-ject to the same historical sensibility, which included a distaste for the "disorder" of the city. It is a symptom of the simplemindedness of public discourse that the National Commission on Urban Problems blamed architects for the failed housing projects, overlooking, for example, the influence of agencies like the FHA. However muddy the thinking was, a series of mid-1960s laws, under President Lyndon Johnson's Great Society program, radically changed the focus of federal urban development policy. As John Mollenkopf writes:

Before 1966, urban renewal projects had demolished more than a quarter of a million low-rent central-city units, displacing almost a million people. Only 114,829 new units had been built in cleared areas, and only 45,861 of these were subsidized. After the passage of the 1965 and 1968 Acts, the rate of urban renewal demolition and displacement de-clined, the emphasis shifted to housing rehabilitation rather than clearance, and the num-ber of subsidized units constructed in renewal areas between 1966 and 1972 tripled.[46]

The new approach to urban renewal involved the participation of people from the affected communities, a radical and controversial departure from the top-down development practices. But when the Office of Economic Opportunity's Com-munity Action Program sought to "assist the poor in developing autonomous and self-managed organizations which are competent to exert political influence,"[47] local politicians cried foul. They saw this empowerment of community-based groups as usurping their own control. But it was not until the Nixon administration that these programs were essentially dismantled.

In the mid-1960s, High Modernism had another potent critic within the architecture and design community in the United States. In 1966, Robert Venturi published *Complexity and Contradiction in Architecture*, an unapologetic and influential attack on Modernism's purity:

Architects can no longer afford to be intimidated by the puritanically moral language of orthodox Modern architecture. I like elements that are hybrid rather than "pure," compromising rather than "clean," distorted rather than "straightforward," ambiguous rather than "articulated," perverse as well as impersonal, boring as well as "interesting," conventional rather than "designed," accommodating rather than excluding, redundant rather than simple, vestigial as well as innovating, inconsistent and equivocal rather than direct and clear. I am for a messy vitality over obvious unity. [48]

This message had tremendous influence. The language, easily contrasted to that of Greenberg, is filled with phrases of inclusion and addition—words like hybrid, compromising, and the consistent use of "as well as." *Complexity and Contradiction* is generally hailed as the starting point for Postmodernism (a term Venturi dislikes) in architecture, and it was written in response to sterile and bureaucratized Modernism. The early formulation of Postmodernism called for the return to decoration, symbolism, and a humanized urban vision. When Venturi asked the question, ". . . is not Main Street almost all right?"[49] it was an intentional blasphemy against the modernist dogma of order and efficiency. Venturi saw aesthetic and social value in the vitality of the seemingly chaotic street that Le Corbusier's followers detested and Jacobs loved.

By the mid-1960s the cities of the United States were in crisis. Riots were a frequent occurrence. In 1966 alone, there were twenty-one major riots. In 1967, there were eighty-three. By this time, inner cities were largely African American, but the police forces remained mainly white, and almost every riot was sparked by police incidents; Rodney King had plenty of predecessors. Twenty-three died in Newark, thirty-four in Watts, forty-three in Detroit.[50] After 1968, the riots ceased, but the crime rate continued to rise. Corporate offices and factories were moving from downtown to the suburbs.[51] To this grim picture, add the chaos of the public sector: subway strikes, urban mismanagement, the threat of municipal bankruptcy, and the expenditure of much-needed public resources on the Vietnam War. Here is what the *New York Times* sounded like in the summer of 1967:

TROOPS BATTLE DETROIT SNIPERS,
FIRING MACHINE GUNS FROM TANKS.
DETROIT TOLL IS 31

Rioters Rout Police;
Guardsmen Released to Aid Other Cities
Detroit, Wednesday, July 26—National Guard tank crews blasted away at entrenched snipers with .50 caliber machine guns early today after sniper fire routed policemen from a square mile area of the city. "If we see anyone move, we shoot and ask questions later," a guardsman said. [52]

By this time, the failures of the planning establishment had become crystal clear. Architecture and planning schools broadened their focus to become more interdisciplinary and responsive to "community needs." Starting in the 1960s, people including Paul Davidoff, Chester Hartmand, and Herbert Gans pioneered "advocacy planning*" to aid populations who they say were left out of the standard planning practices that stressed growth and favored the middle and upper classes. [53] The advocacy planners were followed by a second generation, known as "equity planners" in the 1970s, a group that shared an interest in creating planning schemes for the disadvantaged, and gained a foothold in some city governments. A tremendous amount of thought began to center on the reconstruction of communities and saving cities from the excesses of the last generation's renewal projects. It was at this time that artists were called into the fray.

From a bureaucratic perspective, the reintroduction of art into the city coincided with the Percent for Art movement. The first "Percent for Art" law in the United States passed Philadelphia's City Council in 1959 and was called, "Aesthetic Ornamentation of City Structures." [54] Percent for Art laws provide a simple mechanism for commissioning art; around 1 percent of the construction costs of public buildings is set aside in a separate budget line called an "art allocation." There had been provisions for the expenditure of construction dollars for art in public buildings at least since the 1930s, but these provisions were never mandatory, and were often overlooked by Modernist architects and planners for whom "aesthetic ornamentation of city structures" was anathema. There were several motivations for the Philadelphia law. Michael von Maschzisker, a sponsor of the bill, said: "Spread the message that fine arts must be returned to American architecture; that sterility and her hand-maiden, monotony, must be banished from our avenues."[55] Clearly this was an atti-tude hostile to the sort of stripped-down Modernist design that had taken over public building. As Penny Bach says in her history of Philadelphia's program, "It was thought that public art on a more human scale might be able to salvage an increasingly bleak urban environment."[56]

Just as architects were demonized as the destroyers of the city, artists were unrealistically asked to salvage it. At some basic level, there was a hope that art could revive an old idea of the city. It is not so much that people wanted art on their build-ings. Rather, they wanted to return to the sort of urban environment that they imag-ined was present at the time artists were regularly included in architecture. The initial impetus was conservative—a nostalgia for the premodern rather that any sense of the Postmodern. The laws were spawned in an effort to attract people back to the downtown areas that they were abandoning. And, in fact, urban redevelopment is still a primary motivation in many public art programs.

While several laws were in place earlier, the national move toward public art came in the 1970s, just after the nadir of urban despair. In the early days of the pub-lic art movement, the work that was placed in the "increasingly bleak urban envi-ronment," was by the icons of Modernism; Pablo Picasso, Alexander Calder, and Henry Moore were called upon to create symbols of a new urban identity. The au-tonomous object moved outside of the protective walls into the city as museum. And where were these works placed? In the banal public spaces that had been created by the International Style's retreat from the street—the post-public space of the corpo-rate or governmental plaza. Probably the most highly publicized monument installed in an American city during this period was the "Chicago Picasso." In the summer of 1967, as Detroit burned, the *Chicago Tribune* declared a new era for the windy city:

READY OR NOT, CHICAGO ENTERS ITS PICASSO ERA IN CIVIC CENTER
50-FOOT SCULPTURE UNVEILED BY MAYOR

From this day forward, for better or for worse, Chicago and Picasso are joined together as one. . . as the Eiffel Tower and Paris, the Little Mermaid and Copenhagen, as the Vatican and Rome, the Empire State Building and New York, the Boardwalk and Atlantic City, Red Square and Moscow.

It could be worse, Chicago.

It has been worse.[57]

While people on the streets in Chicago had their reservations about the Picasso, the rhetoric from public officials was optimistic, and it was very nice to be optimistic about *something* in the summer of 1967. This sculpture was to be a new image for the city, Chicago's Eiffel Tower.

On the day of the dedication of the Chicago Picasso in 1969, Charles Cunningham, the director of the Art Institute, sounded a chord that would be heard over and over again, as modern art reentered public space, "Those who haven't experienced this type of art may not like it," he said, "but that's alright. Not too many years from now, it will be accepted by the man on the street, as Van Gogh and the others are today."[58] This theme has become a mantra for the defense of public art—you *will* like this in the future.[59] It is strange to think of Picasso, so avant-garde in Paris just after the turn of the century, still shocking people on the streets of Chicago sixty years later. To the art world, Picasso's avant-garde had become routine and passé by that time.

Meanwhile, in Washington, also in 1967, the National Endowment for the Arts created its Art in Public Places Program to "give the public access to the best art of our time outside of museum walls."[60] The NEA's first commission was Alexander Calder's *La Grande Vitesse,* installed at the civic center of Grand Rapids, Michigan, in 1969. Like the Chicago Picasso, the Calder had its share of detractors in the city. However, as it has been reported often, the sculpture soon became popular, even gracing the municipal garbage trucks as a logo for civic pride. Once again, the story goes, people's initial reaction was wrong, but they came around. The image of the Calder sculpture on the garbage trucks proved the worth of the public art project, and defined its goal: civic pride. Miwon Kwon has said in reference to *La Grande Vitesse:*

It is important to note that Calder never saw, nor did he feel it necessary to visit, the plaza before the sculpture's installation. Like a good modernist, he operated under the assumptions of an artwork's autonomy. The site, in the case of this project, then, was conceived as a kind of abstract blankness awaiting some marker (i.e., art, sculpture) to give it what

Left: Pablo Picasso, Untitled (the Chicago Picasso), 1967, Chicago Civic Center, Chicago, Illinois. Photograph courtesy of Skidmore, Owings, & Merrill L.L.P.

Right: Alexander Calder, La Grande Vitesse, 1969, Grand Rapids, Michigan. Commissioned by the city of Grand Rapids and the National Endowment for the Arts, Art in Public Places Program.

could be claimed an authentic identity, even if that identity was created through the logic of a logo.[61]

And, in 1997, this sculpture-as-logo was still popular in Grand Rapids. When Angela Murphy, my research assistant, called the municipal offices there seeking photographs of *La Grande Vitesse,* a city official gladly ran out and took pictures of both the sculpture and a garbage truck, which bears a now somewhat abstracted image of the work. Kwon's analysis, which is just as valid for the Chicago Picasso and many other large-scale works of the period, points to the overriding strength of High Modernism in the early days of the public art movement. Public art simply meant placing large-scale work in open plazas, marking them as "unique," even as the strategy became generic.

If Jane Jacobs and Robert Venturi represent a counterpoint to the rigidity of Le Corbusier's Modernism, it is easy to point to contemporary alternatives to Calder and Picasso's public art in the late 1960s. Two artists who created radically different public art in the late 1960s (their work is discussed in interviews later in this book) were Mierle Laderman Ukeles and Vito Acconci. Though Ukeles was educated in the

Modernist academy of the time, she was confronted with a profound disjunction in her life and art when she had her first child. The essential elements of this transformation were clearly stated in Ukeles's "Manifesto! Maintenance Art" of 1969, in which she declared that her domestic work and her art were one:

I do a hell of a lot of washing, cleaning, cooking, renewing, supporting, preserving, etc. Also, (up to now separately) I "do Art."

Now, I will simply do these maintenance everyday things and flush them up to consciousness, exhibit them as Art.[62]

Ukeles's artistic project since that time has been consistent with the philosophy stated in the manifesto. For the most part using a collective, participatory approach, she has created a series of maintenance-based installations, public art projects, and performances. An important transformation in her work came about as a result of a project called "I Make Maintenance Art 1 Hour Every Day," (1976), which was presented at the Whitney Museum Downtown. Reviewing her Whitney project in the *Village Voice*, David Bourdon wrote humorously that Ukeles's performance might hold the key to additional funding for the financially strapped Department of Sanitation. If they could simply call the collection of garbage, performance art, perhaps they could seek funding from the National Endowment for the Arts.[63] Ukeles liked the idea, contacted the Department of Sanitation, and began their long-standing collaboration. While Ukeles's more recent work has been less obviously feminist, its roots were certainly in "women's work." (The genesis of Ukeles's work is discussed in an interview in Part III.[64]) She ventured out into the city, not to save it from its filth but to understand it, to bridge the gap between artists and public-sector workers, between domestic and public work, between people and the waste they create.

Another artist who quite literally walked out of the gallery into the city in 1969 was Vito Acconci. In *Following Piece* (1969), he followed a different person through the streets until they entered private space each day for one month. He then sent a record of his activities to a member of the art world,[65] a kind of urban report back to the ivory tower. While *Following Piece* was in the mode of the mail art and systems art of the time, it was a precursor to Acconci's more obviously public art of the 1980s and 1990s. While Picasso, Calder, and the countless other creators of sculptural objects for plazas in the 1970s and 1980s worked within the Modernist spaces

Left: Grand Rapids, Michigan, garbage truck with logo including an image of La Grande Vitesse, 1997.

Right: Vito Acconci, Following Piece, Street Works IV, 1969, streets of New York, New York. Photograph courtesy of Acconci Studio.

they were assigned, Ukeles and Acconci challenged traditional notions of sites for art. They imagined fluid intersections with the city, creating public space for their art in a way that had tremendous influence.

While there were suggestions of a new direction in the work of Acconci, Ukeles, Alan Kaprow, and many others, the official monument-oriented public art movement continued unabated in the 1970s, as Percent for Art requirements were passed in Seattle, Miami, Chicago, Cambridge, Portland (Oregon), and as the federal government made its formerly voluntary art allocation mandatory. But the ideology behind these programs was still very conservative. In general, the programs that were created as public art ordinances spread across the United States in the 1970s, following in the footsteps of the well-publicized successes of the late 1960s, such as the Chicago Picasso. The Northwest, particularly Seattle, was a hotbed for public art in the 1970s. Jerry Allen is a longtime public art official and former director of King County's Percent for Art Program. In an interview, Allen described how the percent programs became law in Seattle in 1973. Allied Arts, an arts advocacy group, prevailed on Mayor Wes Uhlman to consider Percent for Art:

[Uhlman] was a strong downtown development advocate. Along with some other "civic boosters," Uhlman decided to embark on a number of issues to turn things around. The county made the commitment to build a sports stadium (eventually resulting in the Kingdome). The city and the county passed a $100 million bond issue to begin building Free-

way Park and to refurbish county parks. Remember, that was a pretty good size bond is-
sue back then, particularly for municipalities that were in financial trouble. The mayor and
the county executive got interested in Percent for Art, as a way of creating opportunities
for artists, and creating a more attractive downtown. The ideas associated with public art
at that time were pretty rudimentary. People were thinking about "placing" works of art,
based on that notion that the city could become an outdoor museum. But the idea that
was driving it initially was economic. It was part of a larger package of initiatives that the
city and the county were undertaking to fix their image and fix their economy.[66]

Seattle's Percent for Art became a national leader. By all accounts, there was an ambitious push toward commissioning art as soon as the law passed. While most Percent
for Art laws have provisions limiting what sorts of sites will be considered for commissioning art, exempting infrastructure work, for example, almost every public construction project qualified for funding in Seattle. Richard Andrews, who ran Seattle's
program, told me, "We were everywhere."[67] One unusual site that qualified for Percent for Art funding in 1976 was an electrical substation called Viewland/Hoffman,
and it is worth considering because of its disproportionate influence. Viewland/Hoff-
man was the sort of site seldom considered for public art in other cities, and as an electrical substation, there simply was no opportunity to work in the traditional manner.
There was no plaza on which to place an artwork, no building to adorn with architectural detail. According to Richard Andrews, the architects at Hobbs/Fukui were instrumental in bringing artists onto the project at an early stage, although the sponsor
agency, Seattle City Light, was dubious. With the artists and architects working together from the very beginning, Viewland/Hoffman is generally considered the first
"Design Team" project. One motivation for the inclusion of artists was the unpopu-
larity of the project in the surrounding neighborhood. So, as often happens, the
artists were brought in to help make the project more palatable. As subsequent generations of design teams will attest, it was not easy going. Richard Andrews wrote:

The first months of the design team's efforts confirmed City Light's concerns, as the par-
ticipation of artists Andrew Keating, Sherry Markovitz and Lewis "Buster" Simpson seemed
to throw the entire design process into chaos. In fact, the architects, who were initially sup-
portive, found themselves in the seemingly endless debate with the artists on how to pro-
ceed with the design process and how the artists might be involved. It was immediately
clear (and this has proven true in subsequent design team projects) that although the

artists and the designers spoke a common language of form and material, they were far apart in their understanding of how the individual creative process of art and design worked, let alone how they might be integrated into a real project.[68]

An example of the difference in approach might have been Simpson, Keating, and Markovitz's insistence on beginning the project by canvassing the neighborhood. The artists wanted to ask residents about their misgivings toward having a substation near their homes, thus opening the process to "lengthy deliberations."[69] The artists were not used to the process of public design. How could they be? This was the first design team, and some architects of subsequent generations have cursed the day that architects from Hobbs/Fukui opened the door for this sort of collaboration.

After intense effort, Viewland/Hoffman substation was completed. The result was a whimsical mixture of electrical equipment whirligigs by Emile and Veva Gehrke (invited to participate in the project by Keating, Markovitz, and Simpson), as well as sculpture and seating designed by the artist/architect team. The project was a success in terms of public reaction, and in the now mythic status that it has taken on in the public art community.[70] Word spread that artists had been allowed into the process early, and had made a significant difference. An electrical substation, an infrastructure facility that was the center of citizen resentment, had been transformed into a focus of local community life. If this sort of team could be created, public art administrators reasoned, artists would be able to be more than merely decorators of a site. They could become "placemakers." Public art administrators are constantly fighting for more power for artists. This is based both on a belief in the creative strength of artists and a desire for more power for administrators. After all, if the

Andrew Keating, Sherry Markovitz, Lewis Simpson, artists, Hobbs/Fukui, architects, Viewland/Hoffman Substation, 1979, Seattle, Washington. Commissioned by the Seattle Arts Commission and Seattle City Light.

artist is only an afterthought, a decorator of a leftover part of the site, then the administrator does not have a very interesting or significant job.

In the mid-1970s, it seemed that some of the cities' efforts to right themselves were working. Neighborhood associations across the country began to oppose highway construction. At the same time, the gas crisis of 1973–1974 made driving considerably more expensive, and mass transit became the new building agenda of municipal governments. Getting to and from suburban bedroom communities became a bit more problematic, as workers had to endure the indignities of long waits at the gas station and even car-pooling. Small-scale projects gained in popularity. "Urban Renewal" gave way to "Community Redevelopment," at least in the names of the governmental agencies.[71] By the late 1970s, optimistic rhetoric became the norm—downtown had been "reborn." Many cities were climbing out of debt,[72] while office construction was revving up for the 1980s boom. Planners and citizen groups tended to favor the redevelopment of existing architecture in their modest ventures. But the recovery in the 1970s was not evenly felt across the country. While prospects did not seem as grim as a decade earlier, Northern industrial cities continued to lose population while cities across the Southwest surged. John Mollenkopf attributes this to conservative urban development policies on the federal level. Conservatives in and out of government were sick of the disorder of the older (minority-dominated, Democratic-voting) cities, and put their support elsewhere:

These newer cities, typified by those in the Southwest, are strong service centers, have little traditional industry but branch plants instead in the new industries, and little or no conflict or even political debate over growth issues. They have benefited most from the private sector reaction against the political climate of the older cities and its search for conservative alternatives. In contrast to the Northeast, Southwestern cities have had weaker public sectors, fewer calls for political accountability, little or no protest, and a far stronger military influence.[73]

The 1970s, then, saw a continued downward trend for the large industrial cities, and the problems that President Johnson had tried to address were effectively neglected under President Nixon.

Robert Venturi and Denise Scott Brown, among others, created a framework for Postmodernism in architecture, but when it became a fad in the high stakes world of corporate image-making in the late 1970s, Postmodernism was literally superficial.

Carlos Ortiz, Untitled (Scene from the South Bronx), ca. 1975.

It became little more than an *aesthetic* style, absorbing many of the urbanistic habits of High Modernism. Now the geometric high-rise buildings had a bit of trim. The Postmodern architecture of the office boom of the 1980s had no new urban agenda. Architect James Wines has argued that the Postmodern style was reduced in the most part to adding detail to buildings—columns, pediments, cornices, entablatures. Ultimately, he says, "the Postmodernist dialogue has been an exclusive interprofessional forum, and the movement's representative built structures have continued to be dominated by Modernist/abstractionist principles."[74] The sort of radical Postmodernism that Venturi and Scott Brown envisioned was, for the most part, ignored or superficially absorbed into business as usual. As Robert Venturi has said, "Simpleton Postmodernism promoted seductive prettiness and nostalgic appeal as a vulgarization of our architecture—which is ugly and ordinary or gauche and tense—and which we refuse to give a name."[75]

If any building signaled the triumph of Postmodernism in architecture it was the Portland Building (1980) by Michael Graves. This monumental governmental office building featured wildly exuberant decoration. The oversized decorative motifs seem intentionally humorous—Postmodern irony. There was an artist, Raymond Kaskey, involved in the project, but he had nothing to do with this decoration. Rather, Kaskey created a huge allegorical figure of Portland set at the base of the building. Taken together, the art and architecture seem to represent the conservative strain of Postmodernism. The building is grandiose, an overblown if gently ironic image of civic pride, while the artwork, an over-scale allegorical figure, lacks the architecture's Postmodern irony.

Raymond Kaskey, Portlandia, 1995, in front of the Portland Building (Michael Graves, Architect). Photograph: Randy Rasmussen, the Oregonian.

Around the same time, a new sort of Postmodern urban renewal was becoming popular: the "festival marketplace." Throughout the country, upscale development projects were cropping up in urban centers: Faneuil Hall Marketplace in Boston, Harborplace in Baltimore, the Gallery at Market East in Philadelphia, the South Street Seaport in New York City, Ghirardelli Square in San Francisco. These developments, mostly owned and operated by the Rouse Corporation, attempted to resurrect the old city by creating historically "themed" shopping malls. For example, the press package from Faneuil Hall Marketplace in Boston is filled with the history of the site. It even begins with a quotation from General Lafayette from 1825: "The City of Boston, the Cradle of Liberty, may Faneuil Hall ever stand a monument to teach the world that resistance to oppression is a duty, and will, under true republican institutions become a blessing."[76] Imagine General Lafayette's surprise if he were to learn that a century and a half later his fiery words were being used to help attract customers for Victoria's Secret and the Warner Brothers store. While there were no neighborhoods bulldozed for these schemes, they did have one thing in common with the development practices of the fifties and sixties: they were built for the well-off. In fact, the manipulative nostalgia of these sites could drive one back to agreement with Le Corbusier's hard-nosed attack on sentimentality.

In her book *The City of Collective Memory* Christine Boyer argues that the festival marketplace and related development projects signaled the move from the Modernist city to the "City of Spectacle":

For this is the reaction against order: to break apart the dominating unity that prevailed for so many years in the City of Panorama. The utopic disruptions of rational town planning, the boredom of their pure crystalline forms, produced in their wake the City of Spectacle, a city in which appropriations of historical styles and restaged scenographic allusions now become bounded nodes within an urban composition cris-crossed by highways and invisible electronic circuitry.[77]

I live adjacent to one of these "restaged" sites in New York City, the South Street Seaport. While the Seaport has brought "street life" back to the neighborhood, it is a sea of strangers, tourists absorbing a renovated slice of old New York. This tourist-oriented street life is fundamentally different from the urban ballet advocated by Jane Jacobs, where the essence of the experience was the creation of a neighborhood of long-term residents. And, as Boyer points out, the life of the Seaport is clearly "bounded." Aside from a short strip of stores on the path leading from the subway, local businesses have seen virtually no benefits from the hundreds of thousands of tourists who visit the South Street Seaport. Rather, the "old New York" feel that people come to admire is a place unto itself. While there was urban optimism in some quarters in the 1980s, there was also continued development in the outlying districts—massive office and shopping centers at highway interchanges throughout the country. Perhaps the paradigmatic example of this sort of development (at least in

The South Street Seaport, New York, New York, 1999. Developer: Rouse Corporation.

name) was Perimeter Center outside Atlanta, which included more office space than downtown Atlanta in 1988.[78] Urban centers seemed to be recovering, but their suburban rivals were growing even faster.

The 1980s were a tremendously active time for public art. Building on the trend of the 1970s, cities across the country passed Percent for Art ordinances, including New York, Los Angeles, Dallas, and Phoenix. But the most influential success of the decade was not commissioned through any of these programs, but through private donations. Maya Lin's *Vietnam Veterans Memorial* (1981) gained widespread acclaim after a controversy threatened to prevent it from opening (see interview in Part I). Lin's interactive, embracing space showed how a nonobjective work could communicate to the elite and the "common" observer alike. While using the aesthetic vocabulary of abstraction, it soon became one of Washington's top tourist attractions, and was hailed in the art and popular press alike. In the summer of 1997, as I was buying some groceries at the Shop 'n Save in Skowhegan, Maine, I noticed a carousel of children's books, and stopped to buy one for my son. I was surprised to see among them *A Wall of Names: The Story of the Vietnam Veterans Memorial*.[79] It was a "Step 4" reading book in a Random House series that also features *True-Life Treasure Hunts* and *To the Top! Climbing the World's Highest Mountains.* I bought the book and in reading it I realized once again how profoundly important the *Vietnam Veterans Memorial* has been in the recent history of public art. The book gave a very good introduction to the war and the memorial, but what was most outstanding was that I had purchased the book at Shop 'n Save. The supermarket, as public a site as you could find in Skowhegan these days, had no other books on art of any sort.

It is emblematic that Lin, who was trained as an architect, created the decade's best known public art work. There was a growing move among artists and public art programs toward "useful" art: plaza designs, walkways, artist-designed seating. Artists like Alice Aycock, Andrea Blum, Mary Miss, Scott Burton, Elyn Zimmerman, and Siah Armajani created benches, bridges, fountains, and plazas that were hard for some to identify as art. This functional art came to dominate public art in the 1980s, becoming somewhat formulaic. Artists had fought for the right to participate on "design teams" on more equal terms with the architects. However, some artists began to feel that their vision was simply absorbed into the setting, bureaucratized beyond recognition in the name of interprofessional cooperation. In fact, Siah Armajani, a leading practitioner of architectural sculpture, and a successful participant in several design teams, said in 1990:

*Siah Armajani, in collaboration with Scott Burton and Caesar Pelli,
the marina at the World Financial Center, New York, New York.
Photograph: Timothy Hursley, courtesy of Max Protech Gallery.*

*Public art was a promise that became a nightmare. Our revolution has been stolen back
from us and now it is our job to get it back. In the first place, the idea of a design team just
doesn't work . . . the kind of design team that just gets together around a table is like a
situation comedy. It is cynical and unproductive. Genuine debate can't take place around
a table in that way. You get what the real-estate developer and the arts administrator want
because they control the money. The whole emphasis in most of these projects is on who
can get along best with the others involved—at the expense of vision and fresh thinking.
It is like that story about the two thieves who hole up in an abandoned restaurant to plan
their next job. While they are plotting in the basement kitchen, the dumbwaiter comes
down and there is an order for fried chicken, Southern style. "What shall we do" asks one.
"Quick, fill the order," says the other, "or they'll come and find us." So they send up some
fried chicken Southern style. But then another order comes down, and another, and they
keep filling them and sending them up. This is what has happened to our revolution.*[80]

The design team had changed considerably in the sixteen years that separated Viewland/Hoffman and Armajani's lament. What had been radical, including
the artists' desire to canvass the neighborhood before proceeding with the project,
had become routine. Can you imagine the developers of Battery Park City acquiesc-
ing to artists' demands to canvass the neighborhood before proceeding with their

construction? While the artists had brought new ideas to the table in Seattle, their ideas were absorbed in the bureaucracy of collaboration by 1990.

It is now rather fashionable to attack work done in this mode because it seems to fit so comfortably into its settings, to blend seamlessly into the context of architecture and urban development. However, there are many examples of this sort of work that created a meaningful hybrid of art and architecture. Elyn Zimmerman's *Sanctuary* (1990) at the University of South Florida is a good example. The work is sited next to the Lee Moffitt Cancer Center, and it creates a peaceful place for people to sit and talk. I was told on a tour of the campus that it is often used by patients to meet with their families. This was easy to imagine. When I sat within the work, I felt embraced by the space Zimmerman had created; the sound of water gently falling through limestone boulders was soothing. In its attention to surface, texture, and small detail, it seemed like the sort of space that a sculptor rather than an architect would design. In its contours, construction, and scale, it seemed architectural. Its use was defined by its physical and social site—a place to speak quietly, to confront and escape the depressing realities of the cancer center. This mode of art is still widely popular in public art, and functional/architectural projects by Denise Scott Brown and Robert Venturi, Michael Singer and Linnea Glatt, and Vito Acconci are discussed in Part II.

But the 1980s are also remembered as the decade in which *Tilted Arc* was removed. Ronald Reagan had been elected in 1980, and his newly appointed bureaucrats were intent on undoing much of what they saw as the misguided liberal legacy of the Carter administration. William Diamond, newly appointed regional administrator of the General Services Administration led the successful battle to have *Tilted Arc* removed, a traumatic ordeal for many of Serra's supporters, one that was watched with some trepidation by public art administrators across the country. Serra was not a participant in the move toward architectural sculpture. In fact, he was frank in his distaste for the new style.

I am interested in work where the artist is a maker of "anti-environment" which takes its own place and makes its own situation, or divides or declares its own area. There seems to be in this country right now, especially in sculpture, a tendency which makes work which attends to architecture. I am not interested in work which is structurally ambiguous or in sculpture that satisfies urban design principles. I have always found that to be not only an aspect of mannerism but a need to reinforce a status quo of existing aesthetics. Most of

Elyn Zimmerman, Sanctuary, 1990, Lee Moffitt Cancer Research Center, University of Southern Florida, Tampa, Florida. Photograph courtesy of Gagosian Gallery, New York, New York.

the architecture that has been built is horrendous. I am interested in sculpture that is non-utilitarian, non-functional . . . any use is a misuse. I am not interested in sculpture that conventionalizes metaphors of content or assimilates architectonic spiritual structures, for there is no socially shared metaphysic.[81]

Given Serra's goal of creating a work that "makes its own situation," some art world critics felt that a problem with *Tilted Arc* was that it seemed to fit a bit too comfortably into the plaza. While Serra routinely built sculptures that overwhelmed the viewer, truly dislocating a 2000-square-foot gallery, an 84-foot-long piece of steel next to a 50-story building was a bit dwarfed. Many, including myself, would have preferred something more astonishing, something that dislocated the plaza more entirely. But there was tremendous support for Serra, and losing the battle over *Tilted Arc* was a terrible blow to many of us.

Urban optimism was tempered in the late 1980s with the stock market crash of 1987. Old problems seemed to be reappearing—fiscal difficulties for the cities, real estate problems in downtown areas. Although there were four race riots following police incidents in Miami during the 1980s, they were generally overlooked as aberrations from the norm. In 1992, the urban optimism of the 1980s officially came to an end with the uprising in Los Angeles: fifty dead, $1,000,000,000 in damages. As urban historian Jon Teaford points out, the optimism of the 1980s had been an illusion. During that period, manufacturers and corporations continued to leave cities, as office space in the suburbs continued to grow. These thriving suburbs are still overwhelmingly white; Levittown in Long Island, famous for its exclusion of African Americans after the war, now has 31 black residents out of a total of 53,286. [82] Teaford says, "Americans preferred the autonomy of the social fragment to some unifying ideal preached by starry-eyed reformers. Thus, Americans opted for dissolution of the city and, with the aid of the automobile, created the dispersed and fragmented metropolitan world of the late twentieth century."[83] And, in truth, great time and energy have been expended in the twentieth century in creating the technical tools of privacy and separation: indoor plumbing replaces the public fountain; the wristwatch replaces the public clock on the tower; records and CDs replace live music; movies replace live drama, and TV replaces movies. All of these could be seen in terms of separation—pulling away from public, toward individual experiences. In fact, privacy has become something of an obsession in recent decades. Jonathan Franzen argues that what he calls our "privacy panic" is based on a false belief that there is less privacy now than in the past because computerized records are kept by our credit card providers, telephone companies, video rental stores, and so on. Franzen counters with a different vision of the past:

In 1890, an American typically lived in a small town under conditions of near-panoptical surveillance. Not only did his every purchase "register" but it registered in the eyes and in the memory of shopkeepers who knew him, his parents, his wife, and his children. He couldn't so much as walk to the post office without having his movements tracked and analyzed by his neighbors. Probably he grew up sleeping in a bed with siblings and possibly his parents, too. . . . In the suburbs and exurbs where the typical American lives today, tiny nuclear families inhabit enormous houses, in which each person has his or her own bedroom, and, sometimes, bathroom. Compared even with the suburbs in the sixties and seventies, when I was growing up, the contemporary condominium development or gated community offers a striking degree of anonymity. It's no longer even the rule that you know your neighbors.[84]

This is life in the fragmented world that Teaford sees as the typical American experience, and our nearly inevitable future.

And what of the interconnection of technology? Certainly we have all heard of how the telephone, television, and the computer can contribute to the creation of a new "virtual agora." Doesn't the proliferation of the Internet speak of the desire for interconnection? The Internet is a huge, untested mechanism for interaction, though it is certainly debatable how attractive a public space can be that eliminates the body.[85] Preliminary data suggest that the virtual contact of the chat rooms may not lead to a feeling of connectedness. An article in the *New York Times* headlined "Sad, Lonely World Discovered in Cyberspace" announced the findings of a study of Internet users in August 1998.[86] To the great surprise of the social scientists who conducted the survey, and especially to the technology companies that funded it (including Intel, AT&T, and Apple Computer), the conclusion of the two-year study was that Internet users experience greater loneliness and depression than those who do not go online. Moreover, it was not the case that depressed and lonely people were drawn to the Web for solace. The Internet users in the study were originally as happy as the less technology-inclined control group; Internet use *caused* the decline in their psychological well-being.[87] Answering your e-mail simply is not the same as talking to someone on the telephone, and talking on the telephone is not the same as speaking to someone in person. In addition, the Internet can decrease the perceived need to live in an urban center. If you can make all the contact you need online, why not live in a peaceful and quiet environment away from the crowds?

Television is also hailed by some as creating the "new public space" because it is one of the few activities that practically every American engages in— that is, we do have collective experience in the fragmented Postmodern world because we are all watching the same television shows. In a research study called "Time for Life," Geoffrey Godby and others concluded that technological advances have increased free time for people in developed countries. And what have people been doing with this free time? They have been watching more television, "even though they rate it among their least favorite forms of leisure." Americans average more than sixteen hours of television per week, up four hours since 1965.[88] John Tierney said, "The increase in tube-watching seems especially perverse considering that it coincides with a decline of two hours a week in the amount of time people spend socializing, an activity they consider much more enjoyable than television. A society of solitary people sitting at home enviously watching the camaraderie on 'Friends' does not seem like a triumph of the communications revolution."[89]

One might despair as Americans fade off into suburbanized isolation, a populace of glazed-eyed Web-surfers glued endlessly to the screen or tube. But there certainly are signs in the late 1990s that the sprawl of suburbia has many people nervous. The 1998 elections saw a widespread reaction against the effects of unfettered suburban development. By passing ordinances across the country to buy open space and confine development, Americans in effect opted for denser suburban neighborhoods. The move has been couched in environmental and social terms. Larry Bohlen, cochairman of the Sierra Club's national campaign to fight sprawl said, "We're not trying to subvert the American dream—we're trying to get back to it. It's that 'Leave it to Beaver' town where all the kids walk to school."[90] It is emblematic of the politics of the 1990s that any initiative needs to be couched in the most conservative possible rhetoric.

Despite Teaford's pessimistic assessment (written in 1993) that the suburbanization of the United States will continue apace, the 1990s have been another period of urban optimism, and using the arts for urban development has become increasingly popular for municipal governments across the country. In 1993, for example, the Port Authority of New York and New Jersey, with Alliance for the Arts and other groups, published a report entitled, "The Arts as an Industry: Their Importance to the New York-New Jersey Metropolitan Region."[91] Among the report's most significant findings was that the total economic impact of the arts in 1992 for the New York City area was $9.2 billion.[92] The frank mission of the report was to change the way people think about the arts. While the spiritual value of art is well known, the report argued, there is another side to art that is quantifiable—economic impact. This report was immediately seized upon by the New York City Department of Cultural Affairs (DCA) as a way of justifying expenditures of public money for the arts. After all, people come to New York for culture, spend a lot of money, create thousands of jobs, and support the tax base. All of this was convincing to public officials, and the DCA continued to hammer away at the arts as an economic engine. This campaign was so successful that when Rudolph Giuliani took office in 1992, he placed DCA under the supervision of his Deputy Mayor for Economic Development. But DCA was in for a bit of a surprise. The Deputy Mayor took the economic arguments so seriously that he proposed deep cuts in the support that the city had been providing to the smaller community-based organizations, in order to increase support for the larger institutions. After all, these were the largest tourist draws and the biggest employers. If art is about economic development, why not pour more money into the Metropolitan

Lincoln Center for the Performing Arts, 62nd to 66th Street, New York, New York. Center: Wallace K. Harrison, Metropolitan Opera House, 1966. Left: Philip Johnson, New York State Theater, 1964. Right: Max Abramovitz, Avery Fisher Hall, 1962. Photograph: Erin Riley.

Museum of Art, which draws 3 million people a year, and pull the plug on the small groups in the outer boroughs? This became an annual battle, but not one that DCA should have been surprised about. Urban economic development once again was structured to benefit the well-to-do.

All over the country, in the new regime, cities are using concert halls and museums to draw the middle and upper middle classes back to downtown. There has been a tremendous growth of what Sharon Zukin calls the symbolic economy—"the intertwining of cultural symbols and entrepreneurial capital."[93] A front page story in the *New York Times* in November 1997 carried the headline, "Cities Are Fostering the Arts as a Way to Save Downtown"[94] The article chronicled the efforts to "build on the arts" through consciously utilizing culture as an urban development tool. According to the article, the model for all of these centers is Lincoln Center, built on the site of eighteen blocks razed by Robert Moses, as the beachhead for the gentrification of the Upper West Side of Manhattan. These new projects ranged from Philadelphia's $330 million Avenue of the Arts to a jazz museum in Kansas City, to the New Jersey Center for the Performing Arts in Newark. One expert was quoted as estimating that there were between $4 and $5 billion spent on capital projects for the arts in the decade 1986–1996, and much of that total was justified in terms of urban development. But these megaprojects are only a part of the picture:

Beyond the big-ticket building projects are myriad other efforts in which cities have imposed designated taxes on hotel rooms and amusements, offered incentives to developers and aggressively leveraged property taxes to raise money. They have created arts districts, financed arts festivals and promoted regularly scheduled cultural events. Often they have invested large amounts of public money in museums, concert halls and theaters to create tourist destinations, burnish regional reputations and stimulate blighted neighborhoods.[95]

In fact, "Urban Development and the Visual Arts" is now required in New York University's Arts Administration Program. Public art projects are only a modest part of this emerging field. However, the rhetoric and goals of the new Arts-as-Urban-Development movement are similar to those of the early efforts in Percent for Art. Mayors and city council members are still looking for ways to bring people back to the cities, to make urban life attractive to the middle and upper classes.

Not everyone is on the bandwagon. A project that has been criticized as an example of the 1990s version of Arts for Urban Development was "Places with a Past," which took place at Charleston, South Carolina's Spoleto Festival. The citywide event was a series of site-specific projects organized by Mary Jane Jacob in 1991. In this project, artists were sent out into the city to uncover its historical and contemporary qualities. The book jacket of the publication that accompanied "Places with a Past" says:

For one year, the selected artists visited the town of Charleston and became engaged with the extraordinary resources—historical and cultural subjects of past and present—that make the city an exceptional environment in which to stage such an exhibition. The 18th-19th- and 20th-century sites became an active part of each artist's concept; the city a canvas upon which the artist could exercise his or her imagination. The artists' installations, in turn, provided a new and fresh look at this beautiful city of the American South.[96]

More or less assigned to address the past in Charleston, an internationally acclaimed group of artists responded in very different ways, but an overriding theme was race relations from the times of slavery to the present. To many of the artists it was an opportunity to examine memory, the notion that for many in the south "ol' times dere am not forgotten." But even as these installations were clearly critical of cultural amnesia, their role in the context of urban development is ambiguous. When an urban project uses history to expose the uniqueness of the place, how far is it from tourism promotion? Miwon Kwon says:

. . . the ambitions of programs like "Places with a Past" . . . ultimately do not seem to veer very far from those of the city officials and cultural leaders of Grand Rapids, Michigan, [sponsors of Calder's La Grande Vitesse*] thirty years ago. For despite the tremendous difference in the art of choice . . . their investment in generating a sense of uniqueness and authenticity for their respective places of presentation remains quite consistent. As such endeavors to engage art in the nurturing of specificities of locational difference gather momentum, there is a greater and greater urgency in distinguishing between the* cultivation *of art and places, and their* appropriation *for the promotion of cities as cultural commodities.*[97]

Kwon is arguing that the temporary and more politically pointed public art of "Places with a Past" can be used for the same sort of urban development goals that we saw in Battery Park City. As the above quotation from the "Places with a Past" book jacket makes clear, one of the goals of the project was to uncover the uniqueness of the city, and provide "a fresh look at this beautiful city of the American South." Kwon points out how similar this is to the goals of the original Percent for Art laws: to attract people to the city, to infuse a site with the sense of uniqueness that any proper "destination" needs.

But the differences between *La Grande Vitesse* and the works in Charleston are profound. Consider David Hammons's contribution to "Places with a Past." For the project, Hammons chose to work in the African American community, selecting as his site, two empty lots within a poor residential section. As Hammons began to work on the site, he was approached by a local contractor named Albert Alston. After some discussion, Hammons enlisted Alston as his collaborator on a project that they called *House of the Future.* The house was a very narrow, two-story structure, with a variety of elements typical of the architecture of Charleston, from the type of roofing materials to the shingles and doors. Everything was carefully marked, and Hammons describes the house as a learning center for kids in the neighborhood. Hammons also invited a young artist from the neighborhood, Larry Jackson, to create a gallery for himself in the lower section of the house. In Hammons's mind, it was important to hand over control of the project to the local community. As an outsider, he was hesi-

David Hammons, House of the Future, 1991, Spoleto Festival, Charleston, South Carolina. Photograph courtesy of Jack Tilton Gallery.

tant to make the site his statement alone, although he is also frank in admitting that the overall direction was his. In the second lot, Hammons created *America Street* (named after the street that ran between the two lots). Here he created a billboard image of African American kids, situated to look up at a flag pole, upon which Hammons flew an American flag created in red, black, and green (the colors of the Black Nationalist flag).

The installations included elements of participatory, community-based art, local pride, racial identity politics, *arte povera,* and architectural sculpture. But it was equally important to Hammons to find a place for the project that would stretch the social limits of the visitors to the Spoleto Festival. He chose a site that made some art lovers so uncomfortable that they would not get out of their cars. But those who did were invited to interact with people in a community far from scenic Charleston. The urban development agenda of the official sponsors is only part of the picture. There are too many directions from which to criticize public art; the same arguments are rarely used to critique art in museums. Is it necessary, for example, for every review of an exhibition at the Guggenheim Museum to refer to the origins of the Guggenheim family's wealth in the abuse of the landscape around Leadville, Colorado? When an artwork reorients memory in a site, it begins to change the psychological environment. Perhaps this is only a partial step, but it should not be ignored. The *Vietnam*

Veterans Memorial is one of the top tourist attractions in Washington, D.C., and Washington is a city that markets its memorials more aggressively than most, while remaining a city intensely divided by race and class. But to reduce Lin's memorial to its tourism function disregards what happens at the site.

By the late 1980s the sort of community orientation Hammons employed in Charleston was becoming increasingly popular among artists and administrators alike. As Suzanne Lacy points out in her book *Mapping the Terrain: New Genre Public Art,* a good way to understand the changing attitudes toward public art in commissioning agencies is to look at the National Endowment for the Arts's guidelines for its Art in Public Places category. As mentioned earlier, the initial goal of the Art in Public Places Program was "to give the public access to the best art of our time outside museum walls." This statement makes two assumptions that would come into question: that the "quality" of an artwork is something that people will agree upon, and that what succeeds in a museum will succeed on a city street. By 1974, Lacy notes, the NEA guidelines said that the commissioned artwork should be "appropriate to the immediate site," and by 1978, that the commissioning agency should "approach creatively the wide range of possibilities for art in public situations." In 1979, the NEA asked for "methods to insure an informed community response to the project." In 1983, grant recipients were required to submit "plans for community involvement, preparation, and dialogue," which were expanded by the early 1990s to include "educational activities which invite community involvement."[98] This transition from a pursuit of the "best" art to community involvement is not complete by any means. Art world representatives on panels convened to select artists for public commissions still often pit "quality art" against accommodation to "community issues." However, interest in local participation has opened the door for artists like Mierle Ukeles to create art within the context of Percent for Art programs. Her artistic practice, along with that of Vito Acconci, so far from the official public artists in 1969, has entered the mainstream.

In January 1999, the city of Portland, Maine, unveiled its community cultural plan.[99] Portland's comprehensive downtown plan, adopted in the early 1990s, reflected the sort of Art as Urban Development that has been discussed above; in fact, Portland's primary goal in declaring an arts district is the economic revitalization of downtown.[100] But the community plan, at least in the idealistic state of its first inception, is inclusive, participatory, and open. The plan was developed through a "communitywide process" that included personal interviews with scores of ethnic, religious, cultural, political, and neighborhood leaders, as well as open public forums. The results reflect this process. As opposed to the top-down approach of the early public art efforts that sought to expose the people to the "best art of our time," the Portland plan assumes that the arts are in the communities, and will flourish with the support of a concerted public effort. "Far from any notion of elite culture," the report says, "our aim has been to thoroughly democratize our cultural perspective and to empower communities that have previously been absent from public cultural discourse. At its core, this planning process has been an attempt to take a measure of our entire community and its constituent cultures, and to devise a set of mechanisms through which our representative civic government might address their needs and aspirations."[101] The recommendations of the report are not gleaming concert halls or museums, but more modest proposals like a community cultural center that would be accessible to a wide range of groups. Throughout the report, there is an effort to find ways to create interconnections among the people of Portland, while celebrating cultural diversity. Within an array of possible initiatives is the suggestion that public art can play a role in the city. The report was refreshing to read. It did not oversell the value of art as an economic engine. Rather, it argued for the value that art can have in the recreation of community.

In his book *Art, Space, and the City,* Malcolm Miles takes a similar tack to that of Rosalyn Deutsche, Miwon Kwon, and Sharon Zukin in his analysis of art and urban development—arguing that it reinforces the dominance of the cultural elites in the city. However, he sees more hope in alternative practices, in the spirit of the plan developed in Portland, Maine:

. . . the methodology of planning privileges the representations of space (in [Henri] Lefebvre's terms) of the expert, just as the law, according to [Ivan] Illich, privileges the dominant interests in society; yet if a doctor describes his patients as "experts on their own health," perhaps dwellers are also experts on their city, and if so, their expertise begins in their awareness of the spaces around their bodies and the lattices of memory and appropriation they assemble as a personal reading of the city. From this it follows that the role of the planner becomes that of enabler, assisting members of communities in acquiring the vocabulary of information added to the empowerment of community identity, to affect planning outcomes. There is a parallel between planning which involves community participation and art which engages with defined publics in participatory work.[102]

Certainly the framers of Portland's new cultural plan see the citizens of the city as experts on their own space, and rely upon their judgment. This is the philosophy behind many contemporary public artists, certainly not limited to the artists in this book, but including Suzanne Lacy, Daniel Martinez, Tricia Ward, Tim Rollins, and many more.

Again, I think back to the moment when we were sitting on the sand at "Art on the Beach," listening to Sun Ra. It would be easy to say that our pleasure that night was only a prelude to the "uneven development" of the site (to use Rosalyn Deutsche's phrase). But the moment also held out the potential of art in a public context. It is a potential for coexistence and dialogue that is at the center of the art discussed in this book. This essay has attempted to set up a rather simple series of dialectics: Jane Jacobs's and Robert Venturi's celebration of the street versus Le Corbusier's clearance of the old city; the Great Society's community participation model obliterated by Nixon, Calder and Picasso's installations in High Modernist space versus Ukeles's and Acconci's navigation through the city; the early formulation of the design team versus the bureaucratized version lamented by Siah Armajani; our moment at Art on the Beach versus the experience of Battery Park City.

Each of the artists interviewed in this book is deeply involved in creating space or time for interconnection and dialogue, in the rather optimistic attempt to reorient the city of fragmentation and separation. The public spaces created by Lin, Venturi and Scott Brown, Glatt and Singer, and Acconci are sites for democratic interaction. Avalos, Hock and Sisco, Ahearn, Ukeles, Jones and Ginzel, and Wodiczko create ongoing opportunities for dialogue, often in collaboration with their audiences. Chin and Moore make the most literal attempt at curative art. Paulo Freire's writings on the theory and practice of dialogue (discussed in Part III) have helped me understand the potential in sharing power in an educational context. In Freire's model, true dialogue, the mutual pursuit of critical understanding among equals, will lead to critical consciousness for all involved. Just so, many of the art projects in this book allow for an open exchange among equals, far from the elitist notion that public art is a gift of the "best" to the people of the city.

Notes

1. Patricia Phillips, "Art on the Beach," *Artforum,* November 1985, p. 106.

2. Creative Time is a nonprofit arts organization that presents public art, performance, and other projects in "unexpected places" in New York City.

3. For a lengthy and intelligent analysis, see Rosalyn Deutsche, "Uneven Development: Public Art in New York City," October 47 (Winter 1988), pp. 3–53. The elimination of middle-income housing is mentioned in the "Time Line" section of Battery Park City's Web site: "http://batteryparkcity.org/time line," November 1998.

4. Jon C. Teaford, *The Twentieth Century American City* (Baltimore: The Johns Hopkins University Press, 1993), p.98.

5. Ibid., p. 25.

6. Ibid., p. 110.

7. Robert A. Caro, *The Power Broker* (New York: Vintage Books, 1975), pp. 863–879.

8. Teaford, *American City,* p. 103.

9. Kenneth T. Jackson, *Crabgrass Frontier* (Oxford and New York: Oxford University Press, 1985), pp. 203–212.

10. Ibid., p. 231.

11. Dolores Hayden, *Redesigning the American Dream* (New York: W. W. Norton and Company, 1984), p. 41.

12. Lewis Mumford, *Architecture as a Home for Man* (New York: Architectural Records Books, 1975), p. 117.

13. Le Corbusier, "The City of To-Morrow and Its Planning" (1929), reprinted in *The City Reader* (London: Routledge, 1996), edited by Richard LeGates and Frederic Stout, p. 373.

14. Ibid., p. 370.

15. "Footsore Here Find Oasis at Seagram Building Plaza," *New York Times,* July 26, 1958, p. 12.

16. Norman Marcus, "Notes on New York City Zoning—1961–1991: Turning Back the Clock—But with an Up-to-the-Minute Social Agenda," *Fordham Urban Law Journal,* Vol. 19, Spring 1992, p. 715

17. Editorial, *New York Times,* December 16, 1960, p. 32.

18. Joseph Herzberg, "Zoning for Living Long Range Plan Could End Flight Of City Residents and Aid Industry," *New York Times,* February 16, 1959, p. 23.

19. Marcus, "Notes on New York City Zoning," p. 716.

20. Ibid., p. 719.

21. *Zoning and Historic Districts,* prepared for Municipal Art Society's Planning Center. (New York: Abeles Phillips Press and Shapiro, Inc., 1990), p. 38. The document presents a series of problems and recommendations. For example:

Problem #4: Much of the city's zoning encourages development that departs radically from the surrounding area's existing built form. This occurs even where the zoning limits new development to the pre-existing bulk and density because the zoning regulations ensure that the maximum floor area can be achieved only through out-of-context design. Within historic districts themselves, this encourages (and often necessitates) the submission of inappropriate designs . . .

Recommendation #4: Undertake more extensive contextual district rezoning, particularly within and around designated historic districts. Contextual zoning now safeguards the built environment within several historic districts in Manhattan's Upper East Side and West Sides, as well as the larger neighborhoods extending beyond the designated districts; but 1961 height factor zoning, hostile to the traditional cityscape, governs development within and around most historic districts.

22. Marcus, "Notes on New York City Zoning," p. 709.

23. Teaford, *American City,* p. 115.

24. Gwendolyn Wright, *Building the Dream, a Social History of Housing in America* (New York: Pantheon Books, 1981), p. 234.

25. Colin Rowe and Fred Koetter, "Collage City," *The Architectural Review,* Vol. CLVIII, No. 942, August 1975, p. 72.

26. "Slum Surgery in St. Louis," *Architectural Forum,* Vol. 94, April 1951, p. 129. The comparison of this article and the later reassessment of Pruitt-Igoe is suggested by Jon Teaford.

27. Ibid., p. 129.

28. Ibid., pp. 129–131.

29. James Bailey, "The Case History of a Failure," *Architectural Forum,* Vol. 123, December 1965, pp. 22–26. It should be noted that the author of the 1965 article made full mention of the praise for the project in *Architectural Record's* 1951 article.

30. Bailey, "Case History of a Failure," p. 22.

31. Ibid., p. 23.

32. Ibid., p. 24.

33. Catherine Bauer, "The Dreary Deadlock of Public Housing," *Architectural Forum,* Vol. 106, No. 5, May 1957, pp. 141–142.

34. Kenneth T. Jackson, *Crabgrass Frontier,* p. 227.

35. Ibid., p. 230.

36. Wright, *Building the Dream,* p. 237.

37. Kate Nesbitt, ed., *Theorizing a New Agenda for Architecture* (New York: Princeton Architectural Press, 1996), p. 22.

38. Clement Greenberg, *The Collected Essays of Clement Greenberg* (Chicago: The University of Chicago Press, 1986), p. 32.

39. Thomas Crow, *Modern Art in the Common Culture* (New Haven: Yale University Press, 1996), p. 9.

40. For a discussion of Greenberg's Marxism, see T. J. Clark's essay, "Clement Greenberg's Theory of Art" in *Postmodern Perspectives,* edited by Howard Risatti (Englewood Cliffs, New Jersey: Prentice Hall, 1990), pp. 20–38.

41. Consider the historical moment as well. After World War II, especially in Europe, many artists turned to abstraction in revulsion against the ways repressive regimes had employed realism. The purity of abstraction was seen in sharp relief against the horrors of propagandistic representation, so Greenberg's reluctant retreat is understandable.

42. Michael Brenson, "Healing in Time," *Culture in Action* (Seattle: Bay Press, 1995), p. 28. *Culture in Action* accompanied a citywide public art project of the same name sponsored by Sculpture Chicago and organized by Mary Jane Jacob.

43. Jane Jacobs, *The Death and Life of Great American Cities* (New York: Vintage Books, 1961), p. 22. As of 1997, Jane Jacobs is still active in urban politics. Now 81 years old, she is living in Toronto, where she is seen as a kind of municipal "guardian angel" according to the *New York Times* ("Toronto, a City That Works, Offers Varied Places to Play," October 17, 1997, p. 1, Weekend Section). She has continued her work since the 1960s, fighting freeways and promoting urban diversity.

44. Ibid., p. 50.

45. Ibid., p. 15.

46. John H. Mollenkopf, *The Contested City* (Princeton: Princeton University Press, 1983), p. 90.

47. Ibid., p. 91.

48. Robert Venturi, *Complexity and Contradiction in Architecture* (New York: The Museum of Modern Art, 1966), p. 22.

49. Ibid., p. 102.

50. Teaford, *American City,* pp. 129–130.

51. Jon C. Teaford, *The Rough Road to Renaissance: Urban Revitalization in America, 1940–1985* (Baltimore: The Johns Hopkins University Press, 1990), p. 210.

52. *New York Times,* Vol. CXVI, July 26, 1967, p. 1.

53. Norman Krumholtz and Pierre Clavel, *Reinventing Cities: Equity Planners Tell Their Stories* (Philadelphia: Temple University Press, 1994), p. 14.

54. Penny Balkin Bach, *Public Art in Philadelphia* (Philadelphia: Temple University Press, 1992), p. 130.

55. Ibid., p. 130.

56. Ibid.

57. Sheila Wolfe, *Chicago Tribune,* No. 227, August 15, 1967, p. 1.

58. *Time,* Vol. 90, August 25, 1967, p. 54.

59. See my introduction to Douglas Crimp's interview on *Tilted Arc,* pp. 61–66.

60. Suzanne Lacy, *Mapping the Terrain, New Genre Public Art* (Seattle: Bay Press, 1995), p. 22.

61. Miwon Kwon in *Kunst auf Schritt und Tritt* (Hamburg: Kellner, 1997), p. 101.

62. Mierle Laderman Ukeles, "Manifesto! Maintenance Art," *The Act,* Vol. 2, No. 1, 1990, pp. 84–85.

63. David Bourdon, "Art," *Village Voice,* October 4, 1976, p. 105.

64. While I do not claim to be an expert on Freudian analysis, it seems obvious that Ukeles's willingness to focus on garbage in her work, and her attempt to destigmatize sanitation workers, is in clear contrast to the High Modernist obsession with cleanliness and order.

65. Kate Linker, *Vito Acconci* (New York: Rizzoli, 1994), p. 20.

66. From an interview I conducted by telephone with Jerry Allen in March 1996. At the time, he was manager of the Department of Cultural Affairs in San Jose, California.

67. From a phone interview with Richard Andrews, July 1996.

68. Steven Huss (editor) and Diane Shamash, *A Field Guide to Seattle's Public Art* (Seattle: Seattle Arts Commission, 1992), p. 67.

69. Ibid., p.14.

70. Ibid., p. 67. This is Richard Andrews's assessment of the project fifteen years after its completion.

71. Teaford, *Rough Road,* p. 232.

72. Teaford, *American City,* p. 156.

73. John H. Mollenkopf, *The Contested City* (Princeton, New Jersey: Princeton University Press, 1983), p. 217.

74. James Wines, *De-Architecture* (New York: Rizzoli International, 1987), p. 117.

75. Robert Venturi, *Iconography and Electronics upon a Generic Architecture* (Cambridge: MIT Press, 1996), p. 319.

76. Undated press release from Faneuil Hall Merchants Association, Boston, Mass.

77. M. Christine Boyer, *The City of Collective Memory* (Cambridge: MIT Press, 1994), p. 47.

78. Teaford, *American City,* p. 165.

79. Judy Donnelly, *A Wall of Names* (New York: Random House, 1991).

80. Calvin Tomkins, "Open, Available, Useful," *The New Yorker,* March 19, 1990, p. 71.

81. Richard Serra, *Richard Serra: Interviews, Etc. 1970–1980* (Yonkers: The Hudson River Museum, 1980), p. 128.

82. Bruce Lambert, "At 50, Levittown Contends with Legacy of Racial Bias," *New York Times,* December 28, 1997, New York Report, pp. 23–24.

83. Teaford, *American City,* p. 169.

84. Jonathan Franzen, "Imperial Bedroom: The Real Problem with Privacy? We Have Too Much of It," *The New Yorker,* October 12, 1998, p. 51.

85. This notion was suggested to me by Simon Penny, who is working on an essay on the subject.

86. Amy Harmon, "Sad, Lonely World Discovered in Cyberspace," *New York Times,* August 30, 1998, p. 1.

87. Ibid.

88. John Tierney, "Our Oldest Computer, Upgraded," *New York Times Magazine,* September 28, 1997, p. 47.

89. Ibid., p. 48.

90. Timothy Egan, "The New Politics of Urban Sprawl," *New York Times,* "Week in Review," November 15, 1998, p. 3.

91. "The Arts as an Industry: Their Importance to the New York-New Jersey Metropolitan Region." Published by The Port Authority of New York and New Jersey, Alliance for the Arts, New York City Partnership, and Partnership for New Jersey. October 1993.

92. Ibid., p. 2.

93. Sharon Zukin, *The Cultures of Cities* (Cambridge and Oxford: Blackwell Publishers, 1995), p. 3.

94. Bruce Weber, "Cities Are Fostering the Arts as a Way to Save Downtown," *New York Times,* November 18, 1997, pp.1; A24.

95. Ibid., p. A24.

96. Mary Jane Jacob, et al., *Places with a Past* (New York: Rizzoli, 1991).

97. Miwon Kwon, "For Hamburg: Public Art and Urban Identities," in *Christian Phillip Muller, Kunst auf Schritt und Tritt, Public Art is Everywhere* (Hamburg: Kellner, 1997), p. 107.

98. All quotations from NEA guidelines are from Suzanne Lacy, *Mapping the Terrain,* pp. 22–24.

99. *Celebrating Community: A Cultural Plan for Portland, Maine.* Prepared by the Celebrating Community Steering Committee (Portland: Portland Arts and Culture Alliance, 1999). On October 5, 1998, the Portland City Council adopted the plan as an element of the Comprehensive Plan for the City of Portland, Maine.

100. *Downtown Vision: A Celebration of Urban Living* and *A Plan for the Future of Portland, A Component of the Comprehensive Plan for the City of Portland.* Adopted by the City Council of the City of Portland, Maine, March 1, 1991.

101. *Celebrating Community,* p. 5.

102. Malcolm Miles, *Art, Space, and the City: Public Art and Urban Futures* (London and New York: Routledge, 1997), p. 200.

Four Controversies in Public Art

In the following five interviews, the stories of four public art controversies are discussed. Two of the four controversies led to the removal of the artwork in question. In the third case, an additional work of art was added at the site to assuage the anger of the opponents, and the fourth case was a temporary work intended to create controversy. Richard Serra's *Tilted Arc* was commissioned for a federal office building in Lower Manhattan, and later removed from the site by the same governmental agency that commissioned it. John Ahearn was commissioned by the city of New York to create three bronze sculptures for a police station in the Bronx, where he lived. When community members objected, Ahearn asked that the bronzes be removed. Maya Lin won a national commission to design the *Vietnam Veterans Memorial* in Washington, D.C. When her design was unveiled, some veterans thought it was gloomy and gravelike, and sought to have the commission halted. After accepting the notion that a realist sculpture be added to the site, Lin's memorial was installed to great acclaim. *Welcome to America's Finest Tourist Plantation* was a bus poster designed by David Avalos, Louis Hock, and Elizabeth Sisco. Mounted on San Diego city buses during Super Bowl week, the posters ignited a public debate about questions of immigration, freedom of expression, and government support of the arts.

Over the years, I have argued that controversy is not such a large part of public art. I have cited statistics like the fact that roughly 97 percent of the public art projects I worked on at the Department of Cultural Affairs in New York City were well received, without a bit of rancor. However, these arguments tend to fall on deaf ears, as witnessed by the National Endowment for the Arts' need to convince critics that the vast majority of its grants are not to controversial projects, despite the occasional *Piss Christ* that festers in the public imagination. However, to be honest, I ran into *no* controversies when I was a curator for nine years, with the exception of a brief flurry of articles when Senator Alfonse D'Amato complained about a red, black, and green American flag that David Hammons hung outside P.S. 1 during the Persian Gulf War— and that, after all, was really a public art controversy. The majority of this book is dedicated to the discussion of public art projects that were not controversial. After this section, only Vito Acconci and Mel Chin discuss controversies in their interviews, and these controversies concerned projects that eventually went through as planned. But controversy is always a possibility in public art, particularly if it is funded through a governmental entity.

In his essay "The Violence of Public Art," W. J.T. Mitchell argues that there is a degree of violence associated with public art. He cites the destruction of public art from the removal of images of Mao in China to *Tilted Arc* and other contemporary works. However, Mitchell is talking not only about the violence done to public artworks, but also about the violence inherent in them. He says:

Violence may be in some sense "encoded" in the concept and practice of public art, but the specific role it plays, its political and ethical status, the form in which it is manifested, the identities of those who wield or suffer it, is always nested in particular circumstances. We may distinguish three basic forms of violence in the images of public art, each of which, in various ways interact with the other: (1) the image as an act or object of violence, itself doing violence to beholders, or "suffering" violence of vandalism, disfigurement, or demolition; (2) the image as a weapon of violence, a device for attack, coercion, incitement, or more subtle "dislocations" of public spaces; (3) the image as a representation of violence, whether a realistic imitation of a violent act, or a monument, trophy, memorial, or other trace of past violence.[1]

Certainly this taxonomy of violence in public art is relevant to the four projects in discussion here: *Tilted Arc* was the subject of vandalism, and was seen as a "dislocation" of the public space of Federal Plaza; Ahearn's bronzes in the Bronx were threatened with damage if they remained on the site, and were seen as the glorification of violent criminals; the *Vietnam Veterans Memorial* was a quiet reminder of the violence that had taken place in the war; *Welcome to America's Finest Tourist Plantation* was a reminder of the violence done to undocumented workers, was subject to violence in the form of defacement, and aroused violent emotions in some of its detractors. However, in different ways, each of these projects sought to reconceive the notion of the public monument in order to avoid the violence or tyranny of traditional public art. Serra sought to contest the oppression of the site through his "dislocation" of its physical and psychological architecture; Ahearn sought to validate ordinary people from the community rather than place oppressive "heroes" on the pedestals in front of a police station; Maya Lin sought an abstract, horizontal alternative to the phallic vertical thrust of the traditional heroic war memorial; Avalos, Hock, and Sisco chose a democratic, nonheroic site on the back of city buses, and sought to create an image in protest against the oppression of a segment of the city's population. Each of these projects became controversial because it did not conform to the expectations we hold for public art.

While some critics say that one of the most valuable things a public artwork can do is create a controversy that stimulates public interaction, debate, and dialogue, the controversy over Richard Serra's *Tilted Arc* was unusually divisive. On one side was an art world adamantly opposed to removing the work from the Federal Plaza. On the other side was a governmental bureaucracy, freshly appointed by Ronald Reagan, intent on undoing anything the Carter administration had left behind. William Diamond, the new regional administrator of the General Services Administration led the battle for the removal of *Tilted Arc*, calling hearings and appointing a panel to judge the case. Despite the questionable motivation for the hearings, they set up a remarkable public forum for the discussion of public art, and many of the New York art world's most prominent figures came forth to articulate their position on the value of public art. Douglas Crimp was among those who testified on Serra's behalf. As opposed to many of Serra's supporters during the hearings, Crimp has consistently acknowledged the difficulty and antiauthoritarian nature of *Tilted Arc.* At the hearing he called for the pursuit of mutual interests between Serra's supporters and the workers in the Federal Building. In his interview, Crimp differentiates between the various sorts of supporters that Serra had, arguing that there were significant differences among the seemingly unified front of the art world, and admitting that differences were put aside to make a concerted effort to support *Tilted Arc*. On the one hand there were more conservative supporters who simply felt that Serra had created a great and "lasting" work of art; on the other hand his more radical supporters applauded Serra's anti-institutional dislocation of the site. Crimp concludes with a discussion of his work with the AIDS Coalition to Unleash Power (ACT UP), and tells how it brought him back to Federal Plaza some years later to protest governmental policies regarding AIDS.

The second pair of interviews juxtaposes the opinions of an artist, John Ahearn, against the ideas of Arthur Symes, a government official who sought to have a public art project removed. There is a difference in the power structure between the Serra and Ahearn controversies. William Diamond, the administrator who led the effort to have *Tilted Arc* removed, was clearly an authority figure, proclaiming and obtaining power over the Federal Plaza (albeit purportedly on behalf of the little guy). Richard Serra and his supporters claimed the authority of the contract, of artistic freedom, and of lasting "quality." On the other hand, Arthur Symes, an African American city official, attacked John Ahearn's Bronzes as an insulted and injured victim of racism, not as an official with the governmental authority to remove the sculptures that were on public land. John Ahearn countered with arguments that claimed empathy with the people who lived in the neighborhood. While Serra fought to the end to save *Tilted Arc*, Ahearn himself made the decision to remove his sculpture. One striking similarity between Symes and Diamond is that they were attacking artworks that had been commissioned under previous administrations. Whereas Diamond was a Republican attacking a work commissioned under the Democrats, Symes was appointed under a liberal, Dinkins administration, and he attacked a work commissioned under the more conservative Koch administration.

When I went to interview Ahearn, I expected to speak only about the Bronzes in the South Bronx. However, he brought up a pair of projects that he had just completed in Ireland. I feel that the projects shed light on his artistic process, as well as on what was missing in the South Bronx. The problem with the Bronx Bronzes was that they were not made *with* but *for* the community, a community that then rejected them. The projects in Ireland show how Ahearn works outside the constraints of an official Percent for Art Program. One of the problems that I saw repeatedly in permanent commissions was that artists were forced out of their normal patterns.

Symes seems comfortable with certain sorts of censorship, which will certainly be difficult for many people in the art community to accept. But there are elements of his critique that are important to hear. Symes, along with every other opponent of the work with whom I spoke, placed Ahearn's work squarely within the framework of two traditions: the representation of black men as dangerous and the tradition of public art as heroic. Symes says he is insulted when he sees the demeaning representation of a blackface jockey on a white family's lawn, but he was *outraged* when he saw Ahearn's Raymond *on a pedestal*. As Symes says, it was "easy" for the community to see the problems with the sculptures; they were painfully obvious. Rather than build a community of support as Ahearn's previous art had done, this project tapped into a community of resistance. Symes claims that the works would have been destroyed if they were not taken down—not as vandalism but as an act of political defiance against what he understands the sculptures to represent.

Just as John Ahearn wanted to speak of projects aside from the Bronx Bronzes, Maya Lin has practically made it a policy that she will not speak about the *Vietnam Veterans Memorial* out of the context of all her work. When I went to her loft to conduct this interview for *Public Art Review*, I was under the impression that the editors had set up a time to speak about her memorial work for an issue they were planning on contemporary memorial art. However, when I told her the plan, she politely declined, saying that she was battling against being pigeonholed. In the more general interview that followed, she spoke about the *Vietnam Veterans Memorial*, but in a broader context. This context is valuable in dispelling certain inaccuracies about her work. For example, in the context of this interview, it should be clear that Lin's influences were not primarily within the traditions of Western modern sculpture. Roberta Smith, in her testimony at the *Tilted Arc* hearings, stated, "The *Vietnam Veterans Monument* [sic], which has been such a hit in Washington, is a result of someone working with Serra's ideas. So now [in *Tilted Arc*] we have the real thing, the original, the genuine article in our midst."[2] The oft-repeated fallacy that Lin either copied Serra's ideas or was a student of his at Yale University (both put to rest in the interview) disregards her background in architecture and interest in Eastern design and philosophy. It also fails to acknowledge the profound differences between their work, as well as their relationships with their audiences. The *Vietnam Veterans Memorial* is not boiled-down Serra, nor a derivative of the tried and true Minimalist aesthetic.

Despite its eventual widespread popularity, Lin's memorial came in contact with some of the same problems encountered by Serra and Ahearn. Chief among them was the popular notion that public art, particularly a war memorial, needs to be heroic, to stand as a hard-won trophy of past violence, as Mitchell might say. As she says in her interview, Lin does not see her work as monumental or didactic in the traditional sense. Rather, it stands mute, with some emotional distance from its subject.

While *Tilted Arc* and Ahearn's Bronzes were removed because of the controversies, the *Vietnam Veterans Memorial* is, of course, still standing. And it stands because Lin was willing to compromise at a crucial juncture. Lin says that she did not follow the path of strict idealism, did not threaten to pull the plug on her design, and waited until the ground breaking. It is interesting that Lin, with absolutely no experience in the field of public art at the time, was able to finesse a solution to her dilemma while Serra and Ahearn could not (though perhaps there was no solution to their controversies other than those that ensued).

The final interview in this section concerns a project in 1988 that generated a tremendous amount of press in Southern California, as well as across the country: *Welcome to America's Finest Tourist Plantation*, a bus poster by David Avalos, Louis Hock, and Elizabeth Sisco, which circulated in San Diego during the month the city hosted the Super Bowl. The work's poke at the town's boosterism quickly became front-page news. But these artists welcomed the dialogue and they proudly assembled every last headline, editorial, and letter to the editor in a self-published, spiral-bound record of the controversy. The xeroxed publication is a part of the piece—a document of the process of dialogue that the posters initiated. But there is an essential difference between the bus poster and the other controversies. First, the poster was a temporary project slated for a one-month period. Second, as Avalos, Hock, and Sisco say in the interview, it was meant to be a catalyst, not a work of art on its own. So, when it was attacked or even defaced, it was serving its purpose.

The problem with learning from public art controversies is that they never appear in the same guise twice. If the Serra controversy warned bureaucrats in New York that they should consult the Community Board before installing a piece of public art, and perhaps aim to commission realist art that is more "accessible," the Ahearn controversy pointed out that consulting the Community Board, hiring an artist from the area, and commissioning realist art is not necessarily any safer. In the case of the *Vietnam Veterans Memorial*, a realist sculpture was added to the site as a compromise, but it is the abstract sculpture that captured the imagination not only of the art world but also of Vietnam veterans and the families of the dead. While I was director of the Percent for Art Program in New York, a pleasant abstract sculpture by Bob Rivera on top of a school in the Bronx made headlines when Governor George Pataki chose it as a symbol for waste in the construction of new schools. Meanwhile, a rather politically charged work by Dennis Adams installed in a school in Queens never appeared in the press at all. This is not to say that it is unimportant to look at the history of public art controversies, only that one should not take the lessons too literally.

Notes

1. W. J. T. Mitchell, "The Violence of Public Art," in *Art and the Public Sphere,* ed. W. J. T. Mitchell (Chicago: University of Chicago Press, 1992), pp. 37–38.

2. From Clara Weyergraf-Serra and Martha Buskirk, *The Destruction of Tilted Arc: Documents* (Cambridge: MIT Press, 1991), p. 103.

Interview: **Douglas Crimp**
on Tilted Arc

Introduction

It is necessary to work in opposition to the constraints of the context, so that the work cannot be read as an affirmation of questionable ideologies and political power. I am not interested in art as an affirmation or complicity.
—Richard Serra[1]

In 1979, Richard Serra, one of the most powerful and respected artists in the United States, was commissioned by the General Services Administration (GSA) to design a sculpture for the east plaza of the Federal Building in lower Manhattan.[2] This plaza faces Foley Square, New York's civic center, which is circled with local and federal courts, the Department of Health, the Department of Motor Vehicles, and other government buildings. The Federal Building, which houses immigration offices as well as other bureaucratic and legal functions, is the largest federal office building outside of Washington, D.C. It is the regional headquarters of a number of agencies, including the GSA itself, so it is a highly visible site in the culture of government.

In 1981, the *Tilted Arc* was installed in Federal Plaza. Serra says, quite plausibly, that he made little or no profit on his $175,000 commission. The same year, Judge Edward Re of the Court of International Law (located in the Federal Building) began a letter-writing campaign urging the removal of the sculpture. This campaign was not successful, and things were fairly quiet until 1984, the year that Ronald Reagan took office and appointed a new Republican administration throughout the federal bureaucracy. At that time, the new regional administrator, William Diamond, with the support of Judge Re, reopened the issue of the removal of the *Tilted Arc*. Word of this effort spread through the art community; William Diamond had called public hearings to decide the *Arc's* fate. Though I was working a block from Federal Plaza at the Clocktower Gallery, the first I heard of the impending hearing was when a young man (working for Serra) came to the gallery and asked if I would post a petition in support of the sculpture. I gladly cooperated, and later, the signatures that I had gathered were a part of over 1,300 names in favor of the sculpture presented at the hearing. An equal number of signatures were presented by the *Arc's* opponents gathered mostly at desks set up in the Federal Building.

In the 1970s, the art world admired Serra's work for its literalness, for its break from the history of sculpture, its respect for materials, and its revelation of process. In 1970, reviewing one of Serra's early shows, Philip Leider praised *Sawing* in *Artforum:*

The work is a process piece in a very elegant sense, for it delivers to us in an admirably straightforward way not only the process of its making, but also the information that the same process of its making is also the solution to the problem dealt with in the work, i.e., the sawing plainly both makes the piece and is also that which unifies the various materials of the work.[3]

Leider is enchanted with the literalness of Serra's endeavor. Serra presents "information" in a "straightforward" manner. The "problem" addressed in the work is the unification of materials and the revelation of the process.

But eleven years later, in 1981, an *Art in America* review by Elizabeth Frank began, "Serra's latest exercise in site specificity was a great big arc of Cor-ten steel called *Slice.*"[4] Her discussion relates to how this sort of work by Serra manipulates the viewer, and how Serra's aggressive sculpture overwhelms the space. But the lead review in that issue of *Art in America* was of Anselm Keifer's show at Marian Goodman; the art world was beginning to stray from Postminimalism to an interest in neo-Expressionism. Serra's works had lost a bit of their power to astonish the art world. As Robert Storr pointed out in *Art in America,* "Coming at a time when the dominant taste was shifting toward new forms of figurative painting and sculpture, [Serra's commission for Federal Plaza] seemed to some to signal the final co-optation of the Minimalist aesthetic into institutional culture."[5] While the art world might have been used to Serra, the workers at Federal Plaza certainly were not. They were astonished, and did see the *Arc* as enormous and threatening. The federal workers were not yet used to the Minimalist aesthetic, but the furor caught many people in the art world by surprise. Wasn't Serra an establishment artist?

While securely anchored in New York's civic center, Federal Plaza is also in Tribeca, the mixed residential and commercial community south of Soho that became popular in the 1970s for artists' lofts. Eight hours a day, city, state, and federal workers circulate through the area, while, at night, the streets are deserted but for a handful of artists. The controversy over the *Tilted Arc* was billed as a contest between these two groups: the workers versus the artists. However, there is another group on the site every day that outnumber either of these groups: people from all over New York who need a green card, a new driver's license, who must meet a court date, or serve on jury duty. They were never consulted in the battle over Federal Plaza because they are temporary visitors. Because their affiliation with the site is so fleeting, they are outsiders; their "community" is elsewhere. The Serra hearings were a cathartic moment for the art world. They pitted the well-educated art world, often speaking in the technical vocabulary of the leftist intellectual, against the workers in the building. The "workers" were a diverse group—not only secretaries from the Federal Building, but also middle managers, lawyers, and government workers from nearby buildings. Serra and his allies insisted that the negative response to the *Arc* was manufactured by the top brass, William Diamond and Judge Re. However, the vehemence of those testifying against the piece spoke of genuine anger. To my knowledge the only worker from the Federal Building who spoke in favor of the sculpture at the hearing was Morris Ordover, the brother of one of Serra's lawyers.

There were technical arguments in favor of the *Arc* based on the government's contractual obligations and the fact that removing this site-specific sculpture would destroy it. But one significant artworld approach to the issue was epitomized by Museum of Modern Art Curator William Rubin's statement: "Richard Serra's *Tilted Arc* is a powerful work of great artistic merit. . . . Truly challenging works of art require a period of time before their artistic language can be understood by a broader public."[6] The workers' response, on the other hand, was summed up by Peter Hirsch: "The public is saying we don't like it, and we are not stupid, and we are not Philistines, and we don't need some art historians and curators to tell us that we will like it. We don't like it." But not all of Serra's supporters appealed to the "test of time." Douglas Crimp has written:

Historical precedents of public outrage meeting now-canonical works of modern art became something of a leitmotif. But this deferral to the judgement of history was in fact a repudiation of history, a denial of the actual historical moment in which Tilted Arc *confronted its public in all its specificity as well as a denial of Serra's intransigent rejection of the universal nature of the work of art.*[7]

In an oft-quoted interview with Douglas Crimp published in 1980, Serra said that he had not found the Federal Plaza interesting at first because it was a "pedestal site" in front of a public building, but that he had "found a way to dislocate or alter the decorative function of the plaza."[8] Serra was actively working in opposition to the "constraints of the context." But Shirley Paris, a worker from the building, testified thus:

This gigantic strip of rust is, in my opinion, an arrogant, nose thumbing gesture at the government and those who serve the government . . . It is bad enough for government and civil servants to be perennial targets of the public and the press alike, but for us to be degraded by an artist as well is, to say the least, compounding the insult.[9]

While Serra insists that he built the sculpture for the users of the plaza, many read the antigovernment message of the piece as a personal insult. Government workers are used to being demonized, and the piece was installed as the United States was entering a prolonged period of intense antigovernment sentiment. The humor generated by Judge Re's concerns that the *Tilted Arc* might be used as a bomb shield must now be tempered a bit by the realities of the bombing of the Federal Building in Oklahoma City. Government workers are defensive, and defensive groups consistently use public art as a focus for their grievances, as demonstrated throughout this section of this book.

For many people in the art world, the hearings were depressingly confrontational. As Douglas Crimp testified, "This hearing does not attempt to build a commonality of interest in art in the public realm . . . This is not a hearing about the social function that art might have in our lives."[10] There was no intellectual flexibility on either side, and the outcome was preordained. On May 1, 1985, William Diamond recommended that *Tilted Arc* be removed. *Tilted Arc* was now both a physical thing *and* a virtual site around which discourse was evolving. Commenting on the *Tilted Arc* controversy, James Wines said:

The court documents may, in fact, stand as a quintessential work of conceptual art, displacing the physical presence of the sculpture with the far more intriguing discourse it inspired. Had an artist of Duchamp's wit and perception been the creator of Tilted Arc, *he would have seized on the potency of this irony by declaring the court proceedings the art, and the clippings the exhibition catalogue. But Richard Serra is not an artist given to spontaneous reversals or trenchant humor.*[11]

Wines is suggesting that a work of public art creates a *process of reception.* While Serra had been a "process artist," the process never included a two-way public dialogue. In *The Destruction of Tilted Arc,* a book of documents of the hearings and subsequent court proceedings, Serra relates bitterly how he worked with CBS News on a segment about *Tilted Arc,* focusing on the notion of site specificity. When the program aired, he was "stunned" to see that it compared the *Arc* to garbage on the streets of New York. "I'd been had once again." He said, "I should have known that television delivers people, that all public opinion is manipulated opinion."[12] Serra saw no merit in his journey into the public sphere of media. He was filled with regret and recriminations.

The ripple effect of the *Tilted Arc* controversy was great. By the time I became director of New York City's Percent for Art Program in 1990, there had been a reevaluation of public art in the United States. Administrators all over the country revised their procedures for commissioning work. "Safeguards" were put in place to avoid the excruciating public display everyone heard about in New York City. Word was out: "the public" must be included in the process. The GSA reshuffled its procedures to be at once more bureaucratic (the GSA staff makes the final artist selection on the basis of an "objective" series of evaluation criteria), and more sensitive to the community, with "diverse" representation at the selection meetings.

The changes enacted by commissioning agencies, in general, were procedural and superficial. They were based on the negative rather than positive lessons of the *Tilted Arc* controversy, based on fear of controversy rather than an attempt to understand what might be truly meaningful to the users of the site.

Douglas Crimp is a critic, teacher, art historian, and activist. He graduated with a B.A. in Art History from Tulane University in 1968, and received his Ph.D., also in Art History, from the City University of New York in 1994. He has edited or coedited four books on contemporary criticism, AIDS, and film. In 1993, he published a book of his own essays, *On the Museum's Ruins,*[13] while another book, *Mourning and Militancy,* is forthcoming. Crimp has been a very visible figure in the arts for the last decade. He has lectured widely, appeared on numerous panel discussions, and published countless articles and interviews. His focus has been on art and politics, particularly the politics of AIDS and the ideology of the exhibition. For many years he was a member of ACT UP, an AIDS activist group in New York. But, for this interview, I asked Crimp to discuss the hearings surrounding Richard Serra's *Tilted Arc,* which took place in pre-AIDS New York, at a time when Crimp was more closely associated with

Richard Serra, Tilted Arc, 1981, New York, New York. Commissioned by the General Services Administration.

Postmodern theory than activist politics, not that he has ever been far from either. The following interview was conducted at Crimp's loft in lower Manhattan in January of 1997.

Tom Finkelpearl: I would like to talk about the hearings that led to the removal of Tilted Arc, *particularly your testimony. At the hearing, you said, "This hearing does not attempt to build a communality of interest in art of the public realm." And then later you said that the General Services Administration's (GSA) Art in Architecture Program "seems now to be utterly uninterested in building a public understanding of the work it has commissioned." What could the GSA have done to promote public understanding?*

Douglas Crimp: That statement was meant as a critique of William Diamond. It was my sense that the hearings were intentionally divisive, an attempt to manipulate people as a way to destroy Tilted Arc. *I'm not sure if I had anything in* mind. I suppose one could imagine that if there had been some sort of spontaneous disapproval of Tilted Arc on the part of the people who worked in the Federal Building, then, given the fact that the GSA commissioned the work, they might have wanted to hold some kind of workshops or make it possible for the artist to meet his critics. There are all kind of things that one might do if there were a festering disapproval. I have mixed feelings about education programs in contemporary art, especially with a work like Tilted Arc. Part of what interested me about it was its defiance, so I wouldn't particularly want that to be ameliorated. I was saying that, on the one hand the GSA commissioned and approved Tilted Arc, paid for it, installed it, and then a GSA official decided that he didn't like it, and he manipulated public opinion against it. The whole thing was done in bad faith. I was trying to speak against this bad faith, more than anything else.

TF: There are some public art programs in the United States that have very active public education programs. They try to make up for the fact that there is so little education about contemporary art. But with the sorts of resources they have, they might try to bring everyone "up to speed" on contemporary art, public art, and introduce Richard Serra's work in one or two workshops. I never pursued this sort of strategy.

DC: In my essay for Serra's show at the Museum of Modern Art (MoMA), I wrote that I and others who favored Tilted Arc could see its relation to a particular history, a very complex history.[14] But you can't just impart that history any more than you can impart any complex discourse overnight, but you might at least try to explain something about the importance of this artist. In the Cincinnati trial over Robert Mapplethorpe's photographs, the jury ultimately decided in favor of the museum because they felt that they could not determine what was art and that people who did know were telling them that Mapplethorpe's photography was art. I wouldn't want to be patronizing or elitist, but I do think that people could be made to understand that Tilted Arc wasn't just some kind of joke at their expense, that Serra is an incredibly serious artist of international renown, that his public works are in cities all across the world, and that most people find them extraordinarily beautiful. It's a different kind of aesthetic, but there are people who respond to this *aesthetic—something as simple as that. This is not to say that the whole history of site-specificity or Contextualism or Minimalism could be made comprehensible to people who hadn't followed the developments of contemporary art.*

TF: *My first experience with Serra was at the Hudson River Museum where I was the public relations director. Serra had a one-person show and installed* Elevator 1980. *We had a minicontroversy because most of our members did not understand the work. In that situation, the museum's education department hired an art historian, who presented a course in the museum that set a context for Serra. But that was a much more definable community, one that started with some knowledge and plenty of appreciation for art. At the Hudson River Museum, it was the community of volunteers and docents who were revolting and canceling their memberships. "Education" worked in that context. They didn't love the show afterwards, but they accepted it. As you said, it gave them a sense that it was serious. It is my sense that this is virtually impossible in a public context.*

DC: **Right, because for one thing, the people who come to a museum or who work in a museum are already a specific, self-selected group, unlike the people who passed by** Tilted Arc. **But there was a primary audience for the piece—the people who worked there, who were there every day and had to live with it. I suppose you could publish a brochure and hand it out to everybody who works in the building.**

TF: *The GSA does that now.*

DC: **Interesting.**

TF: *Though you might not be too thrilled with the contents of these brochures.*

DC: **I'm sure.**

TF: *Do you think that the federal workers' distaste for the* Tilted Arc *was completely manipulated? Was it absent prior to Diamond and Judge Re's campaign?*

DC: I'm sure that it was easy enough to tap into. Serra's work is difficult. It's hard for me to say this because I have followed Serra's work since I saw Splash in 1968, and I have loved his work. I find his work gorgeous, but that's a question of taste. I would furnish my apartment differently than most of the people who work in the Federal Building. I'm sure that a lot of them found Tilted Arc to be just a barrier. One of the reasons that Serra's work is important historically is that it changes the expectations of what a sculptural object is, in so many ways. I think that you could probably put a more conventional kind of public art on that plaza—the Bernard Rosenthal variety—and people wouldn't understand it fully, but they would recognize it as art and as amusing in some sense. But Serra's work is meant precisely to challenge those views. Diamond's cynicism was that he knew he could manipulate people's confusion.

TF: If the Tilted Arc was a critique of Federal Plaza, its architecture and institutional frame, why were people surprised when a conservative, Republican administration attacked it? Isn't that to be expected if you do something that radical?

DC: Well, your question is coming now, in 1997. It was a little different then. We weren't used to having Republican bureaucrats interfering with the arts. Now it seems inevitable that it would happen. For one thing, I think that until the NEA fracas, the people who might oppose public art or public funding for the arts weren't aware of how they could use the issue. They probably felt that they would make themselves look like Philistines, that a more sophisticated group of congresspeople could make them look like yahoos. This was one of the first contemporary instances of that kind of crass attack on art by public officials. When people came to understand who Diamond was, that he was a Reagan appointee and so on, things became clear. We were aghast and horrified and threatened, but I don't think that anybody was naive enough to assume that it would be business as usual. Maybe we were surprised at first, but we had to get over that, unfortunately, fairly quickly.

TF: It seems to me that a lot of the arguments that Serra's supporters were making at the hearings attempted to diminish the radical nature of Tilted Arc. There were a couple of different lines of argument. One argument consistently used by the art

Richard Serra, Tilted Arc.

world was, "You just don't understand it because it's avant-garde art, but you will learn to accept it like Impressionism . . ."

DC: Or your children will.

TF: Yes. But very few people were willing to acknowledge publicly that the Arc was an aggressive act against a certain kind of repressive space. I don't know if that was just a tactic at the time, or something that people genuinely felt. It seemed to me that people were saying, "How can we make this not sound radical?"

DC: In a different context I have written critically of Janet Kardon's testimony in the Mapplethorpe trial,[15] where she described the photograph of Mapplethorpe with a bullwhip up his bum as a "figure study," all about human proportions, lighting and so forth. But this was a strategy. It was a trial. In a sense, the Tilted Arc hearing was similar. People were incredibly antagonistic to the *hearing panel, but one didn't want to make a self-defeating argument. A lot of people talked about freedom of expression—explaining that what is protected as freedom of expression is unpopular speech. In fact, conflict was partly what that piece was about. On the one hand, I think that those of us who were partisans of Serra's work precisely for its radicality were perhaps underplaying the real reasons why we loved the work. On the other hand, many of the people who spoke at the hearings were sincere in their sense that we were simply in the presence of "great art." What makes Serra great for me is not what makes Serra great for William Rubin, and that came out in the conflict that I had with Rubin [then director of the Department of Painting and Sculpture at MoMA] over the catalogue text for Serra's show at MoMA in 1986. He didn't want my text published. His preface to the catalogue is in fact an argument against my text.[16] He refused to acknowledge me in the catalogue and refused to invite me to the opening dinner because he was so opposed to my reading of Serra's work. He would not have published the text, except that it came right after the* Tilted Arc *controversy, and who wanted more Serra controversy? Rubin's testimony at the hearing was about all of the great avant-garde masterpieces that were opposed in their historical moment—the universalist argument that eventually everybody would come to see that this is a great work of art. I opposed that argument, because I think the importance of Serra lies precisely in soliciting a certain kind of conflict.*

TF: *In your testimony you talked about looking out your window at the beautiful cupola of the Municipal Building, a city of New York office building a couple of blocks from the Federal Plaza. You said the Municipal Building "was built at a time when governments commissioned great architecture instead of bleakly functional and cheap buildings." Do you think that the kind of public space represented by the Municipal Building reflects a time in which there was a "truer" public sphere, in which the public sphere was more complete?*

DC: *My simple answer would be no. One of the problems with "public sphere" discourse as it issues from Jürgen Habermas is its nostalgia for a time of greater democracy, and I just don't think that's a particularly useful way of looking at it. I will say there is a huge difference between McKim, Mead, and White and whoever designed that hideous Federal Building. And I do think that there is a sense in which the increasing privatization of public spaces in New York City is a fundamental problem. But I think that the public sphere is something more complicated than whether or not there's a park here and there or whether or not a plaza is privately owned. The real extent of the collapse of public space is reflected in Judge Re's statement about the threat of terrorists behind the wall. It's that paranoid view of public gathering or of public debate, reflected in the manipulation of the Tilted Arc hearing itself. They felt they had to forestall a democratic process, but they had to institute a pretense of one because we are, after all, a democracy.*

TF: *So the hearing was like the plaza—a false vision of public space?*

DC: *Well, the plaza is defined as it is used by a public. If a public takes over that space and holds political meetings or rock concerts, then it becomes public through that use. The designers of the Federal Plaza managed to create a space that was inhuman in its scale, and in the way the wind whips through. The fountain could never be turned on because it would completely sweep the plaza with water. That seemed rather striking to me. They were talking about how Tilted Arc prevented all these wonderful events from happening on the plaza, but we knew what bad faith that was. Have they organized public concerts in that plaza since? Have they put picnic tables out?*

TF: *Well, for years it lay empty until its recent redesign, which is another story. What about the designation of the work as "permanent"? Isn't Serra's enterprise, the enterprise of that kind of site-specific work, that it's contingent?*

DC: *The issue of permanence had two dimensions. First of all, it was a contractual matter. The commission was for a permanent work. Second, Richard made a very interesting argument—that the site specificity determined that the work would no longer exist if it were moved because it was defined absolutely in terms of its site. The opponents of the Arc argued that they weren't destroying a great work of art; they were just going to move it some-*

Federal Plaza, New York, New York, after the removal of Tilted Arc, 1989.

place else. But, yes, there are contradictions. Unfortunately, there are works of Richard's that got removed, and he placed them elsewhere. Certainly Tilted Arc *was conceived for that site, and it wouldn't make the same kind of sense elsewhere. But after all, Richard's vocabulary is very abstract.* Clara-Clara *(the piece that was cited by people in the hearing who wanted to "relocate" the* Tilted Arc*) consisted of two leaning arcs. It was made initially for the pit at the Pompidou Center in Paris, but moved to the Tuileries, near the Place de la Concorde, and finally installed permanently at Square de Choisy.*

TF: *You couldn't have two more different sites than inside the Pompidou Center and the Tuileries.*

DC: *But* Clara-Clara *was more self-contained than* Tilted Arc. *What it needed was the two curves' relation to each other more than anything else. What's important for a work like* Tilted Arc *is the statement that it makes in relation to its*

Federal Plaza after the removal of Tilted Arc.

site. Now insofar as the site hasn't changed and the conditions haven't particularly changed, I suppose that it would be as viable as a statement today as it was then. But, theoretically speaking, you're right. The terms under which Serra is working include questioning universality. But I think that there's a difference between permanence and universality. I don't think he was talking about a permanent truth. If you put that sculpture up and then knocked all the buildings down and replaced them with an apartment complex, then I think you could make a good case that the piece wouldn't have the same meaning as it had before.

TF: *You concluded your testimony with a statement that invited the proponents and opponents of the Arc to act together. Referring to the Arc as a wall, which was the term the opponents of the piece used, you urged both groups to consider the proposition that we "keep this wall in place and that we construct our social experience in relation to it, that is, out of the sights of those who would conceive of social life as something to be feared, despised, and surveyed." Judge Re had said that the Arc was a barrier to surveillance, and you seemed to be agreeing, endorsing his reading from a very different perspective, from the other side of the wall, so to speak. So, what could have been done by the art world to construct that social experience?*

DC: *What I was claiming, somewhat unrealistically in that instance, was that art as a sort of negation or a critique of institutions (that had a whole history in the avant-garde of the twentieth century) was a reinscription of art in social practice. But it seems clear now that the art that makes the critique is not necessarily the art that goes on to construct a means of sociality, or of constructing a public sphere. In other words, I think that you could say that* Tilted Arc *functioned as a critique of the falsity of that plaza. It functioned as a critique and solicited in that whole debate the very extent to which the public sphere in our society has shrunk. But it is not able to move beyond that critique, and offer any sort of solution for the way that public sphere gets constructed. It seems to me that it waits for yet another generation of art practice where you have a reconception of public art. The point is that Serra is a historical figure of, in my mind, extraordinary importance. But his work has a particular historical function, and I don't think that it often moves beyond that function. There is a historical boundedness to Serra's practice. I think I was talking a little bit beyond the capacity of the work itself, although I had the intuition to think that what this critique enables is the thought of social practice, and that it solicits from the other side a fear of precisely that social practice. When you look at this wall and you think terrorism, or graffiti, or rats, you're announcing in very peculiar ways your fears of, precisely, democratic practice.*

TF: *So their fears may have been well founded from a rigidly conservative perspective.*

DC: *Of course an authoritarian position is going to fear this. We can't expect the William Diamonds of this world to want a deepening democratic practice. They want a shrinking public sphere. That's where their power resides.*

TF: *In your MoMA essay you said, "*Tilted Arc *was considered an aggressive, egotistical work with which Serra placed his aesthetic assumptions above the needs and de-*

Demonstration at Federal Plaza (Tilted Arc on right). Video: Dee Dee Halleck.

sires of people who live with his work. But insofar as our society is fundamentally constructed on principles of egotism, the needs of each individual coming into conflict with those of all other individuals, Serra's work did nothing other than present the truth of our social condition."[17] *On the other hand, you were back at Federal Plaza in 1987, as a member of the AIDS Coalition to Unleash Power (ACT UP), a radical collective dedicated to altering an unacceptable set of social conditions around AIDS. Wasn't this an attempt to go beyond pointing to the "truth of our social condition," toward the creation of a kind of radical democracy?*

DC: *I would not be as likely to speak about the "truth of our social condition," or the "truth" of anything anymore. What I was talking about was a false notion of individuality, the sense in which the creative individual—who makes an ameliorative gesture through the work of art that he places in the public sphere—becomes the embodiment of the "creativity of the individual" or the "autonomy of the individual." Whereas, structurally, in Marxist terms, in-*

dividuality exists only in relation to the rights of property. But I'm no longer a pure Marxist, and I think that's too simple a way of talking about our conditions. Now I would be much more interested in thinking about Serra as contesting particular *conditions inherent in that site or that historical moment—not a figure for universal truth, but rather a figure for critique and conflict.*

As far as the ACT UP demonstration is concerned, that is an example of a fairly self-conscious spectacularizing of the demand for democratic rights. That is to say, the demand has an aesthetic dimension. In many ways, ACT UP was an example of democracy in process—creating public space, or taking public space, or using public space was something that ACT UP was very good at. It was very savvy about taking to the streets, but also about the media and images and public discourse.

TF: *In retrospect, might that be the sort of social experience that we could construct on the "other side" of the* Tilted Arc?

DC: *Yes. When I wrote the essay for the Museum of Modern Art, the photograph that I wanted to open with, as the emblematic photograph for the essay, was a video image from a tape by Dee Dee Halleck. (The Museum of Modern Art would only print it at the end of that essay.) The photograph showed police at a demonstration that took place in front of* Tilted Arc, *at the Federal Plaza, protesting the U.S. Immigration and Naturalization Services's policies regarding Central American refugees.*[18]

Notes

1. *The Destruction of Tilted Arc: Documents,* ed. Clara Weyergraf-Serra and Martha Buskirk (Cambridge: MIT Press, 1991), p. 13.

2. The chronology of events outlined here is drawn from *The Destruction of Tilted Arc: Documents.* In addition, I am generally indebted to Robert Storr's article, "Tilted Arc, Enemy of the People?" *Art in America,* September 1985, p. 90.

3. Philip Leider "New York: Richard Serra, Castelli Warehouse" originally published in *Artforum,* February 1970, reprinted in *The New Sculpture* (New York: The Whitney Museum of American Art, 1990), p. 214.

4. Elizabeth Frank, "Richard Serra at Castelli Greene Street," *Art in America,* Summer 1981, p. 126.

5. Storr, "Tilted Arc," p. 92.

6. Clara Weyergraf-Serra and Martha Buskirk, eds., *The Destruction of Tilted Arc,* p.101.

7. Douglas Crimp, *On the Museum's Ruins* (Cambridge, MIT Press, 1995), p. 176.

8. *Richard Serra Interviews, Etc.,* 1970–1980 (Yonkers, NY: Hudson River Museum, 1980), p. 168.

9. *The Destruction of Tilted Arc,* p. 126.

10. Ibid., p. 73.

11. James Wines, *De-Architecture* (New York: Rizzoli, 1987), p. 87.

12. *The Destruction of Tilted Arc,* p. 10.

13. Douglas Crimp, *On the Museum's Ruins* (Cambridge: MIT Press, 1993).

14. Crimp wrote, "The larger public's incomprehension in the face of Serra's assertion of site specificity is the incomprehension of the radical prerogatives of a historic moment in art practice. 'To remove the work is to destroy the work' was made self-evident to anyone who had seen [Serra's 1968 work] *Splashing's* literalization of the assertion, and it is that which provided the background of *Tilted Arc* for its defenders. But they could not be expected to explain within the short time of their testimonies, a complex history which had been deliberately suppressed. The public's ignorance is, of course, an enforced ignorance, for not only is cultural production maintained as the privilege of a small minority within that public, but it is not in the interests of the institutions of art and the forces they serve to produce knowledge of radical practices even for their specialized audiences." From: "Serra's Public Sculpture: Redefining Site Specificity," in *Richard Serra/Sculpture* (New York: The Museum of Modern Art, 1986), p. 42.

15. Crimp wrote, "Expert witnesses for the defense—mostly museum officials—described Mapplethorpe's wider aesthetic preoccupations and detailed the photograph's 'formal qualities,' reducing them thereby to abstractions, lines and forms, light and shadow. Here is Janet Kardon, *The Perfect Moment's*

curator, speaking of Mapplethorpe's self-portrait in leather chaps and vest with a bullwhip shoved up his rectum, which Kardon referred to as a 'figure study': 'The human figure is centered. The horizon line is two-thirds of the way up, almost the classical two-thirds to one-third proportions. The way the light is cast so there's light all around the figure, it's very symmetrical, which is very characteristic of his flowers.'" From Crimp, *On the Museum's Ruins,* p. 10. The Kardon quote is from Jayne Merkel, "Art on Trial," *Art in America,* Vol. 78, No. 12 (December 1990), p. 47.

16. Rubin wrote in the preface to Serra's Museum of Modern Art catalogue, "The Museum of Modern Art disagrees with the rhetorical tone and historical polemic of much that has been written about *Tilted Arc* here and elsewhere." *Richard Serra/ Sculpture,* p. 9. Crimp responded in a highly unusual author's note at the beginning of his essay, "This essay represents my position on site specificity as I was led to consider the issue in relation to the crisis over Richard Serra's *Tilted Arc,* a crisis that pushed my earlier ideas in a new direction, redefining the terms of the problem. That this position may be at variance with that of the Museum of Modern Art, indeed of most art institutions, will be obvious from my argument. Transcending the differences between the Museum and myself, however, is our shared understanding of the importance of Serra's work." *Richard Serra/Sculpture,* p. 41. Crimp told me that the museum demanded this disclaimer—especially the part about "transcending our differences."

17. Ibid., p. 53.

18. Crimp, *On the Museum's Ruins,* p. 178.

19. Crimp's essay on Serra from the MoMA catalogue was reprinted in his book *On the Museum's Ruins.* In this context, the image of the demonstration on Federal Plaza shares a page with an image of a police officer witnessing the removal of *Tilted Arc.*

Interview: **John Ahearn**
on the Bronx Bronzes and
Happier Tales

In September of 1991, John Ahearn installed three bronze sculptures on a plaza that he had designed in front of the Forty-fourth Police Precinct House in the Bronx. Although this might be difficult to imagine to those who are familiar with the events that followed, the installation of the bronzes was eagerly awaited by everyone involved. It was the culmination of years of work including numerous bureaucratic and construction delays,[1] and this was *John Ahearn,* a widely respected artist, one who had considerable community support. We were all aware of the popular public projects that Ahearn had completed within several blocks of the Forty-fourth Precinct. The public "review process," from the Art Commission to the Community Board, had led us to believe that there would be no significant problems. Nobody was quite certain that the police would love the work, but we all felt that the community would embrace the sculptures which, after all, depicted Raymond, Daleesha, and Corey, "neighborhood residents" well known to the artist. But the installation of these bronzes triggered a full-blown controversy. When the controversy broke, discussion of the issue moved from the daily papers and local television into the art magazines, and to a lengthy article on the controversy in the *New Yorker,* which was later published as a book.[2] How could this project blow up after all of the changes that had been made since the *Tilted Arc* controversy? What about the mechanisms for community review?

In the Spring of 1986, less than two years after the hearings over *Tilted Arc,* a Percent for Art selection panel convened to choose an artist for the Forty-fourth Precinct. In accordance with the new standard procedures in public art, the selection panel included not only arts professionals but also representatives from the Police Department, the Department of General Services, which would be building the station, a curator from the nearby Bronx Museum of Art, as well as an artist and a representative from the Department of Cultural Affairs. Local politicians and community leaders were also invited to sit in on the proceedings. The panel quickly came to a decision to award the $99,000 commission to John Ahearn. He was an obvious choice because he lived close to the station, enjoyed a good critical reputation, and had already spent many years interacting with the community. The panel agreed on several recommendations for the artist: the work should be "colorful," the artist should "work with the community," and should "consider amenities within his or her design, such as seating."[3] These suggestions could not have been further from *Tilted Arc,* and Ahearn fit

John Ahearn, Bronx Sculpture Park, opening day, 1991, Bronx, New York. Photograph: Ari Marcopoulos.

the mold for the "post-Serra" artist perfectly. He was well acquainted with the specific nature of the community within which the commission was sited, and worked in a figurative style that is considered accessible. In fact, despite the rejection of the work, this assessment was accurate to a certain degree. Ahearn's artistic *style* was popular, although this made it no more popular than *Tilted Arc.*

Soon after being selected, Ahearn proposed to redesign a traffic triangle in front of the Precinct House as an open plaza, featuring a number of sculptural figures—to create a new public space as a "bridge" between the precinct and the community. This idea was discussed between four city agencies: the Department of General Services (DGS), which manages the city's capital construction; the Department of Transportation (DOT), which controlled the traffic triangle; the Department of Cultural Affairs (DCA); and, of course, the Police Department. In mid-1988, DOT agreed to put up the money for the renovation of the traffic triangle in exchange for the design services of DGS.[4] While Ahearn's project had a budget of $99,000, the construction budget for the plaza, with benches and pedestals, was added through this interagency agreement.[5]

In August of 1989, Ahearn signed a contract to create cast bronze figures for the site. He proposed to cast three sculptures in bronze: *Raymond and Tobey* (a boy with his pit bull), *Daleesha* (a young woman on roller skates) and *Corey* (a young man with a basketball under his arm and his foot up on a boombox). His proposal subsequently received approval from the Art Commission[6] and Community Board #4. Perhaps because of his previous work in the community, there was very little discussion of the new project at the Community Board. People remembered the positive public response to his relief murals, how they depicted local life, and how Ahearn had created them on the streets. The only note of criticism at the meeting came from a police representative who suggested that the work should include an image of a policeman. Needless to say, Ahearn chose not to add a cop to the set of figures.

On the basis of the approvals, Ahearn was given notice to proceed with the fabrication of his bronzes. Soon after I began working at Percent for Art, I traveled with other city officials to inspect the bronzes at the foundry. Although Ahearn had not finished painting the sculptures, we took some snapshots to document the work—as backup for our files to verify that the work was fabricated, and that the artist was due his next payment. Just before the installation of the sculptures, we began to hear rumblings of discontent over the nature of the works. I was pulled aside by a DGS staff member, who told me that the snapshots of the bronzes that we had taken at the foundry were circulating among the senior staff at DGS, and there was *serious* trouble. Around the same time in mid-September of 1991, DGS Commissioner Kenneth Knuckles called Charmaine Jefferson, the acting commissioner of Cultural Affairs. He expressed his opinion on the basis of our snapshots that the sculptures were racist. Both Knuckles and Jefferson are African American. In this conversation and throughout the controversy, Jefferson defended the artist's right to express himself, and argued that seeing the works as racist was a misinterpretation. To her, these sculptures represented people she knew in the African American community—perhaps not the cream of the crop, but recognizable, "real" people. This position was backed up by all the voices of the Department of Cultural Affairs, particularly Linda Blumberg, the (white) assistant commissioner for Public Affairs.

Blumberg and I quickly arranged a meeting with DGS, and found that two of the most active detractors were Arthur Symes, architect and assistant commissioner of DGS, and Claudette LaMelle, the executive assistant to the commissioner. At our meeting, the two reiterated their opinion that the work was insensitive to African Americans; the images were stereotyped, and the figures were not involved in productive activity. They felt that Raymond, the young man with his dog, looked like a drug dealer, and that this would be clear to *anyone* in an inner-city neighborhood. These were not "positive role models" for youth. LaMelle and Symes did not question the selection of Ahearn or the quality of his work. They simply felt that the specific people he chose to represent were not appropriate as public monuments.

As soon as the works were installed on September 26, local opposition began to surface and the exact opinions that Symes and LaMelle expressed were voiced by community activists and passersby in the street: these were not positive images of the community, and they must be removed. We received outraged telephone calls at the Department of Cultural Affairs, and the Community Board district manager called to tell us he was receiving negative calls as well. It is impossible to gauge the breadth of popular opinion from a series of telephone conversations. The calls could well have been coming from a small number of people. However, it was easy to judge the depth of the opposition. These callers were clearly angry. I vividly recall talking to an elderly woman. She tearfully told me that she felt like a prisoner in her home in the South Bronx, that she could not go outside at night because of "people like the ones you put in front of the police station."

Very upset, John Ahearn immediately called us, and had a series of lengthy conversations with a range of city officials. After assessing the situation, Ahearn came to the conclusion that the work needed to be removed immediately. On the morning of October 1, the sculptures were removed from the triangle by a company hired by Ahearn, and moved to a warehouse. Ahearn predicted that if they were not removed, the works would be the center of a very damaging controversy in which he would be cast as a racist. He thought that things were about to get out of hand.

The Forty-fourth Precinct is a site that taps into two of the community's most intense issues: the relationship with the police, and the role of Yankee Stadium in attracting outsiders to the community. The sculptures managed to inflame both issues simultaneously. We heard some version of this complaint repeatedly: "A lot of the traffic on Jerome Avenue is outsiders driving up to Yankee Stadium. These sculptures will simply reinforce those people's prejudices about the South Bronx. We are not all criminals!" *Raymond, Corey,* and *Daleesha* played on the community's worries about its public face, its feeling that the rest of the city thinks of South Bronx residents as drug runners and no-good, unproductive criminals. The "bridge" between the community and the police that the artist and the selection panel had hoped for certainly did not materialize, or if it did, it was in their mutual attack on the art. Here was something that community members and the police could agree upon: The sculptures had to go.

Since *Tilted Arc* was installed the United States had seen the growth of identity politics, often painted along the most predictable lines of race. Despite the fact that Ahearn had lived and worked in the neighborhood for twelve years, he was repeatedly referred to as *not* being a member of the community. Arthur Symes, who lived in Battery Park City, said, "He's not of the community because he's not black—it's as simple as that."[7] But the neighborhood is not even primarily African American. In fact, like Harlem and Watts, this traditionally black part of the South Bronx is becoming increasingly Latino. Between 1980 and 1990, the black population declined by 13 percent to 48,000 people, while the Latino population increased 31 percent to 64,000. The white, non-Hispanic population fell 60 percent in the same period to fewer than 3,000 people,[8] including Ahearn, of course. During this same period, David Dinkins, an African American, had taken office, and the power structure of the city was becoming increasingly black. Symes, though living in an affluent white enclave and working as an assistant commissioner of a powerful agency, felt comfortable speaking for the black community in the South Bronx, while Ahearn, living in the South Bronx, was an "outsider." The popular press, like Symes, saw the issue in black and white. A headline in the *New York Post* read: "CITY PAYS 100G FOR ART BLASTED AS ANTI-BLACK."[9] For most people, this was a race issue, pure and simple. The identity of the artist and the figures held center stage. It was hardly mentioned in the press that Raymond, the model for one of the three sculptures, is, in fact, Latino. The reasons for this are complex, including the specific politics of New York at the time, but perhaps the controversy boiled down to black and white because, as bell hooks argues (drawing on James Cone), blackness is "the quintessential signifier of what oppression means in the United States."[10] The word "black" in the *New York Post* headline stood for the oppressed in general, or at least people of color. And the headline was literally true. Even though the sculptures did not depict only African Americans, and they were not in an African American community, they *were* being blasted as "anti-black."

The notion that the sculptures were "sinister and criminal" fails to consider the figure of *Daleesha,* the girl on roller skates. There were two photographs of the sculptures in the *New York Post* article. The caption under *Raymond and Tobey* read:

"IN THE HOOD: This statue of a hooded youth kneeling beside a pit bull sparked strong objections." And the caption under *Corey* read: "STEREOTYPE: This image of a basketball player with a boom box has South Bronx residents and cops up in arms." There was no photograph of *Daleesha*. It is predictable that the discussion became a discussion of the black male, while the female was rendered invisible for the most part.

In the same *New York Post* article, a police officer commented on the sculptures, "We were stunned. We spend so much time trying to work with the community, and that artwork is so clearly racial stereotyping. The message the art would have sent was at the least, insensitive. At most it could have caused a riot. The pieces were unbelievable." This statement reveals another aspect of the work that we came in contact with: The sculptures were seen by some people as representing the Police Department's vision of the community, and everyone knew how fraught that issue was.

Prior to the Forty-fourth Precinct commission, the public murals Ahearn had created in the South Bronx were gifts to the community. They were self-funded on the whole, and they were *not* associated with any police stations. When confronted with a public commission, Ahearn felt compelled to make it clear that he was not acting on behalf of the police—to clarify his independence. Like Richard Serra, Ahearn wanted to have a voice independent of the institution that was the funding source and physical site for his project. In the South Bronx, with the division of the community and the police, it seemed possible to speak *with* the community, while not speaking for the police, just as Serra had sought, however obliquely, to speak with the workers against the space created by the government.

John Ahearn was born in Binghamton, New York, in 1951. He received a Bachelor of Fine Arts degree at Cornell University in 1973. Starting in 1977, Ahearn worked with Collaborative Projects, Inc., (a.k.a. Collab) on a number of projects, including documentary films, a cable television show, and the "Times Square Show" (1980), which brought scores of contemporary artists into New York's seediest neighborhood. He started showing his work extensively in the early 1980s both in outdoor projects and in galleries and museums. Many of his projects have been created in collaboration with Rigoberto Torres since the early 1980s. While Ahearn is best known for his outdoor, community-oriented projects, he has had numerous one-person exhibitions at commercial galleries, and his work is in public collections ranging from the Hirshorn Museum, to the Boston Museum of Fine Arts, and the Museum of Contemporary Art, Los Angeles. In this interview, conducted in February 1995, John Ahearn describes the ordeal of the commission at the Forty-fourth precinct. Following a discussion of the South Bronx bronzes is a description of subsequent projects that Ahearn undertook in Ireland. The projects in Ireland exemplify his normal process and the degree of community interaction and dialogue that he routinely engages in.

Tom Finkelpearl: I would like to discuss the difficulties that surrounded the sculptures at the Forty-fourth Precinct. One of the problems that we encountered was a basic discrepancy in interpretation. Many of the people who objected saw the sculptures as symbols, *while people who defended them saw them more as* individuals.

John Ahearn: They are both. They did represent individuals, but the problems that people saw in the work were not invented or imaginary. I made some errors in judgment along the way. The work that was created was powerful as it was set up, maybe stronger than the murals that were done previously. But the issues were too hot for dialogue. The critics said that the people in the community have a right to positive images that their children can look up to. I agree that the installation did not serve that purpose.

TF: Were they symbols of the community?

JA: One could say that, but, as much as I agree with the critics, I do not agree that the boy with the hooded sweatshirt needs to be a drug dealer, even with the pit bull. All the kids in the neighborhood seemed to dress like that.

TF: So it's a common look in the neighborhood.

JA: But I did not pick three images that I thought would represent kids on the block. The way it started out was that I had a long-standing relationship with Raymond. I am still in contact. I saw his family yesterday. I have always been inspired by knowing him. We worked out this idea to do a sculpture that included his dog. This preceded this commission.

TF: *So the project involves your private interaction with Raymond. Then there's the relationship that evolves around the actual casting (sometimes done in public), how you carve and paint the sculpture, and then the public display of the image—first at a gallery, in various collections, in front of the police station, later in a museum in Ireland—how do all of these relate?*

JA: *Let me answer by tracing the steps. That project was doomed in its conclusion by so many steps that led us down this path. Let me go back. There was a point between 1979 and 1983 when there was some kind of unity between needs of the art world, needs of the community, my private needs. For me, everything seemed to be in balance. Those first three Bronx murals were done in that spirit, particularly the first two, where I felt that there was a balance between a harsh reality of life that the art world could respect and relate to as a real, an honest portrayal of life that was shocking to them, and interesting. But there was also presented a kind of high-spirited, idealistic, community life at the same time—in balance. First was* We are Family, *then* Double Dutch, *then* Life on Dawson Street.*

I felt, the day that the first two went up, like Martin Luther tacking his proclamation on the cathedral door. This was my statement to the art world—here is where I put my work. This is what I believe in. By the time the third mural went up it was already getting a little mottled—a continuation of a statement rather than the statement itself. I got confused, and did a couple of side projects to get back into it. Then I said, "Let's do a project for the neighborhood." For the Back to School *mural I said, "Forget the art world." This time I felt I would deal with the community itself. The mural was designed to face the school. We put it up and had a big block party.*

I tried to force those [Back to School] images on the art world at the time, including a show at Brooke Alexander Gallery. But the whole thing seemed "off." It was too nice in a way and it lacked an edge. What had been put together very carefully had pulled apart—that unity of speaking to all sides simultaneously, which is a hard thing to maintain, right? In a way I was following a vision that Rigoberto had—the ideal. A "positive image" street scene. But I like the mural a lot. Every day I got up and it sung to me when I went to get coffee. It was a good vibration for me, very nice.

John Ahearn and Rigoberto Torres, Double Dutch, 1981–1982, Bronx, New York. Photograph courtesy of Alexander and Bonin Gallery.

A part of me felt that maybe I had to dig deeper into the life that I was living in the community to find a contact with the art world—something more difficult. It is too simple to say "negative imagery." It has to do with dealing with emotions and feelings that were darker . . . I am a little at a loss to describe it. My own personality in the neighborhood had other sides to it. I had needs as an artist in terms of contact with the people that were maybe more obsessive than what I was displaying in this Back to School image. What brought this out was my long-running relationship with Raymond. It brought out things that were better and also darker and stranger—more complex. I always found him fascinating as a person. I decided that I would work with him.

Raymond was part of the Latino community. Then I started working with Corey. The neighborhood where I was working was split down the middle, and one-half was very Puerto Rican (now going more Dominican) while the other half was black. They got along, but were divided. I was living on the Puerto Rican side so I decided that I was going to throw myself into the other part of the neighborhood as a way to extend my understanding of what was going on.

At that time I started to do life casting on the block more, not so much with Rigoberto but on my own. I would set up the casting process on the north end of the block. I pushed it up 50 feet, and suddenly got it into a different community.

TF: The black end of the block?

JA: Yes. At the same time I was thinking that I wanted to do freestanding figures. Raymond was the best and the first. What I had not foreseen, when I showed the freestanding work, was that the art world went to Raymond like bees to honey. For some reason he touched on something that people really liked. Strange.

At the same time the Police Precinct commission was getting set up. Originally they had asked me to do faces on the outside of the building. I did not like such a close connection with the Police Precinct, and the architect did not want me touching his building. So I suggested that we work with this traffic triangle across the street—a site for freestanding figures.

TF: The traffic triangle was not part of the original capital project?

JA: No. Jennifer McGregor Cutting [then the director of Percent for Art] fought hard to get the triangle into the project, although everyone said that it would be impossible. We spent years working on this, and finally things flipped and the city started supporting the idea. My idea all along was that I wanted to do a group project in the community out of concrete. Freestanding concrete figures using wire mesh. I thought that it would be really great to do all the work in the neighborhood. All the money would have been spent there. [The commission was $99,000.] A group community project. But the city was against using poured concrete. They said that it doesn't last. Bad idea. They wanted bronze.

I had gotten a letter awarding me the commission from Bess Meyerson in 1986, and year after year there was no contract. The advice I was given all around was: do not start this project until you get your contract because we

cannot promise anything. So all of the time that I was going to these meetings fighting for the traffic triangle, I was not developing the artwork for the
project. I kept holding back. All of a sudden there was an announcement that
I was going to receive the contract (this was four years later) and there was
a request—could I have a proposal ready two months later for review by the
Art Commission. It went from "do nothing" to "have it all done." Generally
one of my weak points as an artist is design—I do not tend to be very good
at making designs in advance.

By that time, I already had finished Raymond. Corey was halfway done.
So I started thinking, "If I am going to make bronzes, these would be beautiful." From the beginning, Corey was designed to look sort of like a Greek
athlete, like the discus thrower or something. Meanwhile, what I felt all
along about Raymond—this is very ironic—I felt guilty that these pieces were
going into collections and there was nothing for the community. I felt like I
owed it to the community to give them the image of Raymond, that everyone would love it. It never occurred to me that this would be a negative image. It was so popular in the art world. I figured that the community deserved
to have this image.

What happened to the bronzes was a part of a long process that had
negative aspects to it. I can not help but think that the bronzes represented
a message to the art world more than to the local community. The Back to
School image was overly sweet and idealistic. But the art world kind of liked
these bronzes at the Police Precinct.

TF: What about the reaction to the bronzes?

JA: The moment of the installation reflected the problems with the process. For example, in previous times when we installed the wall murals a supportive community would all come out in strength to view their friends being hoisted up
on the wall. It was a family situation. Whereas the installation of the bronzes
was a little bit removed from the neighborhood that I lived in, even though
it was only four blocks away. It was just far enough away that it only got
a stray group of onlookers that I recognized. Unlike earlier days, the few
friends of mine from downtown that showed up outnumbered the local
community, which made me a bit uneasy. There was a disquiet to the day. Al-

John Ahearn, Raymond and Toby (with Raymond on bicycle), 1991, Bronx, New York. Commissioned by the New York City Department of General Services, the New York City Police Department, and the New York City Percent for Art Program. Photograph: Ari Marcopoulos.

ready as the pieces were unveiled, there were arguments at the site as to the purpose of the work. That had never happened with the murals. In earlier times, the murals were seen as a private thing within the community, but this was instantly understood to be of a citywide, public nature. This was perceived to be a city site.

TF: And it was—a public commission.

JA: People could tell the difference. People felt that this had to do with the city, not with their community.

TF: The reaction then in the tabloids was to paint you as insensitive to race matters.

JA: There was a little twist. They could have targeted the artist, but that was not so interesting as to target the city [government] for foisting this racist art on the public.

TF: That's true actually. And this is almost always true in these controversies—attacking the city for misusing taxpayer money.

I find it interesting to hear how you, as an artist, are being pulled in different directions by the art world, the community, personal concerns, etc. This is a great problem for the public artist.

JA: What gave me a feeling of confidence at the time of the original work was a faith that all of these things could be done at once, that they were not distant things. I believed that answering the needs of the community, answering your own private problems that you are working out, dealing with art historical problems, that these things could all be made in one piece. That this was interesting art—trying to focus on the unity of all of those things rather than the opposition—that it was possible to make a single image that could speak to someone on the street and also the art world—that this could inform the style that you work in to create something fresh and different.

TF: Do you still believe that this is possible?

JA: To say it is possible—that is easy. To say you are doing it is more difficult. I believed that I was doing it.

TF: Can you tell me about what you have been doing since?

[Ahearn brings out a set of photographs.]

JA: This was the installation at the Irish Museum of Modern Art in Dublin, the last week that I was there. This [Raymond and Tobey] was something that they borrowed for the show. I had forgotten that it just happens to relate to our project, by coincidence. But I thought it was kind of cool because he is a Bronx youth, and these casts are sort of the "bad boys" of Dublin.

TF: Can you take a step back? So you were invited by [museum director] Declan McGon-
     agle for a show?

JA: Really I was asked to be "artist-in-residence." I was invited by Brenda McPartland
     of the curatorial department. When I got there they passed me over to the
     community and education department. The education department at the
     museum already had a relationship with a men's group: the Men's Group
     Family Resource Center. The men were mostly older than I am—retired or un-
     employed workers, not artists. Not a women's art group, but a men's art
     group, which is unusual. I dropped by last summer for four days and met with
     the men and we did a cast. We discussed future possibilities so that when I
     came back, I was ready to do the project. Here's a picture of the early meet-
     ing. Aren't they great guys? I was so into it. I would advise them, give them
     council or technical help to fabricate, but they make the work from begin-
     ning to end, and they have their name on it.
          The curatorial department treats artists like princes. In the education
     and community department, you are more like a worker—to help people in
     the area. I like that idea, but I've also had the experience where it can be
     antagonistic. I think in some ways the curatorial department represents an
     upper class and the community and education department represents a
     working class. And when the group saw me, I was the artist invited by the cu-
     ratorial department and passed over to them.

TF: You made a statement in a publication issued by the museum that you surrendered
     control of the project to the men's group, and that the final product could serve
     as a mural in the center. So you were not only relocating the power into their
     hands but also saying that the final product would not be for the museum, but
     for the center. Did this happen?

JA: Yes, they were planning to install the work after I left.
          The men's center was set up with the idea of group decisions. If some-
     one suggested something, they'd say, "Let's wait until all the guys come to-
     morrow and then we will sit and talk about it." They regarded themselves as
     a collective and thought that individual efforts without the support of the
     group were divisive. I did play the devil's advocate, encouraging individual

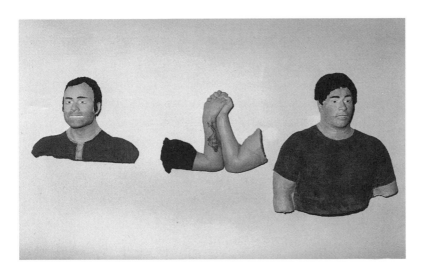

John Ahearn, life casts at the Men's Group Family Resource Center, 1995, Dublin, Ireland.
Commissioned by the Irish Museum of Modern Art.

*men to work with me after class. I told them that they had twenty-four-hour
access because I was living over the workshop. But I felt constrained by the
dynamic within the men's group.*

*I said to the museum, "I want to work on an additional project where I
can be the author of the work. Let me loose with some people, and I will do
everything I can." So they said "Great, we've got a school that we are already
working with: the Christian Brothers School, a boys' school."*

TF: A single-sex public school?

*JA: Single-sex, yes, with Catholic Brothers teaching there. I went over there with Liz
McMahon from the museum's Education and Community Department. We
met [Una Keeley] the art teacher and "Brother Joe," the principal. I showed
them a catalogue from the South Bronx work. As we were talking I was saying, "I would be happy to make work and we could put it on the walls of the
school." I was promising everything. I was brought into a class with twenty-
five kids, around eleven years old. They are tough, Irish "ghetto" kids.*

I went to a mostly Irish American parochial school when I was growing up. The Dublin boys looked familiar. Boy for boy, each kid in my own school seemed to have a counterpart in this group. Brother Joe said, "If you do one kid you have to do them all to be fair." I said, "Let's go for it and see what happens." I give the school and the community lots of credit for the way they set up this program. We met three times a week for two-and-one-half-hour sessions. This was intensive. We met for six weeks. It was late in the school day, so, as the kids came out of the mold, it was time to get on the bus. I was left with all of the molds. At the end of each day my assistant, Danny Pico, and I would start our work. They left us to work, not the way I was guiding the men's group, saying, "Now you pour the plaster. Now you mix up the paint." I got to do my work, and if I wanted to stay up until 1:00 in the morning to work on it, beautiful. Often that is what it was. Twice in the week we would work and they would come the very next day. With art, I like the product to feed into the process. So when they would come the next day, I would want everything sculpted, finished, ready, and on the wall. So I was getting my work done but also inspiring them. The project had a kind of growth and high-spirited energy.

TF: *This was happening at the same time as the project with the men's center?*

JA: *Yes. Often we would meet with the men's group in the morning and then the boys would come in the afternoon. We did about forty-five workshops when I was there in Ireland.*

I felt that I was not getting enough of my own vision into the project with the men's center. It seemed better just to let the men have it to themselves. We had a show at the end of the project at the museum. As I said, after the show is taken down, the work will go back to the community center. What we devised as a final answer with the children—the school had given so much and the museum had given so much, and I gave a lot—I agreed to donate my part in the project to the museum, with the agreement that, after being shown at the museum, the work would go to the school. Still, the museum would be the final owner of the piece, not the school. The school could have it as long as it wanted, and it could go back and forth. The museum was the caretaker of the piece.

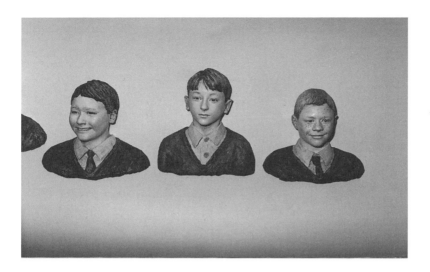

John Ahearn, life casts at the Christian Brothers School, 1995, Dublin, Ireland. Commissioned by the Irish Museum of Modern Art.

TF: *I wanted to ask you about individual expression in terms of the private/public axis. In a way what happened in Ireland is that the project that represented your* individual *expression ends up with a home in the museum . . .*

JA: **Possibly, yes.**

TF: *Whereas the collective project ends up having a home in the community. What are the class implications of that?*

JA: **The class implications are obvious, but I always like my art to function in both situations.**

TF: *The project in which control was given to the community members may have been therapeutic for them—the process was very positive for them. With the boys, you said that you struggled over pieces—carving an eye ten times. There the product was more the focus?*

JA: *The product and the process work together.*

TF: *Your artwork necessitates engagement with a group of individuals.*

JA: *Yes. There is a dependence. [Ahearn brings out some photographs of the early castings at Fashion Moda.]*

These photographs are from 1979. My recent project in Ireland is almost like this project at Fashion Moda, fifteen years ago. When we started casting in the Bronx, it attracted crowds. It was like an accident scene. Everyone would be saying, "Who did it? What happened?" And then people would linger at the doorway and they would look in and feel that it was okay, and would come inside and sit down, and start hanging out. There was nothing organized about it.

There is this core thing, a repetition. But it seems that every time I go back to the very core thing, that is when I do the best work. It is a contradiction because you are always trying to grow and change, but you find that the only way to really be yourself is when you are at your most repetitive. It is a dilemma for me.

TF: *In your work, there is a sense of the psychological identity of the person who is being depicted, and a clear sense of you as an artist. Somehow the sense that it is life cast is very strong, almost like the way people believe that photography is "real."*

JA: *I think these works fail when they breathe too much on the level of life. They should look like art. I like them to become frozen into something iconic, something that is very clear that you could describe. You can do that by simplifying the colors or the shapes. Sometimes Polaroids that I have taken of the person help me clarify the image. I love the idea of the art, and I also love that it is sculpture and that it is painting—not that it is an embodiment of that person. But the life of that person inspires the art and enriches the art. It is not just a print, but there is something of them there.*

TF: *In Ireland, you felt the project with the men's group was too slanted toward the community side to produce a set of works that were wholly satisfactory to you, but the project at the school, it seems to me, represents an interweaving of those*

John Ahearn creating life casts at Fashion Moda, 1979, Bronx, New York. Photograph: Christof Kohlhofer.

concerns. The work will travel back and forth between the school and the museum, and other museums. It's free to travel in a lot of different contexts. Moving back and forth.

JA: *Yes, that is ideal.*

TF: *Some of these projects that you felt somehow dissatisfied with were stuck on one side or the other. While the bronzes from the Forty-fourth Precinct traveled back into the art world, they were not exactly a failure . . .*

JA: *Oh, come on. If works are removed, they are a failure. We've talked about the idea that artworks can occupy multiple positions, in balance. When this works, the art world begins looking to you for guidance. I can remember standing in the Bronx on Walton Avenue, feeling that the world was turning around Walton Avenue—that everything was judged in terms of its distance from this spot.*

Notes

1. See the following interview with John Ahearn for a full discussion of the genesis of the work.

2. Jane Kramer, *Whose Art Is It?* (Durham, North Carolina, and London: Duke University Press, 1994).

3. From unpublished minutes of Department of Cultural Affairs artist selection panel meeting.

4. This bureaucratic process points to two essential aspects of public art. Public art administrators spend much of their time creating an atmosphere of cooperation between the artist, architect, and public agencies, and, if the right atmosphere is created, budget issues become secondary.

5. This sort of manipulation of budgets is very common in Percent for Art commissions. Funds from the construction budget of the site are often transferred to the art project when the artist is providing elements that are functional and/or architectural.

6. The New York City Art Commission, formed in the late nineteenth century, is an independent review body for all publicly funded art and architecture.

7. Kramer, *Whose Art?,* p. 94.

8. Source: Community District Needs, Fiscal Year 1994, City of New York Office of Management and Budget and Department of City Planning, Spring 1993. NYC DCP, 92–93.

9. Peter Moss, *New York Post,* April 23, 1992, p. 3.

10. bell hooks, *Black Looks* (Boston: South End Press, 1992), p. 11.

Interview: **Arthur Symes**
on Fighting the Bronx Bronzes

Introduction

This interview took place in September, 1996, in Arthur Symes's apartment in Battery Park City. Symes and I were acquainted from the controversy surrounding John Ahearn's sculptures in the South Bronx. We had met on a number of occasions on opposite sides of the table—Symes as an advocate of the removal of the sculptures, myself as a supporter of the artist. In the past we had always spoken as public officials. This was our first conversation outside of the official context.

Arthur Symes received a bachelor's degree at Howard University. He earned a Doctor of Architecture degree at the University of Michigan. Over the last twenty-five years, he has been functioning on the educational side of architecture. He came into the Department of General Services, the New York City agency responsible for the design and construction of most capital projects, in September of 1990 as assistant commissioner. Prior to that, he was dean of the School of Architecture at Southern University in Baton Rouge, Louisiana. Since the controversy, Symes has left city government for a position as associate dean/director of the NYNEX Corporate College Program of Empire State College in New York.

Tom Finkelpearl: How long had you been in city government when the controversy over the Ahearn sculptures occurred?

Arthur Symes: I'd been at DGS for a year. But I had learned about the project earlier. I remember one day a project manager came into my office and showed me some Polaroid shots of Ahearn's drawings for the sculptures. I was kind of shocked. In many ways I didn't think the work was appropriate. Later I saw the actual drawings at another project manager's desk. They were even more pointed. Finally, someone gave me Polaroid shots of the sculptures in the foundry, and that's when it really hit home. I checked with Ken Knuckles [then the commissioner of the Department of General Services], and asked him if he had seen the pictures. Well, he'd heard something, but he said, "It's a fait accompli, there is nothing we can do about it now. The money's been expended. The artist has done the physical work, and that's the way it goes. I felt rotten about it, rotten about the process. If it's deemed by enough people that it's not appropriate, I felt that we should have been able to stop it before it was installed. After it's installed, then what can you do? But I let

John Ahearn, Raymond and Toby, 1991, sculptures in foundry.

it go. I left feeling defeated. Here was something that the city was producing that was negative to that particular community, and I thought it just
ought not happen.

TF: Why did you feel the works were so inappropriate?

AS: To be candid with you, I thought they were rather hideous. I don't mean that the
faces of the people were unattractive, because that's not what it's about. But
there was a guy in a sweat shirt with his hood up. He had a pit bull with the
spiked collar. At the time, this was a literal representation of a certain sort of
person out on the street. It was the stereotype of the drug dealer. And then
there was the guy that had the basketball under his arm. He was obviously
out of shape, not what we know of the basketball players in these neighborhoods. The girl looked like a zombie. She was lifeless, not really like somebody that was skating. Now, I'm a rollerblader. I blade hard and fast in the
streets between the taxis and the buses. I'm sixty years old. Blading is my

form of aerobics. This girl doesn't symbolize that. This overweight basketball player doesn't symbolize the athlete. You go in any schoolyard and he is not what you see, generally speaking.

I thought they were negative images. The African American community has too many negatives, real negatives, for those negatives to be emblazoned with pieces of artwork that will be there from now on. It would be a constant reminder. But we don't need to be reminded of young guys running the drugs. They are real, and they establish a sense of fear in the community.

TF: *What about the argument that the sculptures were not symbols, but represent specific individuals who actually lived in the community?*

AS: *Well, I don't have a problem with representing real people. And let me add that I have a real sense that an artist has some rights to produce art that is uncensored. However, if the artist is producing work that is going to do damage to the community, then I think that there should be some limits. Let me give you an example. My son's head is screwed on very, very well. He is not a rabble rouser. All of his life, he's had some understanding of civil rights issues, and he feels very strongly about them. When he was just able to walk, I had him on a picket line. About a year ago, he came from Washington, D.C., to visit. Well, he put some rap music on the CD player. It had the worst language, the real crud of the rap music. I said, "Darryn why do you want to listen to something like that? It's mean, it's horrible. They shouldn't be allowed to produce that kind of stuff and put it out for people to listen to." My wife felt the same way. Darryn was defending the right of people to produce and present whatever they like. I said, "But don't you understand what that music means to young kids who aren't at an age where they can really think and understand the damage it is doing? It's demeaning to black women, but to males also because it's affecting their minds and the way that they act." He understood what I was saying, and I believe he no longer buys it. I don't think that they have the right to demean human beings—not for the sake of art, not for the sake of artists, whether they are building sculpture, or writing music.*

I'll give you another example. You know the amateur hour at the Apollo? If a comedian does a joke or a skit that has to do with roaches, rats, or drugs, he doesn't get a chance to finish the skit. He's booed off. It's not allowed, because those are things of pain, the negatives of the community. I have seen it over and over. They boo them off immediately. If an artist is making a statement to raise consciousness, and it is not seen by the people in the community as being demeaning, I can reckon with that. But as we both know, the community raised up against those sculptures in the Bronx. I felt comfortable knowing that my thinking was on track with the people in that community.

TF: *Some people believe that there is a psychological dimension to poverty, that there is the lack of opportunity, but there is also the lack of self-confidence and self-esteem that is built from "negative representations." Are you saying that these sculptures were contributing to that psychological environment, that people who were already confronted with negative images in their daily lives saw more in this very official place?*

AS: *Yes. And I think this was easy for people in the community to see. I tend to think that John Ahearn was naive to the realities of the community, even though he lived there for nine years. You know, I could move into the thick of the residential area of Chinatown, and live there for nine years, but that wouldn't give me a sufficient understanding of their culture that I could just do anything that I wanted to do. There is a good chance that some of the things I might want to create or do might not be acceptable, because I am not literally one of them. I didn't grow up from birth understanding that culture with all of its extremely fine nuances. I wouldn't understand the pain and the misery. I wouldn't understand all of the joys. Let's say my wife, my son, and I, and some of my friends, colleagues, and relatives, sat around this room with John Ahearn, or you. We could laugh and talk, but some of the things we might say would go over your head. In simple conversation, there are some things that a community just naturally understands. It's not intentional. We wouldn't even be thinking about whether you understand or not, but just talking naturally. Chances are that a black sculptor would not have done what John Ahearn did.*

I am not in any way suggesting that John Ahearn or any artist other than black artists shouldn't be working in that community. Not at all. I am saying

John Ahearn, Corey, 1991, removal. Photograph: John Ahearn.

that, because of his heritage, he did not pick up on the fact that what he did would be rejected. He didn't quite understand the nuances. Now some of the work that he has on the buildings up there in the Bronx is really great. The busts on the buildings are of the people that live in the community. You walk by and you see somebody you know. It's an extremely nice idea, and the fact that these pieces he created for the precinct were real people in a community was great. I've got no problem with that. The problem was in the people he picked or the way he presented them. It was said that the guy with the dog has been in all kinds of trouble—literally, that particular guy. If John Ahearn wanted to bring this guy up out of the mire, he could have found another way to do it, because the people in the community know about that guy. It's taking someone who's thought of as being bad and putting him on a pedestal, literally. We don't need to do that.

TF: *Do you feel that there were any positive sides to the Ahearn controversy? Some people say that these sorts of controversies are important because they bring issues to light that need to be discussed.*

AS: *What was discussed in that community wasn't necessary. The feelings were already there and they didn't have to chew on them. These problems are internalized. The fact that they acted out immediately says that those issues are on their minds. Now, if a work could create a dialogue across the city, then fine. I think dialogue across the city about such issues is certainly very healthy, but this art disrupted and damaged the community more than establishing a dialogue.*

TF: *Do you have ideas of what kind of images might have been appropriate for that site?*

AS: *I could see a mother and child or a father with a child. They would be very different statements, but I could see either one. The father and child could be a statement about what* ought *to exist.*

TF: *Do those images need to be "positive"?*

AS: *I would rather see positive any day than negative. If one could depict something negative and create the opportunity to correct the negative, maybe it would be worthwhile and tolerable.*

TF: *Like an image that depicts Raymond, but shows how his lifestyle is a dead end?*

AS: *Yes but certainly not a piece showing him being arrested by a policeman. That would be horrible. You have to understand the attitude of the community towards the police, which is very difficult for lots of valid reasons. Like most African American men, I've had a real problem with police, starting from when I was a teenager. I was living in Elizabeth, New Jersey. There was nothing to do in that community. There wasn't a playground, or a park. So we stood out on the corners. We weren't raising hell, drinking beer, or anything like that. The police precinct was a few blocks down. Every time the police would go by, there would be some talk about the police. I used to hear stories about the police arresting black men, taking them down to the precinct and beating them up. I recoiled at that. So I developed a really negative attitude, and of course, since then I have seen and heard so much about police misconduct. And I myself have been harassed and arrested for no reason.*

TF: *I think that one of the issues with the Ahearn sculptures was the fact that they were associated with a police station.*

AS: *I think the images would have been a problem wherever they were but, I mean, why would you choose an image of a drug runner to stand in front of the police precinct? The people in the community are not oblivious to the implications. It is not to say that we do not have to have police precincts in our communities. Clearly, we need them, and I am sure that the people in that community would agree to that. But because of the tension, the sculptures are going to take on meanings. There's the precinct and the drug runner and his dog. People would ask, "Do those go hand in hand somehow? Is there some connection? What is the symbolism?" Those are the kinds of things that permeate the minds of people who live in the community.*

I will tell you one thing: make no mistake about it, if that work was not taken down, it would have been destroyed. There is no question about it. If the community hadn't spontaneously risen up against it, within short order it would have been graffitied. And that wouldn't have been the graffiti that you see on the buildings, which I have major problems with. As an architect, and as a citizen, I hate graffiti. I mean, I hate it, because it's unnecessary and damaging to communities. Well, they wouldn't have been spray painting those pieces the way they spray paint buildings. But they would have been doing it to act out against what those pieces represent.

TF: *Political graffiti.*

AS: *Yes. When I was in architecture school, I lived on the fringe of Ann Arbor. A couple of blocks off the main drag there were houses with lots of land around. And there was a house with one of those blackface jockeys. Every time I passed it, I would say I'm going to get some white paint and come by at night and paint the face and the hands, not to make it a white jockey, but to make it a* not black *jockey. I do not think that the people in that Bronx community would have painted the faces white, but they would have found some strong way to say, "I don't like this. It's bad news."*

Interview: **Maya Lin:**
Landscapes and Memorials

Introduction

Any discussion of contemporary memorial art in the United States begins with Maya Lin's *Vietnam Veterans Memorial.* However, a fuller understanding of the memorial is only possible in the context of Maya Lin's work as a whole. Lin's sources are unconventional for a public artist in the United States; she is trained as an architect, had little knowledge of contemporary earth-oriented art at the time of the Vietnam commission, and looks to Eastern sources as much as Western art history.

As most people know, the twenty-one-year-old Maya Ying Lin entered her design in a national competition for a Vietnam memorial when she was a senior at Yale in 1980. Her design was selected and the memorial was completed in 1982. Like much Minimalist sculpture, the simplicity of the memorial is offset by its environmental and participatory nature. The architectural structure of the space draws you down and in to the center, and then leads you up and out. The Vietnam memorial manages to be both more personal and more abstract than the traditional memorial. On the one hand, it does not include an image of the dead, but by naming all of the dead it gives visitors the opportunity to pay homage to the specific person they have come to mourn. While there is a tradition of monuments that include long lists of names, this is unusual for a national monument. Casualties in the Vietnam War were small compared to the numbers killed in wars like World War II, where a list would be overwhelmingly long. When I have visited the memorial and read the list of the dead, I have been reminded of the 1960s antiwar protests that I attended that included lengthy and moving readings of names of the dead from the Congressional Record. Somehow, for the Vietnam War, simply naming the dead became an act of defiance against the forces who supported the war effort. In recent years this tactic has been adopted in the fight against AIDS.

As discussed in the following interview, a realist sculpture by Frederick Hart was added to the site as a compromise with conservatives who threatened to block the installation of the memorial. This group of figures fulfills the traditional function of the memorial. The figures are generic and heroic as opposed to Lin's memorial, which has the aura of fact. In describing his sculptures, Hart has said, "There is about them the physical contact and sense of unity that bespeaks the bonds of love and sacrifice that is the nature of men at war."[1] It is clear that Hart has a very specific agenda in his design. His sentimentality, as clear in his sculpture as in his prose, tends to exclude those who do not subscribe to the notion that "love" characterizes "men at war."

     With the success of the *Vietnam Veterans Memorial,* Lin was invited to create a series of other memorials. She created the *Civil Rights Memorial* at the Southern Poverty Law Center in Montgomery, Alabama (completed 1989) and the *Women's Table* at Yale University (completed 1992). Lin has turned down all subsequent offers to design memorials, refusing to be pigeonholed as an artist of memory. It is interesting to see how Lin describes her *Civil Rights Memorial.* Like the Vietnam memorial, the work is striking for its lack of sentimentality. Her prose style in the following project description is exceptionally dry for a memorial that deals with such emotional subject matter, and an interesting contrast to Frederick Hart's description of his Vietnam memorial sculptures:

Civil Rights Memorial

Black Granite water table (11'-6" dia. × 31" h) inscribed with names and events of the civil rights era, listed chronologically, from 1954—Brown vs. Board of Education thru 1968— assassination of Dr. Martin Luther King Jr. Placed in front of black granite water wall (9' h × 39' l × 18" d). Memorial is situated in a white granite plaza, consisting of an upper and lower level, which separates the entry into the Law Center from the memorial and its plaza (2800 sq. ft.)[2]

     Like the Vietnam memorial, the *Civil Rights Memorial* mentions specific names, individualizing the movement. However, instead of naming all of the dead, Lin chose to focus on a shorter list, and to create a time line. Again, the work is very informational. Here is a sample of the entries inscribed in the black granite:

7 May 1955
Rev. George Lee. Killed for leading
voter registration drive. Belzoni, MS

13 Nov. 1956
Supreme Court bans segregated
seating on Montgomery buses

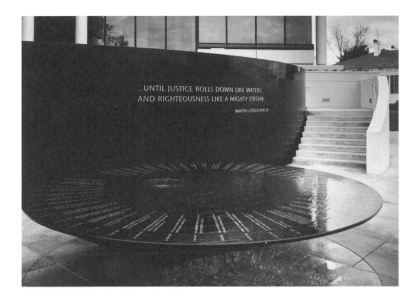

Maya Lin, Civil Rights Memorial, 1989–1990, Southern Poverty Law Center, Montgomery, Alabama.

30 Sep. 1962
Riots erupt when James Meredith,
A black student, enrolls at Ole Miss

20 Aug. 1967
Jonathan Daniels. Seminary student
killed by deputy. Hayneville, AL

As Lin says in the following interview, she takes a rather distanced position in these memorials. As the artist, she tries not to impose a reading on the viewer. However, in a very physical way, she includes the viewer in the works. In both memorials, the viewer is invited to touch the work, to have a direct connection with the dead person who is named. Because of this interactive nature, both memorials are usually photographed with people in them.

The following interview was conducted at Maya Lin's loft on the Bowery in New York City, March 1996. While much discussion has centered on her memorials, it is misleading to isolate them from the rest of her work. This interview ranges from a discussion of her landscape-oriented projects to her memorials, and this broader context reveals her complex approach to art and architecture practice.

In recent years, Lin has concentrated on her sculpture, architecture, landscape-oriented public projects, and design. In 1998, an exhibition of Lin's sculpture was organized at the Wexner Center in Columbus, Ohio, and a line of furniture she designed was produced by Knoll. In the furniture and the sculpture, her interest in minimal abstract form was clearly evident. But, far from the machine aesthetic of Ronald Bladen or Tony Smith, Lin's work has a delicately handmade quality. The nearly perfect curves are hand drawn, not quite symmetrical, asking the viewer for a second look. This same quality is evident in Lin's architectural work, including the Museum for African Art in New York, where Lin insisted upon working directly on certain spaces, drawing the curves herself. This hands-on quality is unusual in contemporary architecture, evidence of Lin's unique status at the juncture of art and architecture.

The following interview was originally published in *Public Art Review,* Fall/Winter 1996, pp. 5–9.

Tom Finkelpearl: How do you think people see your work?

Maya Lin: I realize that the memorials that I designed will be my best-known works, and that's fine. When you do something like the Vietnam Veterans Memorial *at the age of twenty, there is the danger that you will be forever hitting your head against the wall trying to outdo it. I never tried. I was happy with the closure that the civil rights and the Vietnam memorials created for me. They referred to two wars fought by the United States as I was a child growing up: one domestic, one international. By having the two paired, I was able to close a chapter. Though my working process started there, I have really been much more involved in other issues since that time. I have concentrated on the differences and similarities between the making of art and architecture in this public realm, which I would call public art.*

My initial gesture has been toward landscape. In urban projects, I've created works that respond to the hard, urban site, while fighting to get back

Maya Lin, Vietnam Veterans Memorial, 1982, Washington, D.C. Photograph: © Peter Aaron/Esto.

to the land itself. I admire and love the earth artists of the 1970's, but they went out to the middle of nowhere to escape the gallery system. I have worked in what I would call a suburban context. By the time I was doing the piece at the Wexner Center and then the Wavefield *that I just completed at the University of Michigan, I felt a certain voice was emerging: considering landscape and nature based on scientific analysis and 20th Century technologies. That's what really interests me.*

TF: *It seems to me that there is a generation of artists currently in their 30's and 40's who are admirers of the artists of the 1970's like Richard Serra and Robert Smithson. As you say, they have learned from the earth artists, but transposed this sort of art back into more accessible sites. In some cases they are infusing the aesthetic with a more recognizable narrative or social content. Someone like Mel Chin is an example. The* Vietnam Veterans Memorial *has formal similarities to a minimalist work, but it has historical and interactive characteristics, as does the* Civil Rights Memorial.

ML: *It is important to remember that I don't come from an art background. I didn't know who Smithson or Serra were when I designed the Vietnam Veterans Memorial. I wasn't even aware how much the Vietnam Veterans Memorial had in common with the earth artists when I designed it. I can remember walking into the Whitney Museum and seeing one of Smithson's Non-sites in 1982, and I was speechless. I'm much more tied into that aesthetic than a lot of the artists working today that are trying to push other boundaries.*

I think a lot of the interactivity in my work relates to my background as an architect. My reasons for going into architecture were never based on theoretical approaches or learned responses to what architecture is supposed to be. Some say that architecture is a certain language that you need to learn. My approach starts with a psychological understanding. I am only interested in the human response to works. I choose to be much less aware of what either the art or architecture "world" is doing.

The Vietnam Veterans Memorial may look minimalist, but it is really very different. The ideology behind Western minimalist art denies "reference." My piece is coming from a type of simplicity that you can trace back to Shintoism, to Zen. Now, I was never trained in Eastern philosophy or religion, but I always had a real problem with the way that Western European architecture was set up as the end-all. The Western ordering where man is at the center of the universe, where we are able to order our world, is a kind of egotism. I do not find Versailles as engaging as, say, a Shinto temple. Though I grew up in Athens, Ohio, it happens that my parents come from China, and they are both educators. There was a different sensibility. In our home, everything was handmade, crafted, including a lot of my father's ceramic work.

I have a fundamental belief, probably Eastern, that deals with the notion of teaching. There is a proverb that says, "Make a well of knowledge, and allow people to drink from that well." This may seem passive from a Western perspective. I am trying to pose facts and let others interpret them, trusting the viewer to think. Obviously I've been focusing on certain information, but at the same time I'm just asking you to look at facts. The Women's Table at Yale is nothing but numbers.

TF: *Is this approach to information a consistent element in your work?*

Maya Lin, Women's Table, 1993, Yale University, New Haven, Connecticut. Photograph: Norman McGrath.

ML: *Yes. But I've allowed it to be more of an open exploration, looking back to realize the path I've taken. Again I would argue that there is something Eastern about this: You will have found something at the end of your life though you never posed the question as to what you were seeking. Again, I was never trained in Zen or Confucianism, so it is not clear to me where these ideas came from.*

TF: *The history of public art is full of overpowering monuments which are so authoritarian—vertical, phallic. Do you think that being a woman contributes to the less authoritarian nature of your work?*

ML: *Of course there are gender and cultural issues. Though I have a sense, I would rather have someone else decipher that. In a hundred years, when more women have designed buildings, I'd like a psychiatrist to study the way we build, and see how it has changed. In Washington, where there was already* lot of controversy around the Vietnam Veterans Memorial, *things just exploded after an article in the* Washington Post. *The headline read, "An Asian Memorial for an Asian War." The author followed Buddhist tradition. In writing about my background, he pegged it in a narrow and specific way. When I looked at the title of his article, I thought, "We're in trouble now." Of course the veterans were already hearing that I was going to give them a "ditch," and now all of a sudden the race issue came right into play. They didn't see the memorial in terms of the inward-looking nature of my works. I stayed very quiet about my political beliefs through the whole public discussion of the* Vietnam Veterans Memorial. *Obviously I built a memorial that asked us to accept death as the primary cost of war. Having studied countless other memorials, I found that this is rarely addressed at a national level, though sometimes it is dealt with at a local level.*

I have become much more aware of the mix, of the balance between my Eastern and my Western heritage, and this has come forward particularly through my work. As a child growing up, you want to assimilate into your surroundings. But through my 20's into my 30's I became very aware of another voice that is so much a part of my aesthetic. It is a dual voice. It is wonderful to see a balanced mix of two cultures emerge.

TF: *You live at the northern edge of Chinatown. For your commission at the Federal Courthouse you were presented with a site at the southern edge of Chinatown. How did you relate to the site?*

ML: *I love the idea that this area is my neighborhood, that I can do a work, for once, in my backyard. Aside from being a peculiarly narrow site, I saw it as a boundary. It is an interface point between Chinatown and the (solidly Western) regional headquarters of the federal court system. It really is right on the border. In the morning before the judges arrive, the Chinese community uses Federal Courthouse Plaza to do Tai Chi.*

The sculpture I designed for the site consists of four stones, each with a pool of water on the top. Sound is an important element. At first, I wanted wind to whistle through the stones, but I could never get any acoustician to guarantee it was going to work, so I decided to make them into fountains. I think it comes back to this notion of the well. I've built four cisterns, each one its own independent water fountain. In Chinese culture, certain intricately carved stones have been very sacred. Of course the ones I have designed are minimalist blocks. I turned the fountain inside out. The pool of water disappears into itself, but you hear it. These stones are different heights so the pitch and the echoes will vary.

I don't think I would have done a piece like this if I weren't presented with a site on the border of Chinatown. When I was teaching at Berkeley, I talked to a lot of musicologists and anthropologists. I learned that the only people who have used stone as a musical instrument were the Chinese, with their "sounding stones." In public art my site becomes not just the physical site, but the cultural or anthropological site. Knowledge of the specific people who are going to be around a work always comes into play. My hunch is a lot of other public artists do not work this way.

TF: It is interesting to consider the different sorts of relationships public artists have to the various groups they work with. At Yale, you could speak as a graduate. At the Federal Courthouse, you can speak as a Chinese-American "community resident." This is quite different from the civil rights or Vietnam memorial. Was there a big difference in being an insider versus an outsider?

ML: It really depends upon the group. The Vietnam Veterans Memorial and the Civil Rights Memorial presented opposite working environments. At the Southern Poverty Law Center, we were all working as a team with the same goal in mind. The Vietnam experience was the exact opposite. When I started, I was met with an incredible amount of suspicion. My process was the same: go in, immerse yourself in study. For the Vietnam, I chose to study memorials, not the Vietnam War. I was recently having dinner with a journalist who had covered the Vietnam War. He was shocked because his whole approach is that of a reporter: What are the specifics? Get in there and do the research. Find out about the history of the war. I did the exact opposite. I deliberately remained uninformed about the specific politics of the war because I did not think this knowledge would help me do the piece. I felt that these politics might get in the way of looking at the sacrifices made by individual veterans. With the civil rights, I felt that I had to know the history. I grew up through the civil rights movement, but it was not taught in schools. I was really shocked at *how little I knew about that time period. It scared me that we can choose not to deal with history, and it will be forgotten. When I began working on the commission, I think the people at the Southern Poverty Law Center were assuming I would choose to commemorate one or two martyrs, even though it was a people's movement. This is where the creative process gets fascinating. What are you going to commemorate? What should the piece be about? What is your intention? How can you catch a person's attention in an instant and begin to open a matter up? Some monuments act as markers. My pieces tend to be much more educational in nature. For the Southern Poverty Law Center, I chose to create a table inscribed with events and people's deaths, some information about why they died. All of this was intertwined, because there is a causal effect. A riot led to someone's death, which led to legislation. This is how people changed history. By focusing on this, you are subtly saying to the next generation, you can make a difference.*

I made the decision to mention a fairly large number of people in the form of a time line, but I told the people I was working with, "I am not a historian. I am not going to be the one to choose which people to commemorate." While I was working on the logistics of building the sculpture for a year and a half, they got together a crew of advisors, experts, historians. The 43 people who are identified on the memorial all died violently. It was horrible. I came back in at the stage of editing the information, and said, "We need to present the facts, but not in a way that sensationalizes these people's deaths." We needed to present facts which spoke for themselves.

TF: *So it was a tone issue.*

ML: *Yes.*

TF: *Which relates to what you were saying before about how you present information, allowing people to come to their own conclusions as opposed to giving them answers.*

ML: *I've made all these pieces that deal with very difficult issues, and yet I have led a sheltered life. I would argue that it is my weird objectivity that has allowed* *me to do these pieces. I did not really come across racism until my junior year in college when I went to Denmark and people thought I was an Eskimo. The Danes had the same tension towards the Greenland Eskimos that people in the United States have for the Native Americans. There is this huge prejudice against Eskimos. The skinheads would get on a bus and be really nasty, and no one would sit next to me. I finally had to ask someone. If I get a suntan, I can look like a Native American or an Eskimo. It's very strange, because I can cross over and change race. It happened to me in Mexico. When I first got there, the Mexican children were all coming around trying to touch me because I was Chinese, but given two weeks in the sun, I blended right in because my skin goes red. I can relate to the book* Black Like Me. *If you are white you will probably never know the feeling that a non-white person feels in a crowd when you are looked at, standing out as being different in a negative way. To be able to go from being perceived as being one race and then switching over into another race is very strange.*

TF: Are you saying that this sort of identity-switching led to your "weird objectivity?"

ML: I think what happens is that you are brought up not quite fitting in. And because you feel, as a child, somewhat isolated, you distance yourself. Once that has happened, it's both a benefit and a detriment. I think you can really stand back and look and see a different story. You know the phrase, "You are far enough away from it to get a good picture." I was raised not fitting in. I probably have treated life somewhat as a distanced observer.

TF: Would you call your work anti-heroic?

ML: I wouldn't say it is anti-heroic. I would say it is anti-monumental, intimate. No matter how public my work gets, it remains intimate, one-on-one with the individual. Even though I use text, I never use text like a billboard, which a hundred people can read collectively. The way you read a book is a very intimate experience and my works are like books in public areas. I think that is what has always made people respond to my work in a very quiet way. Again, I think gender and my Asian-American heritage play a role.

Maya Lin, Wavefield, 1995, Aerospace Engineering Department, University of Michigan, Ann Arbor. Photograph: Tim Thayer.

TF: But this quiet experience at the Vietnam Veterans Memorial *was almost dislocated with the installation of the heroic bronzes on the site. Were you consulted as to where it would be placed?*

ML: They wanted to place the sculptures at the apex, with the flagpole right on top, and we were lucky to get them out. It would have been horrible. But if I had gone to the press right away, the whole process would have stopped. So I gambled. I felt that we needed to get construction started so I kept quiet for four months, which got us to the ground breaking. I knew that if I couldn't effectively get those realist sculptures moved from the site that was being proposed, I would have had to walk from the piece, or sue. If I had been a strict idealist I would have said from the start, "I will not threaten the aesthetic integrity of the piece," but we would have gotten the heroic sculpture and the monument genre would not have changed at all. I remember a committee hearing where only one person got up to support my design, while countless other people got up to say that they felt I was deliberately trying to hurt the veterans.

TF: *Some people say that when the realist sculptures were installed, they gave your memorial time to be accepted . . .*

ML: *No, false myth. The main person who was behind the compromise was the Secretary of the Interior, James Watt. He had to give final approval in order to start construction. He wasn't going to do that. He held us back from ground breaking until a compromise was meted out. Apparently, what the veterans had been told was that I was giving them a "black ditch," and that the memorial was a negative comment about the war. I kept arguing that we should give it a chance. Let people experience it. Well, the minute the piece was opened to the public, the controversy ceased, and I started getting the most amazing letters from veterans. Even though everyone was responding favorably when the memorial was opened, the sculptures were a done deal. The politicians had already committed. They were put up a year later.*

TF: *It is interesting to me that abstract public art seems to be at both extremes—the easiest and the most difficult sort of art for the public to accept.*

ML: *I taught an introduction to public art at Yale. Some of my students researched this, and found that, statistically, figurative works got into far more trouble than abstraction in the long run, because they are specific. If a work is specific, someone is going to have a problem with it these days.*
     So much of it isn't even the physical presence of the work, but how the work is introduced to the community. The political process needs to give the community respect. At the very early stages, it's about territory, about psychology. I am uneasy with some of the one-man-one-vote approaches that have been tried, but my attitude is to respect the public. And in the end, you should get some controversy, because if you are pushing any limits, people will be surprised.

TF: *Topo [Charlotte, North Carolina, 1991] represents the side of your work that deals more with nature than history. It was a collaboration with a landscape architect?*

Maya Lin, in collaboration with Henry Arnold, Topo, 1991, Charlotte Coliseum, Charlotte, North Carolina.

ML: *Yes, with Henry Arnold who was the same landscape architect from Vietnam. He and I kept in touch. Arnold was the original landscape architect for Constitution Gardens, the site for Topo. I was very conscious of working in someone else's space. In redesigning the space, I figured I should defer to him, call him in on it. It was the right thing to do. We applied as a team to a competition for art at a sports stadium. This is when I was working on the Civil Rights Memorial, and I was becoming acutely aware of getting typecast as someone who only works with the dead. So we decided to do something playful. Also civil rights was a suburban site, and I was trying to get back to working directly with the landscape, like the Vietnam piece. I think they expected an object right at the front entrance to their stadium. But I definitely seek out situations that involve the entire environment. We decided that we would do a completely green sculpture. There was this grassy median strip, 60-feet wide and 1,600-feet long that dropped 75 feet from top to bottom. Henry and I just looked at each other and said, "How can we resist?" Here is a space*

*that nobody pays attention to. So we threw in a game. We designed "balls"
that seem to roll down the hill on that central grassy strip. To this day I think
they worry that we were making fun of them, but we were just having fun
with the commission. In* Topo, *we tripled the number of Willow Oaks that
had been planned for the site. I do not try to compete with the landscape,
but really work with it. This reflects a belief system which I think will color my
whole life, wanting to work with the environment. I want to examine the relationship man has to nature, promoting sensitivity.*

TF: *Do you think you will ever do a memorial again?*

ML: *Yes, one more.*

TF: *Do you know what it is?*

ML: *It will be about extinction, about the environment.*

TF: *So that will put the two parts of your public art together: memorials and landscape.*

ML: *I really care about the environment. It has been my love since I was a child. This
work will probably take my lifetime to do, and it won't be a monument in a
traditional sense. We are the one species that has rapidly caused the extinction of so many other species, and that is unique. We have to stop. We have
to begin to understand that we cannot continue to overuse. Again, for me it
is about teaching. I don't know how it will manifest itself but this is my
dream.*

Notes

1. This quotation is from one of the 2,335 sites my search engine found on the Internet under the category "Vietnam + memorial," a number that far outstripped the number of sites under the name of any
other public artwork or memorial that I could think of. The specific site was: www.newsday.com/The Vietnam Memorial, September 1998.

2. From a project description provided by Maya Lin in 1996.

Interview: **David Avalos,**
Louis Hock, *and* **Elizabeth Sisco**
on Welcome to America's Finest
Tourist Plantation

In January 1988, the city of San Diego hosted the Super Bowl. It was a major event for the city, which had been burnishing its reputation as a tourist destination for some time. However, the publicity juggernaut that the city had put in place was interrupted for a time as news of a public art project grabbed headlines for several weeks. Three artists, David Avalos, Louis Hock, and Elizabeth Sisco, had designed a poster which was mounted on the back of one hundred city buses. The poster focused on three sets of hands; one was cleaning dishes; a second was being handcuffed by a person with a gun, and the third was reaching for a door knob that held a "MAID SERVICE please" sign. The images make reference to the fact that undocumented workers form an important part of the economy of Southern California, filling low-paying jobs like dishwasher and maid, even as they face deportation. When the posters were released into the city, the press responded on cue, and a full-scale controversy erupted.

Welcome to America's Finest Tourist Plantation was not the most visually arresting bus project in recent memory—that honor would probably go to Barbara Kruger's recent project in New York. Nor was it unique in sparking controversy, for many other artists have created controversies inadvertently. Rather, it is the careful planning of the controversy that makes it so unusual. The project was *intended* to create loud public debate, to intercede in the normal public interchange. Avalos, Sisco, and Hock work on the streets, and in museums, but also on editorial pages. Their sites are both physical places in the city and political debates in the media.

As outlined in the group's press release, the poster was meant to counter the official boosterism of the city. But this was not simply a project on the back of city buses. The group's release stated:

Assume that there is no public space in San Diego. The few plazas that lie dormant before their corporate towers await an "art" at the service of public relations campaigns. The City fills its space with work that buffs its image as a fitting housekeeper for tourist attractions. Private enterprise has papered over the space that remains with advertising.

If we further assume that the logical forum for public issues is public space, then it follows that the first task of the public artist would be the creation of such a space.

And if the art that potentially occupies such a space is to continue to be the target of this city's hostility, then public artists will increase their chances of survival by making that target a moving one.[1]

Barbara Kruger, BUS, 1997, Manhattan to Eastern Queens Route, New York, New York. A Project of the Public Art Fund. Photograph: Marian Harders, courtesy of the Public Art Fund.

The public space that the artists created was "moving" in more than one way. Of course, the posters on the back of city buses were moving through the city, but the space of the project quickly moved into the media as well. After the project was over, the group produced a spiral-bound photocopied publication that started with their news release, and assembled all of the local, regional, and national press the project received. This publication includes scores of news articles, both sympathetic and hostile to the group's project. The authors of these articles argued such issues as the role of undocumented workers, the voice of artists, the use of public funding for the arts, and the status of the bus in the city. And these articles were not segregated to the art pages, but visited the front page and the editorial page, and were written by political reporters, art critics, and travel writers. In addition to the articles, there was a large number of editorials and letters to the editor. For example, in the week of January 15, 1988, the *San Diego Union* printed eleven letters to the editor on the project, twice dedicating its "Readers Write" page entirely to the discussion of the group's project, under headlines like, "Posters, artists, buses, aliens, and America's Finest City."[2] The breadth and intensity of the response, as documented in the press accounts, is aston-ishing. There were fifteen television stories on the project. One television station cov-ered it six times. Predictably, tourism officials were outraged, and many in city government felt that the best response would be to make sure that nothing like this happened again, by creating stricter guidelines for advertising on city buses. But the discussion, over many weeks in newspapers throughout Southern California, was quite lively. At least for a couple of months, the project was able to reframe the ar-gument over the role of the undocumented worker, to help create visibility for a group of people whom the business elite of San Diego wanted to hide from sight.

It is interesting to see how the debate became increasingly complex, and how journalists within the same publication felt free to contradict one another. This project promoted intelligent public discussion, so rare in the history of American pub-lic art. While the Serra and Ahearn controversies tended to polarize, while Maya Lin deftly sidestepped damaging confrontations, this project was designed for contro-versy, and part of the art was the group's management of the controversy. This has been their practice in a number of other projects from the late 1980s to the present.

David Avalos received a Master of Fine Arts Degree from the University of California, San Diego. He is an Associate Professor of Visual and Performing Arts at California State University, San Marcos. At the Centro Cultural de la Raza in San Diego, he was the Coordinator of the Border Arts Workshop/Taller de Arte Fronte-rizo from 1984 to 1987. Aside from his many collaborative public works, he has had numerous solo and group exhibitions at spaces including the Museum of Contempo-rary Art, San Diego; ArtPace, San Antonio; and the Spectacolor Lightboard in Times Square, New York. Agencies including the National Endowment for the Arts, Califor-nia Arts Council, and Los Angeles Contemporary Exhibitions have awarded grants to Avalos.

Elizabeth Sisco received her Master of Fine Arts degree from the University of California, San Diego. Since 1988, she has collaborated on a series of public art-works that address social issues. She has received grants from the National Endow-ment for the Arts, Art Matters, and the California Arts Council. Sisco is a resident at the Center for Computing Arts at the University of California, San Diego, and has worked extensively at Southwestern College designing new digital media curricula.

Louis Hock received his Master of Fine Arts degree from the School of the Art Institute of Chicago. His films, videotapes, and media installations have been exhib-ited at institutions including the Museum of Modern Art in New York, the Whitney

Museum of American Art, the San Francisco Museum of Modern Art, and the Walker Art Center in Minneapolis. He has received a number of awards including grants from the National Endowment for the Arts, the American Film Institute, and the Rockefeller Foundation. Hock is a professor of visual arts at the University of California, San Diego. Since 1980, Hock has been involved in public art projects, including a series of collaborations that started with *Welcome to America's Finest Tourist Plantation*.

Tom Finkelpearl: Can each of you tell me how you came to work on the bus poster project, Welcome to America's Finest Tourist Plantation?

Elizabeth Sisco: Okay, I'll start. When the bus poster project was initiated, I had been documenting the police activities of the border patrol officers at bus stations around San Diego, especially around the University of California, San Diego (UCSD) campus, where I happened to be working. I was also curating a show at El Centro Cultural de la Raza, where David [Avalos] was in charge of exhibitions. We started talking about the photographs and the issues of undocumented immigration, and how it was really more appropriate for my work to be out in the streets where it would reach the audience that was most affected by the issues, and not marginalized or ghettoized and in a gallery setting. At that time, we'd known each other for a few years. Louis [Hock] had been making "The Mexican Tapes," a video series about a neighborhood of undocumented workers that he and I were living in at the time. So we got together. We'd all wanted to work together for a while, so we wrote a grant to the Combined Arts and Educational Council of San Diego (COMBO). Some of their funding came from San Diego's hotel/motel tax, and part was from the National Endowment for the Arts. Our grant said we wanted to buy advertising space on the back of city buses to create a mobile gallery, a gallery that would move through San Diego reaching a wide cross-section of the metropolitan population. We said that we wanted to display images of issues relevant to the community, specifically issues of immigration, on this mobile gallery. And miraculously (in retrospect) we got the grant.

David Avalos: I remember I met Liz [Sisco] when she gave me a call, and she asked me to go see an exhibition of photographs that she had made that involved a number of the families who were documented in "The Mexican Tapes." She

David Avalos, Louis Hock, Elizabeth Sisco, Welcome to America's Finest Tourist Plantation, 1988, poster on one hundred public buses, San Diego, California.

had gone and photographed these people in Mexico, and her exhibitions of those photographs really made an impression on me.

ES: Yes. I had gone to Mexico and photographed the families of these Mexican workers who were living in San Diego. I really enjoyed putting on those exhibitions, but I felt that they weren't reaching the right audience. That was the biggest motivating factor for wanting to do something in public—that the gallery is often speaking to the converted, or speaking about the wrong issues. In the gallery, people are focusing on aesthetic issues rather than content.

Louis Hock: In previous years, I had worked as a filmmaker, making films which usually showed in museums and independent spaces. By the third or fourth round of this I found that these spaces were, for the most part, populated by filmmakers, wanna-be filmmakers, film critics, and wanna-be film critics. It was essentially a very cloistered situation. There was no public in the audience. So I stopped making films for that situation, and made what I called a "cine-mural," Southern California, for projection in public places. It was never shown in any kind of conventional screening space and had a mural-like quality, in that it usually was not just shown continuously for one night, but over a series of days, often a week. Its image was the size of a semitrailer, usually, projected 30 feet wide. So one of my interests at the time was mov-

ing away from a more private audience of the art cognoscenti, into a more public arena. I was living in a community of undocumented Mexican people, and I began to make a videotape, which took around five years to shoot. "The Mexican Tapes: A Chronicle of Life Outside the Law" was a home-movie for TV and centered around the life and times of my neighbors. Since I was a player in the community, I operated both inside and outside the narrative. And so, in terms of the content of these works, and in terms of the audiences of the works, I could see how they clearly led into the collaborative public artwork.

Liz and David had already initiated some discussion, primarily around Liz's photographs, and David's ongoing art practice, and then the collaboration congealed among us. But I don't think any of us clearly imagined getting the grant or being able to carry it through as our imagination held it.

TF: When you wrote the grant, you didn't have the image in mind yet?

LH: Oh, no. it was very organic; it evolved through a point-by-point discussion.

DA: Louis and I were having conversations before Liz and I met. In February of 1985, the Border Art Workshop, of which I was a member, had our first exhibition, "Border Realities," at Galeria de la Raza in San Francisco. I had seen portions of "The Mexican Tapes" and asked Louis if we could show them as part of the exhibition, and he agreed. The reason I knew about the video was because he had contacted me about the possibility of showing it to my family, to my folks in particular, just to get some outside-the-art-world response to what he was doing. So we actually met at my parents' home in National City.

Subsequent to that, without my knowledge, Philip Brookman, who was working at the Centro Cultural de la Raza as a curator, invited Liz to put together an exhibition that was about the immigrant experience, but from a more cross-cultural perspective. There were Italian photographers, Cuban photographers. She included Laura Aguilar who photographed lesbians (which was kind of interesting for the Centro). I think it's important to point out that for me, as a Chicano, working with non-Chicanos was more of a possibility because a certain atmosphere existed. For example, in the Border Art Workshop, Taller de Arte Fronterizo, we had Chicanos, non-Chicanos, Mexi-

cans, and Americans. I first heard the word "multicultural" in the 1970s without paying any attention to it, but there was a kind of an atmosphere of issue-specific collectiveness, or collaboration, that wasn't necessarily within the frame of multiculturalism. I think that an open climate existed with the Border Art Workshop, with the Centro, with Liz curating a great show at the Centro. But how do you feel about that, Louis and Liz?

ES: I think that's accurate, and I think that attitude defined how we came together to do all of the subsequent public art projects. It was issue-specific—a group gathered around an issue that was of concern and interest to them, and not so much in terms of their cultural identity.

LH: Although the projects have traveled broadly through the media, the collaborative groups we have worked in together dealt more with the public within a particular, defined region. Our group is a reflection of its audience. A variety of people in the group share concerns that carry over into the audience, which then sets up an intrinsic communication between the particular people who are making the artwork, and the particular recipients of that work. There's no great distinction between the creators and the receivers, as is often the case in museum spaces or gallery spaces.

TF: It is interesting to me that the press coverage of the bus poster did not focus on your identities as Anglo or Chicano.

ES: I think we were able to aim the issue at the power structure. We weren't saying, look at these poor, marginalized people. We were saying, look who's responsible for an economy that exploits laborers.

DA: Also, I think that our premise was that you don't have to cross the border illegally to recognize that this is part of your life in San Diego. In his "Mexican Tapes," Louis realizes, hey, these are my neighbors. Why don't I pay attention to them? And it implies the question, why doesn't society see them as neighbors? Why is there this legal fiction that they're "illegal aliens," rather than part of the community? Louis's tape didn't have a political agenda in the sense of advocating political positions, but I thought it was powerful because *it was looking at people's everyday lives in a way people could relate to, athough they were extra-ordinary because of this legal fiction. We were saying: hey, this isn't an issue that just affects the Mexican immigrant that crosses without papers. This is an issue that affects everyone who lives in this region. And let's not pretend that it doesn't. And to recognize that, and to want to speak to power, as Liz was saying, we don't need to cloak ourselves in the mantle of identity, that we're the only ones who are authorized to speak here. Everyone should be concerned about this because it's defining all of us in this region.*

LH: *When you talk about the border region, multiple ethnicities are inherently in-volved. They're all players. This was clear with the bus poster project. In 1988, it was regarded as a regional art project—dealing with specific regional is-sues. Almost five years later, when we did* Art Rebate, *the idea of the border and immigration had begun to migrate onto the national forum. On a na-tional level, ethnicity was becoming an issue, largely because of its politically motivated exploitation in California.*

TF: *How did you work together to come up with those three images that you use, and the text? What was the process of actually designing this poster collaboratively, hav-ing never worked together?*

ES: *Trial and error.*

LH: *Well, the center image is a photograph of the handcuffed hands of undocu-mented workers being hauled off buses near the University of California. It was from Liz's documentary series. We set up the other two shots to imply the different service industry workers, the dishwasher and the maid.*

ES: *Originally the poster's text read, "Illegal use of hands makes the big game work." [Illegal use of hands is an infraction in football usually called on offensive linemen. The football analogy, then, refers to the illegal use of undocu-mented workers' hands in preparing for the Super Bowl, and the influx of tourists at hotels and restaurants.]*

David Avalos, Louis Hock, Elizabeth Sisco, Welcome to America's Finest Tourist Planta-tion, 1988, poster on one hundred public buses, San Diego, California.

LH: It was a bad football analogy.

ES: I was student-teaching at the time, and I took the poster into the lunchroom and passed it around the table to the teachers from the elementary school, and I just got all these blank stares.

LH: Then we showed it to a bunch of photography students, and got the same reac-tion! This was the day before it was supposed to go to press. I thought we should scrap it and do the whole thing all over again, but I got looks from these two, and they said, let's just play with the text.

TF: The revised text refocuses the project on the tourist industry more clearly, and their designation of San Diego as "America's Finest City." Do you think the change in text made a big difference?

ES: Yes, what we came up with was clearly . . .

LH: Miles better.

DA: It was an intense collaborative process. You know, my idea was we'd write the proposal together, then I'd just step out of the way and say go for it, I've got other things to do. But they were really insistent. There were times when we were around the table, looking at graphics, and our three heads were within inches of each other. I've never worked on a collaboration with quite that kind of intensity. There's a meticulousness about Louis and an insistence about Liz where everything had to be gone over, discussed, determined, and decided upon. It was trial and error, but it was a real sense of all three of us working on it.

TF: There was a rather negative article in an advertising journal.[3] It took apart the poster, questioning the graphic impact, breaking the headline into two lines, and so on. If it's just a political statement, then it's a little hard to read.

LH: Well, often people will want to see the poster itself as the artwork—the graphic itself as the home of the aesthetic content of the work. In fact, the poster's primary function was its catalytic quality. The social performance was a goal, and this was a mechanism, an agent, to be able to allow this to happen. The aesthetic is much more in the social dynamic, the discursive quality of the piece, the performative quality.

ES: The poster was one part of the overall public artwork, which was about putting something out in public that would attract attention and spark debate.

LH: If we were able to have the public dialogue without the physical object, that would be okay. But if we were only to have a physical object with no public dialogue, then it would be a disaster.

DA: When people bring up the question of aesthetics, first of all I think the piece recognizes that it's not about mastery. You know, it recognizes that aesthetic evaluation is not just a determination of the art world, but what's the meaning that's given to a piece? What's the response that people have to a piece? And how do you recognize that the piece can be initiated to begin a process over which we have no control, much less mastery. So I think in that sense it questions a certain kind of traditional aesthetic, and introduces another kind of aesthetic. It's more of an improvisational piece. Once the work's in public, we can not control it. We can only respond to it. There's a need for spontaneity. There's a need for a kind of resilience and resourcefulness, and a kind of willingness to do things out loud and in public. I think it also raises questions about a real problem that we have in the United States, and particularly in the area of public art, and that is a dilemma that's never been resolved, and that's: for a nation with democratic ideals, can you democratize art? How do you get everyone involved? And I don't think anyone has demonstrated that it's been successfully done anywhere.

TF: *It seems to me that you really need to understand local politics to understand the bus poster. I had never heard the phrase "America's Finest City," nor would I necessarily associate dish washing and maid service with undocumented workers. Coming from New York, I wouldn't necessarily "get it" the way somebody from San Diego would. On the other hand, the reason the "powers that be" were so upset about the poster was that outsiders were going to see it during the Super Bowl week, and that it was going to reflect badly on San Diego. It was a complex kind of localism. The critics couldn't see beyond the fact that they understood the critique inherent in the poster, but that people from outside the region might not.*

LH: *Well, I don't think that many people were able to understand what the project was actually getting at just by looking at the bus poster itself. But nonlocal people certainly understood the dynamics of the issues when they were discussed in the newspapers. The politicians understood exactly what that poster was about, and they are the people who spoke about it in the news media. The poster demanded an explanation. When the newspapers or TV commentators or the politicians or we, spoke, we explained, and framed the poster. The poster itself was a mechanism for provoking and giving breadth to the discussion. It didn't have to be self-explanatory.*

DA: Yes, I think there are multiple audiences here, Tom, and I think that Louis is absolutely right. The primary audience was the city fathers (even though at that time we had a woman mayor, Maureen O'Connor) and the media. We had to get them to react in order to reach a mass audience. For a number of years I worked with an organization called the Committee on Chicano Rights, chaired by Herman Baca. One of the things that we used to talk about on the Committee was "dealing ourselves in," when there was some event of regional or national import taking place in San Diego. We'd try to deal ourselves in by having an event that was aimed at the powers that be, as well as the media, using the media to disseminate information that we wanted to get out—a viewpoint, a position. When Herman Baca saw the bus poster on the front page of the San Diego Union, he said to me, "They're going to be talking about this in their bedrooms at night." And later, a Chicano artist who had a family member who worked for the Metropolitan Transit Board told me that in fact they were calling each other late at night—talking about the poster on their bedroom phones: What the hell is going on? Some people said this thing is indecipherable, what does it mean? But there was no doubt in our minds that the city fathers knew what it meant, and the media knew what it meant. Because the media immediately seized on it, and the city fathers immediately reacted to it.

TF: When the three of you were preparing the project, were you conscious of its incendiary nature? Did you expect it to create a controversy?

DA: Look at the language of the application that we made to COMBO. It asked us, "How are you going to publicize this art activity?" And we said, "Posters mounted on city buses are by nature self-promoting, occupying a well-acknowledged advertising arena. Along with the obvious exposure, press releases detailing the project will be sent to all local papers, art weeklies, and art magazines. Each artist involved in the project has been widely reviewed by the press, and critical as well as editorial response to the project will be actively sought." I'd had the experience with a project called the San Diego Donkey Cart two years earlier when I'd been given permission to install a temporary piece in front of the federal courthouse in downtown San Diego. The day after Donkey Cart was installed, the chief federal district judge saw *it, went to a meeting with all of the other federal district judges, and they decided that it was going to be removed because it was a "security threat." (Yeah, right.) So the piece was actually dismantled and put in the basement of the building. However, despite the fact that it was invisible, there were newspaper stories, editorials, letters to the editor, as well as discussions in the art section of the newspaper. We were aware of the* Donkey Cart *experience, so when we said, "critical as well as editorial response will be actively sought," we knew it was something that could be done. We wrote in the grant, "The artists plan to conduct a campaign with large daily newspapers and local papers to determine the public's response to the project." That's something that you could only get with letters to the editor. So right there in the proposal we make it clear that that's our expectation.*

TF: *Some people say that, in our cultural climate, it is impossible to have a true public dialogue because the media is so controlled by certain economic interests—that all public opinion is "delivered." Were you saying with this project that this is not the case, that there can be substantial public dialogue through the media?*

LH: *Well, at the moment the bus poster came out there were three newspapers operating in San Diego, and a number of television stations. Because attention to the bus poster had migrated off the art pages and onto the front pages, there was a hunger for information about this work, and because there were multiple avenues for news information, it allowed our voice, our opinion to be printed in the paper, as we spoke it. In fact, it allowed a kind of dimension of the piece as we understood it to be presented to the public. By the time we undertook* Art Rebate, *we were much less able to speak our voice and have what we said represented accurately. I do think that there was a big difference over that five-year period of time.*

TF: *What were the newspapers in San Diego at the time of the bus poster?*

LH: *The* Union, *the* Tribune, *and the* L.A. Times *San Diego edition. Now the* Union *and* Tribune *have merged, and the* Times *closed its San Diego office.*

TF: *So the different newspapers served to check and balance one another?*

David Avalos, Louis Hock, Elizabeth Sisco, *Welcome to America's Finest Tourist Plantation.*

LH: Well, I think that there was much more of a reliance and trust in the artist to be able to explain himself or herself. Later on, there was more editorialization of what the artist intended to do or say, as it was represented in the press. In 1993, the one local paper was the unchallenged first voice to frame the work.

ES: I agree with Louis that in subsequent projects that we undertook, when there was only one newspaper in town, there was less diversity of voices, and the city fathers knew how not to overreact. The press generally framed our later projects negatively, and assumed that's how the entire populace of the city was reacting to them. We know for a fact that there were many letters of support for the later project sent to newspapers that were never published, but all of the negative sentiments seemed to find their way onto editorial pages.

DA: You know, when I did the Donkey Cart, I was asked by Tim Drescher of Community Murals *magazine to write an article about it. In that article I said, "some people felt that the* Donkey Cart *received its greatest public attention* through the mass media after it was removed from public view. But I think mixed-up ideas about what is public are at work here. I was a willing participant in the daily media coverage of the event, but it also dawned on me that the issues being discussed were not immigration, or public art, or public space, or social interaction. The discourse was reduced to the single issue of government censorship, which explains the high media interest. The mass media like to pretend that the First Amendment guarantee of free expression is their license to make a buck. And while I appreciated all the help I could get, I had no illusions that the media were interested in discussing their own role in the creation of antisocial public space. I think that the most telling response to your question would be that not a single undocumented worker was interviewed by any of the media, press or electronic, as a result of the bus poster project. With Art Rebate in 1993, we tried to remedy that problem. We tried to set up situations where the media would come in contact with undocumented workers. It met with very mixed results, but nevertheless I think it evidences that the three of us recognize that as a problem with the bus poster. I don't think any of us had a delusion that an ideal dialogue is possible with the newspapers. It wasn't a matter of saying, "Okay, mass media, sponsor this free and open community dialogue." But the media is not this monolithic, impenetrable slab of granite. It feeds off of itself. There are people who will put things on the front page that editorial writers don't necessarily like. People will write about issues in the art section that the editorial writers in the paper will disagree with.

The Neighborhood Reporter had promised us that they would publish an image of the bus poster and run our press release in full, verbatim, in the event that nobody else covered the event. We had a back door. Louis was quoted in this context as saying that we wanted to make "a completely unavoidable image," something that they had to respond to, that they could not ignore. As Thomas McEvilley said when William Rubin responded to his Artforum critique of the "Primitivism" show at the Museum of Modern Art, "The bears came out of the woods." And that's the most we could hope for in San Diego.

But the dialogue wasn't always taking place in the editorial pages of the newspapers. I remember Liz telling me that some surfer buddy of hers was talking about being out there, waiting for another set of waves, and other *surfers were talking about the bus poster. Some businessman bought it and put it up in his bar. There was a psychology conference at San Diego State; they were talking about the bus poster and the issue that it was addressing. So there was dialogue taking place in other areas.*

ES: *We even received an award from the Mexican American Business Association.*

DA: *So there was a dialogue that took place outside of the press. But with the press, you're like a flea on a 400-pound gorilla. You can't tell it where to go.*

LH: *Who imagines the press without an agenda? A good example of the current situation in San Diego was the Republican Convention here in 1996. The paper was just a glad rag for the Republican Party. It threw the biggest party for the Republicans during the convention here. But that doesn't mean everyone is blind to bias within this one local newspaper. It's like a movie critic who will always read particular films in a particular way, and you are able to judge what films you want to see based on their take, not based on the direct yea or nay reading. When you say that the news is delivered, I think it's underestimating the people. People understand that, in fact, news is framed when it's delivered to them.*

TF: *You're crediting people with the ability to be critical readers.*

DA: *Yes. But you also need to remember that all of this happened before politicians like Al D'Amato and Jesse Helms began to attack the National Endowment for the Arts, before the attacks on Mapplethorpe.*

ES: *A big concern with all of these public art projects is trying to keep the press focused on the issues that the artwork is addressing, and not the diversionary questions they want to raise: Is it art? Is it the role of the artist to comment on these types of issues in the first place? Then the focus would be on censorship or the use of public funds, rather than the plight of undocumented workers. It's very hard to maintain the focus on the issue in the press. But, as David mentioned earlier, there are also the conversations within class-*

rooms—people discussing issues just casually. I feel people have an ability to discuss the issues from a different perspective, because the artwork raises the questions from a different angle.

LH: *Up until the early 1990s art had been framed by the news media as good art or bad art. The good art was auctioned off for millions of dollars, and you saw pictures of people in tuxedos in the newspaper, and it was good business, and there were monetary rankings of artworks in art periodicals, like stock listings. And then there was the bad art, art that used public money, and raised issues that were controversial. I think that was an overlying paradigm set forth by the news media, within which public artwork was framed. It was a simple way to take a read on art. This read on art had the effect of simplifying a broader and more profound cultural conflict.*

TF: *What about the idea that one of the inadvertent outcomes of this project might have been to close the doors for future art projects, including the fact that the Mass Transit board made it clear that they would censor future controversial bus posters? Controversies make bureaucrats more careful.*

DA: *Well, you know, if a football team creates a defense that shuts down your best wide receiver, you can have him line up in the slot to throw off the defense.*

ES: *(laughs) What's your analogy, David?*

DA: *You respond to conditions. It's an ongoing situation. You need to be creative. My question is, would anyone have raised the issue if there had never been a bus poster controversy? Would anyone have ever said, gee, I wonder if you can use bus posters to make a political point about immigration in San Diego? It's disingenuous to come up with objections like that after the fact. Hey, if you're going to engage in confrontation, first of all, choose somebody that's worth confronting. If you do, that means that they're intelligent and creative. They might even be motivated by a strong sense of belief, so expect to have to improvise and adjust as time goes on. Don't throw in the towel. There's one guy, I won't mention by name, in San Diego, who said "You guys*

*ruined it for us now." Give me a break—as if he was just about to run out
with a set of bus posters.*

LH: *We have always worked with the notion that you have to create a public space,
a space of possibility for these projects. But people react by imagining that
controversy will close off the public art activity. For example, the city might
pass a rule stipulating that you can't be critical of police on bus posters anymore, or you'll be warned if you make art on billboards, or money can't
be used as an art material. But the field of possibilities is large enough that
this small closure after an art project will not stifle the activity of public art
making.*

TF: *How can you judge the success of a project like this? It obviously created a tremendous amount of public dialogue, and you were able to focus it on the status of
undocumented workers. But is the goal to change people's minds about the status of undocumented workers in San Diego, or is it just bringing up the issue in a
kind of complex, public way?*

ES: *I think it's the latter. People change their own minds. I think we had the ability to
bring up the issue in a way that wasn't expected, from an angle that has not
been repeated again and again and again and again and again by the press
and the politicians and the special-interest groups. The success, I believe, was
the project's ability to present a public space that allowed people to think
about the issue from different avenues, in different ways, from different perspectives. And then maybe a few people would change their minds on the
matter.*

DA: *I think it encourages other folks who are looking for ways to reach the public.
And it can influence other artists. I talked to some folks at the San Jose Museum of Art. They had sponsored Edgar Heap-of-Birds to do a project up
there, with bus posters in 1990:* Mission Gifts. *The posters referred to the California mission system, and what it did to American Indians here in California. One poster just had these words: "SYPHILIS SMALLPOX FORCED
BAPTISMS MISSION GIFTS ENDING NATIVE LIVES." I know Edgar, and I've*

talked to some of the folks at the San Jose museum, and they said that there was a move made to remove his posters from the buses. In their defense of the project, they referred to the bus poster in San Diego, and said, hey, look, it was allowed to continue, to be on the streets. So there's a case where an artist and a museum staff were affected by what we did, and it was the opposite effect from the people who said that our poster would make it more difficult to work with this sort of public poster. Even within the San Diego Union *I heard off-the-record remarks like, "Hey, it's really good to see somebody finding a way to get us on this tourist town veneer that we have." You know, the Shamu-and-Surf mentality.*

I don't know what it is but I keep thinking about football analogies. In the recent San Francisco '49ers versus Green Bay Packers game, there was a touchdown pass at the end that won the game for the '49ers and it was a hell of a play. But it wouldn't have made any difference if the score had been 23–0 at that point in the game. Every other play, prior to that play made a difference. I think that it's valid to ask, how do you evaluate this kind of work? How do you give it meaning? How do you understand its importance? But to say that a work has completely turned the tables on a situation, or has to be everything and do everything at one point, is to lose sight of what we're talking about when we're talking about a social/political/economic issue like immigration. It's a long-term struggle, and our project was like one play in a complex game.

ES: *Another indication of the success of the bus poster is that the work became a part of the fabric of the city. You'll often hear people referring to the "tourist plantation." It's a phrase that's been added to the vocabulary of the city to refer to injustices and the plight of undocumented workers within our economy. There were some editorials after the bus poster appeared that asked why it took so long for those plantation posters to appear.*

LH: *I think it's important in a company town like San Diego to introduce a notion of controversy as avenue. We need more than a public relations bureau, something other than the city council to have a voice on critical issues that are operating in the city. Controversy is essentially a discussion marked with opposing points of view. The media coverage of the bus poster allowed an opposing point of view, at least momentarily, to have a sufficient pedestal to be able to look eye-to-eye with those people in power and engage in a discussion.*

DA: When the Donkey Cart *was removed in 1986, Bill Fox, from channel 39, came out with an editorial, and the last sentence of that editorial was "39-Alive calls on Judge Thompson [the federal district court judge who ordered the Don-key Cart removed] to rescind his order and allow this sculpture to be displayed for a few more days as originally intended." Two years later, the same Bill Fox states, "39-Alive calls on San Diego Transit to remove the posters immediately before Super Bowl crowds appear. I'm Bill Fox. We welcome your views." Well, the hell he welcomes our views. If he welcomed our views, why didn't he just shut up and accept our views, which are expressed on the back of the buses? And I think this gets back to your question about the media wanting to control the forum of discourse. We welcome your views as long as we can edit them, decide whether or not they go on the air, decide when they go on the air, how they're contextualized, and so forth. But somehow the media is not a monolith. It's not this lockstep conspiracy. It feeds on itself, undoes itself. It is nothing that we can control—but, rather, something we must constantly challenge.*

Notes

1. This quotation and all others are from the news-clip catalogue that the group assembled and self-published after the project was complete.

2. The *San Diego Union,* Wednesday, January 13, 1988, p. B-6.

3. The *Finder Binder Update,* February 1988, dubbed the bus poster project the "Worst Advertising Pro-gram of January 1988."

Four Experiments in Public Art as Architecture and Urban Planning

In the wake of a number of controversies that arose in public art, administrators across the country began to look for new paradigms for public art, as discussed in the introduction. One of the most popular was "useful" art, art that served a physical function in the site. Across the United States, artists began to be called upon to create "people-friendly" spaces taking on entire sites. Harriet Senie has written:

The expansion of public sculpture from single site specific object to entire site was accompanied by an expansion of the definition of sculpture itself, which allowed for the inclusion of use. The notion of use in relation to art, however, challenged well-established definitions of art in western European culture where art, that is to say high art, traditionally was not functional. In this hierarchy, useful art was relegated to the realm of craft or design and deemed of lesser cultural and economic value. An object without practical use was perforce a luxury item, and ownership was restricted to a monied class.[1]

In some ways, public architectural sculpture maintained this hierarchy. In public commissions, the pedestrian-oriented plazas, enclosures, bridges, and benches were not exclusively for the "monied class," but for the diverse publics that inhabit contemporary cities. Architectural sculpture is rarely controversial with the general public, perhaps because it is so often confused for architecture, and because its uses are welcome and accessible. But there are many artists and critics who have found fault in the sorts of use that art began to serve. As quoted in the introduction, Richard Serra said that he felt "useful" art tends to assimilate with or accommodate architecture rather than creating its own space. And some architects have become increasingly nervous with the role artists feel they might take in the design of spaces.

In fact, I once sat on a public art panel discussion at the College Art Association entitled, "Is the Architect the Enemy?" While the artists and architects on the panel concluded that there need not be an adversarial relationship between the two fields, this is not always the case in practice. Percent for Art programs routinely create forced marriages of artist and architect. Architect and artist are almost always selected by separate panels, often with very different ideas of what the site might need.

The first two interviews in this section, with architects Denise Scott Brown and Robert Venturi, and artist Vito Acconci, address the artist-architect tension directly. The Venturi and Scott Brown interview begins with a discussion of Franklin Court, a museum and public plaza that they designed in Philadelphia. It is an interesting project in this context because it is so close in many ways to contemporary public art. In fact, the "ghost architecture" that they designed to describe the outline of Benjamin Franklin's home is sometimes included in discussions and slide sets on public art. But Venturi and Scott Brown were the architects, planners, and artists on the project, not merely the artists. The discussion of Franklin Court is followed by a more general discussion of the relationship between artists and architects, in which Venturi and Scott Brown take the position that Percent for Art programs can impose an artist into the design process who is hostile to the architecture, who can skew the project by imposing an inappropriate sensibility at the most prominent site in the building.

Vito Acconci presents a vision of the public artist that might represent Venturi and Scott Brown's nightmare. He asserts that public artists are asked to do something peripheral to the architecture, something on the margin. Rather than accept this secondary role, he has sought to make the extra, marginal space into a "cancer" on the building, to cast doubt upon or undercut the main space. Acconci discusses two of his projects: StoreFront for Art and Architecture in New York City, in which he collaborated with the architect Steven Holl, and Arvada Center for Arts and Humanities in Colorado, in which he inserted a ribbon of earth through the building's architecture. The Arvada Center conforms to his notion of public art "infecting" a building, and injecting different aesthetics and uses throughout the space. Acconci's work has become increasingly architectural in recent years, as he has made the transition from an individual artist—Vito Acconci—creating sculpture for exhibitions, to collaboration—Acconci Studio—creating mostly permanent public works. In the light of Acconci's attitude toward architects, it is ironic to note that he read Robert Venturi and Denise Scott Brown's books starting in the late 1970s, and they were highly influential on his work, especially the architecturally related pieces in the early 1980s.[1]

One of the most ambitious architectural projects undertaken by public artists in recent years is the Phoenix Solid Waste Management Facility designed by Michael Singer and Linnea Glatt. This project is the focus of two interviews, first with the artists, and then with Ron Jensen, the government official who paved the way for the project to happen. The interviews treat the project at some length, but the unusual circumstances that led a public official to turn a multimillion dollar construction project over to artists deserves the space. It is important to note that the Solid Waste Management Facility was not being designed by architects, but by engineers. The very straightforward, functional plan that the engineers proposed did not correspond with Ron Jensen's vision for the facility. The artists' approach was much more ambitious—a facility that would actively engage the public in the process of understanding the waste flow and recycling. Singer and Glatt's collaboration was very complex. First, they had to figure out how to work with one another, then with Singer's architectural collaborators, with the engineers, and with the city of Phoenix. They speak about the process of collaboration, and the nature of the compromises inherent in the negotiations that take place at each level: when they could agree to changes, and when they needed to be unyielding. At the end of the interview, the artists seem to be going in opposite directions. Singer, energized by the project, seeks other architectural, landscape and planning commissions. Glatt, satisfied but drained by the project, seeks a bit of refuge in the studio, returning to a more traditional sort of art making.

Ron Jensen was director of public works in Phoenix at the time that Singer and Glatt got their commission to work at the Solid Waste Management Facility. He describes the process that he went through in giving them control of the design of the facility. His story is similar to that of Singer and Glatt, but from the perspective of an engineer. If the building had been over budget or late (as often happens with public construction), imagine the derision he would have encountered in city government for having turned the project over to artists. In the long run, Jensen's vision of a user-friendly facility, and the artists' interest in environmentalism and public participation merged perfectly—the right bureaucrat with the right artists at the right facility.

One of the problems that artists working on public commissions often complain about is their lack of input in the essential nature of the project—the fact that the planning decisions and the basic architectural framework for the project have been settled long before the artist is called in. Vito Acconci addresses this issue in his interview. Project Row Houses is an artist-initiated public art project that includes exhibition spaces, after-school programs, and housing for single mothers in the economically depressed Third Ward in Houston, Texas. Rick Lowe, a young African American artist interested in architectural sculpture, initiated the project and laid the initial groundwork. In his interview, he describes how he went from creating politically inspired paintings and installations to concentrating on community organizing, to mobilizing a group of artists to create Project Row Houses. The Young Mothers Program at Project Row Houses provides housing and support for single mothers. It was the brainchild of Deborah Grotfeldt, who joined Lowe as codirector in the early stages of the project. Assata Shakur was among the first group of mothers in residence in the program, and in the fall of 1998, she started in the doctorate program in sociology at Pennsylvania State University. In her interview, she describes how she came to the program, what it was like to participate, and how it affected her life.

In the late 1960s, public sculpture was created as a complement to architecture. Large-scale works by Alexander Calder and Henry Moore decorated the open plazas that architects left in front of their buildings. By the 1990s, the relationship between artist and architect had become significantly more complex, as the following interviews demonstrate. But, more importantly, artists began to address a wider range of uses for their work, sometimes altering the "program" of the site rather than accepting the essential use as a given.

Notes

1. Harriet Senie, *Contemporary Public Sculpture* (New York, Oxford: Oxford University Press, 1992), p. 172.

2. Kate Linker, *Vito Acconci* (New York: Rizzoli, 1994), p. 113.

Interview: **Denise Scott Brown**
and **Robert Venturi**
on Art in Architecture

Introduction

Since the 1960s Robert Venturi (born 1925) and Denise Scott Brown (born 1931) have been among the most influential practitioners and theoreticians of architecture and urban planning in the United States. Venturi received undergraduate and graduate degrees in architecture from Princeton University (1950) and continued his studies when he won a Rome Prize in Architecture and attended the American Academy in Rome (1954–1956). His first architectural jobs were for Louis Kahn and Eero Saarinen. Venturi has taught at the University of Pennsylvania and at Yale University. In 1964, he started the firm Venturi and Rauch, which Denise Scott Brown joined in1967.

Denise Scott Brown was born in Zambia. She graduated from the Architectural Association in London (1955) and received a Master's in City Planning and in Architecture from the University of Pennsylvania (1960, 1965). She has taught at the University of Pennsylvania, UCLA, Berkeley, and Yale. She is involved in the firm's architectural projects, and is the principal in charge of urban planning and design.[1]

Venturi's first major commission was the Vanna Venturi House (1963), designed for his mother. Although Modernist in its lack of decoration, its façade makes a direct and unmistakable reference to the traditional image of the house. This reference was radical because it was not abstract and made reference to vernacular architecture, to a comforting historical notion of the home. It was far from the antihistorical nature of High Modernist design that held sway at the time. The radical nature of the statement was reinforced three years later with the publication of *Complexity and Contradiction in Architecture*[2] (discussed in the introduction), which was a frontal attack on the purity of Modernist theory and practice.

Guild House (1965) was another of Venturi's widely published early projects. A six-story building of apartments for the elderly, this rather low-budget structure has subtle variations in design (for example, the window types vary as the building recedes from the street) that differentiate it from the cut-rate Modernism of institutional architecture. However, the most striking idiosyncrasy of the building was the large-scale nonfunctional television antenna mounted atop the façade. This sculptural element was clearly symbolic—a reference to the omnipresent TV antenna on buildings (in the pre-cable and satellite dish era), and a gently satirical comment on the amount of television likely to be watched by the elderly inhabitants of the building.

Venturi and Rauch, Guild House, 1965, Philadelphia, Pennsylvania. Client: Friends Neighborhood Guild. Photograph courtesy of Venturi, Scott Brown, and Associates.

In 1972, Venturi, Scott Brown, and Steven Izenour, an important longtime contributor to the firm, wrote *Learning from Las Vegas*.[3] The book is a careful analysis of the iconology and building practices of the quintessential American strip. The book begins:

Learning form the existing landscape is a way of being revolutionary for an architect. Not the obvious way, which is to tear down Paris and begin again, as Le Corbusier suggested in the 1920's, but another more tolerant way; that is, to question how we look at things.[4]

Scott Brown has led the firm in a number of planning projects over the years, including Washington Avenue in Miami Beach (1978), Hennepin Avenue in Minneapolis (1981), Memphis Tennessee Center City (1987), and Dartmouth College (1990). In their firm profile, they say of their planning approach:

Our urban planning emphasizes social issues, economic feasibility and incremental development. We are experienced in putting together and leading interdisciplinary

planning teams and at operating within complex urban and political contexts, where de-
mocratic participation must go hand-in-hand with inter-agency cooperation, and where
legal and financial incentive packages must be devised to meet unique social and archi-
tectural conditions.[5]

During the 1970s the architectural work of Venturi, Scott Brown, and Associates (VSBA) became more obviously influenced by historical and popular sources. A famous example is the addition to the Allen Memorial Gallery at Oberlin College (1976). The addition plays off the colors and scale of the original building in a kind of counterpoint that is neither slavishly imitative nor ostentatiously different. A central element of the design is a fat wooden Ionic column that manages to be simultaneously classical and pop. The Oberlin gallery foreshadowed a series of museum commissions for the firm from the Seattle Art Museum (1990) to the National Gallery in London Sainsbury Wing (1991) to the San Diego Museum of Contemporary Art (1992). While there was a single Ionic column at Oberlin, fifteen years later at the National Gallery, VSBA used Corinthian columns as a primary motif on the façade, echoing the nineteenth century neoclassical museum to which it is joined.

Franklin Court (1976), discussed in the following interview, is a museum and memorial to Benjamin Franklin at the site his house once stood in Philadelphia. It features what VSBA calls "ghost architecture," a steel armature that outlines the form of Franklin's residence. The outline of the house at Franklin Court harks back to the Vanna Venturi House in that it is a simplified, idealized symbol for the house. On the pavement, the architects have inscribed texts from Franklin's letters to his wife, mostly about the construction of the house. This use of text is not unusual in the work of VSBA, both in projects like Welcome Park, an historical site that tells the story of William Penn, and more recently through electronic media in projects like the renovation of Memorial Hall at Harvard University (1995), with its constantly revised running LED texts.

In 1996, Venturi published *Iconography and Electronics Upon a Generic Architecture,*[6] a book that combines some previously published texts with new essays. As the title to this far-ranging book indicates, VSBA has been increasingly interested in the potential of electronic media like LEDs to convey information and iconography in their buildings. While the ultra-modern use of electronic media in architecture might seem to be a radical departure for a firm that is credited with pioneering the reintroduction of historical sources in architecture, it is consistent with their interest

Venturi, Scott Brown, and Associates, Franklin Court, 1976, Philadelphia, Pennsylvania. Client: United States National Park Service. Photograph courtesy of Venturi, Scott Brown, and Associates.

in contradiction, their eclectic embrace of the past and the present. The ghost architecture of Franklin Court is both a well-researched historical reference to the buildings that were on the site and a pop art drawing of those buildings. VSBA is a firm that has kept its supporters and critics off balance for thirty-five years.

This interview took place at the office of VSBA in Philadelphia, January 1996. I asked Venturi and Scott Brown to focus first on Franklin Court because it is a project that bears a strong resemblance to a public artwork, and is sometimes included in surveys on the subject. The similarities and differences in artistic and architectural practice become clear in this interview. The discussion of Franklin Court is followed by a more general discussion of the current state of architecture and public art.

Robert Venturi: The National Park Service. We were relatively unknown architects at the time; I think they came to us mostly on the recommendation of Nicholas Gianopoulos, a distinguished Philadelphia structural engineer, who had worked for the Park Service. They were a terrific client. On Market Street a row of houses was still standing that had been owned and, I think, built by Franklin. They were restored as a part of the project. But when they came to us they wanted a building, a Benjamin Franklin Museum, in the square behind the row houses that was the site of Franklin's house. Some people were interested in reproducing his house, but there was no extant illustration to work from. There were fire insurance descriptions and archaeological remains of the house, so you could tell the exact configuration of the walls, and there were letters about the house exchanged between Franklin and his wife while he was in London and the house was in construction. But, with so little visual information, the Park Service was pretty easily persuaded not to try to reproduce the house.

Denise Scott Brown: The first creative idea was not to put a building there at all; to put the building underground and create a public square over it. The second creative idea was the "ghost" house—an outline in steel of the probable silhouette of Franklin's house, erected over its foundations.

RV: The aim was to create a delightful open place in the center of the dense texture of the city. So the courtyard became a pleasant neighborhood amenity for people who live there, as well as for tourists.

TF: This is unusual. Most museums are designed only for visitors who are there on some kind of outing. This museum creates a central space for the everyday use of the community as well.

RV: Yes, though I would assume the community wouldn't normally go down to see the exhibits.

DSB: The community is office workers, to a large extent.

RV: We also love the idea of iconographic representation. This has intrigued us for a long time. We like representing, we like the words that tell the story throughout the space. But, when we went back the other day for the first time in a while, we thought we should have made the words bigger, given today's "hype" sensibility. The idea of making description part of the architecture was very unusual in that period of minimalist, abstract Modernism.

TF: Who did the historical research to get all the quotes?

RV: Five historians and archaeologists worked with the Park Service.

TF: Who edited the quotes and decided where they were going to go?

RV: It was a joint effort.

TF: In Franklin Court, at several points you are standing in the ghost architecture, and the text in the paving tells what rooms were on the second and third floors above your head. You can't help but stand there and look up at the sky, to imagine the two stories above you. You are there in the space, within the outline of the house, reading the texts, but a lot is left to the imagination. And all those letters from Franklin to his wife etched in the pavers create a very personal experience in a public space.

DSB: Historians talk today of teaching history by helping people "enter into it" personally. Here you literally enter into it.

TF: What about the aesthetic decisions?

DSB: (to RV) You were thinking of minimalist sculpture to some extent.

RV: If you live long enough as an architect, your sensibility changes and you decide everything you've designed is too thin and delicate or else everything is too big and heavy. Let's say you were a furniture maker in the Federalist period, where chairs had such thin legs, and you lived on into early Victorian or Late Greek Revival, you'd say, "Oh, how skimpy all that is." Now we are in a period *when I look at my mother's house and say, "Oh, it's too thin. It's too delicate." Anyhow, I think I'd make it bolder now. The lines in the ghost architecture would be heavier. Our music is louder now, our colors are bolder.*

At a similar project, Welcome Park, we worked on the site of William Penn's house. Here we made a city square. Again, it deals with symbolism and iconography. The paving pattern of Welcome Park depicts Penn's plan for the city of Philadelphia. One bounding wall carries porcelain enamel panels that give information on Penn's life. It's just teeming with information.

DSB: *In Welcome Park, the text is even more important than in Franklin Court. The words are much bigger.*

TF: *One of the things that's interesting to me is that you had the fundamental right as architects to make these big decisions, like putting the museum underground at Franklin Court.*

DSB: *No. We did not have the right to make those decisions. We had the right to recommend them to our client. The client was the one who had to make the decision.*

TF: *Well, for the public artist, those decisions have usually been made by the time they are selected. You had to convince your client to put the museum underground. Nonetheless, it was the sort of idea they might entertain.*

DSB: *In an architectural project, ideas may come from many places. The professional has the responsibility to lay the options out for the client, make recommendations, and explain the implications of those recommendations. It then depends on the client, whether they will or won't accept the recommendations.*

RV: *There is a tremendous difference between traditional and current ideas of the artist. Now we see the artist as his own boss. He makes his own decisions. His art derives from individual inspiration. The artist creates a work of art, and if the public likes it, wonderful. If the public does not like it, he starves. (I'm describing artists of salon sculpture and easel painting.) But historically artists, like architects, worked for the persons who paid for the project. The client-*

architect relationship is a delicate one: on one hand, you are creating your work of art as an artist. Your name is going to be on it. On the other hand, you have to accommodate the client. On a very fundamental level, you cannot say to the client, "I'm going to give you four bedrooms instead of two, and you must just find the money somewhere." But it is not a completely determined situation. There can come a point where the client pushes you to go against your own best judgment, and you may have to make a stand, possibly resign.

DSB: Most architects, most of the time, cannot resign. Clients can fire them, but they cannot resign, because they have signed a contract. To resign irresponsibly would result in legal suits.

TF: That is very similar to how public artists work. They have agreed in a contract to provide certain services (although a good lawyer could probably get them out of it.) Anyway, public artists are working more like architects, but they have no training for interacting with "clients." It can be very frustrating.

DSB: Nor do architects have much training.

RV: I don't blame public artists for getting mad, because I get mad. But they are comparing themselves with their brothers and sisters in the private sector, who really are perhaps exceptionally free. Granted, they may be starving, but at least they are doing their own thing.

Artists who are bitter about their role in the public process are part of the recent, but established, tradition of creating what they want, then putting it on the market. The architect lives by an older and more complex tradition. We sometimes feel bitter that our relationship with the client can be so difficult, but this is really part of the natural process of doing art. One difference between architects and artists is that architects who can't get clients, can't create, whereas artists who can't sell their work, may starve—which is very serious—but they can do their thing.

TF: When thinking about art in architecture, I think about how art was expelled from the enterprise. In the nineteenth century, the presence of art in architecture was

Venturi, Scott Brown, and Associates, Franklin Court. Photograph courtesy of Venturi, Scott Brown, and Associates.

taken for granted, a given. In Modernist buildings, art was largely absent, partially on the basis of the architects' rejection of decoration, but also because the Modernist artist, as you said, sought the isolation of the studio and the museum, away from public life. The problem is that there are so few artists these days who are used to working with architects and vice versa. If you look back, there were probably all these highly skilled artisans sitting around with no work when Modernism took over. Well, now the artists are back.

DSB: *Modernism did not support the notion of civic design, because that was the design of rulers and the Modernists were socialists. So the tradition of civic design and its public art—its equestrian statues, its obelisks—was politically suspect. On the other hand, don't forget that Mies van der Rohe carefully chose a sculpture by Kolbe to go in his Barcelona pavilion. When his Modernist artist companions asked why he hadn't chosen one of them, Mies replied he particularly wanted something in contrast to his own work.*

RV: Denise is raising the issue of juxtaposition versus integration. To the extent that modern architecture accommodated art, the art was, as in the Barcelona Pavilion, juxtaposed upon the architecture without true integration. That was okay, but it was certainly not like a Gothic facade teeming with sculptures in niches, or a Baroque interior composed of scenographic murals. These forms of integration are hard to come by.

TF: Mies decided on the location and nature of the artist and the work for the Barcelona Pavilion. One of the biggest problems for architects with Percent for Art is that there often seems to be an imposition of one sensibility on another. With artists and architects so distanced from one another these days, there is often a clash.

DSB: The English artist, Edward Bawden, had an ironic view of his relationship with architects. I once told him I liked paintings whose compositions were rectangular and geometrical and he replied, "Of course you do, you're an architect: when I work with architects I do paintings like that." This was said with some humor but with an air of tiredness.

TF: Yes, this is one of our problems. Architects often sit on the panels to select artists in the program that I run, but the artist who is selected often is not the architect's choice. Like you say, architects tend to have a predictable set of tastes. The other panelists (curators, artists, community members) are often looking for other aesthetic voices on the site, something different with the 1 percent than you are getting with the 100 percent.

DSB: Ninety-nine percent. I think there are degrees. For an art project that will be intimately associated with the architects' building there should be a friendly relationship between artist and architects. For a piece set far enough away in time or space to avoid the need for inflection between building and art, that's another question. There should also be a doctrine of fairness. Seeing a building you have been hired to design, trusted to execute, and done your best for (and, God knows, made little or no money on) —seeing all this canceled out by an artist—and with money that might have helped enhance the artistry and quality of the building had it been available: there is a level of unfairness in this. And it's not only a question of aesthetics. In Denver,

164

through the One Percent for Art program, the architect for a major public project had recently to accept work of an artist he did not admire in the main space of the building. He has no say whatsoever. He couldn't control the major element in the most important space in his building. The artist he didn't want is one I think is marvelous, I would welcome him in my building. But do you think it's right the architect should have no say in choosing the most important images in the building? Also 1 percent sounds small but in many budget-restricted projects it may be money needed to give a degree of quality to the finish of the building—something to help it survive wear and tear. Seen from our point of view, the artist frequently takes the quality or the specialness out of the building itself and puts it elsewhere.

RV: *That's right. And a parallel to what Denise is saying is that designing 100 percent of the building doesn't give us 100 percent control. Don't forget 40 percent normally goes to mechanical equipment, air-conditioning and all that stuff—and even more in museums that must have high-level environmental controls. There are also huge controlling factors in building regulations, even aesthetic control. Also, you are controlled to some extent by your context. There are many things you can do or can't do in a certain place. Like the artist, who must or should consider the context of the building, the building designer must work within the context of the place.*

The artist can screw up a building by putting something in front of it. Ideally artist and architect should work together. This must have happened on Gothic cathedral facades, with their statues and images, and when Tiepolo painted the ceilings of baroque architecture. But in our modern context, the artist seems often to be a sullen person who hates architects and feels they are rich money makers. Conceptually there is nothing wrong with choosing a work of art that is not analogous to the architecture; aesthetic harmony can be achieved through contrast. But sometimes, the artist's approach is quite hostile.

When we think about public art, we should also consider architecture as a public art form. The art in a building is not only the so-called sculptural component—and now, rather than addressing the notion of artists working with architects, let me talk as an architect who is doing public art. The public design process can be democratic or autocratic. We are all for the democ-

ratic model, of course, but much of the great public art and architecture of the eighteenth century and earlier was produced under autocratic forms of government. Even under Napoleon III the civic art and architecture of mid-nineteenth century Paris was an autocratic imposition. (I don't like it particularly. My favorite city is not Paris. My favorite is a city of no obvious unity, perhaps of chaos—Tokyo.)

A process to introduce democratic review into the public design process has developed in America over the last thirty years. It connects with the idea of citizen participation in urban planning, which evolved, to some extent, out of the city planning department at the University of Pennsylvania in the 1960s. It's a very good thing, basically. The idea is that experts shouldn't act as autocrats. Rather, neighborhood people—particularly people in the lowest-income neighborhoods—should be represented in review processes that, particularly in urban planning and development, will deeply affect their lives. But now you have the "talk show" method of dealing with things, where everyone yells at everybody else. You go to some of these meetings and everyone rudely screams at you. My generation cannot deal with it. It's not the way to talk. It's not "gentlemanly."

Many situations are highly political: if the architect's client is associated with one group, the other group attacks the architect because they want to make a statement to their adversaries. There are often enormous issues of democratic process associated with a project. These may have very little to do with the architecture, but they can either allow or not allow things to happen. Sometimes there are questions of taste. Our designs are frequently called "vulgar"—sometimes by people whose taste we would consider vulgar.

DSB: Today most citizen review groups seem to consist of upper-middle-class people trying, in the main, to protect their property values. I haven't heard "the poor" mentioned at a community meeting in twenty years.

RV: Community design review brings up all sorts of issues of class and "taste culture," as Herbert Gans would say. And these become even more complicated when architecture is no longer abstract and issues of iconography arise. The irony is amazing: When I was young in the 1940s, the radical, daring thing to do *was abstract architecture. Now abstraction has become the old-fashioned, easy thing to do. In the democratic review process, there is seldom objection to abstract architecture, because it has no readable symbolic content; it makes no one mad. And in the context of multiculturalism—particularly the difficulties of one culture resenting another—the abstract minimalist aesthetic raises fewer hackles. But it is frequently bland. Abstract architecture needs art in its foreground. It's often no more than a background for art. Is that where the long tradition of public architecture should end?*

TF: *Of course, the issues that you are laying out sound exactly like what I hear from public artists. They are dealing with democracy, multiculturalism, angry citizens, iconographic interpretation. And, when you have abstract architecture as the background for the art, the art is often attached because it is the only thing that the public can hope to understand.*

DSB: *Except that, as much as there might be problems in common, the artists seem also to resent the architects.*

RV: *Maybe they call* architects *sullen.*

TF: *It seems that a lot of public artists want to act like architects, build things that look like architecture.*

DSB: *Yes, and many landscape architects want to do this too.*

TF: *At the same time, architects want to do art. Everybody wants to do everything.*

DSB: *We want to assert our client's and our own vision of the identity of our building, particularly of its main spaces and main approach. We don't want someone else's interpretation canceling ours out. The central identity of a building is often established by the architectural elements of the facade and the main circulation spaces—perhaps an entry hall and stairway. Today there could be, once again, a strong iconographic contribution to these elements—perhaps from interior or exterior "signs," possibly from moving video pictures or LED texts. These are the changeable elements in the per-*

Venturi, Scott Brown, and Associates, Franklin Court. Photograph courtesy of Venturi,
Scott Brown, and Associates.

*manent building. We would be happy to have Percent for Art money provide
moving images within the architecture.*

TF: *As you know, that is what we are proposing for the Staten Island Ferry building that
you are designing in New York (although we have not yet gone through our democratic process). Here is an area that video or media artists can address that architects might not find difficult to accept, like a changing, moving sculptural
frieze. Of course not all architects would find this sort of media intervention acceptable as you do.*

*You said that you are happy to be working with Ed Ruscha in San Diego.
How did you end up with the* Hammering Man *by Borofsky in front of the Seattle Art Museum?*

RV: *We worked on that with the curator, Patterson Sims. We knew him from
Philadelphia and New York. He said the museum wanted to propose Borof-*

sky, and I said, that's funny, he was at the top of my list. Before that, we had disapproved a project by Chris Burden, to hang a large, wooden galleon over the side of the building. It seemed to us to negate if not humiliate the architecture. The Borofsky, to us, was appropriate, very much at home, and very strong. It wasn't bland.

DSB: There's a complex and playful set of scale juxtapositions on our SAM facade, which take you from the scale of the region and world (the big sign and sheer walls) through syncopated steps, to the scale of one person entering the door accompanied by multicolored "columnets." But, at the end of the sequence, just as you become one person entering a doorway, there is this great guy beside you, who blows the scale to bits again—taking you back to world scale, on many levels. That's what we liked. Burden, I think, was making a social comment.

RV: Of course, anybody who is any good and profound feels socially conscious and antigovernment in many dimensions of our era. But to me, Burden's response seemed sophomoric, not serious.

DSB: But maybe that's what we did in New York when we were asked by a developer to make a suggestion for what to do at Times Square in the context of Philip Johnson's design for the property around it. We designed a 90-foot diameter apple.

RV: It was at the time of Philip Johnson's first design, which was a kind of a Postmodern . . .

DSB: . . . megastatement. Very high buildings on big red granite bases. We used one of these as a base for our apple.

RV: You are right, that was being a bit antiestablishment.

And I'm sure the LED media we're investigating now [the integration of changing text through LED panels is a significant element of several new buildings being designed by the firm] are being interpreted as our "acting negatively," although of course I think it isn't. Just as Modernism derived its *vocabulary from vernacular industrial architecture, so, inevitably, civic art and architecture are going to have to use the enormous vitality of commercial vernacular art as a source. People like Jenny Holzer are doing that and, of course, so did the Pop artists. One hundred years from now, today's billboards will be in museums.*

Notes

1. Biographical information from: Venturi, Scott Brown, and Associates, *Architecture and Decorative Arts: Two Naïfs in Japan* (Kajima Institute Publishing Co., Ltd., 1991), p. 154.

2. Robert Venturi, *Complexity and Contradiction in Architecture* (New York: Museum of Modern Art, 1966).

3. Denise Scott Brown, Robert Venturi, and Steven Izenour, *Learning from Las Vegas* (Cambridge: MIT Press, 1972).

4. Ibid., p. 3.

5. Venturi, Scott Brown, and Associates, "Firm Background," version obtained from the firm in 1997 p. 3.

6. Robert Venturi, *Iconography and Electronics Upon a Generic Architecture* (Cambridge: MIT Press, 1996).

Interview: **Vito Acconci** *on Art, Architecture, Arvada, and StoreFront*

Introduction

Vito Acconci was born in 1940, in the Bronx, New York. He graduated from Holy Cross College in Worcester, Massachusetts, in 1962, with a major in English literature.[1] Acconci then attended the Writers' Workshop at the University of Iowa, where he received his M.F.A. in creative writing. After graduation in 1964, he moved back to New York City. In the mid- and late-1960s, Acconci was a writer, employing a systematic, logical approach that would be the hallmark of his performances in the 1970s. For example, his poem called "Wall and the Ladder" (1968) begins thus:

1. *This one, it's a movement starting down and going up.*
2. *It's a sentence.*
3. *It began with a pointer, to this.*
4. *It is declarative . . .*[2]

In the late 1960s, Acconci made the gradual transition from writing to performing his work, as poetry readings gave way to performances at galleries. But Acconci's performances were not limited to sanctioned exhibition spaces, but included sites in the city. Acconci said, "Going into the street was a way of literally breaking the margins, breaking out of the house and leaving the paper behind."[3] The early 1970s also saw a proliferation of video art in Acconci's work. Acconci's performances and videotapes followed the highly literal, systematic mode of his writing. Repetition and variations on a theme are constants in Acconci's work, as is evident in the prose style of the following interview, which closely resembles the way that he talks.

In 1972, Acconci created one of his most famous works, *Seedbed*, at the Sonnabend Gallery in Soho. For this piece, he built a ramp in the gallery that looked much like the sort of minimal installation art that was common in New York at the time. However, Acconci was lying under the ramp during gallery hours, masturbating in response to the footsteps of the visitors. Two speakers broadcast Acconci's voice as he narrated his masturbatory fantasies. *Seedbed* was typical of Acconci's work in the early 1970s, in that it was an installation that depended upon the participation of the viewer. Kate Linker has written of Acconci, "His career traces a movement from self-isolation to interrelation in which dependency on the other, or others, is a mark of human interdependency necessary for social proceedings."[4] While *Seedbed* is often cited as the polar opposite of Acconci's public work, it was with works of this nature that his investigation of interdependency with the viewer became increasingly evident. Acconci's installations in the later 1970s also began to regularly include places for the viewer to sit, which would become a central aspect of his work later.

In 1980, Acconci began a series of works he called "self-erecting architecture," spaces that were activated and/or created with the participation of the viewer. Whether the viewer was asked to pedal a bicycle that moved scenery, or sit on a swing that pulled up walls as they fell to the floor, the works were incomplete without active participation. In the 1980s, Acconci also created a number of sculptural environments that used the image of the house, often flipped over or turned on angle. These installations always allowed the viewer to investigate, to walk through the space and sit in a number of locations. By the late 1980s, Acconci was becoming increasingly interested in creating permanent public art. As he says in the following interview, "It wasn't until 1988, after I did a show at the Museum of Modern Art in New York, that I began to be asked, frequently, to make public proposals. I had called the show 'Public Places.' It was as if I had to announce my intentions. I thought everybody knew, but they didn't. Only after I told them what I was doing, in the title of the show, did people ask me." By 1990, Acconci had begun to focus mostly on large-scale, permanent commissions, with an occasional museum exhibition or gallery show. His public art is characterized by the variety of social spaces it creates. There are always benches, but they are often in eccentric configuration, and his work is often created in some sort of ironic relationship with the architecture. For these works, Acconci assembled a team of collaborators under the name, "Acconci Studio," as discussed in the interview. This late phase is the focus of the following discussion.

In 1988, I called the current director of the Arvada Center, Kathy Andrews, to get a user's assessment of the project, and she had very positive things to say. She said that the outside portion of Acconci's project is used by people waiting to be picked up and that people use the seating indoors for a wide variety of interactions. Children have a particular fondness for the work. She said that some of the people who come to the center know that Acconci's project is art, while others assume that it is simply a part of the architecture. While there was a controversy at the time the work was commissioned (described in the interview), it was pretty much forgotten several years later. Andrews said that Acconci was very accommodating with the community representatives during the controversy and "did what it took to make the project work."

In general, she reported that the work is weathering well. Panels have broken from time to time, but it is only a matter for routine maintenance. After six years of constant use, the project was in excellent condition.[5]

The following interview was conducted in Vito Acconci's studio in Brooklyn, New York, in May 1996. It was thoroughly reedited by Acconci, so the punctuation is different from other interviews in the book.

Tom Finkelpearl: How do you see the role of the artist in the world of public commissions?

Vito Acconci: When you're asked to do a public art project, you're asked to do something that's peripheral to the building designed by the architect; you're asked to do something on the margin; you don't get the main space, you're put in the corner. And sometimes it's worse than that; we've been working a long time on a project where the architects are saying things like, "Well, we need some art overlay here." So the artist is asked to provide something like paint, or wallpaper, or a carpet. Or sometimes not even that; some architects—maybe understandably—want their walls and floors to be left alone, untampered with; so, what they want is floating art, maybe an "art float," separate from their walls, from their floor. As a public artist, you're asked to do something extra, something unnecessary. The ticket counters have been designed, the transfer corridors have been designed, all of the airport that's actually needed and usable has already been designed by the architect; yet the city has a One Percent for Art law, so art has to come in at the last minute, like a deus ex machina, like an architect's nightmare.

We're asked to do a folly; our program is: to have no program, to do nothing but art. But we—Acconci Studio—work best when we have a program of functions and needs. Usually we have to write our own program; we search desperately for functions to provide. So, if we're asked to do a folly, we try to turn that folly into a joker, a pest.

There shouldn't be a separate field called "public art," there should be only architecture, only landscape architecture; there should be architecture projects, and landscape architecture projects, that everyone—including so-called artists—can apply for. "Public art" gives an artist an excuse to say: this is like architecture, but it isn't really architecture—so it doesn't have to ob-

serve the rules and regulations that architecture has to observe, it doesn't have to be as functional as architecture. If the public artist were in the role of architect, there would be nothing to hide behind.

TF: You often do projects that comment on the architecture.

VA: Yes; if we're asked to deal with extra space, marginal space, we can turn that extra space into a cancer: what this superfluous space can do is disease the main space, undercut the main space. Can you nudge into it? Can you make that main space less sure of itself? Can you cast a doubt, show hesitation, insert a parenthesis, a second thought? And that's the advantage of coming in on the margin, coming in from the outside: you can make a marginal note to the main body of the text of a culture. If you're in a space off to the side, if you're in a lower position, then maybe you can express a minority voice. Which you can't do if you're in the main space, the major position; because then you'd be the majority; you're one of them.

TF: You have talked about getting in the back door.

VA: Yes. And I've talked about coming in from the side, and coming up from underneath, and clinging on like a leech. I'd welcome the chance sometime, the risk, of having to start from the center; then I'd have to make my own center, I wouldn't have the luxury of reacting.

TF: Well, your design along with Steven Holl for StoreFront for Art and Architecture did address the whole space. How did it come about?

VA: Steven and I were approached together by Kyong Park and Shirin Neshat (codirectors of StoreFront).

TF: It was their idea that you collaborate?

VA: Yes; they knew that Steven and I had worked together, starting in 1988, on a seven-block walkway in Washington, D.C. The project never happened. It reached the research and development phase; but, after working together

Acconci Studio/Steven Holl, Storefront Renovation, 1993, New York, New York. Client: StoreFront for Art and Architecture. Photograph courtesy of Acconci Studio.

for fourteen months, we never even got to the design phase. So Shirin and Kyong wondered if we wanted to try again. They asked us to do a piece, an installation; it was us who introduced the idea not of doing something *in* StoreFront but, instead, of doing StoreFront, renovating StoreFront.

TF: *Well, that's certainly a case of writing your own program.*

VA: *It was me who wanted the renovation, more than Steven. After all, he can do renovations all the time. He probably wanted to do art; for me, it was a chance to do architecture.*

TF: *What year was that?*

VA: *It was built in '93; they asked us, probably, a year before that. We knew we had a small budget, $50,000. We knew we had a small space, 10' × 100'. With such*

Acconci Studio/Steven Holl, Storefront Renovation. Photograph courtesy of Acconci Studio.

a budget, and in such a space, all we could do was give StoreFront, literally, a new front, a new facade. By changing StoreFront's face, by loosening its face, we could renovate the whole space.

TF: How did the ideas evolve?

VA: There were so many conflicting ideas, it's hard to say now where they started. Steven starts a project with drawings—watercolor sketches—whereas we start with models. One model took StoreFront's old facade, the wood-panel facade, and tilted it, sank it, panel by panel, gradually, down to the ground. All of us—StoreFront, Steven, Acconci Studio—liked that a lot: StoreFront as a house of cards. But then we—Acconci Studio—drew back, and reconsidered: it was an art piece, it wasn't architecture. Once the old facade had been sunken in, it should have been possible to use the demolished facade as a building, as the gallery that StoreFront was supposed to be. But you couldn't use it, you could only look at it. It would have been only the first phase in a two-phase process: now that the old StoreFront wall has fallen down, another wall had to be put up in its place—ideally, a new wall made up of reused pieces of the old wall that were lying there in front of you. Since there wouldn't have been money for that second phase, we gave it up: we would have been providing a demolition job, but not a construction job, not a re-construction job.

The way Steven and I collaborated, each of us worked alone, separately, and then both of us came together and summarized, reviewed, exchanged ideas. The exchange was agonized, and agonizing. Instead of each of us playing off the other's idea, each of us replaced the other's idea, with one of our own. So, always, we had to begin again, from the beginning. Neither one of us stretched and extended what the other had presented. Or if one of us did, or if one of us anticipated where the other was going, the other had already gone on to something else. Then, after a series of dead ends, something happened. What happened might have been: knowing that now we were down to the wire, now we had to get serious.

So we—Acconci Studio—did a model with a shifting facade: sections of the facade pushed in, or pulled out, making seats within the facade. Steven compared the shifted sections to windows, which made us—Acconci Studio—think of doors, which made us think of shifting walls. Steven wanted to open up the facade to light; so we thought of opening up the facade to people—light could take care of itself. We—Acconci Studio—proportioned the movable panels; we did the drawings; but none of that would have happened without conversations with Steven, arguments with Steven, beating our heads against the wall with Steven.

TF: At StoreFront, were you thinking about opening up the relationship between the gallery and the street?

VA: We wanted to pull the sidewalk into the gallery—the sidewalk would sweep in with the pivoting of a wall—and we wanted the gallery to spill out, ooze out, onto the street. At the same time, we kept in the front of our minds that this was an exhibition space, that different shows were going to happen here. So we wanted a space that would be constantly adjustable: the space could be different for each show—each exhibitor could change the space—outside walls could be inside, inside walls could be outside, part of the gallery could be open while part would be closed.

TF: *Those are two things that architects often do not consider when designing galleries and museums. One thing that has been consistent about galleries has been their complete disengagement from the street. And another tradition has been for architects to design for their own aesthetic statement, not as a space for artists. As an artist, the first thing you are thinking about is how it is going to be used by other artists. So maybe we could say that museums should be designed with input from artists. I think there is such a great tradition of disastrous museum design by great architects.*

VA: *For example . . .*

TF: *Oh, the Guggenheim.*

VA: *Maybe, but it's the best building in New York. And, at the same time that it looked back, to a frontier landscape, it looked ahead, maybe in spite of itself; it's a museum for an electronic age: you can see stuff fast—you can't stop moving, you don't have to concentrate, you're going down, there's a void in the middle, you preserve yourself from suicide and make it out the door. It's like skimming through a book, fast-forwarding a videotape.*

TF: *Yeah, that is fine for a chronological exhibition of easel paintings, in which case you can look across and see what you are about to see; you can look back and see what you just saw. You can scan through it, and you have a sense of where you are in the artist's career. That's what was going on in exhibitions at that time the building was designed. But for sculpture?*

VA: *Okay, okay, I grant you: the art spaces that the Guggenheim provides are wall spaces. As I said before, it's like walking past pages, walking past movie screens. The Guggenheim is a sculpture that you're inside of, inside which you spiral past walls as if you're a spinning top. Anyway, it's not bad for sculpture in the middle; maybe the ramp should be treated as a catwalk—a circle, a spiral, of people to watch a sculpture rise up in their midst and blow out through the roof. Remember, artists who do installations—they crave a space that has its own quirks, its own peculiarities.*

TF: *Well, the space at StoreFront has a lot of character to it. There are a lot of ways for artists to play off of your design in creating an installation. But it doesn't eliminate, for example, a traditional show of architectural drawings.*

VA: *We didn't want to provide a space that other people had to fit into; we wanted to provide a space that other people could fit out for their own uses, their own purposes. Their work could shape the space; their work doesn't have to be shaped by the space. We hope the space can serve them; they don't have to serve the space, or live up to the space. If anything, they might have to live up to change, to the possibilities of change that the space provides. If they want to show drawings on the walls, the walls don't have to stay in one position; if they want to show models, a section of the wall can be pivoted down to function as a table, a shelf.*

TF: *Your public projects always offer the possibility for a lot of different kinds of interactions in the pieces. That's true at StoreFront, because it is so flexible, but even where there are benches, there are always benches for a single person, two people or five people.*

VA: *We try to provide a mix: a space, say, for a large group of people, for an orgy or a revolution, and, at the same time but off to the side, a space for face-to-face contact, where two people might feel each other out as they feel each other up, and, at the same time but around the corner, a single-person seat for a potential suicide, or for a serial murderer looking others over from afar . . .*

TF: *I think that one of the problems in a lot of architecture is that they have an idea of what the right kind of interaction in a public space is. The uniformity of the benches reflects a uniformity in planning . . .*

VA: Since I don't know what a proper interaction should be, all I can do is provide enough occasions, situations, in which other people—through bodily use of those occasions—might come up with different methods of interaction, different attitudes of interaction, different reasons for interaction. When I say "interaction" here, it's an interaction, I hope, not just between person and person but also between person and culture. I hope I can provide the possibility of interaction, but not necessarily the program for interaction. Maybe I can provide a program of programs, a structure of programs.

TF: Well that's the problem with the Guggenheim. It provided one opportunity, which was maybe a good one and a brilliant one, but it didn't provide for enough flexibility.

VA: When our spaces work, it's because the space is flexible. And then maybe people are flexible, more flexible than they thought they were before. We make spaces for adults who can try out being children again. For a space of ours to really work, it has to liberate people. I get thrilled when I see, in a corporation plaza, a person sitting not on the bench that's been provided but, instead, on a step, even if the riser is too short for a seat. The bench functions as an order; you're supposed to sit there. So obviously your reaction should be: "I don't want to sit here, I want to sit over there. I'll sit on a step, I'll sit on a tree stump, I'll make a seat of my own."

TF: A lot of artists are creating tools for interaction. It's like an instrument. You can play it a lot of different ways.

VA: Which brings up a difference between so-called artists and so-called architects. My assumption has been that architecture is an instrument for interaction; the forms are there to allow that interaction to happen. But I'm struck by the difference between our models and the models some architects make. Our models are like model-railroad models; they're models that a child can understand. And our models have figures in them. Actually, putting the figures in the model is the only part of the model making that I do with my own hands. I need to place the figures myself so that I can understand how to use the space—I know where two people might come together as a couple, I know where one person might stand dominantly over another . . .

TF: And you've consistently photographed your projects with people in them.

VA: The only photos that don't have people in them are the photos of StoreFront, because Steven chose the photographer. I don't mean that snidely; it's just a fact. Most architectural photographs are free of people—they're empty.

TF: You know, most public art photographs don't have people in them either. When artists come in for interviews for public art commissions, one after the next will show slides of interesting projects with no people in them.

VA: A professional photographer can certainly take better, more polished photographs than I do; I mess up the scene, I block the shot with people. And I might lie down to get a shot; I shoot with a lens that's too wide an angle; it's a way of trying to get the experience of a space, rather than a view of the space. I want the opposite of distance. First I want people to be smack dab in the middle of the spaces I design; then I want viewers of a photo of that space to be smack dab in the middle of those people.

TF: And it goes without saying that if you look at an art book, there are no people in any of the pictures of paintings, for example. It would be out of the question.

VA: Because the tradition is: you're not photographing a space in which there happens to be a painting; you're photographing the painting, only the painting. So then the book, the mass of pages, becomes the space of the painting as photographed.

TF: Right, and then that's the idea of what a museum is. That blank wall, just like the blank white page of a book.

VA: It was that blank wall, that museum as a repository of blank walls, that was the impetus for many people in my generation to make art; we made art as a reaction to, as a rebellion against, the clean, white space. We made art as a reaction against the "Do-not-touch" signs in the museum. It occurred to us to ask: why aren't there any windows in the museum? Is art as fragile as all that? Does art have to be so protected, so preserved from the world outside? For *many of us in my generation, who are doing public art now, the starting point, the jumping-off point, was the museum. When a person enters a museum, that person is saying, "I am an art viewer." That person is separating himself or herself, then, from all those others who aren't art viewers. Inside the museum, the artist can do anything; the art viewer, after all, has asked for it. But, outside the museum, there aren't any art viewers; there are only passers-by, who haven't asked for art, who are simply passing through the things of the world. Inside the museum, you stand in front of art; you look at it from a distance, you're in the position of desire, you're in the position of frustration. Outside the museum, in the world, when you come upon something for the first time, you pick it up, you touch it, you listen to it, you smell it, you taste it. Outside the museum, the world is in your hands, and you're in the hands of the world.*

TF: *What's interesting to me also is that a lot of artists who began by doing installations ended up in public art. By thinking about space, the next logical step is to think about people in the space.*

VA: *For many of us those installations, from the beginning, involved people. In the mid-1970s, in my audio installations, I provided furniture (though I don't think I would have called it that then) for people to be on, I provided architecture (though I don't think I would have called it that then) for people to walk through, while they listened. If there was a table, with stools on each side, this was obviously a marker for people, an invitation to people, a place for people to inhabit. In the mid-1970s, I was using the gallery as if it were a town square; there was a voice on audiotape calling a group of people to order, as if at a town meeting. Sooner or later, I'd better go to a real town square. The pieces were telling me where to go; I just didn't know how to get out there yet.*

In the beginning of the 1980s, I made equipment for public places. The pieces were interactive, the viewer "made" the piece: a piece consisted of a vehicle, or an instrument, that a viewer could use—the use resulted in, erected, a shelter, an architecture—the architecture carried a sign—the viewer decided where he or she stood in relation to that sign, which functioned as the power sign of a culture—the architecture lasted only so long as the viewer used the vehicle or instrument. But the equipment needed constant maintenance; the use of the equipment needed guidance; in spite of my desire for public space, those pieces could exist only in the controlled environment of a gallery or museum. In the mid-1980s, the pieces were no longer games of making a space, building a space; they were spaces to be in now. But they were furniture, and private houses, and they announced themselves as domestic places rather than public places. I thought people would get the idea; I thought they would realize that I was only waiting for the opportunity, that I could adapt my furniture for—orient my furniture to—a public space. But, until 1988, there were, maybe, four invitations, no more than that, to propose public projects. Two of these proposals were built; but one was for a corporation, indoors, and only for people who worked there, and the other was for a nightclub, and this one was temporary.

It wasn't until 1988, after I did a show at the Museum of Modern Art in New York, that I began to be asked, frequently, to make public proposals. I had called the show "Public Places." It was as if I had to announce my intentions. I thought everybody knew, but they didn't. Only after I told them what I was doing, in the title of the show, did people ask me.

TF: *So, in a way, the ultimate museum show was something like farewell to the museum.*

VA: *In order to go outside the museum, I needed to be, first, inside the prototype museum. In order to go out of the museum, I needed the museum as a distribution system.*

TF: *Well, a lot of the commissions are still controlled by people who read art magazines, who go to art libraries. And everybody looks to the Museum of Modern Art for leadership, so that you can be certified by the Museum of Modern Art as an official public artist, which is interesting . . .*

VA: *And a little sad.*

TF: *It is, but it's also ironic, because the Museum of Modern Art is sort of the essential Modernist museum.*

VA: I'm not sure if modern architecture is as anti-city as all that; maybe it posits a machine city, and maybe we're not good enough machines to use it yet. But that's another story. At the MoMA show, Jackie Ferrara said to me, as she walked in the door, before she had a chance to see the show, that she felt so surprised and so invigorated at seeing a banner hanging outside the museum with the words "Public Places." If the show did nothing else, she said, that was already something.

TF: Before we go on to discussing the next project, can you say what you mean when you say "we" in terms of your designs? Who is "Acconci Studio"?

VA: There are three people who work with me full-time: Luis Vera, Jenny Schrider, Charles Doherty. Two of them are architects; one comes from an art background, and is doing music now. Luis has worked with me for over nine years, Jenny for over five, Charlie for over two. And we work very much with each other; we work at least quasi-collaboratively. I might start a project off with a vague idea, a general structure; but then we work together, we think together, each of us contradicts the others' ideas, each of us plays off the others' ideas.

TF: I think it's a very traditional way of working actually, like the artist's workshop.

VA: More like an architect's office, I think—the kind of architects that work as a studio, a workshop. These aren't people who are there to carry out, technically, my ideas; rather, these people are there so that I can have ideas. We prod each other on. Each of us questions the other, argues with the other, each of us keeps the other honest, and forces the other to keep to a logic-system. I said before that I might start off a project with a general idea. But not all the time. Often I have no ideas, or I can't find my idea, or I can't say my idea. They can push me, shame me, into clarifying. Or, sometimes, we throw all our ideas into a pot, we expose our ideas shamelessly, until one idea stands out, until one idea excites us enough to run with it. When we draw a complete blank, then we start from the ground up: we build a rough study model of the site, before we have even an inkling of a project. So all of us, together, can have *the site in the palm of our hands—we can, physically and literally, push it and pull it in different directions—we can take the site as a tangible thing that we can divide, multiply, shift, pivot, turn upside-down, turn inside-out, etc. We always begin with a model. That way, we're in the space from the start, we don't have to find a way in—we're too big for the model space, but we can get down to its size, we can squeeze our hands and heads inside. I can't move from a two-dimensional space to an experiential space; I need the model as a halfway house. Remember, I don't have architectural training, I don't have art training; I was a writer; I still think as a writer. But talk is cheap; and I need a fact, an implacable fact, in my hands so that I can prove my idea. In front of a two-dimensional space, I understand the space, but only from a distance; I'm a voyeur; I can only visit, I can't stay for a while.*

TF: *Let's talk about the project in Colorado. As opposed to the StoreFront reconstruction, this was a project in which you were presented with an architect's completed design, and you added to it in a very significant way. What was the site?*

VA: *The Arvada Center for Arts and Humanities: a community center, a place for theater and music events, art shows, dance classes, arts and crafts classes.*

    The project started the way most projects start: you're on a mailing list, there's a request for qualifications, a call for slides. Sometimes they ask for twenty slides, sometimes ten, sometimes seven—so you try to foresee the project, you orient the slides toward the project, you pick slides that might relate to the project. But you're always guessing, of course. I remember some requests for three *slides; so, foolhardily, you try to pick that project of projects, the project that demonstrates how you work with every site in the world.*

    Anyway, back to Arvada. On the original application, there were two sites to choose from; one was a blank wall that was the back of a theater; the other was a concrete wall, starting outside the building, that wound its way through the building. My choice was obvious: since my bias is toward a space you walk though and not a space you stand in front of and look at, I chose the winding wall.

    The next step was: we were among a group of finalists, who were asked to make proposals. The form of the proposal wasn't specified. Our tendency,

Acconci Studio, Project for Arvada Art Center, 1992, Arvada, Colorado. Percent for Art, city of Arvada. Photograph courtesy of Acconci Studio.

as I've said, is to make a model; we make a model first to convince ourselves, then to convince others.

They chose our project, which tried to cling on to the site. The center was being renovated; the architect, Ken Berendt, had designed a concrete wall, 20 feet high, that started at the end of a grass spiral, outside the building, and then continued the spiral by winding up to the front of the building, going through the building and curving through it. Berendt claimed that the shape of the wall came from the meaning of the building: this was a center for art, music —the winding wall, then, functioned as a G clef.

Since the architect's scheme had already started a motion from outside to inside, we wanted to continue that motion, do that motion: could we bring, literally, the outside inside? The wall started abruptly, where the spiral of grass ended; could we take the ground up, could we lift the ground up onto the wall? In the back of our minds was Arvada's history: the city began from farming, dirt farming. Our project starts from the ground up, our project starts at the bottom of the wall and ends at the top. A dirt wall rises out of the spiral of grass, a glass retaining wall that holds in dirt, holds back dirt.

The dirt wall grabs on to the concrete wall, it enters the building with the wall. The dirt wall passes through the reception desk, it climbs the stairs, it inserts itself into the building like a parasite. The dirt wall grows, it climbs the concrete wall, covers the wall. To enter a room, you have to walk through the dirt wall; niches are carved into the dirt wall—you sit inside the dirt wall as if in a cave. When the dirt wall reaches the height of the concrete wall, it folds over onto the second floor of the building; the dirt wall bulges out, to make seats against the wall. The dirt wall rises above you like a cut in a mountain; it's four feet deep at the base, and it tapers in to less than a foot at the top— the dirt wall recedes away from you, off in the distance.

They weren't looking for an interactive project. They simply had a wall; and what they wanted, I think, was a picture for the wall, a mural on the wall. Once we provided spaces for habitation, for interaction, they wanted them. But they didn't know they wanted them before that.

Our project was chosen, against the better judgment of two or three people in the community. A lawyer, for example, claimed that a person, sitting within a niche, might bang his or her head when getting up out of the niche. Problems like this are make-believe problems, false alarms; if an overhang of 6 feet is too low, then simply move it up to 7 feet. There's an inherent difficulty in a proposal that's categorized as "art." The implication is that it's a finished fact, it can't be modified—the art is inviolable, the artist can't be interfered with. So, then, if a part is objectionable, then the whole has to be rejected. But a public art proposal is like bargaining for a contract, it's like a business meeting. A public art proposal is the beginning of a discussion: with the client, with the community, with city regulations, with ADA recommendations. A proposal is just what the word says: it's only a proposal, it's a first grasp at the situation. This proposal for Arvada, for example, was made by a person from New York, a person who's only visiting Arvada, who doesn't live there; this is a proposal from the outside, made by a visitor from another planet. Now let's put the proposal up for grabs; now let's hear what the insiders think, what the local inhabitants think—let's have a mix of old and new, region and universe, tried-and-true and untested. When we present a proposal, we're presenting an essay, a theory of public space applied to our myth of a particular city. Now the theory has to be converted into practice, now the myth has to come down to earth.

Acconci Studio, Project for Arvada Art Center. Photograph courtesy of Acconci Studio.

In the Arvada case, when community people brought up supposedly practical problems, I had the feeling that they were talking about something else; I couldn't put my finger on the problem at the bottom of it all. Once our project was chosen, and reported in the press, the problem became clear. And the problem was language, my language. Talking about the project, I used, constantly, the word "dirt": a wall of "dirt." There was a newspaper editorial, then, that said: maybe in New York people want to bring dirt into buildings, but here in Colorado we try to keep dirt out. So I learned how regional language is: in New York, I would plant a flower in dirt, but here in Colorado that dirt was garbage. The problem wasn't in the model—people who saw the model seemed attracted to it; the problem was the word, and the word was in the air now, it became rumor, reportage, it became a rallying cry for people who hadn't seen the model—the word was stuck in their heads, the word became more than flesh, it became a wound, an insult. So I had to eat my words; I had to clean up my language.

TF: *Did you change your rhetoric from "dirt" to "earth?"*

VA: I tried, but it's hard for me to say "earth"; I'm a New Yorker, I'm not from the West, "earth" is a little too mythic, too mystic, for me. But I could at least say "soil." Actually, it wasn't so much that I changed my language; it's more that I tried to make clear to my listeners where I was coming from when I used that language—I tried to mix my language with theirs.

TF: There are different sorts and colors of dirt?

VA: In our model, the dirt is a mass of dark brown. We were thinking in New York terms: dirt is that which isn't buildings—dirt is the generalized substructure under our world. Actually, the look of the dirt in the model was another problem, almost as much of a stumbling block as the dirt. Now, we didn't know how to get around this; dirt is dirt, we thought, and we can't change that; we had reached an impasse. Until I realized that the model was one thing and the experiential space was another; our model could be generalized, but the experiential space had to be specific—we had to use not the idea of dirt but dirt that was specific to the region. So we worked with a local geologist, Steven Schwochow, who told us exactly what the dirt was like on the site. The dirt wasn't a monochromatic brown: it was layers of color, it ranged from reds through tans to medium browns. So it turned out to be easy to satisfy people: all we had to do was see what was right in front of our eyes—or, at least, what was below our eyes, underground. I have to insist, though: we weren't going to make the dirt different colors because people liked it—but we had to make the dirt different colors because that's just what it was, in that particular place. I have to admit: I don't like the layers of color—to me, it looks like a Navajo rug—I prefer dirt as a mass of brown/black. But it didn't matter what I liked; what mattered was what was; there was no reason to impose a New Yorker's idea of dirt on the fact of dirt that happened to be there.

TF: So how site-specific is the dirt?

VA: It corresponds to the layers of dirt below the building—at least, if you trust the geologist.

Acconci Studio, Project for Arvada Art Center. Photograph courtesy of Acconci Studio.

TF: You said that public space is sort of a nostalgic idea.

VA: Yeah. In the late twentieth century, early twenty-first century, the notion of a space that you go to, the notion of an outdoor room the walls of which are the city buildings, the notion of people gathering—I don't know how those notions coexist with an age of computers, airplanes, television, space travel, time travel . . . Why do you need a place to go to when you can take with you all the places you need?

TF: I guess that that's one of the basic problems we're dealing with in the field of public art. Cities are dying. The suburb is the city of the future . . .

VA: Is that true, or is it that there's no difference anymore between the suburb and the city? When we say the word "city," we immediately think of a center, of downtown. But that's not what a late-twentieth-century/early-twenty-first-century city is. We have to think more about the periphery, more about cities joining and blending with cities. Networks and sprawl. It's not that everyone is moving to the suburbs; it's that the city is moving into the suburb, and the suburb is moving through the city.

Remember, in the mid–'70s, I thought that, if I was using the gallery as if it were a town square, the logical next step was to go to the actual town square. But the town square was gone by the time I got there. The town square, the piazza, is made up of talk, political talk: talk that leads to action that leads to change. But you don't need to go to the piazza now to share talk. The talk is already with us, in our minds and on our earphones. We don't have to go "there," to the town square; "there" is already here, "here" is everywhere. But that's not cause for despair; we just have to find out what public space is in a world of private space; instead of traveling into outer space, we have to travel out to inner space.

TF: But the community center in Colorado is public space for that community. The people come together. It still exists, even in the days of people sitting at home and watching TV.

VA: It still exists, but does it have to? Apparently for these people it does. While I was in Arvada, seven-year-old kids would come to dance classes; they wanted to be there; they craved it. The theater was putting on the 795th production of Hello, Dolly, and everybody wanted to go. As Samuel Goldwyn said, "Include me out." It gives me the creeps. Now maybe if they learned to dance on the ceiling . . . maybe if, while sitting in a theater, they watched Hello, Dolly each on a personal computer, while they did some matchmaking of their own, with each other's partner . . .

TF: Everybody talks about the death of the public space, but I am not convinced. There are a million kids who go to school in New York City every day. They are together for six or seven hours of the day. Sure, maybe they go home and watch TV instead of playing in a park after school, but the public schools are public spaces. People still spend a lot of time in public. And I don't think that a desire for certain parts of the past is necessarily conservative. That could be very progressive, like public *transportation, that old idea, is the new idea. That's why you are working on all these public transportation projects.*

VA: *Like everybody else—everybody we probably know, anyway—I have a bias against suburbs. I'm a believer in the position that the suburbs were created to disperse people, to get them out of the city, where they couldn't help but meet and talk and argue and start a revolution.*

I don't drive; I've never learned to drive; I'm a New Yorker. What I love about New York is: it's a city in close-up, a city of close-ups. From Manhattan, you can't see Manhattan; there are no views, no vistas, it's not like Chicago. You can't depend on vision, and from vision we get control; so you've lost control, and you have to resort to other senses: you hear New York, you touch New York, you smell New York, your face is up against it so much that you taste New York. I love to walk, meander, in New York, in between buildings. I love underground New York; I'd rather take the subway than a taxi, I'd rather walk than take the subway. But then I have to wonder: do I prefer the density, the tangibility, of the city because it's cozy, comforting, homey? After all, there's a world out there, beyond the city, a world represented by and reachable by that car that I don't know how to drive—that car that can shoot off on a route of its own, faster and freer than I can be—that unknown scary car that, for all I know, takes off into space once it disappears around the corner.

What I like about living here, under the bridge, on the other side of the river, is the feel of being on the edge of the city; the city falls off into water here. You're not in a Brooklyn neighborhood; you're not in Manhattan; you're neither here nor there, you don't have a place. But maybe you have too much time. What I miss here is the density of the city. It's isolated; you can't go out in the middle of the night to buy a candy bar. When I first moved here, this was my version of the country. Maybe I use the city as if on a computer; I don't use New York very much, I don't have time for movies, for clubs, for restaurants; but it doesn't matter, because other people are using them— they're there to be used even when I can't use them.

Once the computer terminal becomes the institution, you can subvert it with the tangible. But, once you do, you're regressing. In a world where you can have all the information of a city on a computer, what do you need the city for? You need the city for other bodies, you need the city for sex. But maybe the city has so much sex that you don't have to do it any more; somebody else is doing it anyway, somebody else is doing it for you, they're so close you can almost touch them, you can close your eyes and you can almost feel them.

Notes

1. The information in the introduction is largely drawn from: Kate Linker, *Vito Acconci* (New York: Rizzoli, 1994). The book is an excellent overview of Acconci's career.

2. Linker, *Acconci,* p. 13.

3. Ibid., p. 15.

4. Ibid., p. 60.

5. From a telephone interview with Kathy Andrews, October 15, 1997.

Interview: **Linnea Glatt** *and* **Michael Singer** *on* *Designing the Phoenix Solid Waste Management Facility*

Introduction

The Twenty-seventh Avenue Solid Waste Management Facility and Recycling Center in Phoenix, Arizona, is a groundbreaking project in which the design of an $18 million building was entrusted to a pair of artists: Michael Singer and Linnea Glatt. These two artists were selected under Phoenix's Percent for Art Program to create art for the facility. However, when the schematic designs were presented, the artists took the unusual initiative of putting forth an alternative scheme that asked different questions and presented a different set of answers than the engineers. The city officials were convinced that the artists had a more complete, more beautiful, and better functioning design than what the engineers were proposing. In an unusual and courageous move, the city of Phoenix, led by the director of public works, Ron Jensen, turned the design control over to the artists—working, of course, with architects and engineers. To my knowledge, this is the only example of artists *leading* the design team for the construction of a major infrastructure project in the United States, or anywhere else.

The resulting structure, which was completed in the fall of 1993, is an example of "Green Architecture": building toward greater environmental sensitivity and consciousness. The artists' stated goal is to "open the entire operation to public view," to bring the visitor into direct contact with the recycling operation, hoping to help transform the public's attitudes toward waste and waste management. This project makes an interesting comparison with the interview with Mierle Ukeles in Part III. Where Singer and Glatt create a physical environment to open the sanitation process to the public view, Ukeles engaged in a similar endeavor through participatory performance.

The building is dominated by enormous central trusses which, though functional, are enlarged for aesthetic effect. As clean fill is deposited around the building in years to come, the building will gradually be submerged into the environment, and these trusses will take on an even greater visual prominence—like the top of a building (or bridge) that has sunk into the ground. Great care was taken to make the facility "user friendly" for both the Sanitation Department and the general public. On a regular basis, school groups are invited to watch the recycling process, and the citizens of Phoenix are asked to participate in recycling. The space is inviting, including attractive plantings and unusual vistas—especially when compared with average station/recycling facilities, which tend to be dreary and uninviting buildings designed by engineers. Consider the following paragraph in a glowing review by *New York Times* architecture critic Herbert Muschamp:

> The design details throughout the complex are excruciatingly refined. Windows are carefully aligned with dramatic vistas within and without. Huge machines are installed with the precision of classical statues. Translucent panels and skylights bathe the interior with Gothic light. The effect is not pretty. Instead the artists have reached for awe. Like the great Galerie des Machines at the 1889 Paris Exposition, the center extracts from industry its aura of holy terror, fusing it with the American landscape tradition of the pitiless and the sublime.[1]

How often has a New York architecture critic traveled across the country to review a transfer station? The artists were given control of the design of this building because the engineers were thinking in traditional terms. Their uninspired design was based in part on the notion that a facility of this nature need not be attractive, that it exists only to get a job done. Ron Jensen and other Phoenix officials understood that there is a great social need to get the public more involved with recycling, and that they would have to look to new sources to make the operation itself more attractive. What the artists came up with was more sophisticated architecturally than

Michael Singer and Linnea Glatt, with Sterling McMurrin, Richard Epstein, Dino Sakellar, and Black and Veatch, Solid Waste Management Facility, 1993, Phoenix, Arizona. Commissioned by city of Phoenix Percent for Art Program. Photograph: Michael Singer.

the standard warehouse, but also demonstrated a more complete understanding of the environmental and symbolic needs of the facility. To top it off, the artists contend that the project came in $2 million under budget, although a depressed construction environment at the time may have had something to do with the low cost of the final project. In any case, it is clear that their design did not break the bank.

Linnea Glatt received a Bachelor of Science degree from Moorhead State University (Moorehead, Minnesota) in 1971, and a Master's degree from the University of Dallas in 1972. Starting in the 1980s she created a series of simple architectural spaces that indicated a particular use: *A Place to Gather* (1982), *A Place to Perform* (1984). Five of these projects were installed permanently. Michael Singer received a Bachelor of Fine Arts degree from Cornell in 1967 and attended Rutgers University in 1968. He had a series of one-person exhibitions at galleries and museums starting in the mid-1970s. He has worked on a series of projects that navigate the territory between landscape design, sculpture, and planning. These include, for example, a river walkway for Grand Rapids, Michigan, a building at Millay Colony for the Arts, and a master plan for Long Wharf Park in New Haven. Both Singer and Glatt came out of a landscape/architectural art background, but neither had ever worked on a project of the scale of the Solid Waste Management Facility.

This interview was conducted in New York City in 1996, when Singer and Glatt were in town working on the educational and interpretive aspects of the project.

Tom Finkelpearl: It is an exceptional process that leads to artists designing a major public building. But I gather it started in a very conventional manner.

Linnea Glatt: Yes. The city of Phoenix Art Commission simply had my slides from a previous private project that never materialized. Out of the blue, they called me and said that I had been selected for a recycling facility project. What was perhaps a bit unconventional was that we did not even know that we were being considered for the project. This was 1989.

Michael Singer: Someone had told me that Phoenix had a Percent for Art Program. I was curious about the desert, so I sent them some slides. Next thing, I got a call from Gretchen Freeman, the manager of the Percent for Art Program, saying that I had been selected for a public art project and they needed to know if it was something I'd be interested in. They invited me out to Phoenix, not for an interview, but to meet with the people involved in the project, and, by the way, there was another artist. I asked how they put us together, and Gretchen said that this was the largest public art project that they were doing and the site was big enough to accommodate two artists doing separate projects. But there was also the possibility that we would choose to work together on something.

LG: I think the selection panel saw Michael's work and my work, and they said, "Hey, this looks good together." Looking back, if we had taken that Percent for Art money and said, "Well, I'm going to do a piece over here, and you do something there," it would have been these two little blips, totally insignificant to the larger picture. The city had already hired an engineering firm, Black and Veatch. They had prepared a study that actually included a building design and site plan.

MS: Linnea and I reviewed this preliminary design book and decided we really wanted to work together. I was working with a group of students from MIT, where I was teaching at the time. They helped me understand what the engineers' original proposal was all about. When we sat down at the first meeting with Ron Jensen and the Black and Veatch engineers, we said, "So okay, you can spend that money on a couple of sculptures, but nothing is going to humanize this site plan other than redoing it." The engineers were shocked when they heard this.

LG: Gretchen Freeman had already primed us. We had told her that we were going to come and lay out what we saw as the problems with the original design and how we'd like to affect it. She told us, "Ron Jensen [the director of Public Works] is very special. He's the best person in the city to work with. If you've got ideas, you really can tell them to him, and I think he can hear you."

At our first meeting with the city and the engineers, Ron told us that he had this vision of a transfer station, and then a recycling center, and that he also wanted it to become an educational center. He was looking to the artists to give him some suggestions. The most important part of that meeting was the fact that Ron Jensen really indicated to us that we had the opportunity to start over, to in effect conduct our own study.

TF: What were some of the specific problems with the engineers' original design?

LG: Well, the first thing that we wanted to change in the site plan was the "out of sight, out of mind" attitude that says you do not put garbage in the view of the visitor. The self-haul area is a really wonderful spot because this is where neighborhood people come and dump their recyclables. In our plan it is located very visibly and in close proximity to the other functions of the facility. The original plan by Black and Veatch had the self-haul area in the back of the lot where no one could see it.

MS: So the public would never understand this connection to the facility.

LG: It was like, "Don't let anyone see what is going on here." The visitor came in, did what they were doing, and then they left. They didn't have any experience of the site or interconnection with the functions of the facility.

TF: So it was segregated into public versus private, in a way. The public workers and the private citizens were separated.

LG: Yes, very much. So the overriding concern on our site plan was to integrate as many functions at the facility as we possibly could.

MS: The function of the building was also hidden in their design. It could have been a corporate headquarters, a factory, or a mall. Another thing that bothered me right off was that the entire 25-acre site was to be paved. There was one spot where it said "Retention Area," that was landscaped. That was a little island around the visitor parking.

LG: Necklaces, everywhere. Little "landscape-y" edges.

MS: The other thing that jumped right out was that the visitors center and the administration were placed on the east side of the facility. The prevailing winds *are from west to east. So basically they had visitors and administrators down-wind from a 2-acre enclosed space filled with garbage. I said to Ron, "If you think we are totally obnoxious pointing out all these problems that we have found, if you just simply turn the building over, flip it from east to west, you'll be one hundred percent ahead of the game." This was one thing that really caught Ron's attention at our first meeting.*

LG: *We also pointed out the fact that there were twenty-some-odd columns in the building. They said they wanted flexibility in the interior space, but how could they have flexibility with all those columns?*

MS: *We pointed out that their traffic pattern mixed 500 tractor-trailers a day (which is 1 a minute) with visitors, with administration people, and with people bringing their own garbage. It was unsafe.*

LG: *I think we are sounding very disparaging about the original plan. In defense of Black and Veatch, this is pretty standard. This is the way things are done in engineering firms. You have a design and you plop it down in any situation.*

MS: *The design was generic for any waste facility. They had an office in Kansas City, and this design came out of their computer. It had nothing to do with Phoenix specifically.*

LG: *Just the approach, an artist's approach is going to be different. It was obvious at this first meeting that we had given a lot of thought to how one comes to this place, what one experiences as one moves through this place, which is not what engineers do. They just flatly didn't do that, which is why this process was so important. I'm sure they were very skeptical at first. Ron, however, in a very courageous move, gave us two months to develop an alternative site plan. It was a limited time.*

MS: *They had a fast-moving train. Their landfill was closing in two years, so they had to get this new facility going. Ron said, "Look, if you can get into our schedule and come back with your alternatives and how you would solve these problems, we'll listen to them."*

LG: Which is very unusual. Both the Art Commission and the Public Works Agency were going out on a very big limb.

MS: So, in that two-month period we prepared a booklet that had four or five alternatives.

LG: And we came in with three models. Michael worked in Vermont with his team, and I worked in Dallas with an architect that I hired. Michael and I came together in Vermont, and, in one weekend, we put together a whole new model, which incorporated my ideas and Michael's ideas. We presented that along with other ones.

TF: When you were up in Vermont putting together this model, did you believe they were going to accept your designs?

MS: I had no idea. I thought they were going to say, "Compromise. We can do some of this." Some of our ideas were not quite functional, but they were important to put out on the table as part of a process.

LG: Well, I felt more optimistic about it because we really thought about what we were doing. When we made our presentation to Black and Veatch, Ron Jensen, and lots of other city officials, I think they were very impressed. We had drawings all over the wall.

MS: We had traffic studies. It was really great. They had no idea what they were getting into. It was kind of fun.

TF: So you had your foot in the door?

MS: Yeah. And three models on the table. I must say I was more skeptical than Linnea about their accepting what we were doing, even though we answered all their questions. But then, at the meeting, they turned to us and said, "Well, which scheme do you like the best?" We turned back to them and said, "Which one do you like the best?" And they chose the one scheme which we all felt was the best one. They said, "Let's work with that."

TF: So what were some of the characteristics of the new site plan?

MS: I think that one of the main things we did is really respond to the site. We placed the building off the grid that Phoenix is built on. The engineers had the building on the grid. Looking at our plan, one of the engineers said, "You are not square to the world."

TF: So, Phoenix is on an abstract grid, which had nothing to do with this specific site?

MS: Yes. This building is going away from the grid. To us that deals with movement and transformation. *Every element of our design contributes to the idea of transformation, reclamation, educating the public towards issues of waste, the need to recycle, the relationship of the building to the landscape around it. On their approach to the site, the visitor goes to the top of the landfill, where a view allows people to look south to the mountains and the natural system and north to the city and the built system. We saw the facility's site as being the place that mediated between those two. And it was a great opportunity to provide vistas so people could see the city (where the garbage came from) and its effect, if it is not recycled, on the natural environment, which is also in clear view.*

LG: As I mentioned earlier, we tried to integrate all of the functions. For example, we brought the self-haul area, which was in the back, way up to the front and adjacent to the building. We really wanted the area where the building is situated to be the focus of a transformation. It is very apparent in our design that all garbage is routed into the facility and something happens there and sends it out as a salvageable resource for the most part.

We separated the different sorts of traffic. Large dump trucks move directly into the building. Recycling vehicles travel underneath the bridge and around the back to pick up the recyclables. As Michael mentioned, we had visitors and employees coming up to the top of the landfill and getting an overview of how the whole site is situated in terms of the surrounding landscape. And then you proceed down, go across an effluent channel, and you pass all of the activity in the self-haul, which is a terraced and planted sunken *area. You proceed to parking and then cross the bridge into the facility. We separated the traffic for safety and function, but there is a sense of inter-connection. You can see where everyone is going, what their destination is, and there is a lot of interaction and openness. The overriding concern was what you encounter on your way in and out.*

Another important site consideration was landscape. What often hap-pens is that a building is designed and then decorated with landscape. In this case we saw the landscape being as important as the structure itself. The land really began to inform what this building was going to be. Over time you won't be able to tell if the building is emerging from landscape or is sub-merged in it. There is going to be a whole area that will be built up over time with rubble, virtually burying one part of the building . . .

MS: *Which is another kind of recycling. We also had an idea for the effluent channel, which runs through the site and comes from a sewage treatment plant. We wanted to divert water from the effluent channel and put it through a built wetland. When we suggested this in 1989, this was a very recent technology, so we were skirting on the cutting edge. Basically we created a pond, a "wa-ter feature." This would present another possibility for recycling, showing that clean water could be obtained without using chlorination.*

LG: *Actually, at one point we found out that some effluent was being diverted di-rectly into the Salt River . . .*

MS: *So it was something that we wanted to correct.*

LG: *We wanted to bring this effluent to the site, plant the appropriate plants to pol-ish it naturally, and then let it divert back into the Salt River. This is not built, by the way.*

TF: *Will it be built?*

MS: *We have created the possibility. It's there to be built. This facility is sited in a flood plane, so one of the big expenses they had was bringing in fill to raise the land to build on it. And carting in materials is very expensive. So what we* ended up doing is actually digging the pond for this water system, which they are using now as a retention basin for run-off water. They used the earth from digging the pond as the fill for the site, which probably saved a million dollars on the project.

Of course, we put the visitor administration area on the west side rather than the east side to correct the odor and ventilation problem in the original Black and Veatch plan.

TF: Upwind instead of downwind.

MS: Right. Later, in the building design, we eliminated the interior column system. But on the site plan, the building looked like a solid block, really schematic.

LG: The site plan also included a sunken employee courtyard so that workers could come out into this open planted area, to have a wonderful space.

MS: Basically, the engineers' site plan did not consider the environment of the workers in the building. We found out these workers were prisoners on work release, and there was no place for them to be out of the building, in a safe area. We considered their environment and created that space. It's one of the nicest areas. And we did offer a design that revealed the facility's operation rather than concealing it.

TF: You've talked about the functional differences a lot, but what are the symbolic or social differences between this design and theirs?

LG: I think the most obvious is that it just turns around the whole notion of what these places have always been in a community. Usually they are just tucked away in the most undesirable area, and this indeed has been a very undesirable area in Phoenix. For many years, the area adjacent to the landfill was used as sludge ponds for water treatment, and "borrow pits" for the landfill. We felt it was important to take a stand at that site where these past abuses had occurred, because this is the only way that you are going to turn things around—to be aware of the abuses and try to point the way in a new and responsible direction.

We went to a community meeting that was very heated, very interesting. This is a low-income area, and all the undesirable infrastructure of the city is located here—the water treatment facility, etc. They were just so angry. They said, "You are not building this facility here. You are not going to dump on us again." That meeting reinforced what we were doing, trying to turn the whole thing around and make this an important place, a salvageable place, a resource; otherwise the area would have no hope for recovery.

MS: And it is important not to simply cover up what those abuses were. There were plans to, you know, put a golf course on the landfill.

LG: . . . to make it look like something else. We always felt that the landfill should remain just that. It is a huge, monumental form 1 mile long, 6 stories tall, which really drives home the idea of how much garbage we generate. We did not want to disguise it with another function. There was talk of mining it for its resources, which would be fantastic.

MS: Basically, the big move, and this is part of Ron Jensen's genius and brilliance, is that the facility really is a place for the public. Infrastructure facilities in the past were never considered to be for the public. They would put a wall around them, hide them, try to make them go away. I think our project has raised the issue of infrastructure projects generally, and their need to involve communities. It is important to understand how they affect the communities around them, and consider their design in relation to their context, and not just the traditional definition of function. A facility won't function if the community is not considered in the design.

LG: We have offered an invitation to come in. And, indeed, people have receptions and parties at the facility. Isn't that incredible?

MS: In our design for the educational components, we don't want to put exhibits in the courtyard because people use it for receptions. We are talking about a dump!

LG: We're talking about weddings at the facility!

TF: Do you think that this openness was made possible by the recycling movement, that public officials like Ron Jensen were affected by all of the rhetoric about participation in recycling?

MS: One of the things that Ron said was that it's going to take us a long time to change people's attitudes. He often used the example of people throwing litter out the window. He said when he was growing up no one even thought twice about just throwing anything out the window. We've taught our children something about that, like Smokey the Bear and forest fires. He said these are things that take a generation to go through, and that this facility was in some way the beginning of educating kids in the next generation to understand some important environmental issues.

TF: So you presented your site plan. Did they say they would put it under advisement . . .

MS: No, they accepted it right then and there. And then we said, "Look, we really also need to be involved in designing the building as well as all the details."

LG: The engineers were a bit shocked, and the subsequent months were extremely difficult.

MS: We had to play a bit of "circle the wagons." It was like they tried to redo the site plan to their liking, and we just fought with them and had to show them why each thing was where it was and why we couldn't redo it.

LG: When we started to work on the building design, we would give them verbal direction, and we would get a plan back that just had nothing to do with our ideas. This went on back and forth for quite a while, and then finally we decided the only way we could get information across was to actually give them very specific drawings.

TF: You were working together on these drawings?

LG: Yes, but, well, this is where it gets a little tense.

Linnea Glatt and Michael Singer, Solid Waste Management Facility. Photograph: David Stausbury.

TF: Well, it's not surprising that there could be problems. You never worked together before.

LG: Michael and I have been rather vocal about this idea of the Percent for Art Program throwing artists together. In the end, I think it worked out really wonderfully. I remember the first time Michael and I saw the building complete, we were standing there in awe, and realizing that I could point to certain things and Michael could point to certain things, but it was this wonderful combination that would have never occurred without our working together. But, the fact is, it was difficult. When I look at it, I don't think it was so much a personal conflict. I think it was much more a conflict about what we do individually as artists.

MS: You know, what it eventually came down to, after we went through that period of figuring out if we could trust each other, was that Linnea had to present a very good argument why something that I had suggested wasn't going to work, and I had to do the same for her. And then we had to sit there and say, "Well what will work?" Out of that came a respect and an understanding that we really were working together, when we could really critique each other in a way that didn't say, "I'm trying to get the better of you or you're trying to get the better of me. I'm trying to make it more mine, and you are trying to make it more yours." Now we are working on the educational part of the project, and it is delightful to be confronted with problems and to sit here and look at each other, and we both can come to the answers very clearly.

When we were given the direction to work on the building, we generated drawings that were very specific. We did drawings about the structure, and the concept that there be large trusses, which would allow the columns to be outside the building. We worked out the visitor administration area, though it went through a couple of changes. At a certain point, we made a list of opportunities for our specific involvement, and I remember picking the columns, and Linnea picked elevations. We each picked a series of things that we were going to work on and then would send back and forth for critique to each other.

TF: How did you present the building design?

LG: We presented a very detailed model.

TF: With the trusses?

MS: Yes, and most of the final design was there. And we presented drawings.

LG: It went through some transformations from this point, but most of it stayed intact.

TF: The transformations were on the basis of what?

LG: Most of it was budgetary. We had to give up things. I remember we did all these surface wall panels. We had a model, wall samples, but we had to give a lot up for budget reasons.

MS: *They just went nuts over one column. They just didn't understand it. So at a certain moment—I think it was the guy who was the head of city architecture— looked at us, and he said, "Well, this is a very interesting presentation. All your ideas are very creative. It's wonderful. Now we have to get down to the real issue here of how to design this building. Now comes the time of compromise." And I looked at him and I said, "Compromise? There isn't a compromise. You didn't hire us to compromise, you hired us to give you a vision. And there isn't a compromise to be made here unless it's justified by function or by cost. There is no compromise in terms of vision, or else we should go home tomorrow and the Arts Commission will have wasted its money." And Ron Jensen actually supported us, saying, "That is what we've paid for, I want to see this built as closely to what the artists have described in this presentation as we can possibly get."*

LG: *And, again, I think that is the way most things get built. It's a matter of compromising, compromising, compromising. But I think with Michael and me what was always intact was the vision of this place. We did make some budgetary compromises. I mean we were not unreasonable. But actually in the end we were able to give the city much more for less money than in the engineers' original plan.*

MS: *We always asked why these compromises were necessary, and we had people who could interpret that for us, and to know if it was because it was going to cost too much because the engineer had to do the drawings, or if it was really an issue about function or cost in construction. And in some cases we disagreed when they said it wouldn't function and we showed them why it would. In other cases, on the cost issues, we would get an independent assessment of it and show them that they were wrong. Part of this project was what we call "The Great American Memo." We wrote a zillion memos.*

LG: *As you can imagine, it was difficult for some people to understand our role. Michael and I always joked that if there were a red stripe around this building, it would be recognized as the art. We knew that people were going to say, "Where is the art in this?" So one time we got to the site and indeed there was a red stripe around the building. It was a water line that they had put right at the zone where the "Kal-wall" meets the concrete block. They had put a red pipe entirely around the building. Talk about a fight.*

MS: *It was because the construction manager on the project probably just never paid attention. The installer said, "I'm here to put in the emergency water pipe. Where should I put it?" And he probably told him to put it where it's going to be convenient, and never thought of its visual effect. We went out and saw it and we actually had to spend six months fighting to have them raise it.*

LG: *And they did it, they raised it for us.*

MS: *But we won because of a functional issue. The pipe was along the walkway where people go, and you could literally reach up and grab it. So we began to show them how kids were going to jump on the pipes.*

LG: *We stuck to it and said, "This is really important." They really came through for us.*

MS: *Yeah, Ron did.*

LG: *You know what I think was extremely important on this project in that respect? We had Sterling McMurrin working with us, who really could speak the language of function for us. Even if we knew it ourselves to begin with, it was great for us to have someone else argue our point for us.*

MS: *Sterling is a graduate of MIT architecture school, and he works with me. Rick Epstein was also working for me. Rick is now an architect, but he had just graduated from MIT architecture school when he came to help on this project.*

LG: *In terms of the building design, we really wanted it to have a different kind of look and to express in some way that something important was happening here. We wanted the facility to be well designed, well put together, well thought out. We wanted the facility to be totally unlike the standard, a to-*

Linnea Glatt and Michael Singer, *Solid Waste Management Facility*. Photograph: David Stausbury.

tally unexpected experience. The tradition is that it doesn't matter what these places look like. We thought the opposite, we used very ordinary materials, but put them together in a very considered way. I remember at one meeting, I told the engineers that this was an excellent opportunity for them to strut their stuff as engineers.

MS: It was one of the ways we got them excited, when we first said, "We want the structure to be shown." In the 80s people wanted to clad everything and cover everything, so Linnea said, "Strut your stuff."

LG: Being the only woman in a room filled with men all the time, it may have been the wrong thing to say.

MS: It was the absolutely right thing.

LG: Well, I think they began to see this as an opportunity. As a matter of fact, at the end, the project architect for the engineers said, "You've really reminded me *about what it means to be an architect,"* which was an extremely rare and fine compliment.

TF: What about the iconological as opposed to the functional meaning of the trusses?

MS: The meaning relates to the landscape as well as the building. When you look at the south mountains, there's this divide, and there are two sets of mountains, reflected by the trusses. It also defines function in the building. The larger part of the truss is over the part of the building that's a transfer station, and then it shifts, and the other part is over the recycling area. There is a third area that has a secondary truss that lowers one quadrant of the roof. That allows for the administration area to look out and have a view over the city. We could have done one truss across the whole structure, but we really love the idea of this change within the building, and that's expressed in the columns that are outside, and the trusses.

LG: This is very much like Michael's and my work. There aren't hidden areas. It's all there to see. So even when they requested a dropped ceiling, we put a translucent material in so that you could still see the structure. It's very much our aesthetic.

MS: The trusses express what is going on inside the building to the outside.

LG: And this truss is becoming this incredible landmark. You can see it for miles, the way that the mountains just happen to work behind it. And there is something about the coloration of the building that we didn't realize until we saw it, somehow it just looks like it's part of the landscape.

TF: Are there any "green" elements in the building?

MS: There are solar tracking skylights on the roof. We designed the whole south face of the building, which is an enormous length, to have a solar panel screen, which would also cut the glare on that walkway. And we were told by the city at the time that there was a law in Phoenix against any solar installations on municipal buildings. Isn't that outrageous? They had this enormous south-facing wall, and a whole landfill, with a mile of it on a south-facing slope. But they didn't want to hear about it. Now I think things have changed in the city, and part of our meeting today is to go back and propose that they revisit the solar panels, because they need to do something to cut the glare coming in the walkway, and we want it to function as solar panels as well. That was part of what we wanted to do and they cut it.

LG: While we were designing the facility, a lot of the areas that we included were not requested by the city. There's a multipurpose room, there's a library, there are additional offices for potential uses. Now every nook is used, and expansion is already imminent. We created a large visitor courtyard and an administrative courtyard around which the offices are grouped. We created viewing windows in the ramp area, viewing windows in the courtyard, and the amphitheater. So there were all these opportunities that we built into the place to be developed later on in an educational plan. We were really pushing them to consider an educational plan.

MS: The city hired us under a new contract along with Albert Woods, an interpretive design firm. We were asked to coordinate with the team so that there would be a continuity and understanding of how the design of the facility is meant to work with interpretation, so now we are basically designing an interpretive program.

TF: So what are your goals?

MS: Recognizing all the opportunities that we identified in our design of the building.

LG: And some things are not working so well, so this is an opportunity to make those places better. Basically, it's a place that raises questions, we hope, so we are trying to push the educational plan in the same direction.

TF: Aren't school kids already coming in there?

MS: Yeah, they are. The city has recognized that the place has been a huge success. They have groups coming every day. They've had thousands of visitors, a lot of visitors from Europe. They're getting calls from all over the country about replicating this project, so they are setting up a consulting service for other cities. Some of the people who were very skeptical about our involvement and about the whole design are now running the facility. I guess what's very satisfying for us is that they really have seen its success and are very support- ive of our continued role. I think we have our work cut out for us. The chal- lenge is going to be to get them to deal with interpretation in the way that we were dealing with the building, and not do what is obvious.

LG: One of the major things that we are trying to drive home is the seriousness of the garbage issue. We would like to find a way for kids to make sense of the place visually, to start making connections between what they are seeing in the city and what they are seeing inside the building. Also, we do not want the interpretation to be static. It should be a system that is changeable over the years, something that creates a life, that begins to create an energy of its own.

MS: Ideas about recycling and waste management are changing every year, every month.

TF: You've had the unusual opportunity to be able to continue to work on the project af- ter the construction was complete.

LG: Which is really advantageous, because we know the place so intimately. We know the opportunities.

MS: For anyone else to do it, they would have to spend an enormous amount of time at the site.

TF: So what is next for you as artists?

LG: While we were still working on the project, we gave a presentation, and some- one asked me, "What are you going to do now that this project is over?" As you can imagine, this project was very, very demanding. It has since faded in my memory a bit, but at the time I said, "I just want to go back to my studio and lock the door and not come out for a while." I think some people in the audience thought that that was bad. Now that I have some distance from it, I know why I felt that way. Haggling, being persistent, really being true to your vision in an extremely convoluted process is extremely difficult. Luckily, I was able to work on my own projects in that five-year duration, which was very important for my own progression. Working on your own projects is like feeding your soul. Large city projects can take that soulful element, and just nearly squeeze it dry. I could not do city projects without having a sound basis in my own investigations, because that's what keeps me spiritually alive, intact as an artist. And that's what I have been doing exclusively the last two years. Only recently have I taken on a new city project, a small one. I have been committed to the idea of working in the public realm. It has been an interest of mine for years. But this interest can be manifest in many ways that I continue to explore.

MS: For me the project really opened the door to something that I was very interested in. I think at the time the project came up, I was really asking myself the question of how I could take the problem-solving process that I go through in my own work in the studio and bring it to a community problem, or to a problem outside in the world. Artists bring a process that's very different from the design profession. It comes out of a different place. The Phoenix project opened the door. I continued to work in the studio on projects, but at the same time, I got involved in several others that were very much in the same scale as Phoenix in some ways, and very, very challenging.

   The major difference is that I set up a team around me to work out the kinds of issues that would drive me nuts if I were working alone. Without this structure, I would probably feel the same way as Linnea does. I could not face the kind of arguing or the administrative parts of a public arts project, but I put together a group of people who really understand how to do that. My role on this team is to be creative and to answer questions and problems, and their role has more to do with implementation. And there is a real balance. They are people in different fields. But just as Linnea said, it's grounded in what I do in my studio. My studio work informs all of the other things that I *do and helps me make decisions about what I am working on. The public projects come directly out of issues that I am working on in the studio. The constraints and opportunities in a public project are clearly defined by someone else. In your studio, you define them, or you choose not to define them, or create your own world. But when you work outside, you are given real constraints, and those constraints are tied to opportunities that I found very, very rewarding and exciting.*

TF: *The studio has constraints. The constraints in the studio have to do with connection to the "outside" world, relevance to different audiences. I'd say* reception *is the constraint in the studio, as opposed to* creation.

MS: *I guess I see my studio work as research. I've always felt that way. I feel I have a certain responsibility, which is part of being an artist, to share that research. If I didn't have to, I probably wouldn't. I'm happy just doing the research. I love that, and I don't work in order to show what I do, but I show what I do because there is a responsibility that comes out of working.*

Notes

1. Herbert Muschamp, "When Art Is a Public Spectacle," *New York Times,* August 29, 1993.

Interview: **Ron Jensen**
*on Commissioning the Phoenix
Solid Waste
Management Facility*

Introduction

Ron Jensen was the public works director in Phoenix, Arizona, until 1996. An engineer by training, he worked for the city of Phoenix for twenty-eight years. While some city officials across the country have gradually given artists their trust, Jensen is unique in handing the design of a building over to artists. This may have come from the fact that he was secure in his power. A former director of the Public Works Association of the United States, he was a well-respected leader in his field. Where lower-level bureaucrats are always looking over their shoulders, Jensen was in a position to take a risk, and to create something unique for which he could be remembered. Since the completion of the Solid Waste Management Facility, Jensen has retired from the public sector to teach at the University of Arizona.

Tom Finkelpearl: What kind of interaction did you have with public art projects before the Solid Waste Management Facility?

Ron Jensen: Not much. I was generally aware of the Arts Commission and some public art projects that were proposed, and I was aware that there was a requirement that capital improvement projects involved public art, but I hadn't gotten directly involved. For the Public Works Department, the Solid Waste Facility was the first direct involvement. It all began when I met with Deborah Whitehearst, the director of the Phoenix Arts Commission in 1991, and she explained the public art program in more detail. She asked to review our capital improvement program, to see what projects might be coming up. We had projects primarily in equipment management on the fleet of 6,000 vehicles, landfill operations. We also had regional shop facilities and a large central shop, so there wasn't much that was conducive to art when we turned to the Public Works Department pages in the book of capital projects. Of course there was a project where we were closing a landfill and converting to a transfer station. We looked at that and said, "Well, that's just a garbage handling facility," so we skipped over it to see what else we had, but we really didn't find anything. So I said, "The more I think about it, the more I think that's an area that we may want to highlight, because there is a strong interest in solid waste, a lot of media attention being given to the environmental impact of landfills and incinerators." We really need to educate the public and get them involved, and public art means public involvement. This facility is going to be in an industrial area next to a landfill, and the attitude is "out of sight, out of mind." It's a facility that provides a basic service. Even though it is essential to people's daily lives, they aren't aware of it. White-hearst said, "Let's just put a check mark on that project and get back to you later."

I don't know how much time went by, but she came back with Gretchen Freeman, who worked for her as the manager of the Percent for Art Program. The two of them wanted to talk about the transfer station project some more. I was warming up to the idea as well. I've been involved in the process of finding sites for regional landfills, and I've dealt with the NIMBY [not in my back yard] syndrome. Anytime you try to do something for the public good, if someone perceives it as having negative impact to property values they oppose it and kill it. So I thought, here is something where we could create a positive to offset some of the negative. In fact, we were considering implementing a recycling program and an educational program. At that time, we were already into the conceptual design of the transfer station. We had hired Black and Veatch, an engineering firm, to do the studies on travel distances to the regional landfill, which was 45 miles away, including the number and size of the trucks necessary to haul the garbage out there. We had gone through a public hearing trying to site the transfer station at a different location, but the NIMBY syndrome had killed us, so we just settled on some property we owned adjacent to the existing landfill. Since we weren't encroaching in a new area, we got approval easily. We had the engineering, technical wheels turning as to how we were going to operate, and some of the basic studies and information that would go into the sizing of the transfer station. In fact, somewhere along this time period, Black and Veatch submitted schematic plans—a square box transfer station that they had designed in other locations—kind of the cookie cutter approach that engineering firms use on standard facilities that provide basic services. We were somewhat in the defensive mode, wanting to protect what was going to be a very large investment. So I thought it might work well to have something that's attractive, and maybe public art could just provide something of public interest. So Gretchen and Deborah got enthused that this might be breaking some new ground. Instead of having an art piece at a public park, out in the open, we could involve it in this "out of sight, out of mind" location. They cleared it with their committees, and we started the artist selection process.

TF: Had you heard of any other public art projects that were related to environmental issues or sanitation at this point?

RJ: No. As I said, I did not have previous experience or knowledge in working with artists. I was an engineer and manager. But I was well aware of changing times—that we needed more public involvement. I was aware that we were perceived as degrading the environment with projects we were building and that we were having projects killed on us. Phoenix has always been very citizen oriented. In fact, in getting funding for this and other solid waste projects we had a citizens bond committee, and early on I went and talked with the chairman about doing something innovative, and got support from them.

You have to keep in mind that this was not a very public place. We do have a lot of traffic to solid waste facilities. On weekends people might clean out their garage, hop in a pickup truck, and go to the landfill. In other countries, I can think of Australia, the social meeting place was at the "tip," the landfill.

TF: Where I come from, a small town in Massachusetts, the dump was something of a social meeting place throughout my childhood. But, with the advent of recycling, this has become even more pronounced because it is so labor intensive. A trip to the dump takes time to sort everything out. There are even volunteers there to help sort.

RJ: Yes. Recycling has done that. This plant was built at a time when we were getting ready to implement a residential recycling collection program in Phoenix. Initially, we hadn't planned that this facility would be anything more than a transfer station, where the neighborhood trucks dumped into big hoppers, which loaded into eighteen-wheelers to haul the garbage off to the regional landfill. But the advent of recycling was changing the whole dynamic.

When the Arts Commission was ready to solicit proposals from the artists, I gave them an idea of what the project was: the basic functions, the *location, what we intended to do on a long-term basis, what the budget was, and so on. They made this information available to artists who were interested in public art projects. I sat in on parts of the selection, and sent deputies to other parts. It was narrowed down to six finalists. We looked at slide presentations and written materials on previous art projects. Included in those were Michael Singer and Linnea Glatt, who were completely independent—didn't even know each other. Quite frankly, we liked some of the things that Michael had done, including environmentally based work that appealed to me. And Linnea had done some interesting outdoor art projects in Dallas. So the Arts Commission talked to them about working as a team. My understanding is, from talking to both Linnea and Michael, that they didn't know if it was going to work or not. They didn't know each other, but they were both willing to give it a try. They came to Phoenix, looked at the site, and both became very enthusiastic—the proximity to the Salt River, the view of the south mountains and downtown high-rises, the backyard of the city, the industrial area—all of this was appealing to them.*

So they shared some ideas and came to me and said, "Hey, we like the project, can we talk to you a bit?" I said, "What I want to do is set up a meeting with city engineers, my own staff, the Arts Commission, building inspectors, and with Black and Veatch, because I'm going to have to put them on hold and they aren't going to like it." It was a "get acquainted" meeting, and I guess everyone thought that they were going to come in and hear what the artists had to say about plunking down a statue in the corner of the project. Anyway, what I decided to do was to lay it on them, so I did: a thirty-minute "vision" talk. I said I want a new project. This is a public works project. We've got challenges from the public. We have new programs and ideas for dealing with the NIMBY syndrome. We want this to be state of the art. We want it to be an outstanding project. We want it to reflect new design, new ideas. I went through all of this—here's the vision for the future: we would like to bring in recycling. We want public involvement and public access, and we are going to have tours. We were going to do a lot of different things nobody had really thought of. (I was just rambling on.) And then I said, "We want to put Black and Veatch on hold, and here are the artists with some of their ideas." So they talked about how they felt about the site, a new approach. Everybody left the meeting not really knowing what was going to happen.

Linnea Glatt and Michael Singer, Solid Waste Management Facility. Photograph: David Stausbury.

The engineers from Black and Veatch came to me afterwards and said, "Hey, this is a million dollar design contract. Our people aren't going to like it." I said, "Refer them to me and I will deal with it." So Larry Shaper, the vice president out at the main office in Kansas City, called me and said, "What are you doing?" I said, "I think we have a great approach." We were both going to an American Public Works conference in Orlando, so we agreed that we would get together for lunch there. When we did, I explained our vision. He said, "We are concerned that you are going to turn something over to the artists, and there's the budget, plus we are concerned with public safety and structural stability." And I said, "We are not going to let them go over budget. I know that they have told me that they have some architectural students and some architects that they will bring in who would watch out for building design standards. But I'd like to have you work as a team. Initially, let's see what they come up with in the way of design, and would you just go along with me and hold off for a couple of months? You are still in the project. You are going to get paid your fee." He said, "Okay, I am willing to go along with you. We'll have a gentlemen's agreement." I said, "Mark my words, you will not regret it. This will be a project that will help your reputation as a company." So he went along with us.

Two or three weeks later, the artists came back to town. They had gotten together and worked day and night. They showed up with a cardboard model that had a new vision. As opposed to the schematic and preliminary plans that Black and Veatch had laid out along straight lines on the city's grid, they had angled everything, and they came up with a model that had structure on the roof—just a completely different layout, while still providing the area inside and the basic facility. They also brought a couple of architects from MIT. I think the engineers were a little more comfortable that maybe these weren't artists who were way out on cloud nine, but they were still skeptical. That was the start of a series of joint meetings in which the engineers would comment on the basic model and ideas that the artist team came up with, and then the artists would go back and work. They started designing some details—the office part and the roadway layout. We exchanged faxes, and then they would come to town to have another meeting. It moved toward a team, but let's say it was still somewhat of a shotgun marriage. They were not in love with each other. The engineers felt like second-class citizens. Even though I am a registered, professional civil engineer, I sided with the artists most of the time, because I wanted to take a few more risks, to have more innovative design.

TF: I am sure that it was good for the artists to have an engineer on their side—not only an engineer, but one who happened to be the client.

RJ: An engineer is a rational thinker. You are trained in college to do things following standards and mathematical formulas and scientific methods. The artist is a free thinker who has a lot more flexibility and can explore new arenas, and is not operating within any boundaries or conventions or standard ways of doing things. Of course, there were times when I had to take the side of the engineers. I remember, for example, when the artists came up with a very fancy design for the main columns that support the building. The column narrowed down to a pin and it was made of all kinds of metal. It was an interesting design, but it looked extremely expensive. While they had done some of the structural analysis that showed it would carry the load, I said I don't think it is worth all of the construction costs and problems, so I vetoed that one with the engineers. As we got into the final stages, a little more teamwork and camaraderie and pride developed to where they didn't need me as much.

Black and Veatch put out the final design drawings. The artists reviewed them, and while there were some things that they still weren't happy with, I said, "Okay, we can work it out with change orders." So the project finally went out to bid. At an earlier stage, the engineers had done an estimate on what the bid costs should be, because that is a required part of the process. The engineers' estimate was $15 million for the basic design, and when the sealed bids were opened, the low bidder came in at $13 million, or $2 million less than the cookie-cutter box. The artists were ecstatic. They said, "Our involvement saved you money!" Well, we let them take credit for it, but you have to remember that these were tough economic times. There wasn't much construction work, and the contractors had sharp pencils. It is clear, though, that they did not come up with things that were overly fancy, or detailed "art" that would create extra costs. In fact, Linnea may have mentioned to you that she had proposed some major artwork in the visitors area. We vetoed it. I wanted it to be clear that in phase one, the artists' involvement was in the design of the whole project. I didn't want to have a somewhat controversial piece of art attached to phase one even though I thought it was interesting. I wouldn't mind incorporating some "pure" artwork in phase two or later on down the road, but I didn't want a statue plopped down or anything hung on the building at this point. We wanted the artistic involvement in it. So we stuck with that.

As we got into final design, most people saw the huge trusses (the A truss is the largest metal truss ever erected on a structure in Arizona), and said, "Gee, the engineers really had a lot of influence to design that truss." Wrong. That was the artists' design. The artists said, "We want people to see what holds this building up, plus we only want two columns in the center of the building," which I liked for flexibility. We can change the interior design from transfer to recycling, to new technology, and we are not stuck with a lot of columns that make it difficult to do things inside the building.

During construction, we had to bring in the contractor. I thought he was a willing player up to the point where it would cost him money. There were some cases in which the artists argued that the engineers didn't write their intent clearly enough into the specifications. They said, "You are going to ruin the whole thing if you do this." Did they mention to you the red pipe?

TF: Yes.

RJ: That was a real interesting one because, quite frankly, it didn't catch my eye until Michael pointed it out to me, and then I immediately went to his side on it. Down below the roof line is a sprinkler system pipe that runs the entire perimeter of the building. It was part of the fire code, and fire sprinkler systems are painted red. The artists came to town to see their beautiful building, and here's a red pipe all the way around it. Michael came to me just incensed. He said, "They have to tear that thing out of there! They've ruined the project." I said, "Look, it's required." He said, "When people come up, they'll look at that and say "I understand this is an artist/engineer design project, and I can see what the artists did: they put a red ribbon around it.'" I could see his point. He said, "It should be raised up, under the eaves, out of sight." But there were the webs of the major beams that cut across. And the engineer said, "Gosh, you can't pierce the webs." And I said, "Look, I'm an engineer. You have a 24-inch web there, and to put a 4-inch hole in it does not weaken the structure. Give me a structural analysis that says it's going to weaken it." And they couldn't do that. They just didn't like the idea. Then they said, "It's going to cost a fortune to do it." I said look, "Along the back we have a walkway, a viewing arcade for visitors to look in the windows. This pipe is low enough to be a safety hazard, where teenagers could jump up and play games. It needs to be raised up, and we'll pay for raising it up on the back side, and on the other side, I don't know, but let's talk to the contractor." So they made some kind of concession so the pipe was moved and raised, and they got it all worked out. I wasn't even privy to all of their final trade-offs.

I can think of another example when I went with the artists right away. Standard procedure for poured-in-place concrete construction is that you "form up" and you pour into the forms. After you pull the forms off, there are ridges and form lines. There is a standard process called "sacking." That's when they take a slurry of cement and water and they dip a burlap sack in it and they rub it all over the concrete. It gives it a uniform gray color, fills in all the little voids, so you would have nice smooth, gray concrete columns, which can easily be painted. The artists didn't want them painted, and they didn't want them sacked either. They wanted all the form lines to be seen. Well, in the specifications in the contractor's bid there was $12,000 for sacking the entire facility. The contractors said, "We've always done it that way; it's a standard practice." I said, "Is it just appearance?" They said, "Yeah." And I said that the artists like the appearance and I don't see any big problem, it looks okay to me. We deleted the sacking. The artists said, "We saved you $12,000." Nobody complained and nobody commented. In fact, we had a tour with a group of architects from the university, and two of them commented, "Gee that's really neat seeing all the form lines. We like the artistic look of that."

TF: *What is the future of the facility?*

RJ: *Part of the original design for phase two was to take the effluent from the adjacent wastewater plant and bring it behind the facility to a big open drainage area, which will have natural wastewater treatment through open channels using reeds and water hyacinths and all of those kind of plants that naturally treat wastewater. It's an environmental research project. So you have solid waste, and then you will have wastewater treatment, and then I proposed that sometime down the road we could get into mining the landfill next door to see if we can bring out aluminum cans and other valuable resources. The facility is flexible, and has the expandability of going into solid waste and landfill mining and research into other environmental activities, all the while including the public with educational tours and recycling drop-off points and all of that. So it goes far beyond just a basic single-function dumping facility or a wastewater plant or an environmental center. It's all of those wrapped up in a unique design.*

TF: The thing that is interesting to me is that obviously there are several different visions here, and they worked together to create this facility. There's your vision, including these progressive environmental ideas that are on the drawing board in a lot of places, but haven't actually been executed much. There are the visions of the two artists, which had to come together. But even if they had, they needed your vision and power to get the engineers to agree.

RJ: Well, that's a major problem that I think artists are faced with. You get engineers that quite frankly aren't interested in some of these other things. They just want to do the basic things and get out. The timing was good. And I don't want to say we concealed this project in any way, but this was not a front-page issue. We sort of kept things quiet until the dedication. When we had the dedication, the building was complete, and the mayor came out to the site. We had a stage and a microphone, and there were 400 people there. As we climbed up the steps onto the stage, the mayor kind of whispered to me, "Where's the art?" And I had to say, "It's the whole thing, mayor." The mayor and city council, of course, approved the budget and the capital improvement program, and, of course, they created the Percent for Art Program, but they were not that close to it to know exactly what we did. We made reports to the council periodically and said projects are under way, but some of the innovative things didn't hit the front page or didn't go into council reports. We didn't do anything wrong, but it just wasn't a hot issue, and we were not going to make it one. Sometimes there are people that are looking for negatives just to challenge the system, so by not having it on the front page of the newspapers, it was out of the way of criticism. If it had been laid out in the limelight, there may have been some naysayers who would have said that you do not need to build a monument to garbage. The only criticism we got is one council member who was running for election looked at the facility and said, "You've got landscaping out there—why would you want to put plants out on a garbage dump?" When people get out there, they are absolutely amazed. It is just a nice, bright, open, modern, well-designed facility.

TF: What do you think is the essential difference between this and other facilities?

Linnea Glatt and Michael Singer, Solid Waste Management Facility. Photograph: Michael Singer.

RJ: I think the big difference is this is a multiuse facility. In the past, facilities have basically been for a single use. A transfer station was simply a transfer station, and that is basically what Black and Veatch were originally hired to design— a building that trucks come in and dump their garbage, and larger trucks haul it somewhere else.

    I said, "We need to name this place something other than 'The Twenty-seventh Avenue Solid Waste Management Facility,' which is its legal and official name." I wanted to call it something catchy. So I proposed to call it "Treaxeros." It's Greek sounding, a new word. Here is the meaning: "T" is for transfer. "R" is from recycling. Half the building is recycling, with bailers, processors, and all of that. "E" is education. We provided an educational element, a multipurpose room, a library, tours to educate the public. "A" is art.

Linnea Glatt and Michael Singer, Solid Waste Management Facility. Photograph: Michael Singer.

The whole thing is public art. "Xeros" is a Greek-derivative word for arid. All of the landscaping we have is xeros-scape, meaning low-water-consuming plants in an arid environment. Part of the design that hasn't been completed is rubble and rocks and desert plants that are going to be in front of it, so as you drive up to the building, it seems to rise out of the desert. It's a giant warehouse with total flexibility. We have the viewing arcade, the multipurpose room, the library. We have parking for school buses. We have guided tours. We have all kinds of educational programs. We cater luncheons. We have an atrium that can have art displayed or educational displays. So my name sums up my sense of the place. "Treaxeros": Transfer-Recycling-Education-Art-Xeros. So that's what I think is different. The name describes it.

*Interview: **Rick Lowe** on Designing Project Row Houses*

Introduction

As discussed in the introduction, cultural centers have been built in downtown areas across America in recent years, inspired by a wealth of evidence that suggests the arts are a potent economic engine. But the group most affected by diminishing city resources is the urban underclass, and their needs are rarely alluded to in the creation of glittering new concert halls and museums. Large-scale art initiatives have almost never originated within underserved, underprivileged, minority communities. An exception to this state of affairs is Project Row Houses in Houston, Texas. As described in a handout from the organization, "Project Row Houses is an art and cultural community project sited in Houston's Third Ward that encompasses public art and education programs, community service, neighborhood revitalization and historic preservation."[1] On a more concrete level, Project Row Houses is twenty-two buildings that have been purchased and renovated by a coalition of artists, administrators, and community activists, led by a young African American artist named Rick Lowe (born 1961).

For several years prior to his initiation of Project Row Houses, Rick Lowe had been creating art that dealt with the image of the house. His work took the form of architectural sculpture, incorporating themes from African American experience. He was inspired by the work of John Biggers, an older African American artist, whose work often employs the image of the row house in the depiction of African American life. In 1992, Lowe first saw a group of derelict row houses in Houston, and began to imagine creating a project within them. He wanted to bring life back to the houses, which are situated in the midst of a poor African American community. It is interesting to note that Lowe's first reaction to the site was primarily aesthetic—it reminded him of John Biggers' work and the forms that he employed as an architectural sculptor. However, Lowe's aesthetic is intertwined with a strong social and political sensibility. To make a long and complex story short, within a year, the twenty-two houses had been purchased, and a renovation effort was well under way. It was a tremendous volunteer effort, including the involvement of many institutions and individuals in the cultural community, as well as public and corporate support.

Project Row Houses encompasses two city blocks: One block has fifteen houses, the other, seven. In the first block, eight of the houses are used for artists' projects. One house is an open house/office, another, the more business-oriented office. Behind these ten houses are five more: two neighborhood galleries, a facility for af-

Project Row Houses, first house opened in 1994.

ter-school programs and workshops, a storage facility, and a wood shop. On the other block, there are seven houses, six of which are used as rent-free housing for single mothers. Each of these buildings is a row house, a vernacular American architectural form that is said to have origins in Africa. Because the three rooms are lined up, row houses are also referred to as "shotgun" houses; you could stand at the front door and shoot a bullet through the house and out the back door without hitting a wall. Modest in scale, the row houses are associated with poor communities, but they also have positive associations in African American history. The ever-present front porches created public sites for community interaction, and for better or worse, the "shotguns" were a common form of housing for blacks in the south for generations.

Perhaps the most traditionally art-oriented aspect of the project is the eight row houses dedicated to art exhibitions. Reminiscent of project rooms at contemporary art centers, these are spaces where artists are given free reign to create installations. In general these installations have focused on African American experience, and the majority of the artists have been black. However, the audience for the art exhibitions has been mixed from the start. In part this is a result of the "House Challenge," in which cultural institutions from across Houston "adopted" a house and assumed responsibility for its restoration. These institutions included mainstays in the arts community, such as the Contemporary Arts Museum, DiverseWorks Artspace, the Menil Collection, and the Museum of Fine Arts, as well as local organizations like Trinity United Methodist Church. Each group raised several thousand dollars for materials and mobilized a group of volunteers to make the repairs needed for their house. It was a unique opportunity for the people of the Third Ward and for the people mobilized by the museums to work side by side.

The community's need for economic and cultural redevelopment is stated clearly in Project Row Houses literature: "Project Row Houses is in the heart of one of the poorest neighborhoods in Houston. Problems of poverty, deteriorating infrastructure and housing conditions, poor health, employment, and educational opportunities as well as lack of economically viable private enterprise are factors contributing to the neighborhood's designation as one of Houston's 'Pockets of Poverty.' 90.8% of the Third Ward population is African-American; 51% of live births are to teenage mothers; 51% of the children are being raised below the poverty level, and 23% of neighborhood youth aged 16–19 are not in school."[2] These are the sorts of social problems that planners have found intractable, and the sorts of urban issues that art-as-urban-development projects rarely address.

While he continues to work on Project Row Houses, Rick Lowe has initiated similar projects in Watts, a traditionally African American section of Los Angeles, and in Birmingham, Alabama. He has given up on making objects for the moment, citing Joseph Beuys's notion of "social sculpture." In each of his new projects, he has entered into a long-term dialogue with the people who live in the neighborhood where his project is intended to take form. Part of the power of Project Row Houses is the energy that came from within the community. It will be a test of Lowe's skills as an organizer to see if he can be as successful when he is brought in as an outside "expert." Each of the projects that Lowe has undertaken has the goal of using art as a vehicle to enrich the lives of people outside of the power establishments. The last thing that Lowe would want to do is create an unwanted project that is alienated from the community where it is sited.

This interview was conducted by phone in February 1996, then updated and augmented with an additional telephone interview in October 1998.

Tom Finkelpearl: I would like to talk about Project Row Houses, but first let's talk about how you came to that point. I know that you had been doing installations that were politically and socially based. It's not like you were painting landscapes and all of a sudden decided to develop the row houses.

Rick Lowe: Right. But I was doing landscape paintings before I started my political work. I was trained as a landscape painter at Columbus College in Columbus, Georgia. It was a really small school. There were only five faculty members in the art department. When I first got to college and I was playing basketball, most of my friends were black athletes. As I began to get more into the art department, I found myself shifting into a whole different community, leaving behind old friends and making new. I studied landscape painting mostly with a professor named Jamie Howard, whose personal work, ironically, dealt with a make-believe world of events and characters from the Holocaust. Well, I did the landscape painting, but it was not related to my life. Shortly after leaving school, I started trying to deal with issues that were relevant to the world that I had grown up in.

TF: *Did you also investigate different sorts of contexts for showing your art?*

RL: Yes. I was dealing with politics on two levels. I was trying to interject content that was relevant, but I was also trying to find a form that was relevant and accessible to people whom I considered my community. It didn't matter if I used political content if it was going to be limited to gallery spaces and audiences. Early on I started doing things that were out of what the art world would consider "legitimate" exhibition places. In 1983, when I moved to Mississippi just after art school, I did a drive-through exhibit at a friend's place that was right off the main tourist route in Mississippi. We posted signs and encouraged people to drive off the main drag through his little U-shaped driveway to check out the art. That was my first effort to find a different audience. After moving to Houston, I started doing a lot of work with political action groups like Amnesty International, for Human Rights Week, and the like.

TF: *What was the nature of these pieces?*

RL: Like the piece in Mississippi, they were cutouts and paintings on plywood. Without really knowing it, I was progressing toward a format that I could build in components—put them together, take them down, move them around: 4˝- × 8˝-foot sheets of plywood and house paint. The imagery was dealing with domestic violence, police brutality, hunger, poverty.

TF: Was it specifically related to the African American community?

RL: No. At that time, my work was very broad. Around 1988, I started feeling the need to focus my efforts to become more effective. I've always considered my community to be working people, poor people, regardless of race. These days, I express strongly that "my community" is the poor, African American community. As a tactical thing, I found that it was more effective to work with a focus, as opposed to trying to speak for the world.

TF: In the late 1980s, were you beginning to show in museums and galleries?

RL: Yes. In 1986 and 1987, I started showing in all the alternative spaces in Houston, while still working with Amnesty International and other groups. My first museum show was in 1988. It was the Texas Triennial at the Contemporary Art Museum in Houston. I did an installation about the lynching of a young black man in Mobile, Alabama, which had taken place in 1983. That's when I started having thoughts of trying to focus more on community-based work as opposed to galleries and museums. I was thinking not only about trying to put the work in the community, but also becoming a part of the community.

TF: What was it about that experience at the Contemporary Art Museum that made you want to change your focus?

RL: I did what I thought was a very strong piece. One day during the exhibition, I was giving a gallery talk, and I got really emotional. I had been living in Biloxi, Mississippi, about 60 miles from the site of the lynching that was the subject of my piece. At the time, I was about the same age as that person who was killed. It could have been me. Well, I was talking, and my audience was mostly white artists and patrons, a middle-class audience. I felt that I was talking to a group that didn't have the same kind of emotional feelings that I had about this event. They did not appreciate it in the way that people who shared my life experiences would. After that event, I distinctly remember watching people go from the paintings and sculpture into my installation. The whole gallery scene just seemed like a shopping mall, where people shop around for ideas. I didn't sense sincerity among the viewers in relation to my work. It was at that point that I decided this was not the right place for my work. I was dealing with the wrong people.

I stopped making objects for almost two years. Because I had made the decision to address issues concerning African Americans, I decided that I needed to get more deeply involved with the African American community. I should be a part of that community, and that community should be a part of my audience. I sat back, did a lot of reading on the civil rights movement, African American artists, African American history.

TF: How were you supporting yourself at that time?

RL: I always supported myself as a building craftsman, either carpentry or painting.

TF: So you were living a working person's existence, while thinking about art and history.

RL: Oh yeah. During that time, I started doing volunteer work at this place called the S.H.A.P.E. (Self-Help for African People Through Education) Community Center. I did everything from help them distribute fliers, to sit in on all the meetings. There were all different kinds of action groups. I joined the Ida Delaney Justice Committee, formed to fight for justice in the killing of two blacks from the neighborhood.

TF: Which neighborhood was that?

RL: The Third Ward in Houston. It is a low-income community, mostly black. I was working on becoming a concerned citizen within the African American community. That's where I was getting my nourishment. It was kind of funny because I felt distance growing between myself and my friends in the art community. It was the same kind of experience that I had when I first went to college, and left basketball for art. But now, I saw the reverse. I was going from the mainstream, white community back to the black community, realizing that when you cross those lines, normally you cross them alone.

TF: This is 1990?

RL: Yes. At that time I started to feel this desire to contribute more. I knew that my value to this community was more than just passing out fliers. I suggested to the Ida Delaney Committee that I could do an installation that would address the issue of police brutality to heighten the awareness of people in the community, as well as maybe get some press. When I proposed this to the group, they kind of ignored me. Their attitude was, "Well, if you want to do it, you can." But I was pretty excited about it. It was an opportunity for me to make some art and do something really rewarding. So I started working on these pieces dealing with police brutality.

TF: Were you still working in the same kind of artistic vocabulary, with the cutouts, that you were using when you had stopped making art a couple of years earlier?

RL: Yes. I put the installation together, and people started coming by, checking it out, getting interested. A couple of the leaders asked if they could hold a press conference in this piece. They thought it would show the strength of the group, and the injustices of police brutality. I agreed, and it was a big success for them. It was very important for me because it showed me that there was an appreciation for aesthetics in the African American community. I had somehow been convinced that it wasn't there. You know the attitude, "Uneducated, poor people don't have the ability to appreciate the fine arts." Photographs from the press conference were on the front page of both of Houston's major newspapers, and there were a lot of repercussions. There were probably four or five articles dealing with that particular issue in different papers.

TF: Did the art press respond at all?

RL: The art critic of the Houston Post was very supportive of my attempts to stretch the boundaries of what was traditionally called fine art. But the person at the

Houston Chronicle *was very much against it. The critic for the* Chronicle *had been there for years and years, and was close to Houston's old guard of artists. That's what she treasured, and it was mostly a white, male arts community. She wrote an article that was really biting about what I was doing, saying that I was crossing the thin line between art and propaganda. That gave me even more incentive to stick with the community. I thought, "Who cares if the arts community can't appreciate what I am doing, as long as my target audience respects me for it?"*

About six months later, I put together an installation in front of the Convention Center. It was about creating a platform for different community groups to speak from, a visual platform. That was right around the time of the Persian Gulf War, so there were groups forming around that issue. I got them involved with the piece, as well as the Houston Area Women's Center, a very mainstream organization. I even had a police officer come and address the crowd about the troubled relationship between the police and the African American community. That went really well, lots of response. But it also created a problem for me, because people started asking me if I would make a piece for their cause. I like my independence, and I like to be able to work on issues that I feel passionate about at the time. I can't do it otherwise. I've never been really good at doing commissioned work.

In the project at the Convention Center, I built some rooms for others to use. I was hoping that different artists would just plug into this structure. I did manage to get one other artist to participate, a photographer, who makes a living as a photojournalist for the Houston Chronicle. *He took one of the rooms and did a piece that was up for a week. But what I was not considering was that I had spent years developing a form that was temporary and portable, using plywood and house paint. Other artists, even if they were dealing with highly political issues, were dealing with them in media that could not survive in the environment that I had created.*

That was late 1990. In 1991, I took advantage of the energy that was generated by the Convention Center piece to do some community organizing. It gave me a kind of recognition that I wanted to take advantage of. My approach took me right back to the arts community. I founded a group called the Union of Independent Artists. I thought that artists are pretty progressive, and they are affected by a lot of the same things that affect the poor. I figured if I could get a group of politically active artists to deal with things like freedom of expression, then maybe I could get those same artists to deal with issues that were affecting the black community. It worked for a while, but I found out, when you really look deeply, there are a lot of conservative, middle-class people in the arts community that don't see themselves as having the same problems as working people in poor communities.

Then there was a whole series of overlapping events that made me think about houses. In the last part of 1991, I was invited to do a piece for Snug Harbor. [Snug Harbor Cultural Center in Staten Island, New York City, sponsors an annual outdoor sculpture exhibition.] My piece needed to survive outdoors for six months, so I decided to build a little house for the installation, to make the house a part of the piece and the piece a part of the house. I built a little structure that was 10-feet wide by 12-feet deep with a door in the front and one in the back. It was a little "house of justice," focusing on how African Americans have fought for justice through the church and educational institutions. I liked the way that worked out, and started thinking that maybe that would be the idea—to make houses for other people to use in their own way.

At the time, I was meeting with six African American artists, talking about ways to do projects together in the black community. We discussed the idea of each doing an installation in a house. Then, I was curating an exhibit of emerging African American artists for the museum here, and one of the artists wanted to build a house and work within the structure. Finally, I was enrolled in classes at Texas Southern University, where John Biggers was the founder of the art department. When I was taking classes at TSU, where his work still has a strong presence, I saw that Biggers was pointing out how African Americans don't have a deep appreciation for our own culture and heritage. We don't respect it, and we don't demand that other people respect it. I started seeing all the different things that he was pulling into his work, and how he was putting them in a different light—like the mamas carrying the babies. Usually when people see that now, they think of it in terms of welfare babies, these irresponsible women. But he showed it in a different light—a kind of strength in emotional commitment to family.

Most importantly, I saw the shotgun house in John Biggers's work. The way that he used the houses was pretty incredible. He used them as the foun-

Project Row Houses, the site before renovation.

dation for his composition, but also he used them as the foundation for the people that he was portraying in his work. It was around that time that it hit me that we should find an area that was historically significant to the community and bring it to life.

After some other investigations, I came across the site of the Project Row Houses. I was thrilled by these houses. I thought they were ideal because they were so much like a John Biggers painting. I was visualizing how these houses were when there was a lot of activity in the past, and what could happen in the future. It was the perfect place to create the form that I was looking for, to bring a lot of different artists to work here in the community.

TF: So to some degree, it was an aesthetic decision, based upon your appreciation of an older artist's work.

RL: Yes that was a big part of it, the aesthetic quality of the site itself. Talk about found objects! It was perfect. They were abandoned. At first I was thinking of a one-shot guerilla art show. I thought it would be pretty neat to do installations in these abandoned houses, to get whatever we could out of the site and move on. But I've always had this commitment to doing ongoing, long-term projects for the community, not just hit-and-run.

I went on this long, solo journey of researching the properties, finding the owner and trying to figure out how to set up a mechanism that would allow this idea to grow. That's when I started seeking the support of artists and arts organizations in the area. I was on the board of DiverseWorks Art Space, the alternative art space in Houston. We talked about the idea, and they agreed to allow me to apply to the NEA for a grant to start the project. That was the beginning. In the application, we didn't mention the fact that the houses needed about $280,000-$300,000 worth of renovation before anything could happen. But there is always a risk. Whatever you are creating, whether it is a painting or a sculpture, it's just a chance that it's going to work. Some of the people at the NEA saw the same vision that I could see, and thought that it was worth taking a chance. Burt Kubli [at the NEA Art in Public Places Program] stuck with us all the way on that first proposal. He didn't press any of the hard questions that we couldn't answer, and guided the grant through for us.

At that point I started talking to city officials about the idea of saving these properties and contributing to the revitalization of the neighborhood. Michael Peranteau at DiverseWorks helped get some money so that I could stop working at the carpentry and painting jobs and spend a bit more time doing this. The Firestone Graham Foundation came up with a $10,000 grant.

TF: At what point did you actually get some sort of agreement to purchase these houses? You must have had much more money committed by that time.

RL: No. We didn't. Finally, in December of 1992, I contacted the owner of the property in Taiwan. He had these abandoned properties, and the city was nudging him about tearing them down, so he was looking for an out. I started talking to him about a five-year lease, and he sent me a letter committing to negotiating a lease deal. But there was a lien on the properties. The owner kind of backed out because he didn't want to get me tied up into an insecure situation. He was pretty honest and straightforward about it. He mentioned *to me that he was trying to get community development dollars to rehabilitate the houses, and that's where I got the idea to go to our community development department and talk to them about funding to buy the houses. They were lukewarm to the idea at first, but they sent a bunch a people out and got a bit excited about it. There was a complex set of financial options. Really, I just wanted to get the houses, but it was necessary to get the money before the lien holder foreclosed on the property. I was very naive and idealistic. In fact, we still haven't gotten the money from community development. But they said it could be done. (Whether I had the political clout to get it was a different story.) So that was the encouragement I got from the city, and, in fact, it was pretty significant.*

I contacted a lawyer friend to draft a lease-purchase agreement, and we got it signed. This was in August of 1993. Once I got the agreement signed and a little bit of money, we started to organize the community. First, I went back to the African American artists who were in the earlier discussions about how we could contribute to the community. I share studio space with five other artists, so they came and helped out. We just started cleaning and clearing the site, investigating what was under all this junk.

During the time that I was negotiating with the owner, I brought a bunch of contractors whom I had worked with to the site to get an idea of how much it would cost to rehab each of these houses. These were people who were pretty good friends, so they were giving me good, honest, friendly advice. And that honest, friendly advice was, "Forget it!" These were contractors who were used to doing jobs to make money. If there is too much trouble, they don't bother. Well, we went ahead. The first big effort was to renovate the houses for artists' projects.

A majority of the volunteers were cleaning and clearing the site. I do carpentry jobs and rehab jobs with one of my studio mates, Dean Ruck. Dean and I started renovating one of the houses while we worked with the volunteers on tearing out other stuff. We approached the houses as if we were working on a sculpture. If there was an old window frame that couldn't be purchased for less than $1,000, we just made a piece that fit, whereas most contractors don't think that way. We started tearing out the rotten parts, moving along, kind of sculpting this house. We made it work. It took from September to January cleaning and clearing the site. It was in March of 1994

Project Row Houses, during renovation, 1994. Photograph: Steve Clark.

when Dean and I completed the first house and started on the second. At that point, we held a reception for all the volunteers to show them a piece of the progress—this one house that was completely renovated, with electricity and plumbing. That was another step toward proving that it could be done, generating hope among people who were still doubtful. During the cleaning and clearing stage, there were very few community people involved. It was mainly just artists. But that changed as we moved into the beginning of 1994.

After we had the open house for the volunteers, we had an open house for potential funders. At that point, the Brown Foundation gave us a $10,000 grant. We were called in by the department of Community Development to talk to a potential corporate group that was looking for a project to work on. It was the Amoco Oil Corporation.

While she had been working with us for some time, it was at this point that Deborah Grotfeldt came to work with Project Row Houses full time. Debbie and I went to meet with Amoco to sell them on this community project. We only had one house completed, and the site was still pretty ratty looking. A lot of vagrants were still coming through. But Amoco had a vision also, which I thought was pretty unusual for corporate people, to want to take on something that is at the budding stage and could still fail. They came out and we walked the grounds and kicked around the drug needles. This one executive from Amoco, Cory Webster, got really excited. He felt that they could make an impact. And they agreed to renovate the exterior of twelve houses.

TF: Amoco adopts a specific charity each year?

RL: It's a summer program in conjunction with their "Corporate Olympics." They invite all the top-level management to travel to a city in which they will have these sporting events. (I say upper-level management because they don't pay for anything. They get the week off work, but they have to pay their own way.) They have a big sporting event, but they also reserve one day for community service.

TF: You had a bunch of Amoco executives out there painting and scraping?

RL: Well, it turned into something that was really a lot bigger than they had imagined, which is why I was really shocked that they accepted it. Normally what they do is a hit-and-run project—something you can complete in one day, like painting a gymnasium. But this took an incredible amount of planning. They were going to bring out about 400 people on one day to replace the sill beams and rebuild porches. Knowing a bit about construction, I realized right off the bat that it would not work. It's like saying you are going to have the sheetrockers hang sheetrock, coat it, and paint it all in one day. You can't do it. People would get in each other's way. So Amoco put together a team that came up with this plan. They formed smaller groups to come out and prepare the foundations and start building the porches, so that when the big day came, and all the other volunteers got here, they could snap things together.

At this time, in the middle of 1994, Paul Winkler, the Director of the Menil Collection, came by and got really excited about the idea of renovating these little houses. The Menil Collection has had an ongoing interest in issues of housing. They have sponsored the design of low-income housing, for example. He asked how much it cost in materials to renovate the first house. We told him, minus plumbing, probably about $3,000. [The houses that are used for artist installations have electricity but no plumbing, since they are not residential.] He said that they could come up with that amount of money and bring the volunteers out to do the work. He proposed to challenge the other museums to do the same.

Winkler has about as working-class an attitude as you'll ever find in a museum director. He drives a pickup truck. He was one of the first people to roll up his sleeves and come out and start tearing stuff out and building stuff up. He challenged the other museums to adopt a house. First to accept was the Museum of Fine Arts, then the Contemporary Art Museum, and Diverse-Works. Once that happened, we saw the possibility of spreading that whole concept and getting other groups to take on a house. Trinity United Methodist Church adopted a house, as did The Links, which is an African American women's group, the Coleman/Whitfield family, and finally, an individual, Betty Pecore. All of these groups mobilized a lot of people to come out and actually do the work. There was a tremendous amount of volunteer effort, but that was also part of the point—all of these people working side by side in the Third Ward. And that's how we renovated the other eight houses that are devoted to artist installations.

TF: During the time that you were getting all the physical structure together, were you beginning to imagine what is going to happen inside these houses?

RL: Yes. My core group of artist friends and I were talking about how the houses could be used. We realized that the best approach was to let people take the houses and do whatever their creative impulse encouraged them to do, just let it go. Art and aesthetics weren't that important to me at the time. I understood that I was doing work that was stretching the boundaries of art, but I always tried to understand how it fit within the development of mainstream art. Who are the other people out there who are doing work that is related? I was aware of people like Hans Haacke, and the painterly artists like Leon Golub. As an artist, it was something that I needed to do. It's an intel-

lectual process. But during those early days of Project Row Houses, there was not a lot of time to consider that. I was lost in work.

TF: *What about the relationship with the community groups when you had the Amoco executives and the museum staffs out there renovating the houses?*

RL: *The community involvement was kind of interesting. The neighborhood people finally started coming by and helping after six months or so, because I was here all the time. A lot of weekends, I was the only person here working. So they would come and help out. I think they actually felt more comfortable coming when I was the only person because they didn't have to interact with people that they didn't really know. There may be kind of a fear of not understanding each other.*

I know our state representative from this area, Garnet Coleman. I met with him early on to talk about the project. When we did our event for potential supporters, we had hors d'oeuvres and that kind of stuff. We had a police officer to watch people's cars. I got word a few weeks later that Garnet's reaction was that the community didn't need a wine and cheese place for middle-class white folks to come and hang out. That was an interesting community response. It was a great thing for me to hear. I needed to know what the perception was. In the beginning, when white groups started coming in to volunteer, I'm sure a lot of people thought it was just going to be something that a group of white people were going to do in their community, kind of taking over. But then the church groups started to respond. They preach about doing stuff in the community, but they did not have much of a record. This was an opportunity.

TF: *They got people from the congregation to volunteer?*

RL: *Right. To actually do work. That's been an ongoing relationship. One young woman named Karen Jennings dove in completely. She would spend basically every weekend here doing loads and loads of work, and constantly telling other people at the Trinity United Methodist Church across the street, "You'd better get out and practice what you preach," kind of embarrassing* them into coming out and working. She is now on one of our committees for the Young Mothers Program. A lot of those volunteers have moved into the committee work now.

TF: You have set the basic theme that artists are asked to address in the houses. They do exhibitions, projects, installations that address issues of African American experience?

RL: Yes. We throw that out as kind of a basis that they can work from. But it is not only African American artists, and the approach is not always so literal. For example, we had this collaborative team, Paul Kittleson and Carter Ernst [both are white], who did a project based more on the house, and its meaning to people who had lived there. Their piece didn't have an overtly African American look or feel about it. But at the same time, the essence of it really did deal with the lives of people who may have lived in row houses.

TF: You have spoken about the houses dedicated to art projects. What about the other houses?

RL: Everything is all in place right now. The site has two blocks. One has fifteen houses, the other has seven. In the first block, there are eight houses for the artist projects. There is one house that is used as a partial office, partial lounge, a general hang-out facility. There's an office. These are the ten houses in the front. There are five in the back; one of those is a neighborhood gallery. One of them is a school house, where we do after-school programs and workshops. There is a house that we are using as a gallery space for some of the young students that have volunteered, allowing them to get some experience with showing their work. One house is still storage. The last of the fifteen houses on this block is a wood shop. Some people are interested in using the shop to teach building—general skills, like how to build a table.

On the other block, there are seven houses. We just completed these houses, and they are actually the most exciting part of this project right now. We had a series of meetings with people from Texas Southern University, discussing the programming for these houses. There was a lot of group discussion, but I credit Debbie Grotfeldt for coming up with this idea to create housing for single mothers.

In any case, the US Homes Corporation, a major home building firm, partnered with Masco Home Furnishings to renovate them for the residency program for single mothers. Every year at the Astrodome they hold the National Home Builders show. Something like 5,000 home builders are here for a week or so. For that show, US Homes usually builds a $200,000–$300,000 house in one of the suburbs. Masco Home Furnishings provides all the furniture, and Woman's Day magazine features the house in the magazine. Well, this year, we managed to convince the president of US Homes to do a different twist to the home show. (It didn't take too much convincing. He was really excited about it.) Instead of doing houses in middle-class suburbia, he decided to help us with the renovation and furnishing of the houses here. These would be their model homes. Along with Woman's Day magazine they selected five different interior designers, and invited them to design the interior of the houses. (There are six of them, because Chevron completed one of those houses.) Each house looks like a little suburban town home. It's pretty funny, actually. So those houses are all ready, and we have all the young mothers selected who are going to be living there.

TF: What are the criteria for their selection?

RL: They are single mothers, ages eighteen to twenty-five, who are working toward some kind of educational goal, whether it's completing high school or college. It's set up as a one-year renewable contract. They live in the houses rent free. At the end of the year, their progress will be assessed and it will be determined whether they are able to move on or they need more time. At first we thought the entire group would move in and out at the same time, like a class in school. What we didn't take into account, is that some people will not complete it and then we'll bring in other people.

TF: But the program is not just housing. The young mothers are also taught "life skills," for want of a better phrase.

RL: Yes. Again, this was driven by Deborah. In the process of her research on how to write about the program, she kept coming up with information on single parenting. And so she started thinking about what would it take to help these young mothers. Then Dr. Nelda Lewis came in as the coordinator of the program. She had a lot of experience working with black parents. She began to actually shape the program.

TF: There are some pretty strict rules—no overnight guests, a curfew.

RL: Yeah, but the rules were probably a lot stricter than they needed to be at first, at least in some cases. (In other cases, probably not as strict as they should be.) Some of the young mothers were eighteen. For the most part they had never lived on their own, and they didn't necessarily think about the responsibilities. The thought was that they would have some kind of structure, some kind of guidelines. And as it turned out, the youngest woman (who was seventeen) could not deal with rules at all, and she ended up leaving the program. The rules are a little more relaxed now. We're always playing around with what works best. For instance, there was one woman who had this boyfriend—not the father of the child—who was very supportive of her and the child. They've moved in together. And it was a situation where we were thinking, are we going to drive a wedge into this family?

TF: Of course, there are famously divisive rules for welfare recipients that have made people hide their relationships, because they'd lose their benefits if their partnership was revealed. Many have blamed these regulations for breaking up families, or keeping single mothers single.

RL: Yeah, we have to be careful with that; we don't want to play that role.

TF: Have there been any recent developments in the Young Mothers Program? Are there any plans for expansion?

RL: Yeah, we're already building our first new house in the block. We're not sure exactly how it's going to work. But there's a possibility that it may be used for

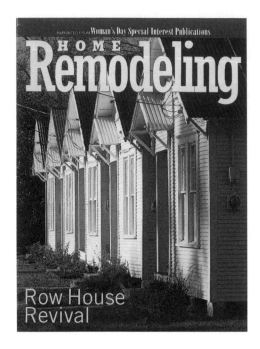

Project Row Houses, Houston, Texas, on the cover of Home Remodeling, *1996, reprinted from* Woman's Day Special Interest Publications.

the Young Mothers Program. There are many complexities. It's going to be complicated to keep a connection between the art part and the residential part, making sure that there is that merger between the two. The other difficult question will be how to deal with these social issues, and finding people that can work on them in a reasonable manner. Nelda Lewis grew up across the street and has her Ph.D. in sociology. But most of the people that we have been able to get to support the program have been upper-class, wealthy, white women. They see it as an opportunity to be very active in the project, which is fine, but there are some problems as well. One example is that the director from Planned Parenthood came and asked if we would want to work with them in dealing with the issue of parenting, planning a family. But one of our major supporters doesn't support abortion at all, and didn't want us to deal with any organization that supported "choice." Her thing is abstention. You've got to be kidding! You are not talking about the real world. So there are all these conflicting values. There have also been problems with specific people who have consistently made bad choices, like marrying a guy who you've known for two weeks who is out on parole, then back in jail in less than a month. In any case, we have these beautiful houses, and an active program that is always in transition.

TF: Can you talk about the future? What do you think about your creative involvement with Project Row Houses at this point?

RL: I think my creative involvement for this project is basically over. I think about something that Mel Chin said, that artists need to create a form or forum and step away from it, let it go and do its own thing. As soon as I am comfortable with the organization's stability, I'd like to see my participation become more like volunteer work in the community. The creative work is pretty much over. It's a machine.

TF: How will this experience with Project Row Houses be relevant to your art in the future?

RL: I think it has totally shifted my way of viewing art and seeing myself as an artist. Doing this has proven to me that I don't have to rely on making objects to utilize my creative energy, my creative spirit. When I started thinking that, I had to once again find some grounding for myself in art. I started doing a lot of reading about Joseph Beuys and listening to the thought patterns that he was going through and his ideas about "social sculpture." I started looking at that as being a legitimate form.

TF: What about your relationship with art made for the gallery-museum context?

RL: I try to tell people that just because I am abandoning object-making as a form for myself, doesn't mean at all that I have any less respect for the object as an incredibly powerful form.

TF: That is something that almost every public artist I have talked to says. Many people think that artists who choose this sort of route are completely divorced from the history of art.

RL: That's not the case with me at all. Last week I was looking through a catalogue and came across some very powerful work created by a Japanese artist in response to the bombing of Hiroshima. It was traditional in its medium, but that was not a problem. I still have a lot of feelings about "museum" art. It's not in the cards for me anytime soon, but who knows, it may creep back in.

Notes

1. From press material provided by Project Row Houses, 1997.

2. Ibid.

Interview: **Assata Shakur**
on Living in
Project Row Houses

Introduction

Because of the acute needs of the community, Project Row Houses has taken on the role of a service provider, attempting to address social issues directly. Since half of the babies in the community are born to single mothers, and since these young women have a notoriously difficult time finishing their education and developing professionally, Project Row Houses has dedicated a significant amount of its space to serving these young women and their offspring. The Young Mothers Program is the brainchild of Deborah Grotfeldt, former managing director of DiverseWorks Art Space, who joined Project Row Houses in 1993 as executive director. (Rick Lowe retained the title of founding director.) In this program, young unmarried women live in row houses that have been renovated for residential use. Only women who are enrolled in educational institutions are eligible for the program, and they participate in weekly meetings on issues ranging from long-range planning to parenting skills. Here is how Project Row Houses describes the program:

Since February of 1996, The Young Mothers Residential Program (YMRP) has offered one-year renewable residency contracts for young single mothers and their children who are provided free housing while they work part-time, further their education, and participate in twice-weekly formal programming, including individual and group counseling, job/life skill training, and parenting programs. The goal of the YMRP is to assist single mothers and their children in achieving independent, self-sufficient lives through their residency in a positive emotional, physical, economic, and social community.[1]

There is an ongoing effort to integrate the young mothers into the artistic enterprises of Project Row Houses, but this has had its downside as well. When the Young Mothers Program first opened, visitors to the eight art installations tended to wander over to see the rest of the site. Assata Shakur told me that the young mothers felt a bit as if they were on display. The need for privacy for these young women had to be acknowledged, even though their homes were a part of a public art project.

This interview was conducted by telephone, October, 1998.

Tom Finkelpearl: How did you first hear about the Project Row Houses?

Assata Shakur: Well, at the time I was living in a small apartment complex, and Project Row Houses was getting ready to start their Young Mothers Program. The original "mentor mom" was staying in that apartment complex. She told me, "I think it's a good program. I think it's a good idea." She gave me application forms.

TF: Were you living nearby in Houston's Third Ward?

AS: Yes.

TF: Did you grow up there?

AS: No. I grew up in Houston, but in another neighborhood, in South Park.

TF: Were you among the first group of Young Mothers who moved in?

AS: Yes.

TF: And you have one child?

AS: Yes.

TF: What was the process of applying and being accepted into the program like?

AS: Well, you had to write a story, an essay about why you wanted to be in the program, and what your plans and objectives for your life were—your educational goals, personal goals. It was a very personal experience. You had to reveal certain things about yourself. Then you met with people from the organization, then you were simply chosen or not chosen.

TF: Was it a highly selective process?

AS: There was a lot of publicity, so I think they had quite a few people to choose from, which is always the case.

TF: *Once you were accepted, and you moved in, what were the requirements of the program?*

AS: *There were a lot of requirements. You had to be in school. And we had to work at the same time. And then we had to attend workshops twice a week, and we had to do some volunteer work at particular houses. There are also behavior requirements. We had a curfew. Our curfew was 12 on week nights, and 2 a.m. on weekends.*

TF: *Were there programs for kids?*

AS: *Yes. There was a day care center right in the backyard, right in the backyard on the campus courtyard. And so everybody there took their child to the day care center. Then we had a play area for the children. So it was like having everything you needed in one place.*

TF: *What level of school were you in at the time?*

AS: *I had started college a couple of years prior to 1991, and I had gone for a couple of years but I had stopped going to college. I don't know if you would say I dropped out, but I had some problems, and I stopped going. I had decided that I wanted to go back. But I owed the university some money, so I decided to join the Americorps program. Well, this Americorps program, it was like a volunteer kind of pay; I made around $600 a month, and I had to pay rent, and I had to pay for insurance on my car. I had a lot of different expenses, and I had no money. It was very, very constraining on me. And in fact, before I moved into Project Row Houses, I was living in a . . . I don't know how to describe it . . . well, a not-nice apartment. It was really very, very difficult, and I was having a lot of problems, just meeting my financial responsibilities, and owing money. I had experienced quite a bit of instability in terms of housing, because I decided to go back to school, and I left a pretty good job, making a pretty good amount of money, to making $600 a month. Two people, $600 a month—that's not any money, you know? But that was the decision I made, because I wanted to go back to school, and I didn't want to work from one job to another job for the rest of my life.*

Project Row Houses, interior of Young Mothers Program residence, with Maya Angelou quotations on wall. Interior design by Anita Webb Smith. Photograph: Hal Lott.

Coming to Project Row Houses was very emotional for me because I didn't come from great poverty. The poverty I encountered was when I was an adult, trying to live an independent life. So it was very difficult, having a child, and not really having the type of environment or surrounding that you know you need to raise a healthy, happy child. What can you do? Either you work full-time, or you try to dedicate yourself to an academic pursuit. It's very hard to do both.

TF: *I understand the Young Mothers Program at Project Row Houses is for women who are in school, trying to finish up.*

AS: *Yes, but they are at different stages. Several people had not started college. I was one of the people who had started. When I came, I had been through the try-*

ing-to-go-to-college stage, and I had been through full-time employment, and I knew that that's not what I wanted. I didn't want to be at a job 8:00 to 5:00 or 8:00 to 6:00. So I came with the goal of getting myself back into school full-time. In the course of being at Project Row Houses, I finished my Americorps project and got $5,000 scholarship money, paid off my school debts, and then started college full-time. It was like starting school all over again. It was a totally different experience than it was the first time around. Totally different.

TF: *What college did you go to?*

AS: *University of Houston. It was so amazing, because I think when I was at Project Row Houses, I was probably still classified as a freshman. I was only in one sophomore-level class. I really hadn't had very much success in college—not because I couldn't, but because school just really didn't have an interest to me. And I think I just didn't have the support network that I needed. But when I went back to school, school was my thing, 24/7. I did school as a full-time occupation, and I really had the support that I needed. People at Project Row Houses were really interested. They'd say, "How's school going?" If I had a paper, I would tell Rick my ideas and he would help me. I really had someone. My family had moved out of Houston. I grew up with my grandparents, so I don't really have a strong nuclear family base in Houston. So, it was really very hard to go to school the first go-around. But the second go-around, it was like starting all over again. And everybody was so concerned, and I could study all the time while the other young mothers were watching my son. You know, it was just a total support system available to me.*

TF: *How many years were you living at Project Row Houses?*

AS: *I was at Row Houses for a year and a half, officially living there.*

TF: *Well, what do you mean? Were you living there unofficially at another time?*

AS: *No. I mean I never really left Project Row Houses. That's the essence of it. When I stopped living there, I started working in the after-school program, so my connection became even more embedded. Since the time I moved there, I never left Project Row Houses. That's the truth. Once I couldn't work in the after-school program, I started working in the arts program. I was never involved in the arts. I was the only young mother who had no interest in art, and I never went to any of the openings. You know, I just didn't see the connection. But when I started volunteering, that really merged me more with Project Row Houses.*

Rick Lowe worked with me. This is what happened, really: Project Row Houses put a great investment in me. They became really concerned about my schooling, and things I was going through, and they were really of great assistance to me in other parts of my life. And so I wanted to reciprocate that, and that's why I tried to get involved and learn more about it. And then I began to see really the way Rick's program and Project Row Houses was transforming not only my life, but the lives of so many other people in the community, and so many other people who came through Project Row Houses. I did tours. To watch people come and just be overwhelmed by the project made me take a step back and really recognize the greatness of the project. People would come from all over the country, who had heard about Project Row Houses or were interested in doing similar projects in their neighborhood, and I could really see the effect that it was having on other people.

TF: *Are you still in touch with any of the young mothers?*

AS: *Yes. Some more than others, of course, but we are in touch. I am very close with another young resident who worked in the after-school program. We all didn't finish at the same time. Three of us finished instead of five. One chose to leave, and one was removed from the program. The woman who was actually terminated from the program is now deceased, but she was able to do training—which upgraded her job skills tremendously—and get a higher paying job. It matured her a lot. But the project was very strict. They had curfews, we couldn't have overnight guests, you know, but it was also very nurturing. We had classes in spirituality, in sexuality, in wellness, very intimate subjects that really built the character.*

TF: Who was supervising those classes?

AS: Dr. Nelda Lewis. She grew up in Third Ward, and, in fact, she grew up in the house across from where we lived. That's actually how she got involved with the program. She has a Ph.D. in psychology. And that was good; we had some- one who had been through school, who had done it.

TF: Why did you decide to leave Project Row Houses?

AS: You can stay two years, but I left because I had maxed out all the things that that program had to offer. I had been able to learn the skills necessary, even just basic skills like goal setting, personal discipline. I mean, these are skills you need to deal with your life that you don't necessarily gain along the path in life. And we worked in the program—we were a family. I can't express it any more than this: we went to the grocery store together; we cried together; we fought together; we argued together. We were a family, very much a family, and we were able to grow. And as you learn, and you get skills, then it's time for you to go and apply those skills in your life. And so it was time for me to go and apply my skills to my life. So that was the leaving part, when I said, "I can do this. OK, I can do this."

Nickesha Sanders, a member of the Young Mothers Program, with her daughter Nahla at Project Row Houses, Houston, Texas, 1998.

When I left Project Row Houses (of course, I was still there every day), I was still going to school. At that time, my son went to a private school. I needed him to be at that school for more than one reason, because it was an extension of our lives, and they helped you a lot in terms of the care during the day. But I was faced with, "What do I do? I'm going to have to work more hours to keep my son in school." And then the Project Row Houses board assisted me by giving me a scholarship for my son. The money that I was spending for him to go to the school, I could spend on rent. So my life didn't shift totally. In a year and a summer, I finished school!

TF: What are you studying now at Penn State?

AS: I study sociology, social movements. I'm in the Ph.D. program. I'm just getting started. Rick came to visit me with my diploma, which was such a big shock, still. Sometimes I just think about it, and don't even know how I did it. And I said to Rick, "I don't even know why you brought this here. You should have put it up at Project Row Houses," because it's so very true. They helped me every step along the way. But you know, they helped me pay for the application. All the letters came to Project Row Houses. They are my family. When I got here, I was very homesick the first day; they were the first people I called, and I was like, "Oh, God, I don't know how I can do this."

I can't really describe the impact that Project Row Houses had. You have children who live in the neighborhood who come to Project Row Houses, and this may be the only source of encouragement that they receive. And you can see that and get to involve yourself in something that's greater than who you are, than your personal situation. Project Row Houses has a very communal nature. It makes you understand your relationship to other people. We feel the sisterhood, and the ability to assist someone else outside of ourselves, and understand how important it is to have those types of relationships with other people. That's one of the principles and lessons that I learned while being there.

TF: At Project Row Houses, there are art exhibitions, after-school programs, and the Young Mothers Program. Do you think there's a good interchange among all the different parts?

AS: I do think there is an interchange. I don't know if everybody's able to make the same transitions, because we are so trained to think that one thing is isolated from another. But I think that since I've been there, the connections have become much stronger. The Young Mothers Program is maybe on the fringes. And it's on the fringes because that's how we created it. You have to understand, the program was very new at the time. And so a lot of people came to Young Mothers as though we were on exhibit. They would want to walk through our houses as we lived in the houses. You're in a very private experience, in such a public realm, so everybody's kind of gawking at you. And so to provide some security for ourselves, we tried to insulate ourselves a little bit from the other side. That's the challenge—keeping a situation for the young mothers that is personal and private, and yet giving them the exposure that they need to the other parts of Project Row Houses.

TF: Do you think that that's more resolved now?

AS: Yes. Much more so. At the end of the program, we spent a lot of time going through the installations. As I said, I never really attended the openings, but then we went through the installations. Another thing that really helped out a lot is that the artists started doing projects related to the Young Mothers Program. And so, we had an interchange through that.

TF: What would be an example of that?

AS: Well, one lady did an installation on African hairstyles, natural hair. And she did workshops. One of the young mothers was really interested in learning all of these styles, and she ended up being an intern with the artist, and ended up working with her. She had a shop on site, and there she was working with the artist. So, that was a perfect connection between an artist and a young mother. You have a lot of resources, and hopefully you are able to match the resources with people who need the resources. So she was able to learn a skill that she enjoyed and liked, and she was able to make a living off of that. Another young mother was an artist. So it was perfect for her. She had a lot of opportunity to expand her art there.

Let me ask you a question. What is the book on, exactly?

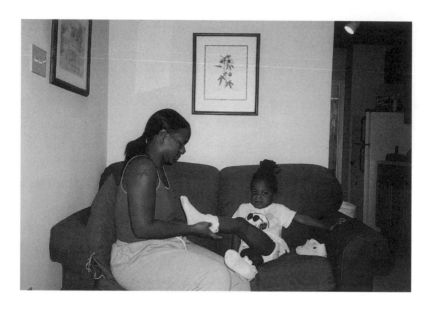

Keneesha Johnson, a member of the Young Mothers program, with her daughter Kayla at Project Row Houses, Houston, Texas, 1998.

TF: Well, it's about public art, including a number of projects that are stretching the whole definition of what art is. I mean, Rick Lowe is an artist who ended up doing this urban project in Houston in collaboration with all of these other people, this huge project that combines housing, art, education, and more.

AS: You know, this is one thing that I wanted to mention, and I told Rick this. One day we were talking about school, and when I said, "I'm your art." I am really here in graduate school at Penn State because Rick created Project Row Houses. It is not that I wouldn't be successful otherwise, but it was something that was necessary for me to move myself further in my life. And without them at the time, the journey could not have been possible. Almost definitely. You know, he invested; he saw; he created; he put these ideas into being, and this is the result of his ideas and his creativity. We are his living art forms, which function throughout life. When I was able to see it like that, then that's when I thought that art was a beautiful thing. It wasn't some-

thing that you just hang on the wall. It could be that, but it could be manifested in so many ways. And he also taught me that I am creative. He would always say, "You always say you have no creativity, and you're not very artistic, but what you do in school is creative, and it is artistic." He said, "Creativity is about recognizing creation. You create in different forms, not on a piece of paper and not on a wall, not with paint. You can create in whatever medium. And your medium happens to be academic." So, in that way, Project Row Houses is very tangible and accessible. When working there on Saturdays, I was so amazed that not only people who came from strange places, but also people who were going to church would stop by and just walk through the houses, and be quite amazed at what was there. They were people who never would go to the fine arts museum, who would never go to one of the galleries. They could see art, in a very nonthreatening way, art that related to them, that had some connection to them. That is a pioneer effort, when you bring something to a community, instead of bringing a community to a museum. That's a challenge that many people don't always meet.

Notes

1. From "Project Row Houses Organization History" (Houston, Texas: Project Row Houses, 1999), p. 2.

Five Dialogues on Dialogue-Based Public Art Projects

In the introduction, I discussed how Clement Greenberg decreed that art exists in its own aesthetic realm, separated from the world of politics or other social interactions. The thinkers and practitioners in this section could not be farther from this notion of aesthetic purity and isolation. They embrace the notion of dialogue, of sharing power and creating through a process of social interaction.

As a counterpoint to the Greenbergian notion of aesthetic isolation, I start this section with an interview with Paulo Freire (1927–1997), an influential activist and educational theorist from Brazil. Freire's philosophy (which I summarize in an expanded introduction to his interview) has tremendous appeal for me in a discussion of public art for several reasons. It seems relevant to mention that I first heard about Freire in the mid-1980s from artists who were involved in public action. I learned what a dialogue-based approach could mean by experiencing their art projects—and later learned about Freire's philosophy of dialogue; I progressed from practice to theory.

Translations of Paulo Freire's work have been available in the United States since the early 1970s, including *Pedagogy of the Oppressed,*[1] *Pedagogy of the City,*[2] and *Pedagogy of Hope.*[3] Reading these three books convinced me that Freire is a philosopher whose theories are firmly based on action and experience, whose activism is infused with theory. When I interviewed Freire in São Paulo, Brazil, where he lived, I was inspired with his open-mindedness, the continuing evolution of his approach, and the relevance of his notion of dialogue to public art practice. In the interview, Freire discusses the nature of dialogue and how his ideas intersect with art. Freire, even in less-than-perfect health, was lucid and energetic in his discussion. True to his philosophy, he was intent on listening as well as presenting his own point of view.

Mierle Laderman Ukeles has been working in collaboration or in dialogue with the New York City Department of Sanitation since the late 1970s. In her interview, Ukeles discusses how she went from a graduate student in fine arts, to a young mother looking after her baby, to a professional artist working on a day-to-day basis at the Department of Sanitation. The interview traces Ukeles's work from her early maintenance art projects, to her manifestoes, to her early projects in collaboration with sanitation workers.

In creating *Alien Staff,* Krzysztof Wodiczko has collaborated with a series of immigrants to the United States and other countries, often undocumented workers. For example, working together, Wodiczko and Jagoda Przybylak designed an instrument with which she could tell her story of immigration in the city. The staff includes a series of transparent compartments that hold small objects that Przybylak felt were important in telling her story. At the top of the staff, there is a video monitor that plays a tape of Przybylak relating a series of emblematic stories regarding immigration. On a number of occasions in New York and in Houston, Przybylak has taken this instrument out into the city and used it as a device to interact with strangers, to stimulate discussion on the issues of immigration. There are several levels of dialogue: the staff is created through a dialogical process between Wodiczko and Przybylak, and it is meant to stimulate discussion and debate. When it is being operated in the city, it is an instrument for dialogue.

The first interview is with Jagoda Przybylak, a woman who, like Wodiczko, grew up in Poland and emigrated to the United States. As opposed to Assata Shakur (interviewed in Part II), Przybylak was not helped out of economic hardship by the art project. By the time she collaborated with Wodiczko, Przybylak was certainly "on her feet" in the United States, teaching photography and showing her work. The *Alien Staff* had a different sort of effect on her, helping her to come to terms with and make public her early experiences as an undocumented worker, when she was employed as a companion to an elderly woman and as a cleaning woman in New York's financial district. It is also interesting to note that Przybylak credits *Alien Staff* with opening up a dialogue between herself and Wodiczko regarding their immigrant experience. It has a public role, but it functions in a very intimate way as well, revealing personal stories.

The interview with Wodiczko is more theoretical. He discusses his philosophical motivations for *Alien Staff,* and how it relates to other projects, including his well-known projections. He discusses the psychological nature of *Alien Staff,* how it acts as a sort of public/political psychotherapy. In the United States, Wodiczko has run into resistance to *Alien Staff,* because of the general perception that immigrants are welcome here, and that suffering is simply an acceptable part of the experience. But immigration is changing the face of America in a way that makes some people uncomfortable; opening up the experiences of immigrants to public view is desirable to counter the increasing hostility. *Alien Staff* is an instrument developed to create dialogue in the tradition, I believe, of Paulo Freire.

In the introduction, I discussed the development of Battery Park City. At the north end of the development is a New York City public school, Stuyvesant High School. Stuyvesant was founded in 1908 and operated on the same site on the east side of Manhattan until moving to Battery Park City in 1992. Under New York's Percent for Art law, the school was required to spend 1 percent of the construction costs on permanent public art, and Kristin Jones and Andrew Ginzel were awarded the commission. In Paulo Freire's educational technique, prospective educators first spend a great deal of time in the community, develop their educational materials in dialogue with the community, and create a mechanism for ongoing dialogue. Without any direct knowledge of Freire (as far as I know), Jones and Ginzel created a very Freirian project—spending time at the old Stuyvesant High School, creating a project with thousands of current and former students, and making an on-going project for the members of the school community over an eighty-eight year period into the future.

One of my great regrets is that I was not able to complete this book before Paulo Freire passed away. I would have loved to discuss it with him, to hear his criticism. Freire was inspiring in his openness, his ability to listen to criticism, and to continue to move forward intellectually. He insisted that education, learning, and social change were a process, not a goal. This emphasis on process is also evident in the projects in this section.

Notes

1. Paulo Freire, *Pedagogy of the Oppressed* (New York: Continuum, 1970). Translated by Myra Bergman Ramos.

2. Paulo Freire, *Pedagogy of the City* (New York: Continuum, 1993). Translated by Donaldo Macedo.

3. Paulo Freire, *Pedagogy of Hope* (New York: Continuum, 1992). Translated by Robert R. Barr, with notes by Ana Maria Araujo Freire.

Interview:

Paulo Freire: *Discussing Dialogue*

Paulo Freire was born in Recife, Brazil, in 1921. He received a law degree from the Universidad Federal de Pernambuco, but never practiced as a lawyer. Instead, Freire chose a career in education, first outlining his philosophy of education in his doctoral dissertation at the University of Recife in 1959, and as professor of the history and philosophy of education at the same school. He was the first director of the Cultural Extension Service of the Universidad de Recife. Freire, a well-known leftist, was jailed for seventy days by the military government that seized power in Brazil in 1964 and "encouraged" to leave the country. This led to fifteen years of exile, in which he worked in Chile, taught briefly at Harvard University, and joined the World Council of Churches in Geneva. Freire passed away at the age of seventy-five on May 3, 1997.[1]

Freire is best known for *Pedagogy of the Oppressed,*[2] a book that outlines his approach to education and liberation. He came from a middle-class family, but the Great Depression hit Brazil as it did the United States, and the severe poverty he experienced as a child influenced his later writing and action. *Pedagogy of the Oppressed,* written in exile and completed in 1970,[3] is both a political/philosophical treatise and a description of the educational methods that Freire developed in working with adult illiterates. Because his philosophy seems so relevant to the projects described in Part III and there is some unique terminology in Freire's philosophy, I will provide an expanded introduction.

Freire was never content with the goals of traditional education. Rather, he developed an educational approach that sought to teach critical consciousness, learn from students, redefine the power relations between teacher and student, promote dialogue across the economic, political, and educational lines that divide society, and inspire action on the part of the underclass. He saw the roots of oppression not only in illiteracy and poverty, but also in a "culture of silence" among the oppressed. His educational goals do not center on a single problem, but approach the larger social arena within which the problems exist.

Pedagogy of the Oppressed begins with a discussion of the relationship between the "oppressor" and the "oppressed." While these categories might seem a bit too clearly drawn, it is important to remember the context within which the book was written. First, Freire was writing in the late 1960s, a time when political lines seemed clearer than they do today. But "oppression" is a word that still comes to mind when one visits Brazil, where the divisions between the lots of the rich and the poor are so extreme, where the two classes are so physically proximate and unmediated by a large middle class. Glittering high-rise buildings abut directly on the *favellas,* slums in which living conditions are almost incomprehensible to people from the United States. The oppressor and the oppressed, however, are not separate in Freire's view. The power of the oppressor is evident in the oppressed people's acceptance of their lower status. Freire says, "Self-deprecation is a characteristic of the oppressed, which derives from their internalization of the opinion the oppressors hold of them."[4] In the classroom, this makes it difficult to open a dialogue, the essential goal of Freire's educational approach, because the (oppressed) students are waiting for the teacher to assume the mantle of authority, to pose the questions and supply the answers. Freire states the problem thus:

A careful analysis of the teacher-student relationship at any level inside or outside school, reveals its fundamentally narrative character. This relationship involves a narrating Subject (the teacher) and patient, listening Objects (the students). The contents, whether values or empirical dimensions of reality, tend in the process of being narrated to become lifeless and petrified . . . Education thus becomes an act of depositing, in which the students are the depositories and the teacher is the depositor.[5]

This dialectic can be applied to the artist-audience relationship. In the context of the museum (the equivalent of the school), artists, through their work, often take on the role of moral/intellectual/aesthetic teachers, while the audience takes on the role of the passive student. And in the narrative structure of the museum, artwork can become "lifeless and petrified," dead in the mausoleum. Of course this does not need to be the case. When it is not, it is because the viewer takes on an active and critical position in viewing the work—a position for the viewer that is only occasionally encouraged in the structure of the contemporary museum.

Against this model, Freire suggests the "problem-posing" model of education, which is based upon mutual communication rather than a one-way transmission of information:

Through dialogue, the teacher-of-the-students and the students-of-the-teacher cease to exist and a new term emerges: teacher-student with students-teachers. The teacher is no longer merely the-one-who-teaches, but one who is himself taught in dialogue with the students, who in turn while being taught also teach. They become jointly responsible for a process in which all grow.[6]

We might call the art discussed in Part III problem-posing art, which is created jointly by the artist and the audience. For Freire the process of problem-posing education is creative. If problem-posing dialogue is the essential technique of *Pedagogy of the Oppressed,* critical thinking is the goal. "In problem-posing education, people develop their power to perceive critically *the way they exist* in the world *with which* and *in which* they find themselves; they come to see the world not as a static reality, but as a reality in process, in transformation."[7]

It is worth looking at the specific techniques that Freire developed for his literacy program, because they reveal the depth of interaction to which he was committed. Freire's notion of dialogue did not involve a couple of "community meetings," as it seems to for some public artists and bureaucrats. Rather, it involved a flexible and intense series of collaborative interactions over a protracted period. Here is how Freire describes his educational process in *Pedagogy of the Oppressed* (including the key words that Freire used to describe his work). A given project would begin with a team of investigators researching the area within which they planned to initiate an educational program. After reviewing secondary sources, the investigators made contact with people from the area and organized a meeting to talk over their objectives, ask for their blessing to proceed on the project, and seek participation in the investigation. Freire does not say whether people ever rejected the investigators' request to work in their area, but it seems unlikely that anyone would turn away a literacy program.[8] After gaining local support, the investigators called for volunteers to help in the process of investigation, and subsequently included the volunteers in the team meetings. Team members then made a series of visits to a variety of sites in the area, including homes, schools, and churches, and individually recorded everything they saw and heard.

The next stage consisted of a series of evaluation meetings, in which the investigators reported their findings and through discussion began to consider the "nuclei of contradiction" within the community. These contradictions are the basic questions, the "meaningful thematics" of the area (usually centering on social issues of one kind or another). After coming to some preliminary conclusions regarding the nuclei of contradiction, the investigators researched the awareness of these themes for the local people. Then, acting as a team, the investigators selected some of these contradictions to be developed into "codifications" (sketches or photographs), which would be the basis for the discussions that would follow. The sketches and photographs were designed to be neither too explicit nor too obscure, so that they might open issues up, to stimulate dialogue when they were used in group meetings. When the codifications were completed, the participants analyzed them to understand the process. Then the group returned to initiate dialogue about the codifications in "thematic investigation circles" of up to twenty local residents along with a psychologist and a sociologist. These meetings were taped for subsequent analysis. This "decodification"[9] process was not simply listening to the local response to the images, but also a chance for the investigators to challenge the local residents, posing problems. Once the decodification meetings were completed, the investigators undertook a systematic interdisciplinary study of their findings. Finally, the team prepared the materials—what we might call "teacher packets" in a museum education program—which would be used for the educational project in the area.

This thoroughly dialogical process was meant to be the *starting point* for dialogue: "With all the didactic material prepared . . . the team of educators is ready to represent to the people their own thematics, in systematized and amplified form. The thematics which have come from the people return to them—not as contents to be deposited, but as problems to be solved."[10] The aim of Freire's educational program was to stimulate critical consciousness, help the local residents to gain understanding of the political, social, and economic conditions they lived within, and by taking their input seriously, to help increase their self-confidence. Freire insists that the process must be true to its philosophical underpinnings. While Marshall McLuhan says that the medium is the message, Freire might say that the process is the product (or conversely, the product is the process). If liberation is the goal of the educational program, then the design of the educational program itself should be one of dialogue and power-sharing. One can imagine the education that the investigators received in creating their educational materials.

Some have argued that Freire's philosophy is essentially powerless because it is based upon a transformation in consciousness as opposed to a transformation in social institutions. bell hooks is one of Freire's strongest advocates. In *Teaching to Transgress* (certainly a Freirian title), she addresses the objection that creating critical consciousness falls short:

Many times people will say to me that I seem to be suggesting that it is enough for indi-
viduals to change how they think. And you see, even their use of the enough *tells us some-*
thing about the attitude they bring to this question. It has a patronizing sound, one that
does not convey any heartfelt understanding of how a change in attitude (though not a
completion of any transformative process) can be significant for colonized/oppressed
people. Again and again Freire has had to remind readers that he never spoke of consci-
entization[11] as an end itself, but always as it is joined by meaningful praxis.[12]

Stanley Aronowitz has said that the basic point for Freire is not to create a
new *technique* for teaching, but to "offer a system in which the locus of the learning
process is shifted from the teacher to the student. And this shift overtly signifies an
altered *power* relationship, not only in the classroom but in the broader social canvas
as well."[13] Aronowitz goes on:

The teacher-intellectual becomes the vehicle for liberation only by advancing a pedagogy
that decisively transfers control of the educational enterprise from her or himself *as sub-*
ject to the subaltern student. The mediation between the dependent present and the in-
dependent future is dialogic education.[14]

One of the basic criticisms of Freire's work is that it still depends on the
teacher, the presumably middle-class, educated leader, who will open the minds of
"the people" for their benefit, whether they like it or not. This objection has been
leveled against dialogue-based art as well, and it is a difficult objection to overcome.
In a 1996 review of the Three Rivers Art Festival, Miwon Kwon cited the risk of projects that claim to be created through an interactive process with non-artists. She says:

With return plane tickets in their back pockets, artists enter "communities" as outside ex-
perts to mediate between the daily lives of underprivileged social groups and Art. In turn,
these "communities," identified as targets for collaborations in which its members will per-
form as subjects and co-producers of their own appropriation, are often conceived of to
be ready-made and fixed entities rather than as fluid and multiple.[15]

Kwon is critiquing the "community art" in which the nonartist participants are little
more than a new sort of material to be manipulated. And she is right: interactive art
can be manipulative. As Kwon points out, there is nothing inherently good about col-

laborating with an audience. If one is to collaborate, it needs to be done with caution and respect. Just like traditional public art that is thrust upon the local residents, superficially conceived community projects could qualify as "cultural invasion" in Freire's terminology. "In cultural invasion," Freire writes, "the actors . . . superimpose themselves on the people, who are assigned the role of spectators, of objects. In cultural synthesis, the actors become integrated with the people, who are coauthors of the action that both perform upon the world."[16]

Kwon's argument posits a weak and naive "community" and an artist who has not entered into a complete dialogue in Freire's sense. But the "underprivileged" people to whom Kwon refers often have their own personal or political goals that they hope to accomplish in collaborating with artists. In addition, the artists whom I put forth here as examples of dialogue-based art have worked together with their "community collaborators" for extended periods. They do not have "return plane tickets in their back pockets," but dedicate years, if not decades, to their collaborations.

Dialogue-based art or education is a balancing act between "cultural invasion" on the one hand and mere reflections of popular values on the other hand. If one believes that "the oppressed" have something to offer, shouldn't the "people's voice" be unmediated by any input from the outside? By the time Freire published *Pedagogy of the City* (in the early 1990s) he had been asked about the balance between the teacher-student and the student-teacher repeatedly. His response reflects the approach he outlined in the last part of *Pedagogy of the Oppressed,* though (as Aronowitz points out) it lacks the revolutionary rhetoric:

To be with the community, to work with the community, does not necessitate the construction of the community as the proprietor of truth and virtue. To be and work with the community means to respect its members, learn from them so one can teach them as well. . . . The mistake with the sectarian community-based program does not lie in the valorization of the people of the community, but in making them the only repositories of truth and virtue. The mistake does not lie in the criticism, negation, or rejection of academic intellectuals who are arrogant theorists, but in rejecting theory itself, the need for rigor and intellectual seriousness.[17]

The teacher-student and the students-teachers enter a process of dialogue, to which all contribute. To construct *only* the "community as the proprietor of truth and virtue" ignores the contribution of the teacher-student.

Freire's emphasis on process and transformation is relevant to the art discussed in this section of the book, an art in which process and product are one. This is essentially different from traditional works that are created out of sight of the audience—finished and stable, created for the autonomous, permanent, unchanging context of the museum. Just as Freire questions education that seeks to transmit a set of immutable facts from teacher to student, the artists discussed in this section question the one-way communication between artist and audience, and create art through a problem-posing process.

In recent years, there has been increasing discussion of the notion that *all* communication is dialogical. Invoking Bakhtin, theorists, including Rosalind Krauss and Johanne Lamoureaux, argue that meaning is constructed *between* the speaker and listener, rather than simply given.[18] Certainly it is easy to see how the meaning of *Tilted Arc* was constructed between Serra and his various audiences. From the moment it was sited on Federal Plaza, its meaning was in flux, constructed and reconstructed by a series of different audiences in an intense contest for the authority to fix the meaning. If all communication is dialogical, all art is dialogue-based. But it is a matter of degree. The artists interviewed in this section are dedicated to an ongoing process of dialogue. They acknowledge dialogue and accept the instability of meaning as an integral and *desirable* element in the ongoing creation of their work. It is this approach that allows for a critical art that is not based in conflict. When an artist embraces dialogue and sets out to create a process that involves sharing power, this can reorient the process.

Freire's approach is based on a series of ethical decisions. If oppression is wrong, then one must develop a way to fight it that is as sound in its process as it is in its goals. Dialogue is not a means to an end, but a process, an ongoing project of intersubjective investigation.

Of course, public art does not need to be created through a dialogical process. I am presenting this process as a particularly fruitful strategy *among others*. For example, the works discussed earlier by Vito Acconci, Linnea Glatt, Michael Singer, and Maya Lin were not designed through dialogue, although they have all created sites for dialogue. And as Freire points out in the following interview, *any* work of art can be situated in a problem-posing context. He states, for example, that one can interrogate the notion of beauty in a still-life painting and discuss how "beauty" is distributed in our social system. Freire's approach, then, is not only relevant to work that is created through dialogue, but also to the way all art is presented and consumed.

Freire's work is hopeful because it offers us not a goal but a process, and it is achievable. We *can* initiate a dialogue, even if we cannot immediately dismantle the oppressive institutions that constitute contemporary politics. The sort of dialogue that Freire advocates can be carried out on a small scale, out of the spotlight, across lines of division. Paulo Freire named one of his books *Pedagogy of Hope,* and therein argued that dialogue-based action depends on *critical hope.* He says, "I am hopeful not out of mere stubbornness, but out of existential, concrete imperative."[19]

I was once told that in turn-of-the-century Vienna it was common practice in the Jewish community for people to go over to a friend or relative's home, lie down on a couch, and discuss their problems at some length. The story goes, then, that Freud was simply adapting an everyday mode in the structure he designed for psychoanalysis. I was reminded of this story in visiting Brazil and Paulo Freire. Brazil is a place where human contact is simply more highly valued than it is in the United States. Freire himself is also a person who clearly enjoyed interpersonal dialogue. Though he complained about it good-naturedly, he related how university students were always coming to interview him, and how he always agreed. When I first went to meet him, he was too exhausted to conduct a formal interview, but he offered me coffee, and we chatted for around a half-hour. He was eager to talk about the United States, particularly the trials of O. J. Simpson and Mike Tyson, which he analyzed in terms of class and race. When I left, I thought that Freire's philosophy was a true extension of his cultural and personal circumstances. A great conversationalist, he is the great advocate of dialogue. My gratification in meeting Freire and seeing how true to his philosophy he was mirrored the experience of bell hooks. In her book *Teaching to Transgress* she writes, "When I first encountered Paulo Freire, I was eager to see if his style of teaching would embody the pedagogical practices he described so eloquently in his work. During the short time I studied with him, I was deeply moved by his presence, by the way in which his manner of teaching exemplified his pedagogical theory. (Not all students interested in Freire have had a similar experience.) My experience with him restored my faith in liberatory education."

Note: This interview was conducted in May 1996. I sent the interview to Freire for revisions. However, I received a letter back form his office several months later saying that Freire was not able to make revisions, and asking that this be noted upon its publication.

Tom Finkelpearl: In the United States the influence of Pedagogy of the Oppressed *and your other books is very broad, not just in education. However, since the practical techniques you discuss relate to an educational process, there can be problems with the translation of these notions of dialogue into other fields. Have you had this sort of experience?*

Paolo Freire: Yes, yes. I think that the only possibility for one not to have this kind of experience is not to produce and think. The moment you make proposals, you risk both understanding and misunderstanding, distortion and respect. For example, personally, one of the great problems I had in the '70s was the misunderstanding of the concept of "conscientization."[20] If you ask me, "Paulo, what should be done in such a situation?" I answer that I think that the author who perceives that he or she is being distorted cannot commit suicide, but has the duty to make it less easy to be distorted. How? By becoming clearer, more explicit, by discussing the propositions with more rigor in order to help people, including ourselves, understand. I'm sure, though, that the comprehension of a text is not only a task to be accomplished by those who write the text. That is, the readers also have to produce the product, the comprehension of the text.

TF: So the reader is in dialogue with the writer.

PF: And because of that I think that the writers must be clear concerning the task they have in writing. For example, in the seventies I perceived the distortion in the "conscientization." It seemed that people were saying, at that time, that it was a kind of aspirin. You went to the pharmacy and you bought 50 aspirins, 10 aspirins, 3 aspirins, depending on the quantity of reactionary ideology. For a very reactionary person, you would need, I suppose, 100 aspirins. [laughs] Pills of conscientization. I began to fight against that, trying to make it more clear what I was meaning by conscientization. Today I think that is not a problem.

I am not sure whether I was able to explain to you how to struggle against the possibility of misunderstandings that provoke bad use of your proposals. For me, there is no solution. The answer is not to be angry, but to be morally more clear. Sometimes the distortion is innocent, sometimes it is preestablished, it is programmed. In any case, we have the duty to clarify.

TF: *The sort of distortion I am talking about, for example, relates to artists who go into a neighborhood to set up a "dialogue" and report back to their peers, without ever really leaving room for the people to speak for themselves. People employ the rhetoric of dialogue, but it's a false dialogue. For example, what if I went to an African American community to create a "dialogue," but I knew beforehand what I want the results to be?*

PF: *Yes, it is absolutely false. But look, I don't want to say that I am prevented from knowing what I would like to say before going there. Because, as a person, I am a project. If I am a project, it means that I have objectives, because if I did not have some objectives and some ends that I am fighting for, I could not be a project. And it is part of my project to conceptualize what kind of arguments I can use in order, for example, to work against racism. For me, this is legitimate. What is not legitimate is to try to impose on them precisely the arguments I thought of beforehand. It is not legitimate, because a true conversation cannot be preestablished. I cannot know beforehand what you will say to me in answering my question. I have to become engaged in order to follow our process of conversation. Do you see? Of course, I have to program my conversation. Nevertheless, I have to know that my conversation cannot be precisely as I planned it.*

TF: *When I came here today, and I have my questions . . .*

PF: *Yes. You have your questions, and you have anticipated a way of answering your questions. But these are not necessarily my answers.*

TF: *You talk about the "nuclei of contradiction" in* Pedagogy of the Oppressed: *getting to these essential questions for a community.[21] Some artists, I believe, working in their studio, with no dialogical process, have the ability to reach these "nuclei of contradiction" intuitively, almost. They create images that are very valuable to everybody else, that help us ask questions and create dialogue, without themselves being in a dialogue. I've noticed that your house is filled with art. Do you have a feeling about the artist's ability to help us ask questions?*

PF: *Oh yes. In the last analysis, the artist, in the silence and intimacy of his or her studio, creates scenes like these. [Gesturing to paintings in his living room] First of all, even when the artist is not interested in making a "protest art," still, the artist cannot escape from the social dimension of his or her existence. In many respects, when the artist creates, the artist is projecting, in his or her work, the social influence, the political influence, the ideological influence with which the artist lives. It is social and not only individual, no matter if the artist is working alone. The artist is a social being. There are possibilities of different readings of the production of the artist. Nevertheless, it is possible that all of us find some nucleus, and this nucleus in the artist's production, is the reflection of the social condition.*

Of course, sometimes that is the intention of the artist. For example, this piece here [walks over to a small framed painting] was made by the former minister of education of Brazil. In 1963, when he was minister, he invited me to come to Brasilia to organize the campaign for adult literacy in the country. Maybe twenty years ago, he became an artist. He made this work for me. This represents Brasilia. For him Brasilia is something that is rising up, in a transcendental direction. And here, stenciled on the painting is the word tijolo, which means "break" in English. [The word itself is broken into three parts on the canvas: ti jo lo.] It was the first generative word[22] we used in Brasilia, because Brasilia was a city being constructed from nothing, so tijolo was a very strong, generative word for the literacy program. It was a very present word. This is the artist's vision: Brasilia, the future, the dream, the Utopia. It is Brasilia wanting to be something. The artist has all the right to put his or her imagination to work, to transcend the concrete. And, in any case, we can discuss the imagery. For example, we can use this work of the artist as a codification.[23] I can show this work to a group of workers, and we can discuss that.

TF: So the artist's work may or may not intend to make a social statement, but his or her work can open discussion. But one of the things that we discussed the other day [in a previous, unrecorded discussion] related to social class. A problem that we have with art, is that it is associated with the upper class, while public art relates mostly to places that are used by the lower classes.

PF: I've not had concrete experience in this area, but I think that it is not difficult to understand the possible difference of appreciation and the reaction to projects of public art according to different classes. What I think, nevertheless, is that without wanting to reduce the artists, without trying to instrumentalize the artists, we can use their production independently of their intentions. This still-life painting [pointing to another painting on his wall] is by a very famous Brazilian artist. We could discuss this with a group of workers. Of course, the discussion, a priori, would lead us to aesthetic dimensions of the work—that is, to the question of beauty. But in discussing beauty, you can easily discuss ethical questions, because of the relationship between ethics and aesthetics. In discussing ethics and aesthetics, you discuss politics. For example, you can discuss the right to beauty, the right the poor people have to be beautiful, to have beauties, to create beauties. Nevertheless, the poor people have been prevented from getting beauty. What does it mean? Why? Then you can discuss politics, organization of society, of the state, and so on.

TF: I have a friend who is an artist who said that he felt the most radical thing that he could do was to plant trees in the communities where there are no trees, to give some living beauty to the people in that community, to give them a sense of hope, the living presence of the tree. To take care of a tree, to help it live, to help it grow in a community is a transparent metaphor for life.

PF: Yes, yes, yes. Planting a tree can be also a creative and artistic job. Undoubtedly, the very movement of the body in order to make the hole—there is ritual, there is harmony, there is contradiction in this. The very process of planting is very interesting; in some aspects it is a violent process also. By making a hole, we are interfering in the nature of the being of the earth. Nevertheless, we can discuss the beauty of the objectives. This is also an artistic job.

TF: There is an artist at the Sanitation Department in New York City, and one of her performances involved following sanitation workers on their normal trip around the city to understand the movements that they had to go through, to understand the beauty of their ballet of picking up garbage. She learned their dance, their skill.

PF: This is beautiful. When I was a child in Recife, there was a profession: the men whose job was to move pianos from one house to another. I will never forget how they did the job. It, too, was a ballet. I am sure that, from the point of view of physics and mathematics, we could make calculations to explain how they divided the weight of the object through the different movements of the body in order to put the piano on the heads of each one, and also how to continue to divide the weight by ritual of the walking and singing.

TF: They sang?

PF: Yeah. Fantastically. I am very sorry because we have lost that profession.

TF: I am sure they sang to synchronize their movements. That sounds very beautiful, the sort of beauty that artists can investigate.

I would like to ask you about the issue of cultural difference. I've been in Brazil now for a week, and I've noticed a completely different relationship with time and with space. Everybody is constantly touching one another, and then time . . . is later. You meet someone at maybe, around a certain time of day.

PF: Yes, [laughs] maybe we meet around a certain time. And remember, you are in the center, the most modernized city of the country. If you go to North East Brazil, a professor in the university there tells you, "We'll meet tomorrow at ten o'clock." Well, maybe it's twelve. In São Paulo, we have lots of punctuality, comparatively. [laughs]

TF: With all these differences, what about the translation of ideas, understanding across time and space. You lived in the United States for a while during your exile?

PF: I lived in 1969, in Cambridge, Mass., for a year.

TF: You found those differences?

PF: Yes, yes. But, first of all, I am very curious about cultural programming. I am always open to the difference. One of my convictions is that we learn, above all, when confronting difference. What is important is to be different, and to respect the difference. I am always convinced, for example, that there are sides of a behavior, sides of a discourse, sides of a sign, which we are not seeing clearly, and that culture explains this. Because of that, I always try to learn. For example, I remember that one time I was in Chile in the beginning of my exile and I needed to resolve questions of my documents, so I went to a public office, but no one looked at me. And then, after a while, I gestured like this [waving toward himself]. A man came to me, very angry, and said "I am not a dog to be called like you did." I said, "Look, I am very sorry but I am a Brazilian." And he said "You must know that you are in Santiago." I said "Of course, I know I am in Santiago, I am just trying to tell you that I was not being offensive. I was ignorant, and now I have learned and I will never will do that again." When I left, I said to myself, "The man is right and wrong." When I told him that I am a Brazilian, I was not being arrogant. On the contrary, I was trying to explain my mistake, my error. I remember also that one day when my daughters were adolescent, they were protesting, making very harsh criticisms of the Chilean way of life. I said, "No, no. You are wrong. The Brazilians are not good or bad, because they are Brazilians. The Chileans also, the Americans also. Look, my daughters, we people are not, we are becoming." Culturally becoming. Historically becoming. Then the question for us, when we come into a strange space, is to begin to learn how we can try to become in the strange space: how the natives are being, what are the social tastes, the way of smiling, the reason why people smile. Humor is very difficult. Sometimes, in the States, I understand the English, but not the language of humor. It does not touch me. It is cultural. But I have discovered possibilities of reinventing myself in the States. I continue to be myself, I am very Brazilian. In my way of speaking, my taste for food, and so on, I am very, very Latin. But I also have good relationships with the public in the States. I create words in English, not just Portuguese. But somehow, people are smiling, understanding me.

TF: I would like to ask you about theory and practice. In your life, you have gone out to teach literacy, back into the study, out into government to run the school system in São Paulo, and back to the study. In a way, that is like an artist going into his or her studio and back out "into the world." Can you comment on that?

PF: I think that this question of the relationships between action and reflection, thinking and doing, practice and theory will always be a very important question for us. We became historical beings. We became social beings. We became beings programmed for learning and then for teaching, and because of that, we became beings of memory. We became beings of interfering, or for interfering. That is, we are called upon to change the world and not to establish it, not to stop it, or immobilize it. Because of that, it is impossible for us to separate thinking and acting, as if they were two different things. The contradictory unity of it is so strong that by telling you I am a theorist, I am telling you I am a practician, and vice versa. What I want to avoid is to say that we have different times—one for acting, the other one for thinking. It does not exist. What nevertheless exists is that we have preponderant-action time, preponderant-reflection time, but we always are inserted into both action and reflection.

The existence of any action without evaluation is impossible. That is, the evaluation of the action implies moments of reflection upon action. The evaluation process is very theoretical. When we get distance for evaluating, we are theorizing the action. It is impossible to separate, to consider two different things. Maybe we have two different moments inside of just one—of making theory and making action, making practice.

TF: So, what we are doing right now is both.

PF: Yes.

TF: We are reflecting, but this reflection is a part of our practice, and we are also engaging in a process which will be a public manifestation, in a book, which will be published. People will have it in their home, in a library, in their moment of reflection/action. So our reflections and their public manifestation will result in other reflections which can become a part of the practice of the readers.

PF: Yes, and I remember now a fantastic morning I spent more than ten years ago with an artist in Chicago. We were visiting the murals of Chicago. Fantastic. Afterwards, he gave me a book with the murals. In one part of the book, reference is made to my ideas of codification. Because the painters on the walls of churches, and everything, are painting, exactly, the people of the community. A text in São Paulo was a part of a mural in Chicago.

Notes

1. Information from: http://www.irn.pdx.edu/kerlinb/hotsite/Paulo_Freire.html

2. Paulo Freire, *Pedagogy of the Oppressed* (New York: Continuum, 1970). Translated by Myra Bergman Ramos.

3. From Richard Shaull's foreword to Freire, *Pedagogy of the Oppressed.*

4. Freire, *Pedagogy of the Oppressed,* p. 45.

5. Ibid., pp. 52–53.

6. Ibid., p. 61.

7. Ibid., p. 65.

8. At the Percent for Art Program, we instituted a policy where we would ask local community leaders to "sign off" prior to initiating a public art project in their community. Almost without exception they agreed. When a question is asked, and under what circumstances is, of course, key to the answer that will be given.

9. As Ann Berthoff has pointed out to me, there is a difference between decoding and decodification. She says, "Paulo Freire differentiates decoding—matching of graphic sign and sound—and decodification, interpretation, meaning making." She says that Freire and I. A. Richards are the only pedagogues that she knows of who make this differentiation. (From a letter Berthoff sent me, July 1998.)

10. Ibid., p.104.

11. The neologism "conscientization" is the central term in Freire's activist pedagogical philosophy. In the 1993 edition of *Pedagogy of the Oppressed,* the translator, presumably with Freire's consent, says that the word, "refers to learning to perceive social, political, and economic contradictions, and to take action against oppressive elements of reality." (p. 17)

12. bell hooks, *Teaching to Transgress* (New York and London: Routledge, 1994), p. 47.

13. Stanley Aronowitz, *Dead artists Live theories* (New York: Routledge, 1994). See the essay "Paulo Freire's Radical Democratic Humanism," p. 219.

14. Aronowitz, *Dead artists,* p. 229.

15. Miwon Kwon, "The Three Rivers Art Festival," in *Documents,* Number 7, Fall 1996, p. 31.

16. Ibid., p. 161.

17. Paulo Freire, *Pedagogy of the City* (New York: Continuum, 1993), pp. 130–132.

18. Johanne Lamoureaux, "Questioning the Public: Addressing the Response," in *Queues, Rendezvous Riots,* ed. George Baird and Mark Lewis (Banff: The Banff Center for the Arts, 1994), p. 150.

19. Paulo Freire, *Pedagogy of Hope* (New York: Continuum, 1994), p. 8.

20. As noted above, the translator of the 1993 edition of *Pedagogy of the Oppressed,* says that "conscientization" "refers to learning to perceive social, political, and economic contradictions, and to take action against oppressive elements of reality," p. 17.

21. As outlined in *Pedagogy of the Oppressed,* Freire's literacy program consists of a number of steps. After a team has been assembled, investigators observe the area where the literacy program will take place, under a variety of circumstances. As these investigative teams (who are both outsiders and locals) meet to discuss their observations, they come up with the "nuclei of contradiction" that will produce "meaningful thematics" for the interaction with people who enter the literacy program. These are developed into "codifications" (see footnote 4).

22. "Generative words" are words that are used in the literacy initiatives to generate meaningful dialogue.

23. After identifying the "nucleii of contradiction," the investigative team selects contradictions to develop as "codifications." These codifications are sketches, photographs, objects, or even sounds. They represent situations that are familiar to the community. As described in *Pedagogy of the Oppressed,* they are meant to be not too explicit, yet not too obscure. The former would verge on propaganda, while the latter becomes a puzzle or a guessing game. These codifications are analyzed in "thematic investigation circles" and later used in wider "culture circles."

Interview: **Mierle Laderman Ukeles**
on Maintenance
and Sanitation Art

Introduction

Mierle Laderman Ukeles has been active as an artist since the late 1960s. Her work has generally centered on issues of the environment, the city "as a living entity," and service labor, although she has undertaken a number of projects outside of the realm of public art, including installations in museums and galleries. For example, in 1997, she created an enormous installation at the museum of Contemporary Art in Los Angeles, *Unburning Freedom Hall,* examining the meaning of fire in the city. However, in this context, I will focus on Ukeles's long-standing collaboration with New York City's Department of Sanitation (DOS), where she has been the official artist-in-residence since 1977. Since her role at DOS has never been funded by the agency or clearly defined, she has had the opportunity to chart her own course, to claim the *whole* city as her site (through a system that keeps it running), and to define her "community" as *all* New Yorkers. Ukeles has been able to work her way through the various divisions of DOS to create sanitation-based art works that have included performance, video, temporary installations, and (to be completed) permanent artworks.

After an education in international relations and art, Ukeles had a child. The transformations that this brought to her life changed her art as well, as discussed in the interview that follows. The essential elements of this transformation were clearly stated in Ukeles's "Manifesto! Maintenance Art," of 1969, in which she declared that survival work—maintenance—and art, including her domestic work and her art, were one (quoted in the Introduction). With the manifesto as a backdrop, she created the seventeen different performance works including "Maintenance Art Performance Series" (1973–1974) and "I Make Maintenance Art 1 Hour Every Day" (1976).

Ukeles's first year and a half at DOS (1977–1978) was spent getting to know the agency—from the workers to the history of waste management in New York to the structure of the bureaucracy. The commissioner assigned Gloria Johnson, an assistant for Special Projects, to help Ukeles through the department. In turn, Johnson introduced her to a series of foremen and workers. Ukeles began going to DOS every day, either to do research in the city archive, to talk to employees, or simply to go out on shifts with the workers. As Ukeles became a fixture at Sanitation, Gloria Johnson realized that Ukeles would need a desk of her own. She offered Ukeles an office in Waste Disposal Planning, which she occupied for sixteen years (1977–1993) before moving to her current, larger office in Sanitation's downtown headquarters for Solid Waste Management and Engineering and Waste Prevention, Reuse, and Recycling.

Ukeles's first official work at DOS was *Touch Sanitation Performance* (1978–1980). This performance had two parts: *Handshake Ritual,* which consisted of visiting all of New York City's fifty-nine community districts, and facing 8,500 sanitation workers, shaking hands and saying to each, "Thank you for keeping New York City alive," and *Follow in Your Footsteps,* which involved replicating the sanitation workers' actions as they collected trash. As in many of her collaborative projects, Ukeles wrote a letter to the sanitation workers to explain what she was up to:

I'm creating a huge artwork called TOUCH SANITATION about and with you, the men of the Department. All of you. Not just a few sanmen or officers, or one district, or one incinerator, or one landfill. That's not the story here. New York City Sanitation is the major leagues, and I want to "picture" the entire mind-bending operation.[1]

Over the next five years, Ukeles intensified her collaboration with the Department of Sanitation, culminating in the "Touch Sanitation Show" in the fall of 1984 (cosponsored by Creative Time). This vast undertaking involved a huge exhibition at a Sanitation Department station on Fifty-ninth Street, a garbage barge ballet on the Hudson River, an environmental exhibition at Ronald Feldman gallery, and "Cleansing the Bad Names," a performance on Mercer Street with 190 participants.

In 1984, she wrote "Sanitation Manifesto!," this time speaking as the artist-in-residence at DOS. She saw the public system of sanitation as a bond that ties us all together; the subtitle of the manifesto was "Why Sanitation Can Be Used As A Model For Public Art." As opposed to other documents she had written, this text was clearly aimed at the art world, not sanitation workers. She speaks to every citizen's public interdependency and interconnectedness:

We are, all of us, whether we desire it or not, in relation to *Sanitation, implicated, dependent—if we want the City, and ourselves, to last more than a few days. I am—along with every other citizen who lives, works, visits, or passes through this space—a co-producer of Sanitation's work-product, as well as a customer of Sanitation's work. In addition, because this is a thoroughly public system, I—we—are all co-owners—we have a right to a say in all this. We are, each and all, bound to Sanitation, to restrictiveness.*[2]

While her primary focus had shifted to work in a public agency, she continued to work in traditional art world venues, often with the cooperation and collabo-

Mierle Laderman Ukeles, "Follow in Your Footsteps," performance, with the New York City Department of Sanitation, 1978, New York, New York. Photograph: Marcia Bricker courtesy of Ronald Feldman Fine Arts.

ration of DOS. For an exhibition of community-interactive projects at Project Studios One (P.S. 1) organized by Glenn Weiss and myself, Ukeles created a multifaceted collaboration that required cutting through three gallery walls. It included a 90-foot long, 18-foot wide, 13-foot high work with twenty tons of recyclables forming the walls, ceiling, and floor, and a sound work created with the sounds of recycling. The work, *Re:Entry,* was fabricated from all of the materials that were being recycled by DOS at the time.

While *Re:Entry* was an ambitious project for P.S. 1, it was only a maquette or prototype for a part of Ukeles's permanent work called *Flow City,* which will be the public portion of a marine transfer station at Fifty-ninth Street and the Hudson River. Ukeles's contribution will be made up of three basic components: a 248-foot ramp (much like the P.S. 1 model), a "glass bridge" for viewing the mixed waste and recycling operation, and a 24-monitor multimedia wall, including live camera images from sites such as the Fresh Kills Landfill.

This is an unusual public art project in that Ukeles intends to change the meaning and use of the site. Without *Flow City,* the facility would never be open to the public. Instead of allowing the building to remain separated from the city, she wants to draw the people into the transfer station's inner workings, or more accurately, to help them understand viscerally that they are already implicated in the plant's inner workings.

At the present time, Mierle Ukeles is beginning to participate on a design team that will address the 2002 closing of Staten Island's Fresh Kills Landfill and its eventual opening to the public as a park. Her participation on the team will be funded by New York City's Percent for Art Program. Fresh Kills, the city's only operating landfill, covers 3,000 acres, and its enormity is mind-boggling. The *New York Times* described the landfill thus:

It grows cell by cell, each 20 feet high and 1,000 to 2,000 feet in length, advancing 75 feet a day as giant trucks dump more and more, and 35-ton vehicles with giant metal rollers compact the earth . . . Nearly 600 people work [at Fresh Kills Landfill] unloading the barges that arrive 24 hours a day, six days a week . . . The fill rate, at 14,000 tons per day, 306 days a year, equals five million cubic yards per year.[3]

While certainly not our greatest achievement, the landfill *is* the world's largest manmade structure. Though Ukeles has spent many years observing the landfill and has been working on related issues for the last thirty years, her budget for work on this design team calls for hundreds of hours of additional research. She plans to know the landfill "inside out" before beginning to contemplate what design might begin to address the needs of the site. She will undoubtedly consult with a wide range of people within and outside the Department of Sanitation, a range that would be impossible if she were not already *in* the agency.

Ukeles's presence at Sanitation is a complex fusion of outsider (independent artist) and insider (long-term fixture in the Department). In working on Percent for Art projects, I met many Sanitation administrators, *all* of whom know Ukeles personally. A typical response to Ukeles and her work came from a contract officer who had been at Sanitation for over thirty years. (Ukeles's two-and-a-half decades at DOS, by the way, is not a particularly long tenure by department standards. Many workers go to Sanitation for job security and spend their entire adult life there.) When Ukeles's name came up, the officer chuckled, and said that she was a "pain in the ass" who had put him through a lot of extra work. "But seriously," he said, "she's really a dynamic lady. Do you know she took the time to meet every sanitation worker when she came on board?" His attitude was one of amused bewilderment mixed with appreciation for what she had done for the agency and its workers.

In a 1994 *New York Times* article, Emily Lloyd, then the new commissioner of Sanitation, discussed how she had overcome initial doubts about the Department's artist-in-residence. She said of Ukeles:

Her philosophy is my own . . . She's saying, We have to understand that waste is an extension of ourselves and how we inhabit the planet, that sanitation workers are not untouchables that we don't want to see. She advocates having our facilities be transparent and be visited as a way for people to be accountable for the waste they generate.[4]

This is a remarkably succinct summary of Ukeles's goals, and it demonstrates the commissioner's commitment to environmental consciousness rather than simple waste removal. What is left out is the means that Ukeles employs. After all, she is an artist, feminist, environmentalist, and social activist, probably in that order.

This interview, conducted in spring of 1996, focuses on Ukeles's early work, and how she came to collaborate with the New York City Department of Sanitation. The manuscript has been edited and revised by the artist in Winter 1999. Certain word usage, punctuation, and capitalization are Ukeles's addition, and they reflect the emphatic way that she talks and writes.

Tom Finkelpearl: Where did you go to school?

Mierle Laderman Ukeles: My undergraduate degree is in international relations and history, at Barnard. While I was an undergraduate, I would return home every summer to Colorado, where I was born, and go to art school at the University of Colorado at Boulder. I was leading two lives. I wrote my senior thesis on Tanganyika, but after a trip to Africa, as an appointed aide to President John F. Kennedy's Delegation for Independence in 1961, I decided that the diplomatic world was too constricted, too diplomatic, so I chose art. I got into Pratt Institute, and I went there in the early 1960s. I was making very personal works. The artist Bob Tannen had thrown out a whole bunch of cheesecloth. I found this soft, sort of translucent / transparent, wonderful material, and started wrapping, binding, pouring huge amounts of watered glue to stiffen it, tying over and over, in a very ritualistic way that ended up looking quite organic. I wanted to see how much I could stuff these forms until they were so completely full of energy they would almost burst. I recognized that I was in a new ballgame; I both didn't know what I was doing, and yet I was the only one knowing what I was doing; I had entered my own zone, and became a real artist.

The dean and the chairman of Pratt Institute told my teacher, Robert Richenberg, that I was making pornographic art, and I had to be stopped. This was in the beginning of the sixties when the rumblings of students beginning to get very uppity was happening, and they said to him: "Obviously, she's oversexed, and we have to put a stop to this!" They were hysterical. But Richenberg kept saying: "This is terrific, original," kept my work openly displayed, and encouraged me to keep going. So I kept working, and they fired him. I was some kind of last straw for them. I thought the whole school would march out on this issue of academic freedom, that the faculty would leave. I was so naive. There were a few demonstrations. Tom Hess wrote an article in the New York Times, and then things slid back to quiescence. The cause died. I switched for a semester to the University of Colorado at Boulder, and got a lot of support from my professor, Roland Reiss. Then I tried Pratt again for one more semester, but the tone there sickened me. I just couldn't stand being there; so I quit. I went back to Colorado again, to the University of Denver, and got a teacher's certificate to teach art. For the art education degree, I wrote several curricula—a one-year curriculum on Love & Hate, and one on Peace & War. I liked thinking about art education very, very much. I subsequently returned to New York, and in 1967, started grad school all over again at New York University, in a program called Inter-Related Arts, where, eventually in 1973, I got a master's degree.

While in Boulder and Denver, I continued developing the stuffings that I had started at Pratt. They turned into room-sized installations. I was looking for structures to wrap, stripping away the canvas and using the frame as an armature. Soon I needed stronger structures: window frames, doors, bedsprings, baby furniture—cribs and playpens. My being drawn to the baby furniture really scared me. I was buying rags by the hundreds of pounds, then started buying stuffed animals—hundreds of pounds of stuffed animals, because they had more coherence than rags, and I liked them better. I was stuffing these animals into tubes and rags, but my pieces would get troubles. I would be stuffing and pouring one piece all day long, sliding around, sort of skating, in gluey water. I would push past the point of tension it could withstand, and it would get hernias—explode on me—all the stuffing was so wet, full of glue, drowning in glue, and all this crap running all over the floor.

Then in the summer of 1966, I got an idea that I could stuff these things with air—inflatable sculptures. I could make very big work (because I always wanted to make big work), and these things could be in the water, on the land, in the air. When they weren't being used, they would fold up. The central image was a giant piece that, when I was finished showing it, I would fold it up, put it in my back pocket, and I was free. I wouldn't have to take care of these works, schlep them around and worry about them.

This was the sixties when materiality was suspect. There was something wrong with occupying space, something imperialistic about it. This was the time of Vietnam, where the United States essentially was spreading beyond its borders, dominating, controlling. Art, on the other hand, was about utter freedom. Freedom was Art's only ally. Any connection to an institution was corrupting. The de-materialization of the art-work really came out of pulling away from materiality itself, the marketplace, selling objects. It was also an ecological idea.

All this was aimed at work that would be free, unencumbered, and not imperialistic. But it ended up differently. I worked in heat-sealing factories in New York and Philadelphia, trying to make these inflatables, where they use di-electric radio-frequency sealing. I didn't understand until later that I was still trying to hand-make my art even though I was completely dependent upon industrial processes. So there was a big glitch between concept and process. And they all leaked. They had horrible maintenance problems. I got deeply involved in valves, chambers, openings and closings. I was also dependent upon getting materials from companies that weren't used to working with artists, and they neglected to tell me basic things, such as the vinyl cracks and the seals break when the temperature drops below a certain degree.

At the same time, I became pregnant. I sort of became an inflatable myself. My own body was expanding, which seemed not unrelated to what I was *doing. I was the favorite student of a famous sculptor. The first time I came to class when it was obvious that I was pregnant, he took a look at me, and said: "Well, I guess now you can't be an artist." You know, things were different then. It threw me. I got amazingly angry and disappointed in him. So we had our baby, that we wanted so much. Then I entered this, this time of "Who am I?" and "How am I going to do this?" I literally divided my life in half. Half of my time I was The Mother. I was afraid to go away from my baby. I was very nervous about leaving her with people that I didn't know. And half of the time, I was The Artist, because I was in a panic that if I stopped doing my work I would lose it. I just had this feeling. Maybe it was a lack of confidence, or maybe I had struggled for so many years to become an artist, I felt that if I stopped working, it—the magic "it"—would evaporate, because that happens to a lot of people.*

TF: *Yes. Like me.*

MLU: *I was so rigid. It was 2.5 days of the 5-day work-week: 50/50 down the middle. But things were a little confused. When I was with my baby, changing a diaper for the 200th time, I would actually feel my brain saying to me: "Is this what I'm supposed to be doing?" The repetition was astounding to me. You know, I hadn't baby-sat; I hadn't stayed inside at home when I was growing up except when I was sick. I focused on being an artist, being free, being like Jackson Pollock. Like Marcel Duchamp. I wanted this baby. It is obviously not a superficial thing if a human life is dependent on you, in your hands. So, nothing in my whole, long, long education, in international relations, in sculpture, nothing educated me for how to bring a wholeness to taking care, not only creating life, but maintaining life. The creating, the originating, that's the easy part. And that's actually always true, even in art. The art, the creation, is often like that [snaps her fingers]. It's the implementation of getting it out there, follow-through, hanging in there, deepening, not throwing up your hands and running away. I had no models, none, in my entire education to deal with repetitiveness, continuity. I had the best education that this society provides but nothing in my head to help think about getting from this minute to the next minute. I was doing work that's so common; yet there was no cultural language for this work. People would ask: "Do you do anything?" I had never worked so hard in my whole life as when I had a little baby. Ever. Trying to be a decent parent, trying to keep myself alive as an artist, trying to make some money. I was working like a maniac. But there were no words in the culture that gave value for the work I was doing.*

So I had a crisis, an absolute crisis. I felt like I was two completely different people. Inside I could physically feel my brain separating from my hands, and I think I became an artist because I liked having my brain connected to my hands. I had spent my childhood making up games while playing around in the mud, outside, in Denver. I was one person. I was all connected. My notion of being a free person was being a whole person. I had to come to grips with how vastly selfish the ego was that my education directed me toward "refining." The way I was educated to construct my perception and thinking through almost all my education was "I want," or "I think," you know, "I think that Africa blah . . . ," you know "I, I," it was "I."

If anything got in my way of being an artist, I was out the door. It was painful, scary, and hard. Before we got married, my husband, Jack, and I took three years of yelling and screaming at each other before we could get to a "we." I mean, this was serious. It was hard for me to get to a "we" where I felt that my artist part would not get disintegrated. But we kept working at it. I mean, we are still working at it and we're doing a great job. It's not an easy thing. I know what I'm scared about. I'm scared about something that's legitimate—to lose freedom. It's hard. You can lose it, at any moment.

But when I had a baby, I realized that my language needed to open up out of the "I." O.K., I'm changing my baby's diaper. The baby's crying. The baby needs, the baby; the baby needs. The need is not in me, it's outside in another human being. At the very same time, in my work, so much trouble with maintenance of the inflatables whose purpose was to be so free, unfettered, and ended up being a complete list of maintenance nightmares— leaks, this, that, this, that. I spent four years trying to make these things. Four years of factories. Total maintenance troubles. And out of free choice, we had this child. I wanted this child. I fell madly in love with this child. So, I became a maintenance worker. I no longer understood who I was. I got so pissed-off. I became utterly furious at not feeling like one whole human be-

ing. Then the fury turned into an illumination, and, in one, sitting, I wrote a manifesto calling maintenance "art."

TF: *This is now 1969?*

MLU: *Yes. I wrote that if I'm the artist, then whatever I say is art, is art. It isn't an ego-thing, it's what the artist needs. It's the work conditions that you need to make art—to be able to say what your work is. I loved Pollock because he was so physical, and I swallowed all the propaganda about action, about abstract expressionism, moving into the unknown, making freedom. For him, make a work and it's behind you, it's not even there for you anymore. Your job is to move into the unknown. Alone. This model was so phony. Pollock appeared autonomous, didn't need anybody, hardly needed gravity itself. It wasn't living in the world, in a planet that has finite resources, where we need to stay alive, in connection with other people. It was a total phony thing. It had an evil underside of autonomy, only the "I"; not acknowledging who holds you up, and who supports you, and who's providing the food, and the raw materials, and who are the people who are taking them out of the earth, and what are* their *working conditions, and what are the pollution costs of moving materials all around the world, who's paying for what, and any fact of human life. The model of the avant-garde that I swallowed, that I lusted for, presented images, embedded within and contiguous with individual art works, of human freedom and free expression. The exquisite articulation and refinement of free expression in these works are among the greatest accomplishments that have ever happened in the world. But there can also be an evil side to that model of freedom.*

TF: *So the disconnection of modernism created a personal crisis for you.*

MLU: *Right. But I was having the privilege of taking care of another human being to the extent that her life was dependent upon what I did, and that gave me a connection to most other people in the world who live their lives having to deal with how to stay alive, how to keep their families alive. I went to the school of diapering my baby, feeding my baby, putting the needs of another in front of my own needs. That was the basis of the connection. I had a re-*

sponsibility, and my "I" could provide the needs. I had the ability to provide the needs for a child, and the child could thrive, or die depending upon what I did. It was that powerful. And through that, I got the beginning of an understanding of working to get from this minute to the next minute; to get that close to the unfurling of basic existence. It's as if I looked up suddenly, after all my formal education in autonomy, and I saw people doing support work, to keep something else going, and not necessarily only themselves. Workers.

TF: How were all of these ideas in your Manifesto?

MLU: First of all, the Manifesto proposed an exhibition, called "CARE," where I would move into a museum with my husband and my baby, and I would do my family things, and also take care of the museum, maintain it, as well as taking care of, servicing, the visitors who came to the museum. The museum would be home. And that would be the art-work. In other words, I would clean it, I would change the lightbulbs, whatever was necessary to keep this place operating. The museum's life-processes would become visible. That would be the art-work.

Second, the Manifesto's exhibition proposed to ask all different kinds of people in society, "What do you have to do to keep alive? How do you get from minute to minute?" There would be many tables where people would be interviewed about what they did to stay alive. In Western culture, you're not supposed to talk about this stuff in polite company. Certainly in 1969, there were very few words to talk about ongoing sustenance.

The third part of the exhibition was constructing an image of the earth (outside) as a needy and finite place. Every day, containers of ravaged earth, air, and water would be delivered to the museum. Each day, scientists and pseudo-scientists (artists) would process and purify these elements in the museum, and then return the elements to the city in a healthy mode. My image of the museum was the site of alchemy, where polluted earth, polluted water, polluted air, could become transformed and returned to the city, revived. It was such fantasy, right? But I actually believed that creativity and restitution sit right next to each other, that scientific pursuit of knowledge can teach us how to use a material without destroying its integrity and poten-

tiality for re-use. But the creative jumps come from artists. Sort of leaps across things, crashing categories.

That was the Manifesto. I sent it to Jack Burnham, whose writings I admired. He published an article about the end of the avant-garde in Artforum *in 1971, and excerpted most of the Manifesto in there, using my work as an example of another way to proceed. I just sent it to him and he published it. I thought, "This is a snap!" So I sent this proposal to the Whitney museum. I got a letter back—on half a piece of paper—from James Monte, a curator, and he said: "Try your ideas on or in an art gallery before approaching a museum." That was it. A slap on the wrist. But he misunderstood. You see, I felt that it was the museum that could be the site where the public comes to understand itself. Well, I dropped the museum proposal; but continued on with maintenance as art.*

TF: After the Manifesto, what sorts of projects did you undertake?

MLU: In 1973, I was invited to be in "C. 7,500," a show that Lucy Lippard organized of women artists. I sent several photo-series documenting maintenance tasks such as Jack [Ukeles's husband] diapering the baby, me dressing the children—by now there were three—to go out in the winter and undressing them to come in, doing the laundry, washing the dishes, other workers in my neighborhood doing repetitive tasks. The exhibition traveled, and I got jealous. I thought, if my work can travel, how about me? So I started contacting these locations where the show was going, asking them if I could come do a maintenance art performance work. I ended up doing about 17 different maintenance art performance works. I dealt with maintenance of continuity in nature, personal maintenance, institutional maintenance, maintenance of ethnic traditions. In these art institutions, I'd take over the persona of The Maintenance Worker, who is supposed to be unseen, and cleans behind the scenes, after hours. Or the guard, who keeps the keys silently. I was trying to bring maintenance out in public.

In 1976 I was invited to be in a group show called "ART <--> WORLD," at the Whitney's branch at 55 Water Street. I went to check out the site and said, "Oh my God, a skyscraper!" I had been waiting for years to get my hands on a skyscraper. Why? Because a skyscraper needs tremendous main-

Mierle Laderman Ukeles, "Hartford Wash," 1973, part of Maintenance Art Performance Series, 1973–1974 at Wadsworth Atheneum, Hartford, Connecticut. Photograph courtesy of Ronald Feldman Fine Arts, New York, New York.

tenance. In this sort of high-end commercial building, the maintenance people are supposed to be completely invisible. There's an Apollonian ethos in a skyscraper. Its maintenance mission is to create, during the property owners and their clients' prime action hours, an appearance of stasis, beyond time. The goal is to look publicly as if nothing has happened and everything is always clean, always quiet. Which is actually shocking if you think about it. In other words, everything is secret. At 55 Water Street, for example, the maintenance workers were supposed to wear ties, and keep their long-sleeved shirts buttoned, while cleaning, because that was the proper presentation for the real estate interests that owned the building—that one could do this maintenance work without even sweating. Of, course, at night, when the office workers went home, when no "one" (important) was watching, people would wash the floors in their undershirts.

The branch-museum concept was actually a utopian idea of the Whitney: a branch in an office building, so that people could have art right in the

Mierle Laderman Ukeles, I Make Maintenance Art One Hour Every Day, 1976, Whitney Museum of American Art Downtown, New York, New York. Photograph courtesy of Ronald Feldman Fine Arts.

middle of their work day. I loved that idea. You didn't have to leave your life to go to the art museum, the art museum would come to your life. Except that the 300 maintenance workers in the building never, ever came into the museum, except to change a lightbulb and wash the floor. So I tried to turn the tables, make a piece with all the workers that kept this building operational twenty-four hours a day. The Whitney got me connected up with the owners, who said they would allow me to do this. I wrote a letter to 300 workers in this building. I invited them to do an art-work with me. The piece was called I Make Maintenance Art One Hour Every Day. *I asked them to select one hour of their regular work, and think of that work, that one hour, as art. It was completely up to them if they wanted to do this or not. Opening up the power to choose and power to name was critical.*

I went around with a Polaroid camera documenting their work. There's an inch of white space at the bottom of each picture, which always intrigued me, so I made labels that fit that space. One label said "Maintenance Work," and the other said "Maintenance Art." I would approach a worker, and I would say, "Can I take your picture?" If they said yes (and they all said yes), I would show the picture to them when it came out of the camera and said, "Is this art or work?" In other words, have I crossed your path during that hour that you picked? Some people would say, "This is art." Sometimes, when people were working together, one person would be making art, and one person would be making work. I also gave everyone a button that said "I Make Maintenance Art One Hour Every Day," which, shockingly, most people wore for the seven weeks of this exhibition.

I remember one guy who was probably the greatest maintenance worker of all. He was a star, every single move looked effortless. His name was Bruno. This building is huge. The hallways are literally a block long. One day the elevator door opened up, and there's Bruno. He had stuffed the elevator with huge garbage bags; then he saw me. I was a block away. He yelled, "This is not art! This will never be art! This is not art!" And the doors shut. It was so great! I caught up with another worker, Vanilla, at 4:00 a.m. in the sixth week of the performance work. "I've been waiting for you every night for six weeks," she told me. Then she took me on rounds. She was making Art.

There was a tremendous testing of me by workers, which was a fine learning experience. First, they needed to check out if I worked secretly for the owners of the building. Second, did I work for the unions? Third, did I work undercover for the immigration service, because a lot of people had a shaky status. What got me accepted was that I kept showing up every day, just like they did. I entered their work-patterns. I actually worked two shifts a day. I just kept coming back.

The building at 55 Water Street was the headquarters of Chemical Bank. Much of the cash in New York City is stashed there, five levels below ground. There were levels and levels of security. The Whitney tried to get me admitted into these places, and everybody said nothing doing, but the maintenance people took me right down there with them. Maintenance people have access. Every day I mounted the photographs I had taken in the museum. When I started the show, "my space" was empty. Over the seven weeks, there was a gradual accumulation of photographs that recorded the choices of the people: this is art, this is not art.

TF: How many pictures did you take?

MLU: By the end, over 700. It ended up looking like a grid, like the building itself, actually. But it was a grid of voices of the people who didn't have a way for their choices to have a cultural venue. That was the function of my piece in the museum—700 choices whether or not to call their activity art—part of the culture. Of course, there were many, many stories that people began to tell me about how they didn't like being invisible.

      When I wrote this Manifesto, I had come to understand that, as a woman, as a mother, I was connected to most people in the world—the whole entire world of maintenance workers. Women were never invited to become a maintenance class, we were just told: "You are like this. We know what you think. We know what you are. You take care of us." Women have been defined like that within the domestic sphere, while service workers, of either gender, do this stuff outside, to make a living. That's most of the people in the country, and most of the people in the world. If women could get together with service workers, as a political coalition, they could become a majority with great potential power. Society could get reorganized. Taking care of the planet could grow out of ancient work-wisdom, and would be attached to great power. Now the feminist movement failed to a large degree because it never understood the inherent power of what women were walking away from, the power to connect with other people who did a similar kind of work. The feminist movement failed to take into consideration, for example, the millions of women of color who were already working. They had always worked, because they had no choice. They always had to balance several lives; they didn't want to starve to death; or in a more luxurious longer view they wanted to lift themselves and their loved ones up from day to day subsistence. Those women never felt connected to the angst of identity that asks work outside to provide the answer to: Who am I? What do I want to become? It was a privileged, thus limited discourse in the feminist movement. However, it is a great discourse in human history, that came out of the civil rights discourse of, Who has rights? Who are we? What is this country about? Who is free? The questions raised by early feminism are a continuation of a great movement in human freedom. Again, like the avant-garde, it was unconnected, not understanding that unless everybody is ask-

ing those questions to each other, we don't yet have a complete conversation.

It was a partial image, not a very whole image. A lot of things, I think, have actually gotten better, largely because more people, including women, have entered into public life. I've been around men who also accepted a dirty deal for many, many years. Where they accepted, as a given, that they might get injured at work, that they had a very, very unhealthy, unsafe work environment. Now, I think that there's a lot more room for people to say, "Hey! I shouldn't have to get silicosis for United States Steel." You don't automatically trade away your health to make a living. I really believed that there could have been a revolution linking up feminism with service workers, crossing gender with economic class; that did not happen. Instead we got partial and mainly middle class measures: health clubs, preventive maintenance, flextime. There was no major reorganizing.

TF: Was it just after this project that you hooked up with Sanitation?

MLU: Yes. David Bourdon wrote a review of the project at the Downtown Whitney. He ended with a very tongue-in-cheek statement. Remember, this was in the fiscal crisis in the seventies, when the city was laying people off like crazy, and there was great fear that the city itself was going to go bankrupt, and die. So Bourdon said that perhaps the Sanitation Department could think of its work as performance art, and replace some of the budget, which had been cut, with a grant from the National Endowment for the Arts. I read this comment, and I thought, "Sanitation Department!" I had dealt with 300 workers in a skyscraper, and I thought that's the most people that any artist could ever work with. I looked up the address and sent a photocopy of this review to the Sanitation commissioner. I got a call from a person on the commissioner's staff, and she said to me, "How would you like to make art with 10,000 people?" And I said, "I'll be right over." And I met the commissioner.

TF: Who was the commissioner?

MLU: Anthony Vaccarello. He had a great influence on me because he said, "Go talk to the workers. They're great people." He arranged for me to have some-

body introduce me to many people and to show me various kinds of sanitation facilities: garages, "sections," (locker rooms), incinerators, marine transfer stations, landfills. Then I met Superintendent Leroy Adolph. He was the head of the training center for new sanitation workers. I spent a lot of time there. He insisted on teaching me every aspect of this department. He gave me a big view—cleaning, collection, waste disposal, all the shifts, twenty-four hours a day. He sent me out on field research; I started talking to sanitation workers, going to incinerators, landfills, bumping into people. I had already done many works with different maintenance workers, so I recognized the maintenance talk right away, but there was a whole other layer of the stigma from garbage. It was so bad. There was such a level of disconnection ratified by almost everybody that I met, I'm invisible, I don't count, I'm part of the garbage. It was sick.

Here's the picture around 1977. In a sanitation garage, there are no women, but there are entire walls of photographs from raunchy pornographic magazines well beyond Playboy. It's a very hard, ugly environment, very unforgiving, so that these men would fill up entire walls with images of women who were soft, yielding, and available.

TF: *And demeaned, lower than them.*

MLU: *Right. These facilities, in the seventies, were in abandoned jails, condemned firehouses. I mean, these were utterly disgusting places. They had no furniture of their own. If the city wanted to give a message to the workers that they are garbage, they couldn't have designed a more efficient environment than what sanitation workers had in those days. So, I'm standing there, a feminist, in front of all these pornographic photographs, and I'm talking away about my connections to them, how they keep the city alive. And then they would say things like this: "Do you know why everybody hates us? Because they think we're their maids," or "because they think we're their mother." There were always images of women, but it never occurred to these people that this would be an insult to me. I was supposed to automatically understand, oh, of course they hate you because they think that you, the man, are a woman, that if you were a woman it would be natural to hate you for this. It was so split, Tom, so alienated, so sick.*

Mierle Laderman Ukeles, "Touch Sanitation Performance," 1978–1980, with the New York City Department of Sanitation, New York, New York. Photograph courtesy of Ronald Feldman Fine Arts.

These workers would say, "Nobody ever sees me. I'm invisible." I mean, they're out performing their work in public every day in New York City. Why aren't they seen? I mean, the disconnection between what is in front of your face, and what's invisible, what's culturally acceptable, thus formed and articulated, and what is outside culture, thus formless and unspeakable, was almost complete. It was so severely split, that I thought to myself, "This is a perfect place for an artist to sit, inside of this place, because things are so bad that they've become very clear." The level of denial was so extreme outside in the general culture, and at the same time, inside the Sanitation Department, that I felt I couldn't find a more valid place to make an art that aims to create a new language.

Initially, I proposed a series of works that I called "Maintenance Art Works Meets the NYC Department of Sanitation." The first was a performance work called "Touch Sanitation." I felt that I had to establish a certain validity for an artist to be present and counted inside this heavy work system.

It was also a way to gain a level of credibility for myself, so that I would get approval to proceed to the other works that I wanted to do. I saw "Touch Sanitation" as a portrait of New York City as a living entity. To create this, I decided to do the opposite of what social science or the mass media does. Social science samples, abstracts, selects. The media takes a huge, vastly complex system and boils it down to a sound bite. I wanted to do the opposite. I went to every single place, every single facility throughout the New York City Department of Sanitation. I tried to face every single worker, person to person, as if there were no means of mass communication. I faced each person, shook hands with each person, and said to each person, "Thank you for keeping New York City alive." I was saying that we have to start over again, that culture begins here with maintenance and survival. Culture and survival are twins; they go together. Art begins at the same time as basic survival systems. Art doesn't wait to enter after everything else is all put together. The only way to do this was the simplest, human way, by walking out into the city, and facing each worker, and walking out into the streets, and staying behind the trucks, and listening to people, and seeing the city from garbage can to garbage can, from bag to bag, from street to street, through all the weather.

I modeled my performance work on work shifts, constancy, endurance, on all kinds of virtues that didn't have too much value in culture. I thought it would take three months. It took eleven months. I'm always amazed that nobody asks me, "Well, how did you find all the workers?" I spent a lot of time designing the mapping of this piece. I modeled the work on the same mapping processes the Sanitation Department uses to go find the garbage. I liked the idea that sanitation goes everywhere, and they never, ever stop. That's a great model for art. Art should go everywhere all the time. There's no special place, no special time. The Sanitation Department divided up the city in districts, and then subdistricts. So I did the same thing, and I went to the first district in Manhattan, then the first district in the Bronx, first district in Brooklyn, first district in Queens, first district in Staten Island, then the second in Manhattan, and so on. I circled the city. I could have done all of Manhattan, then all of the Bronx, but I felt that if I did that, then the people of Manhattan would think that I ran away and never came back. This way, I did a circle, came back again. It took something like ten circles. Little by little, the word got out; it grew.

At 6:00 a.m. roll calls, I started making fiery and fiery-er speeches. I would say, "I'm not here to watch you, I'm not here to study you, to judge you, I'm here to be with you. That's the art, and I want to say thank you." What a great way to see the whole city!

I got some grants, which I used for audiotaping hundreds of hours of interviews and videotaping during seven days, which was all I could afford throughout the eleven months of the performance work. When we took video, I always said this was going to end up in a show. Then I would ask the sanitation workers, "Where should the show be?" A lot of sanitation workers said, "Let them come to us." One of the best things a worker said was, "Look. You're not a normal artist. You're a real artist. This show has to be real with trucks and barges. So why can't they see what it's like here?" Then I asked, "Would you bring your family, if it were in a sanitation facility?" And many would say no. I'd say, "Why not?" And they'd say, "'Cause it's a dump. It's awful here." And I'd say, "But you feed them out of what you do here." And they'd look at me, and they'd say, "You're right, but I'm not bringing my family here. Why can't we be seen in a nice place. In an art place." So I realized what I was hearing was that Sanitation has no place that's understood as being inside culture, as a place for everybody. So I chose to re-present my citywide portrait journey as one exhibition, called "Touch Sanitation Show," sundered into two separate kinds of places: one in a workplace and, simultaneously, the other in an art gallery. It was divided, disconnected, because the reality is disconnected, because there is no one place where this could really be fully manifested.

It took four years to raise the money, get the zillions of permissions required, and make the works for this show.

The workplace part of the show, called "Transfer Station Transformation" was in the old marine transfer station at Fifty-ninth Street and the Hudson River. It began with a barge ballet that I choreographed, with six garbage barges and two tugs. I asked to work with the best tugboat captain in New York Harbor. I said to this guy, when I sat down with him, "What have you always wanted to do, if the Coast Guard wasn't watching you?" He responded immediately, "I always wanted to make a figure eight across the Hudson River." But he took out his tide book, looked up the date that we had picked, and said, "It's too dangerous. I'll do a spiral." For me, the spiral was perfect.

Mierle Laderman Ukeles, "Marrying the Barges," part of "Touch Sanitation Show," 1984, Hudson River, New York City. Commissioned by New York City Department of Sanitation and Creative Time. Photo: Marcia Bricker courtesy of Ronald Feldman Fine Arts.

We did a ballet called "Marrying the Barges," which is a sanitation term for linking up four barges. The transfer station itself was a 35,000-square-foot facility.

I did a sound work with Stephen Erickson, called Trax for Trucks & Barges, *selected from the hundred hours of very frank, unscripted interviews that I had with sanitation workers. They used to say to me, "If only the trucks could talk." So I had 18 trucks lined up, a full array of vehicles—equipment for snow removal, street cleaning, flushers, garbage trucks, and humongous equipment from the landfill. Five of the trucks spoke with different voices. Many expressed deeply felt emotions, sometimes painful to hear. The trucks were empty, because I was trying to set up a condition where the visitors to the exhibition would hear human voices coming out of the trucks, but there was nobody there. And I was hoping that as a visitor approached the big* truck, with the driver's door slightly ajar, speaking, the idea of, "Who is talking? Maybe that could be me," a role reversal possibility would get moved into the visitor's head.

These localized voice parts were interspersed with an all-over eight-track audiowork composed of field recording sounds harvested by Stephen and me from the entire Sanitation system, from the garages, to the transfer stations, to the landfill, recorded with exquisitely sensitive equipment arrayed as impeccably as if in a fine audio studio, as, for example, we tromped through the deep garbage at the landfill, capturing the rhythms of Athay wagons, cranes, and bulldozers. This part of the sound work was played through many concert-quality speakers installed throughout the entire station, deep in two barges in the slip of the Hudson River, one floor below the tipping floor, and lashed all over the steel girder ceiling. The whole place became saturated with real industrial music. The first time we turned it on, it sounded like the building was crashing down. It was fabulous.

Cut through the end wall of the transfer station, we cut this sentence, "What are we going to do with the garbage? No more landfill space RE-." A collection of giant boxcars of recyclable materials was welded to the wall, as if rising up out of the deep below. There was one big container of soda bottles, bursting through the roof, up at the top.

At the Ronald Feldman Gallery, in Soho, the site of the second half of the two-part exhibition, I was again presented with the problem of distilling Touch Sanitation Performance's citywide spatiality and year-long temporality into one place.

Again, I started with a performance work called Cleansing the Bad Names. It came from one of the thousands of stories that I had heard. The sanitation worker told me: "We were in Brooklyn. It was over 90 degrees, humid; we were very tired. We loaded a lady's garbage into the truck, and sat down on her porch steps for a minute. She opened up the door, and she said to us: 'Get away from here, you smelly garbagemen. I don't want you stinking up my porch.'"

This story, to me, crystallizes denial; it was garbage from her, not them. Then he said to me, "That stuck in my throat for seventeen years. Today you wiped that out." Bang: the best thing that ever happened to me as an artist *to date. And then he said, "Will you remember this?" His last question blew my mind. It was as if he were saying that, while, for him, I healed his ancient wound, but maybe, for me, I would forget about it by the next day. Was that the deal with me? He wanted to know. He sent me down a path, that guy. He understood the power of art. I realized he was saying to me, Listen, artist. This that I am giving you, this piece of my gut and my soul, isn't personal for you, even though I trust you enough to enter into this healing with you. This isn't your personal property; it's your job. He was really giving me a job description: My job is to take this deep-inside 1:1 exchange and make it public.*

So for the performance work at Feldman Fine Arts, I rebuilt the lady's porch on the gallery's front steps on Mercer Street. One of the functions of art is to play time over again and remake history better this time. I sent out a telex, from headquarters, all over the Sanitation Department, asking workers to tell me if anyone ever called them a bad name. I got back hundreds of names. We copied the bad names all over 75 feet of plate glass windows along the Mercer Street facade of the gallery and its neighbors. We built a two-story scaffold in front of the windows, because they were very high. For the guy who asked if I would remember, I rebuilt the porch, and 190 cleansing participants washed away all the bad names. These 190 individuals represented different cuts through society, because I felt that it's the job of the whole society to wash away the bad names, not me. I was playing out my half, enlarging this exchange of my unspoken deal with him: just as Sanitation cleans the city for all of us, it's our job to take away the stigma from our "stinking" garbage from them.

Inside the gallery there were two installations. One was called Maintenance City. *I aimed to set up a valence between an all-over installation in this large whole space and the ubiquity of one Sanitation year: Sanitation is all over the city, works everywhere, all the time. Every inch of the walls of the large front gallery was filled with a continuous print installation, a collage of thousands of clocks showing every hour of work, all the work shifts, one folding into the other, season flowing into season: a whole year's work in one room. Sanitation workers picked the colors for each season. Just overhead, a 1,500-foot transparent map painted with all of NYC's fifty-nine districts was suspended by a support web of fine wires. I wanted the weightiness of supporting the city to be a palpable presence. Four 12-foot-high video towers,*

Mierle Laderman Ukeles, Touch Sanitation Show, 1984, Ronald Feldman Fine Arts, New York, New York. Photograph courtesy of Ronald Feldman Fine Arts.

representing four seasons pierced through the map, played a multi-monitor videowork of the whole system. In the center, an old telex spewed out telex messages from me to sanitation workers endlessly.

The second installation, called Sanman's Place, *was a recreation of two Sanitation "sections," an old one and a new one. Sections were places where sanitation workers had lockers, a place to eat, wash up, go to the bathroom, a place to change from being a person to being a sanitation worker and back again. During snow emergencies they were required to sleep there. Real old sections that I encountered all over NYC, showed, I believe, how the city and the public felt about Sanitation workers. During my early research, it was one of the ugliest things I encountered: many sections all over New York City were in condemned real estate, abandoned firehouses, jails, only half a roof, bathrooms—one toilet for forty workers. Most toilets had no doors on them. Many had no heat. Sanitation never, in the history of NYC, had their own furniture, only that which someone—cops, kindergartens—threw out and what* they scavenged for themselves on the street. They began to get their own new furniture during the time I was creating Touch Sanitation Performance. Many told me this policy shift had a lot to do with the attention I was getting for the workers from my artwork.

I wanted this installation to ask the question, "What is the place of sanitation workers?" I sent another telex from headquarters all over the department asking: "What is the worst section? What's the worst locker room? The ugliest facility? The most disgusting, demeaning?" We got hundreds of responses: "We do. Us. Come see us. We have the ugliest, the worst, the most demeaning in the whole city." I went around with the official, who had been appointed to get the first new furniture for the sections in the history of New York City. We collected chairs, a desk, a table, that people had gotten from the streets, like a thrown-out, broken kindergarten chair that a 200-pound man ate his lunch on. "Take this," he yelled, "show this, what people want me to sit on. What are they telling me? Wait a minute, I'll sign my name on it." What does that tell you? When we took this furniture it was on the condition that it would never be returned; they would get new for old. We got the best of the worst.

Out of these things, I made the installation with many craftspeople from the department. Every single item came from a real section somewhere. Even the siding of the walls, one miserable toilet, stained sink, and broken, cruddy shower. We marked each board as if we were doing a historical reconstruction and these were the most precious materials. Besides furniture and bathroom, I crammed the section with a decor of "Mongo," items workers selected from the waste flow, that they refused to put in the truck—art, religious figures, dolls. I got great stuff, parts of collections from several famous treasure rooms in sections in Brooklyn and the Bronx that most workers knew about. You could see the creativity arising from the discerning selections plucked out of the city's dross in flux by these masters of flowing material. Their fascinating taste made a certain luster rise from these objects and lit up this bedraggled space.

Juxtaposed with the old section was a spanking new section, the first new furnishings. Well, the new furniture was ugly as sin, brown, fake-wood tables, and still reflected old rigid values: backless benches. "How about a back to lean on for a tired sanitation worker on lunch?" I asked an officer. "I lean," he replied, "the worker gets a bench." So even though there was still a long way to go, they were first-time use just for Sanitation workers. It meant real change was possible, and that overturned the old received wisdom that weighed down the whole department. My art had a lot to do with it.

My biggest coup was getting enough fixtures for a really humane, sufficiently large, new, clean bathroom for the new section. To me it was the culmination of clinching a new place for Sanitation. That meant several toilets with doors that locked, individual sinks, not horse sinks, and several private showers, so you didn't have to take a shower with everybody. Good lighting. I sweated blood to get them. The bureaucracy was dragging its heels on this one, even though they had turned themselves inside out for me on every other thing I had requested. I hung in there refusing an offer of one sink, one toilet, one shower, even though new, because it was the same old message: forty workers, one-half hour for lunch, one bathroom, one toilet. Nothing doing. I said I would shut down the show. (This was a few days before the opening.) The bottleneck got released only from a direct order by Commissioner Norman Steisel to "Just do it!" They appeared and they signaled a revolution! How ironic: bathroom/icon/Sanitation!

High on a locker, between the old section and the new, a one-hour videowork circled on a rotating disc, showing hundreds of workers talking, as I made my journeys around the city in "Touch Sanitation" about the deal of their "place" with the citizens, seen now in the context of the old section and now in the context of the new section. I was trying to raise the question about where these people with our garbage belong—trapped in the old place, which itself is made of garbage, or in a place that we can create anew.

Postscript (written by Ukeles in 1999)

I look back at this "show" that took place fifteen years ago and happened seven years after I landed in Sanitation. I am amazed at the level of cooperation, participation, and interaction I got from every single layer, office, bureau, division of an entire city agency—who were not known before as contemporary art specialists. For example, at the transfer station, for a five-

week show, to counter municipal nervousness about allowing the public into an old, dangerous workplace, they erected a waist-high steel fence along the 350-foot tipping floor. Three kinds of electricians—automotive, in-house, exterior—wired the station for sound. Everyone pitched in: people from different, sometimes competitive parts of the department itself, to completely unrelated people. A private commercial gallery turned itself inside out, literally, to become a public art installation with sanitation trades working next to sanitation workers working next to gallery preparators. We just did it.

I dreamed that I could make public art grow from inside a public infrastructure system outward to the public and that the growing would affect both the inside as well as the outside. When I first got here, people said that the way things were—the terrible way—was the way things would always be. "That's just the way it will always be." Hundreds of people said that to me in great sorrow. It's simply not true. I learned in Sanitation that vision and will can change just about anything. Didn't Art always know that?

Notes

1. Mierle Laderman Ukeles, "Dear Sanman," letter to Sanitation workers inaugurating *Touch Sanitation Performance,* 1979.

2. Mierle Laderman Ukeles, "Sanitation Manifesto!" published in *The Act* No. 4, 1990, pp. 84–85.

3. Matthew Weld, "Buying Time on Mount Garbage," *New York Times,* May 11, 1993, p. B4.

4. James Barron, "Art Work Is (Yes, Really) Garbage," *New York Times.*

Interview: **Jagoda Przybylak**
on Alien Staff

Introduction

The following two interviews discuss *Alien Staff,* a project initiated by Krzysztof Wodiczko. He has created a number of different versions of the staff in collaboration with immigrants in Europe and the United States. The particular version discussed here was made in collaboration with Jagoda Przybylak. Przybylak received her graduate degree in architecture at the Warsaw Polytechnic Institute. Her experimental photographic works have been shown in Poland and Europe. In the United States, her photographs have been presented at the International Center of Photography in New York and the Hirshhorn Museum in Washington, D.C. In 1981, days before martial law was imposed, she left Poland for New York City. The political situation in Poland forced her to remain in the United States, living and working in limbo while waiting for the legalization of her immigration status. During this period, her experiences were similar to thousands of Polish immigrant women in New York, employed as low-paid office or domestic workers. Since 1986, Przybylak has been teaching photography at the New York Institute of Technology.

  Krzysztof Wodiczko has created a number of interactive projects (summarized prior to his interview). In *Alien Staff,* Wodiczko has experimented more directly with public interaction—starting with his own interaction with the operators of the *Alien Staffs,* interactions between the operators and the instruments as "transitional objects," then the multiple interactions that are created on the street, the documents and reflections on these interactions in print, the attempted recreation of the interactions in the gallery, and so on. Here is how Wodiczko described the *Alien Staff* in a handout at Galerie Lelong in New York city, at a 1996 exhibition that brought together all of the *Alien Staffs,* and other immigrant instruments, along with written, photographic, and video documentation:

The Alien Staff (El Xenobàcul)

  The Alien Staff *is a piece of storytelling equipment and a legal and ethical communication instrument and network for immigrants. It gives the singular operator-immigrant a chance to directly "address" anyone in the city who may be attracted by the symbolic form of the equipment, by the character of the "broadcast" program, and by the live presence and performance of its owner.*

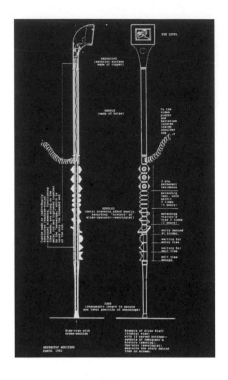

Krzysztof Wodiczko, drawing for Alien Staff, 1992. Photograph courtesy of the artist and Galerie Lelong.

The Alien Staff resembles the biblical shepherd's rod. It is equipped with a mini video monitor and small loudspeaker. A video player and batteries are located in a specially designed shoulder bag. The small size of the monitor, its eye-level location and its closeness to the operator's face are important aspects of the design. Since the small image on the screen attracts attention and provokes observers to come very close to the monitor and therefore to the operator's face, the usual distance between the immigrant, the stranger, will decrease. Upon closer examination, it becomes clear that the image on the face of the screen and the actual face of the person are of the same immigrant. The double presence in "media" and "life" invites a new perception of a stranger as "imagined" (a character on the screen) or as "experienced" (an actor off stage—a real life person). Since both the imagination and the experience of the viewer are increasing with the decreasing distance, while the program itself reveals unexpected aspects of the alien's experience, his or her presence becomes both legitimate and real. This change in distance and perception might provide a ground for greater respect and self-respect, and become an inspiration for crossing the boundary between a stranger and a non-stranger.

The first model of the Alien Staff was built and tested in Barcelona in June, 1992 by Dgenevou Samou, an African immigrant from Burkina Faso, with the assistance of the Fundacio Tapies and the help of SOS-Racisme. A second model was built, and its design further transformed in Brooklyn, during the summer, fall and winter of 1992-93. This variant of Alien Staff differs from the first model in the way it was developed specifically for, and with the input of, a singular and individual person as a storyteller, video-performer and life performer-presenter of her own experience, as well as a legal and ethical advisor for other immigrants. This version has a vertically oriented screen of the "xenoscope" (the top or crook section of Alien Staff) for a closer view of the owner's face, which is made of stainless steel in order to look more powerful and respectable in the New York context. The new "xenolog" section (the central part of the rod of Alien Staff) is made up of interchangeable cylindrical containers for the preservation and display of precious relics related to the various phases of the owner's history. This version thus becomes something of a reliquary, with containers for relics like rejected visa applications, immigration and legal documents, apartment keys, old photographs and the various identity cards acquired by the owner. Through video and live performance and narration these memories from the immigrant's past are recalled in the face of the immigrant present, and become a work of critical history and a vision of the future. The first operator of this version of Alien Staff was Jagoda Przybylak, a prominent Polish artist-photographer, who moved to New York in 1981. Forced by immigrant circumstances, she took various jobs of Polish women: "plejsy" (cleaning private apartments), "ofisy" (cleaning corporate offices), and "kompaniony" (accompanying elderly American women). Jagoda Przybylak presented herself with her "Alien Staff" in Greenpoint, Brooklyn, and at the New York Institute of Technology where she teaches photography, to give the students, professors, staff and maintenance personnel an opportunity to hear and see her stories of "plejsy," "ofisy" and "kompaniony." The process of telling these stories required recording and much editing. She found that publicly recounting and revealing her hellish past emotionally difficult but morally constructive in terms of regained respect from others. Details forgotten or suppressed return, providing the possibility of the discovery through language, both Polish and English, of identities old and new which go far beyond what is usually taken for granted.

The newer gesture-responsive and digital version of Alien Staff invites an improvisation and virtuosity in replaying the pre-recorded content. The electric field sensors respond to the operator's and interlocutor's gestures modulating both sound and image. Unlike the previous versions, the monitor does not expose the entire face but only the eyes of the operator. The quality and strength of the speaker has been improved. Additional covers give the operator the choice to expose or conceal the relics. If necessary the containers can be easily detached during the performance for closer examination of their content.

This sort of carefully crafted description of his artistic projects is typical of Wodiczko's artistic practice. Far from formalist art that is left to "speak for itself," Wodiczko's projects are theoretically and technically complex, and the artist works hard to make their layered complexity available to the various audiences. The *Alien Staff* was used by many immigrants in Barcelona, Brooklyn, New York, Paris, Marseille, Houston, Stockholm, Helsinki, Warsaw, and Rotterdam. These newest versions of the *Alien Staff* were designed with the technical assistance of Joshua Smith of the Media Lab at the Massachusetts Institute of Technology. All variants of these instruments were built by John Kuntsch of Brooklyn Model Works.

The following interview was conducted at DeRobertis Café, in New York City, June 1995.

Tom Finkelpearl: When you were first approached to create and operate an Alien Staff, *what was your reaction?*

Jagoda Przybylak: You know, my experience is that people do not like to talk about how they started out in this country. At first, I was not sure about the Alien Staff, *about telling everybody my past experience. But, you know, Krzysztof is a very convincing person.*

TF: When you agreed to participate, was the first step to make your video statement?

JP: No. First, we went together to the workshop where they made the Alien Staff. *We discussed it. In the meantime, of course, we discussed my experiences. Then we started with the choice of objects and discussed the best way these relics could be displayed in the containers of the* Alien Staff. *We also worked on the shape of the* Alien Staff. *I looked through my old drawer and thought, "What can act as a reference or an illustration to my beginning here?" Krzysztof asked me to write down two or three important experiences—the things that I remembered the best. This was, of course not enough, I had to tell these stories in front of the video.*

Krzysztof Wodiczko, Alien Staff operated by Jagoda Przybylak, 1992–1993, Brooklyn, New York. Photograph courtesy of the artist and Galerie Lelong.

You have to remember that when I speak with Krzysztof, we speak only in Polish. To speak with him in English is unnatural. When we made the tape, I was sitting facing Krzysztof, who was operating the video camera. Standing in back of him was our American friend, who does not speak Polish. It was easier for me to speak in English when I talked to her, not to Krzysztof. We arranged this for a reason.

TF: *Were you speaking only in English?*

JP: *Yes, and because I was speaking about these matters to her for the first time. I forgot about this video camera. I wanted to explain my story to her, as a typical American. I saw how interesting it was to her. Here are the stories I told her:*
       In America, as fresh immigrants, we do not have much choice in jobs. The safest thing is to work in a home. Nobody knows about it. One sort of work is taking care of children, which I do not like. It is too big a responsibil-

ity, especially here in America where children are so independent, not like Poland. I could have tried to take care of sick people, but I do not have experience. Or you can take care of an old lady, too old to be alone, as a companion. I thought she could help me learn English. This would be the perfect job, although this is not the truth. The old lady who I met was not sick. She was full of energy, but her mind was not straight. Finally, she wanted not just a companion, but wanted an extra advantage over me. Never in my life had I been so lean. I lost weight (fifteen pounds!) because she gave me just a little food. She controlled every piece of bread. She repeated constantly that I "didn't need energy," that I had an "easy time" in her house, and to be her companion was "not a job, but a pleasure." She wanted to have my attention all the time, every minute, every second, even when she watched TV. She treated me like her slave. This was one of the stories that I told—how difficult it was for an independent person like me. In Poland, I was an artist. I wanted to remain independent, but finally I started to be like the woman I was caring for.

The other job I told about was cleaning offices from 5:00 to 11:00 in the evening. Offices are so full of life. A lot of girls (and sometimes men) go and clean. Many are Polish, and from South America. This was a good job because we got insurance. It was not easy to get this job. It was what everybody wanted. Finally, you got it through connections and a bottle of alcohol or something like that. I liked working in the evening, having the morning free so I could look around the city, meet somebody, see galleries. I could be normal, or like a tourist. And from 5:00 to 11:00, I was a different person, cleaning. For me this was a very interesting job because I met a lot of people from South America, or from Poland, or from small countries, people I could never meet before. I like people, so I was so happy. A lot of friendly girls.

The end of this job was a "visit" from Immigration. This was still not official work. We were still without green cards. Immigration came. How afraid we were. This sort of thing could never happen when you worked for a family in a house. Our boss shouted, "Go out! You are not here!" But how could we go out when we had a special blue uniform? All of our clothes were locked in a closet in the basement. We hid on the fire escape. Imagine several girls in the blue uniforms in this very cold place—afraid, so afraid. Maybe they will open the door at any time. But nobody came. One hour, second

Krzysztof Wodiczko, Alien Staff, operated by Jagoda Przybylak. Photograph courtesy of the artist and Galerie Lelong.

hour. I told myself that I was not so afraid. (This was before martial law.) If it were necessary, I would go back to Poland. I had an interesting experience, a little bit of money. My position was all right. But not the position of the girls from South America. They were from very, very poor places. Especially one who was planning to get married in a few weeks. She was so afraid. Deportation for her was like the end of her life. It was funny because she took off her blue uniform. She was just in her underwear—very sophisticated because she had a boyfriend. In this cold, damp place she was saying, "No. I don't work here." It was funny. What was she doing here if she does not work here?

In the end people said to me, "Okay, if you are not afraid, go. Go and look. Maybe they left." When I went out, I was in the rest room. When I saw my face in the mirror, oh, my god! My face was white like paper. I thought, "This is me? I am not afraid?" I never had a problem with the law before. In Poland I never had a problem. Here I had a good job and enjoyed compan-

ionship, and some money. At that time I was earning big money compared with Poland. But anything could affect you if you did not have papers.

TF: So the objects in your Alien Staff *reflect these experiences?*

JP: I found a picture of this old lady who I worked for, looking very sweet. This was how I saw her when I first met her. Second, I have deportation papers. They were sent to me by mistake. They told me "Oh, sorry, this was a mistake." Do you know how much sleep you lose when this happens? It almost cost me a heart attack. I have a picture of all of the girls in the blue uniforms when we went out to dinner together. I also have a small dictionary that I always had with me the first years I was here. This dictionary was so used that finally it did not look like a book, but like a little sculpture. Also I had documents from Poland, and a student ID. I looked so nice.

TF: Where have you shown your Alien Staff*?*

JP: Several places. At first, I resisted showing this Alien Staff *to the students where I teach [photography]. No. I did not want to do this, but finally Krzysztof convinced me, and it was a very interesting experience. Now the students interact with me much more closely. Before I used to be just a teacher. At the end of the semester, they forgot me. I did not exist. After seeing the* Alien Staff*, they started to trust me like a different person who was more interesting to them. There was a different connection. There are a lot students, especially where I teach at New York Tech, who are new immigrants, and they started to have conversations with me. But the connection was not only with the new immigrants. All of the students were interested that I had my own* Alien Staff*—something that is new. It is not sculpture, not a TV, but uses a language that they know very well from TV, and they appreciate it. I have this new device, and my own story is right here. I started to be somebody with roots.*

TF: Have you shown it in your neighborhood?

JP: Yes, I took it out where I live in Greenpoint, Brooklyn, a Polish area.

TF: *In Greenpoint, were you mostly interacting with Polish people?*

JP: No. Mostly young people. Mostly Americans, and the reaction was very good. I also showed the Alien Staff *in Houston, Texas, when Krzysztof had his opening there. When I walked with the staff in Houston, white-shirted businesspeople, out during their lunch break, did not care about it. They did not understand, and they did not want to show that they did not understand. They also might have been afraid that it is against them. But the people from south of the border, they wanted to talk. I had conversations with them. When one person started to talk, others joined in. This is something very new and interesting, although the problem is very old, from the beginning of the United States: immigration.*

TF: *It is interesting to me how little people talk about their families' immigration experiences. I never spoke with my grandmother and grandfather about coming to the United States from Hungary and Russia. Perhaps your students had the same sort of interaction with their parents—hiding the stories.*

JP: *Let me tell you something interesting. Krzysztof showed my* Alien Staff *in Warsaw. There, in Poland, America is like a dream. A rich country. The reaction to the staff in Poland was, "Why? Why do you do this work?" Someone wrote me a letter saying, "You have friends and a good job. Why would you agree to participate in this?" People do not want to talk about these things. But if you start to talk, they become more open. They become less ashamed that they also had a bad beginning.*

TF: *I am not really clear on why the people in Poland were so upset.*

JP: *These are people who have not visited America. They do not have experience with the "American Dream." So they still want to keep their image, their dream.*

TF: *It is interesting. It seems to me that they would want to hear the truth.*

JP: *They were dissatisfied with me for opening my secret life. It is as if I should be ashamed.*

I think that Krzysztof has started the Alien Staff *project for several rea-sons. You must remember that he has been thinking about immigration is-sues for a long time—not only since it has become a popular topic in the newspapers. I think that Krzysztof is a bit tired of always working within in-stitutions and being associated with institutions. All of his projects are con-nected with the city, with public institutions and bureaucracies. The* Alien Staff *is more independent. Also, I think this new direction in his art relates to Krzysztof starting to think about himself. Even though I have known him for a long time, he never told me about his hard experience in this country, how he was in Canada without a normal position, with no papers. Though every-body at the university appreciated him, nobody took note of how he lived, the circumstances of his life. He was living in a cold, small room. Sometimes he even had to use his projectors for heat on cold nights.*

TF: *That is actually a great symbol for Krzysztof: his projectors keeping him warm.*

JP: *(Laughing) Yes, you are right. But, since I remember, he never discussed this with me before. And now, when I opened my past, through the* Alien Staff, *he opened also.*

Interview: **Krzysztof Wodiczko**
on Alien Staff

Introduction

Krzysztof Wodiczko was born in 1943, in Warsaw, Poland. He receiving his M.F.A. in industrial design from the Academy of Fine Arts in Warsaw in 1968, and worked for ten years as an industrial designer. His early work, and indeed much of what has followed, was deeply influenced by these years in industrial design. An important early work, for example, was his *Personal Instrument* of 1969. The device, which was strapped around the forehead, ears, and hands, created a range of variations of reception of environmental sound, depending on the motion of the operator's hands in relation to the sunlight. Wodiczko himself "performed" the piece. In the early 1970s, he developed a vehicle that he propelled through parks and streets in Warsaw by walking along a tilting platform and causing a seesaw motion, which was translated into the rotation of the wheels, causing the vehicle to move. This sort of machine-subject-oriented project was typical of his work throughout the early 1970s. In 1977, Wodiczko moved to Toronto, Canada, where he received permanent resident status in 1980. That year, he started to experiment with outdoor projections, a medium that would be his primary form of expression for some time. He went on to create nearly seventy large-scale public projections over the next ten years. Often employing large-format transparencies and high-powered projectors, these projections were created in direct relationship with specific architectural sites.

In 1988, Wodiczko said, "My work doesn't necessarily have a specific political message. It reveals the contradictions of the environment and the events actually taking place there. It is to do with the politics of space and the ideology of architecture. City centers are political art galleries."[1] This quotation reflects the critical approach that Wodiczko took in his projections. It places his work within the tradition of site specificity and the critique of space, along with artists like Michael Asher, or perhaps Richard Serra. There was a consistent critique of the hidden social meaning and function of architectural form in these works.

In his more recent work, Wodiczko has undertaken projects that are not tied so closely to a specific place, that can move around the city. This started with a series of functional vehicles that addressed the image and status of the homeless in the city. While discussing his *Homeless Vehicle* (1988) and Union Square projects, Wodiczko told me in 1988 that he considered himself a "critical real estate artist." After the exhibition and early tests of *Homeless Vehicle* in 1988, *October* magazine published three articles that discussed the vehicle.[2] First was Rosalyn Deutsche's influential ar-

Krzysztof Wodiczko, projection, Campanile, San Marco, Venice, Italy, 1986. Photograph courtesy of the artist and Galerie Lelong, New York.

ticle, "Uneven Development," on public art in New York City, followed by an article written by Wodiczko and David Lurie about the vehicle, and finally, a conversation about the project by three homeless men, who were the project consultants, and Wodiczko. All three of these articles had an influence on this book. Deutsche's article was the first time I had seen a critic place public art within a serious examination of urban development. While many studies of public art pay lip service to urban development issues, they are generally superficial, subsumed into the standard discussion of the development of style. The conversation reinforced my trust of the form of dialogue. I was surprised and moved to see the comments of the three homeless men, "Oscar, Daniel, and Victor,"[3] in the pages of *October.*

Tom Finkelpearl: You have worked in many different media and under many different circumstances. How do you see the continuity of your work?

Krzysztof Wodiczko: As I read more and reflect on what I have done, I am developing a sense of the method of my work. In general, I have employed urban sites that are charged with some meaning, representing something that Walter Benjamin called the "history of the victors," or one might say, the "culture of the victors." The sites are monuments or other structures, and now the city at large. Into this, I insert what Benjamin calls "the secret tradition of the vanquished." By doing this, it is possible to interrupt or disrupt, Benjamin would say, the continuity of the history of the victors. He was talking about the philosophy of history and the necessity to see history from the point of view of those who do not take anything for granted, who have a need to speak, for they are usually deprived of history, for example, people who are perceived and treated as strangers. They are people with "no history," and these are the people who have been the focus of my work and my collaborators, whether it is the Homeless Vehicle *[1988] or the* Homeless Projection *in Boston [1986–1987] or the* Leninplatz Projection *[1990] of a Polish shopper in East Berlin. The tradition of the vanquished is the point of view of those who have no voice: those who are newcomers, those born of the transformation of the city, or of global transformation. They must somehow regain the right to become legitimate members of the community or have a legitimate relation to the monument and the history it represents. I would like to stress the present project:* Alien Staff *(also called the* Baton d'Etranger *in French, or* Laska Tulacza *in Polish), which began in 1992. This project occupies my mind at this time. I am excited especially about the psychological dimension of the new project. The* Homeless Vehicle *and* Alien Staff *are both operated, or performed, or transformed by the operators who do not have a "voice," people who have no recognized, legitimate presence in the urban environment or in the media.*

These projects have a psychological dimension, because the operators become legitimate members of the so-called "urban community." They operate tools or instruments designed for and with them. In this society, once there is a product designed for specific users, they are taken seriously. Even if onlookers do not know exactly what is going on, they recognize the seriousness of this design engagement. The operators, whether homeless people, or immigrants, or undocumented workers, feel legitimate as human beings, as presenters of equipment newly designed for them. They have

Krzysztof Wodiczko, drawing for Homeless Vehicle, 1988. Photograph courtesy of the artist and Galerie Lelong.

something to offer and explain through this object, and other people ask them questions through this "machine." This object, as a "third party" in this social interaction, helps to initiate communication.

Through the creation and operation of the new equipment, the operators gain necessary distance and come to terms with their own conditions of life, the pathos, tragedy, and comedy of their experience, as something somehow rich and complex, no matter how terrible it is. This condition should not exist, but, at the same time, it is something human because they are human. They are witnesses to disaster, and they have comments about it. They are born of it. They can find form and communicate the history of becoming. They remember other times. They can, in the midst of a crisis situation, empower themselves through certain abilities and skills. Strangely enough or perversely enough, they are not just survivors. Out of their alienation and displacement and marginalization, through the fact that they managed to survive, they are strangely powerful, frighteningly okay. (Of course, we do not see all of those who die in the process.)

With Alien Staff there is an aspect of empowerment and transformation of the self, and therefore the possibility of seeing one's map of displacement. This happens through the performative act on video, recorded and edited and then continued in front of, or surrounded by, people who the operators have never seen before, in the space of the very city from which they were alienated. That part is much stronger in the new projects. It has a psy-

chotherapeutic effect for those who choose to use this artifice, this double, this companion or magic object, around which they hope for new discourse to develop. It is something that relieves them from responsibility of telling their story alone, providing an extension of their own displacement. In this way the Alien Staff alienates their alienation. In the process of recording, in the process of performing, in the process of displaying in the museum, as a museological object or artifact—in all of those cases, I feel that it is much more effective [than the Homeless Vehicle Project]. The new projects are also much more provocative in terms of the necessity to respond.

TF: For the Alien Staff do you conduct a series of interviews with the operators that are then edited and screened on the monitor at the top of the staff?

KW: No. [emphatically] Not interviews. It is more like a video history, a video psychology. It is not an interview in which I ask questions. In fact, when people start talking to the camera, they have less difficulty, over time, saying things to the camera than to a person. It suddenly becomes a kind of confession, but also a liberation for many people—to finally find the words without any time constraint, like in a psychotherapeutic situation. Then they can edit the tape, or help in the process of editing.

Strangers have an incredible ability to see problems in a new place and recognize them immediately. They can even criticize the ways in which people try to be nice to them. On the tapes for the Alien Staff, they can say all the things that they haven't had an opportunity to say, acknowledge all of the aspects of their own displacement, and recognize their transformation. They can relate how they have changed since they crossed the border, and how many more borders they have crossed internally. They try to find the words. Very often they speak many languages, though not necessarily fluently. Often, they help themselves with all kinds of baroque phrases and metaphors, the particular language of strangers. They repeat the same story in various languages, and of course the story is different each time. The final edited version combines them all.

In other words, the Alien Staff is truly an instrument. Not everyone will make the same sort of art with it. It requires the operators to become artists to some degree: Performers, storytellers, oral historians, or existential *philosophers. According to United Nations statistics, there are between 35 and 50 million refugees on this planet, most of them without documents (although the number is probably much higher).*

      As an analogy, I have considered the history of the Jewish nation that managed to develop sacred texts in the form of an ethical companion-manual for ethical choices to be made under changing circumstances. *But those millions of refugees might not have a Talmud yet. My opinion is that they should have one. The* Alien Staff *points to the possibility of a World Wide Web link. It could create a bank of memory in public workstations that could be operated by the equivalent of rabbis, people I call "xenologists," meaning doctors of displacement (both ethical and legal, since the law here is a very important point). In fact, democracy is being tested here by everyone who can act, or demand the right to speak, those who try to convince others that the world should be changing according to the viewpoint of the displaced people.* They *are the future of the world.* They *are the prophets. The texts accumulated through such an interaction could be called the "Electronic Talmud." Of course, it is an absurd one because there is no sacred literature as a base. There is no Torah. But, I do believe that there is the possibility to create a "Torah" on the basis of assigning a particular set of testimonies, statements, and stories that are the most general sort of initial responses to the experience of displacement. This initial base could be changing with no stable Torah, always in transition. This is a loose proposal. There is a history in many groups, and there is a philosophical body of work of a nomadic kind: Nietzsche, Benjamin, Kristeva, Deleuze, Guattari, and Levinas. The idea revolves around people who have experience with crossing and trespassing, and transgressing different frontiers, like Jagoda Przybylak. She is already doing it because she is running an informal network for Polish immigrant women workers.*

TF: On the Internet?

KW: No, on the telephone, on her answering machine. But there is no reason why it could not be on the Internet. It is about giving advice, listening and giving examples, transmitting stories and facts so that people will not feel alone, because they are not alone. The situation of the Polish illegal worker in

Greenpoint, Brooklyn, might be very similar to someone from Haiti living in Paris. Once people see this, it will probably help. The "Electronic Talmud" is a project that is still very far from beginning, but I have to mention this as a horizon. Between this horizon and those performative instruments there is still a gap. Fortunately young researcher-students and Ron MacLean at MIT's Media Lab have already helped in developing an initial computer program as a seed for the "Electronic Talmud."

TF: *Are you familiar with the nineteenth century woodcuts of the "Wandering Jew" with the staff?*

KW: *Yes.*

TF: *Was this a source for your* Alien Staff?

KW: *As a cliché, of course, and there were many more clichés, like Moses, or the tribal chief. This project relies heavily on the cliché. As strongly as the* Homeless Vehicle *relied on the cliché of the shopping cart. Why not? If there is a cliché, why not use it? But it has to be immediately transported to the contemporary world and infused with a new meaning.*

TF: *The cliché of the low-tech walking staff as a magical communication device is then contrasted with the more contemporary technology of magic: video.*

KW: *Yes. The top and the bottom. There are Plexiglas containers built into the staff, display containers for relics of the immigrant experience. These are contrasted to the electronic part, another kind of container—the electronic container. It is like science fiction, somewhere between the ancient and the future. But the actual basis for this project is the present, where the past and the future dwell, as Benjamin would say. And the present experience is the base of utopia. Utopia is hope lived in the mode of the present. So you have the present combined with hope. It is not that you have an image of the future on the horizon to which you are walking. Rather, you have hope that despite the present, there is a future and there is a past, so there is some possibility of having a past and also creating a past. You are infusing the pre-*

sent experience into the past, transforming your identity to a more and more unfamiliar form. You might not be accepted by your old community or by the people who are around you. But you have no choice, you are creating your own history, a kind of critical history infusing the present with the past, a little like projecting images on monuments [laughs]. And then you have a kind of history of the present which is unacceptable and for which there should be no place in the future. The immigrant utopia, then, is a future place in which there is no place for the present experience.

One problem with the Alien Staff *is that people strongly believe that it is not necessary in the United States because it is a country of immigrants.*

TF: Does this objection come from the new immigrants as well?

KW: No, from Americans, those who were born here. They think that they are all strangers because their parents were. So they do not see that there is much of a problem. They feel that it is a better place than any other place in the world for newcomers. They feel that the project should be for Europe. And, in fact, these projects were born from the European situation, but as seen by me, an American. I started this project because I realized that the situation for immigrants is really awful in Europe, perhaps worse than in the States. However, once I was working on the project in Europe, I realized that the situation in the States is getting worse, and perhaps the project is much more applicable to America than I thought.

There is a discrepancy between the actual situation of foreigners in this country and the public image of their experience. It is not possible to explain to an American-born person that immigrants don't have to go through the hell that their parents or grandparents went through. Their idea is that, in order to be properly American, you have to "go through the showers," through hell. That makes you a real American. They say, "So, welcome to the family." Unfortunately, some immigrants and naturalized citizens hold this opinion as well, who expect the newcomers to go through the same hell as they did. This is a foundation of American identity—suffering through the unbelievable hardship of immigration as a rite of passage. I think this has to change. One reason is that, according to statistics recently published by the federal government, the 1980s and 1990s saw a wave of immigration almost equal to the wave at the turn of the century. But the second wave is arriving after the first wave, so it is not a frontier situation in which the world is still open. We are talking about the possibility of ethnic wars now, when the new groups arrive and are competing for resources and rights.

Birth rates indicate a predictable decrease of the population of the United States, but that is being corrected by immigration. That is, the population remains at the same level as a result of an influx of immigrants. It is possible that by the year 2010, nearly half of the overall population of the United Stated will be foreign-born. If this is the case, then you will have an overwhelming majority of foreign-born people in the larger cities. The differences between them will be very severe in terms of their experience. It is quite possible that America is already very different from what most people think. In Minnesota, the majority of children in public schools will be of Asian origin. But people still cannot imagine that this is Minnesota. So there is a possibility of a backlash, of isolationist reactions. Perhaps pogroms. Everything is possible. I cannot believe that things will not happen because they have happened already in the past.

That is why I think that these projects are applicable to the United States. Right now, if I took them to California, they would feel at home, as they were in Europe, certainly after Proposition 187, and the abandonment of affirmative action.

TF: So far, you have spoken of the experience of the Alien Staff *from the point of view of the "operator." What about the interaction?*

KW: Incredible conversations develop around the instruments, both with immigrants and nonimmigrants. This can be seen from the videos made with a hidden camera in Paris. The person carrying the staff—here I am a bit utopian—this woman in Paris, is discovering within herself the kind of community, mental community of different discourses and dialogues with her own past, projections into the future, problems with the present, acknowledging how mobile this is. She is projecting this to the outside world, opening it up. This becomes contagious because there is often someone in the group that forms who understands, who has a close relationship with an immigrant or who is an immigrant, and then there is someone who is not. And then it becomes a discourse around this staff and this operator who is disrupting herself. This staff is speaking, but she also is taking her prerecorded comments as tips. She is saying, "No, no, no. It is not like this, not exactly as the staff says." It is actually worse or better, or funnier, or more tragic.

TF: *Commenting on what she herself had said?*

KW: *Yes. Because she is always in the process of transformation. It opens up a different kind of discourse on identity of community. It is born of what is happening to that person, and that is why I feel that this is a project that is both cultural, psychological, and political. And there is an ethical dimension, because each time she uses the staff she is speaking to the world, confessing or explaining the decision-making process and her impossible circumstances. For example, she put a broken coffee cup into this container, which was a very important relic. In the videotape you see her trying to reassemble this broken cup, but explaining that the parts do not fit anymore. It is not possible to reassemble. She cannot reassemble herself, and she does not want to. In many ways, she has been liberated from an identity that was partially a prison for her. Now she is in another prison.*

Also in the container is a picture of her baby. She used to be totally dependent upon her husband to sign any documents. Now, her baby is a French citizen because it is a baby of a French father. This immediately gives her the right to have a work permit, because the mother of a French citizen is entitled to one. So now she is not dependent so much on her husband as on her child. She says in this videotape to everyone, "What if my child misbehaves?" Imagine this monstrously powerful baby. People identify or are amazed. They are shocked, they act against it, or they dismiss it. On the hidden camera videotape, you can see some French tourists from the provinces talking to the woman. They are right-wing, and refuse to acknowledge that there is any problem. [Looking at video documentation of the interaction] Here she is standing in front of them almost naked, with all of those stories, ready to discuss them, and they refuse. But then there is someone else standing behind making faces, understanding.

One thing that I like about this project as opposed to my projections is that it is not attached to a particular, fixed physical site. It may be a "projec-

Krzysztof Wodiczko, Alien Staff, operated by Patrica Pirreda in Paris, France. Photograph courtesy of the artist and Galerie Lelong.

tion" in terms of inserting or inscribing something into the everyday life of the city (as an alternative kind of architecture or design), but it is not fixed. So, in other words, it is not site specific. I do not know why I am so happy about this. It may be because it is more able to integrate and interconnect with the person. It is very difficult for me to project, for example, an illegal domestic worker from Haiti on the body of a monument of Abraham Lincoln. It is ironically possible. In fact it would make quite an interesting comment— but the monument will always be seen as dominant. You are making a hero ironically, but still you are monumentalizing someone who is marginalized. In the case of the staff, there is not this sort of monumentalization. In fact, it is relying on the tradition of people who are crossing boundaries. It is relying on the popular art of storytelling or magic, performance, tricks. Making artifice in order to communicate. The stranger is the maker of an artifice using gestures, songs, music, stories—a trickster of some sort. It is partially artificial, partially natural. It is a cyborg of sorts: someone who is artificially implanted into something that is called natural, but who is denaturalizing it.

She is learning how to reflect, use, pervert all of the expectations that are imposed on the stranger—stereotypes, entertainment value. You want entertainment? You have it. But my entertainment will be better than yours. I will maintain entertainment value, but I will also tell you something that you do not want to hear in the process. Like in the blues or jazz tradition.

What I am saying is that this project is not an appropriation of monuments of victors or dominant environment. It is actually a reinforcement of the other tradition that already exists, the unacknowledged tradition of the vanquished that I mentioned earlier. Clearly, those operators are agents. Angels and agents. They are acting not only on behalf of their own life and their own transformation and empowerment, but also they feel that they are acting on behalf of the others who are in a similar situation, or they would not be participating in the project. There is a certain prophetic component without being monumental in the manner of an official monument.

TF: *That is so unusual to do in public art—like David Hammons selling the snowballs on the street, fitting in with the street vendors, creating a mechanism for interaction. You are opening up this very private discourse. Even the television set is associated with privacy and domesticity in our culture. By bringing it out to the street you are confusing all of these public and private categories.*

KW: *Clearly, you do not usually have the person who is speaking on the television standing behind the monitor. So from the beginning it is quite comical, because you have both the character and the actor at the same time. One is alive and can actually correct or put in doubt what the same person recorded [laughs]. It becomes an exposition of the impossibility to explain things. That part relates to private/public. Sure. It goes without saying that the experience of immigrants, especially illegal immigrants, is "illegal" experience. Therefore, it is secretive, not public. By making it public, you are offending people's expectations of what is to be said in public. In this way it is a brave act on the part of the operator to open up stories, to import deported history.*

There is one aspect that is difficult to explain. This is the psychological part. Freud believed, according to Kristeva, that it is very hard for people to come to terms with their own strangeness: You feel stranger and stranger as life goes on, because you have to learn things, and once you learn some-thing, it is no longer a "natural" state of being. You have a theory for things. You have words, cultural norms, patterns, and proscribed identities. Plus, there is the history of being rejected or rejecting someone, a whole set of fears and repetitions or uncontrollable drives. So, when you face someone who is properly a stranger, who comes from somewhere else, who speaks in a different accent, who is lost, it invokes your own strangeness. Rather than acknowledge this strangeness in yourself, because it is repressed, you expel this strangeness together with the stranger. This is a Freudian explanation of xenophobia. Of course it is much more complicated than that. In life, differ-ent categories of strangeness are in conflict with each other—the stranger within the stranger within myself, and so on. However, expelling the stranger outside without recognizing and confronting the stranger inside is a general problem. Freud thinks that it is easier to come to terms with the un-canny feeling of strangeness if it is presented in the form of artifice, some-thing partially artificial, partially real, such as telling about a nightmare, or a fairy tale. The hope for strangers is to produce themselves as artifice.

So, I feel that the situation when 50 percent of the people in the United States are foreign-born will have a major impact on American culture.

TF: *And psyche.*

KW: *Yes. I feel that artists, together with strangers, are in a position to prepare the ground—at least to propose a different way of being, different experience as "truly American." Second, it is quite possible to say that there exists a long tradition of the artistic avant-garde for the artist who paints a self-portrait as a stranger. Courbet portrayed himself as the "Wandering Jew" in the painting* Bonjour M. Courbet *[1854]. He was on a mission, a journey, but also on a mission to say something to this dealer, this member of the art world and the established world. Though he is opening himself up to this dealer of culture, he positions himself on the side of the marginalized, of the no-madic.And he also carries the moral responsibility to give a warning or ex-plain things, to act as a prophet. This kind of position was further developed by movements of the avant-garde—groups of utopian artists, who continue this sort of "Judaism" or utopianism in a nonreligious way. There is a certain link with the promised land, the world without boundaries, some sort of peace, an international world without nationalism that connects also with the wanderers' utopia—a world with no borders.*

I am making a lot of shortcuts, but there is a lot of similarity between the avant-garde kind of "nomadology" and "xenology" and the experience of the strangers that cross the borders in massive scale today. What I am saying is that it may be time for artists to recognize that in their veins there is an avant-garde tradition that still circulates, despite the fact that they spit at it, and there are some good reasons to spit at it as well: the utopian vision of a better society engineered toward a preconceived notion of a better world— this is questionable. However, affinity, empathy-bridges, attempts to recognize the world as seen from the point of view of those who are in transit, who are marginalized, who are in the process of becoming, these are serious matters. I think that artworld artists are still in the position to recognize other artists. To be a stranger is to be a kind of artist. It is a way to survive—the ability to manipulate language, to find artifice, and forms, and metaphors, and gestures, and sneak through different boundaries, to disappear and reappear, to change forms, to be as Kristeva says, a "Baroque personality."

The issue is: What can art and design do in this era of displacement? It can examine all of those notions of identity and community, questioning the media presentation in the contemporary world and creating alternative means of representation and communication. I do not mean that the world will change for the better because artists do those things, but my utopia is based on the belief or hope that if we did not do those things the situation would be worse. It is not that I am providing a new horizon, but clearly just to come to terms with the present situation is an incredibly utopian project— just to figure out where we are now and where we should not be in the future.

Notes

1. Krzysztof Wodiczko, quoted in *Public Address* (Minneapolis: Walker Art Center, 1993), p. 163.

2. *October,* Winter 1988, pp. 3–77.

3. While naming these men only by their first names could be seen as an insult, this is often a necessity. Not everyone is comfortable being identified as homeless in print. In this volume, a formerly homeless woman named Jackie McLean is interviewed and identified with her full name. There is a difference, of course, in that McLean is now living in her own apartment.

Interview: **Kristin Jones** *and*
Andrew Ginzel *on* Mnemonics

Introduction

Kristin Jones (born 1956) and Andrew Ginzel (born 1954) have been collaborating on site-specific installations and public artworks since 1985. For many years, their work was characterized by subtly designed kinetic environments. They did not make "machine art," but landscapes that used motion, along with materials drawn from nature like sand, water, and fire. Their first permanent public commission was a Percent for Art commission at the Portland, Oregon, Convention Center, completed in 1990. Since that time they have worked on a series of commissions in both the private and public sectors, along with a smaller number of gallery shows. At the time of publication of this book, they are completing a huge project for a residential building at Park Avenue and Fourteenth Street in New York City. The multimillion dollar project includes a massive terracotta wall and a variety of timekeeping devices from digital to lunar. Also in 1999, they installed a permanent work called *Oculus* in the World Trade Center stop of New York City's subway system. The work is executed in mosaic and consists of scores of eyes based on photographs the artists took of a wide range of New Yorkers. The work discussed here is *Mnemonics,* a permanent work commissioned by Battery Park City Authority, the New York City Board of Education, and New York's Percent for Art Program. Completed in 1992, it is installed throughout Stuyvesant High School in Lower Manhattan. In this interview, Jones and Ginzel discuss the structure of the project and how it came to be. With extensive participation from current and past Stuyvesant High School students and others, Jones and Ginzel created artworks within four hundred hollow glass bricks placed randomly in walls throughout the school. Wherever you walk in the ten-story space, you see at least three or four of their blocks: over drinking fountains, in glass brick or masonry walls, along the run of the numerous escalators.

Stuyvesant High School was founded in 1908, and it is a selective public school. Any student who passes the entrance examination can attend the school regardless of where they live in New York City. (Many people feel that it is no mistake that this exclusive public school became a part of the exclusive public space of Battery Park City.) Given the challenge of working in this environment, the artists chose to create a project that would include the history of Stuyvesant High School, as well as a reminder that the world exists outside of the city, the state, the country.

The blocks are divided into three groups. The first group consists of a block for each of the eighty-eight classes that had graduated from Stuyvesant. The blocks

Kristin Jones and Andrew Ginzel, Oculus, 1998, throughout the World Trade Center Subway Station , New York, New York. Commissioned by the New York Metropolitan Transportation Authority, Arts for Transit.

are filled with memorabilia: photographs and objects that chronicle the school's history and the history of American culture. Each block was sandblasted from within with the appropriate year. Another eighty-eight blocks were left empty, again with a date sandblasted from within. For eighty-eight years (starting in 1992), each graduating class will have the opportunity to open the appropriately dated glass brick and place significant objects within it before permanently resealing it. The third set of blocks, around 230 in number, contain objects from around the world. These were obtained through an ambitious mailing campaign—contacting embassies and consulates around the globe and scores more of people, most of whom had never heard of Stuyvesant High School, participated in this aspect of the project. The three sets of blocks are mixed randomly. Walking through the school you see objects, empty blocks, and historical blocks in a variety of sequences—so you are encouraged to think about the past and the future, as well as north, south, east, and west simultaneously.

The title *Mnemonics* means, literally, a system to improve or develop memory. Both in its process and its permanent presence, the project asks the school to remember, but it is essentially different from traditional memorial artworks. First, the artists asked the users to define their own history in the eighty-eight blocks from past classes and the equal number of future classes. In addition, each individual block is very modest, implying that history should not be boiled down to a series of great monuments or "great men," but exists as multiple experiences. Although the project was a massive undertaking over four years, each block is personal and approachable. This project, through the participation of literally hundreds of people, creates an image of what education is, in a mode quite similar to that undertaken by Paulo Freire (although Jones and Ginzel were not influenced by him directly). Not only were all of the past classes included in the project, but eighty-eight future classes will need to participate before the project is complete. The artwork insists upon ongoing dialogue, and the artists have asked the community of the school to define itself, to decide which objects will represent each class in a kind of self-portrait of the first 176 years (88 past and 88 future classes) of the school. Demanding eighty-eight years of participation is an optimistic gesture in the context of the New York City Board of Education. Jones and Ginzel were able to weave a project through this building that has an individual, as well as interdependent voices—of the artists, the school community, and the hundreds of people worldwide who participated in collecting objects for the glass bricks.

Mnemonics was created at a time of an intense building campaign for the Board of Education in New York City. Between 1989 and 1994, the Board of Education, the School Construction Authority, and New York City's Percent for Art Program commissioned well over 100 artists to create new site-specific works for public schools in every borough. It was the largest and most significant series of public art commissions in New York City since the WPA.[1]

Tom Finkelpearl: Let's start from the beginning. You went in for an interview at the New York City Department of Cultural Affairs for the Stuyvesant High School project?

Andrew Ginzel: Yes. We were asked to interview without creating any kind of proposal, although we were asked in a general way how we might approach the school.

Kristin Jones: All we could do was explain that our work is varied and evolves from a specific understanding of the context and site. We could not even begin to fathom what we would do.

AG: We had never been faced with a challenge such as this, with a directive to create a work that was meant to last, to endure 100 years. We believed that it was important to consider the entirety, the school as a whole—the present and past, as well as the future. It seemed logical that you'd have to spend time in the old school before proposing something for the new school.

KJ: We had built a single public art piece before in Portland, Oregon. That gave us credibility for permanent commissions because so much of what we had done had been ephemeral. It's surprising to be chosen for a project when you haven't made a specific proposal. It is an act of faith to choose artists on the basis of their past work, on the seriousness of their intent.

TF: Of course, this is a philosophical position of New York City's Percent for Art Program. If the artists are going to work for five years on a project, it doesn't make sense that they be bound by a proposal developed over a couple of weeks. With design competitions, which are favored by some cities, the artist locks in to a design at the start, and then you spend five years executing it. After selection, how did you get started?

KJ: Even before meeting with the architect, we went to the old Stuyvesant High School.

AG: Neither of us had experience in a big city public school. I grew up in Chicago, but the school I went to was not a science/math high school and was much smaller. Kristin had also attended smaller schools.

KJ: It was wonderful, all of a sudden, to be immersed within the environment of eighty-eight years of accumulated history, of this New York City public school . . .

AG: . . . where nothing was ever thrown out. It seemed like the Board of Education never had any way of deaccessioning things. The school was an incredible museum of late nineteenth-century education.

KJ: The spirit of the school was really contagious. The place has an enormous amount of pride as a public place. We sensed this spirit immediately.

AG: The old school was endowed with an incredible sense of history of the city as a whole, a microcosm of New York. There was a really organic quality—different phases and different lives. And the makeup of the school population has changed so dramatically through the years.

KJ: It's really a gauge for the . . .

AG: . . . waves of immigration . . .

KJ: . . . the ambitious immigrants who flow into this country and create the energy of the city. You can feel the sense of striving and integrity in the school. Many students are not necessarily even born in this country, and oftentimes they are the only ones in the family that speak English. There is a definite sense of excitement within the place, a sense of the appreciation of the gift of intelligence.

AG: Even though the old building was physically inadequate for the rapid evolution of contemporary education, there was this real lament about having to abandon ship. The building had a distinct patina about it. While the school community was excited about the move, and had worked for years to create a new school, the sense of nostalgia, of history, was very real.

KJ: The physical building was very much a part of the identity of the school.

AG: The stone steps in the main staircase were literally worn down. The concave steps bore evidence of the generations of graduates.

KJ: In this city, in this country, there is so little sense of accumulated history, and however brief the history of the school, it just seemed very pertinent. There was so much humanity, so much history of the country captured in the place. It all seemed very poignant.

TF: I've heard that the three most traumatic things in life are marriage, death, and moving. Moving can be traumatic, especially if it's a place that you really identify with.

KJ: It really does challenge you, your whole sense of identity, because all of a sudden . . . who are you? You've established yourself. You've laid your roots. It is a shock to move to a school that's ten stories high, that has express escalators skipping floors.

AG: Also, the turf. The land that the new school is built on had never existed before. It's landfill. It has no history.

TF: The old school was on Fifteenth Street and First Avenue. What neighborhood would you call that?

KJ: Stuyvesant Town.

AG: The whole neighborhood is associated with the school or Stuyvesant in a lot of different ways.

KJ: Peter Stuyvesant is buried at St. Mark's Church nearby [the old site]. But the school itself was not necessarily tied only to the neighborhood. The wonderful thing is that students attend this special public school from all boroughs. It really is representative of the city. Like the island of Manhattan itself, Stuyvesant draws people from the entire city. Students come to Stuyvesant by choice, if they are smart enough to pass the qualifying exam.

AG: You sense right away that the vitality of the school really is the kids that are in it. It's not that there aren't some great teachers, but the faculty and staff are pretty much standard Board of Ed. people on a Board of Ed. budget.

KJ: The selection of the faculty and administration is not . . .

AG: . . . as specialized as the selection of the students. When we were selected, the building was in a relatively advanced planning stage, but many of the details were still pretty open. We were introduced to Joe Lengeling, the project architect for Cooper Robertson, who was responsible for the building with Gruzen Samton Steinglass. Cooper Robertson were the design architects, while Gruzen were the mechanical/programmatic planners. But Joe, luckily, was a very sympathetic figure who spent a lot of time with us, trying to explain how this very complicated machine of a building was going to operate.

KJ: We could sense that he was completely passionate about this project. And he was also completely open to the mystery of what we might do. He wasn't afraid of us as artists. He was really curious, and interested in working with us somehow.

AG: And then there was Renée Levine, who is . . .

KJ: . . . the self-ordained matron of the school.

AG: Early on we found ourselves being drawn into the school, and wanted to be. We started spending a lot of time at the old school. For example, we went to the school's theatrical productions, like South Pacific. We were watching what was going on, talking to people, exploring the floors and classrooms. Trying to get a feel for the place.

KJ: Digging around in the hidden recesses of the school was an adventure. It seemed to us that the place did not need an isolated art object per se, a special chandelier hanging from the skylight or a sculpture of Peter Stuyvesant in the entryway. We realized that our audience was going to be present for four years, and that it would be important to us to make something that could somehow stimulate, intrigue, and mystify them, perhaps forever, to sort of haunt them.

AG: We started to realize that the alumni of the school were remarkably attached to their memories. Many of these students had gone on to become accomplished in later life, but still had this attachment. We would mention that we were working on this project for Stuyvesant, and people in the city would immediately react, because they knew it was a special place, a legend of sorts. By spending time in the school, we realized that the place not only embodied a treasury of memories, but also was a treasure trove of broken scientific models, of musical instruments, violins and beautiful wax toads . . .

KJ: There was a history of the evolution of science in the closets of the school.

AG: The cabinets in the chemistry lab were filled with beautiful hand-blown glassware. There were piles of old surveying equipment down in the basement. So it seemed like a resource. It also became very clear to us that the whole sense of education had radically changed, that the sense of the empirical, of investigation, was going to be transformed in this new building. The new building is now filled with fiber optic communications. Every classroom has a very large monitor in it. The students are largely on computer. So there is this radical shift in the way that education is being addressed. It seemed to us that this change in sensibility, away from the more empirical investigation had . . . an aura.

TF: From your previous work, it is clear that you love the look of old science—old beakers and stuff like that. So, one of the kinds of things that you are very attracted to happened to be filling all the closets in the old school.

KJ: We use a wide range of materials and have used scientific glassware before. It seemed like such a crime to have a completely sterile new building that, aside from the name, had no connection to, no memory of the old school.

AG: We started to believe that the new building should be somehow infused, in a way that you could never grasp totally. So, a student coming into the school for four years would never quite be able to see all of what we had done.

KJ: Dispersing the project throughout the school was an attempt to try to affect the whole place, and suggest that perhaps every block that the school is built of is a potential clue to something else.

AG: The school was built extremely solidly, for a contemporary building. The interior walls of the school are all masonry. They break down into 8- x 8-inch increments of glass block and structural, ceramic-glazed tiles. So it seemed logical, in a certain way, to use this increment and infuse something into the infrastructure.

TF: Did you talk about these ideas with the architect or with Renée Levine?

KJ: Yes, with the architect. We were trying to think of something to really involve the current and future students, the alumni, and faculty, so it was theirs, so it wasn't some sort of apparition that came from nowhere that didn't relate to the place. We wanted to combine a lament of the loss of the empirical approach to the world, with the alumni lament of leaving the old school. We imagined that the alumni who meet the first Thursday of every month in the library might want to be involved in the project, because they were so sad to leave the old school. We also saw that the students were incredibly active with a million clubs. (Apparently, in order to get into college, it looks good if you are president of a club. So every single senior class member is a president of a club.) We thought maybe this could be like a club. We would get a lot of the students to participate.

AG: And everyone kept on saying how they wished they could take a sense of the old school with them. Through all of this, we started developing this sense of addressing memory: the memory of the history of the world, the memory of the old school. We also wanted to project into the future, creating a point, a reference point in this history of the school, where one side is a reflection of the other, projecting something into the future while looking into the past. The school was eighty-eight years old. In eighty-eight years, the new building will probably be considered obsolete. People will start thinking about what to do next.

Kristin Jones and Andrew Ginzel, *Mnemonics*, 1992, Stuyvesant High School, New York, New York. Commissioned by Battery Park City Authority, New York City Board of Education, New York City Percent for Art Program. Photograph: T. Charles Erickson.

TF: Can you describe the blocks physically? What is in the blocks? How many are there?

AG: Officially, there are exactly 400. It's funny, things are so regimented until you actually get on the site and start working. We actually put more blocks in the building than anyone knows about.

TF: What sorts of objects are in the blocks?

AG: There are three basic categories. The first group is eighty-eight empty blocks. They have future years sandblasted into them—eighty-eight years from the date of the new school's opening in 1992. They are made to be filled and resealed by each graduating class.

KJ: So there are individual blocks, dispersed throughout the building, that mark the inevitable passing of time, up to the year 2080.

AG: Then there are eighty-eight blocks that are sealed and mortared into the interior walls. They contain artifacts that refer to the eighty-eight years of the school's history, starting from its inception. These "past" blocks are composed of artifacts and documents that were solicited from the alumni, gathered from the old school itself, somehow culled from various sources. Then the third category is a field of various disparate things from all over the world. Some of them are enigmas, some are clearly defined by an inscription in the glass.

KJ: It's a field of relics.

TF: Let's talk about each set of blocks. The eighty-eight blocks with dates stretching into the future are going to be opened, and . . .

KJ: Filled by each senior class.

TF: How does that work?

AG: There is a special cabinet in the principal's office, mounted high up on the wall. It contains the instructions, the tools, all the documentation on the extensive campaign to obtain the artifacts, as well as the apparatus for opening the "future" blocks. Once a year, a representative from the senior class is given access to the apparatus to open up the block and insert the new material selected by the seniors. So the work continues to grow, but is no longer our work. It becomes theirs. In the last three years, the students have simply done it themselves.

KJ: Although the blocks are mortared into the wall, we provided a very serious suction cup to pull out the front face, and then set it back in with one-way screws.

TF: What sort of objects are they meant to put in each year?

KJ: The thought is very much related to Proust's idea of biting into the madeleine. The elements placed within are meant to bring back a flood of memories, *of vivid remembrances. So it's a trigger for memory. Hence the title,* Mnemonics.

AG: The first year the new school was open was a particularly poignant one, because of the bombing at the World Trade Center . . .

TF: . . . which is two city blocks away from the school.

AG: At the end of that year, students petitioned the FBI and they were actually given this piece of evidence, a piece of concrete with a tire track on it.

KJ: From ground zero.

AG: I think they chose this particular relic to put in their block because that day the earth shook. It was a memorable occasion. The students were highly restricted in what they could do during the investigation of the bombing. For example, they couldn't go out and use the empty lots as playing fields.

TF: So they had a particular personal relationship with that bombing, as opposed to the public relationship . . .

KJ: In a way, it's perfect, because it was a moment in time that everybody can absolutely remember where they were.

TF: So, students will be placing these objects in blocks after we are all dead. As artists, you've initiated something, but it is also out of your control. You are passing on some of the essence of creation to the public that you are addressing. You are allowing them . . .

KJ: . . . to leave something behind. You inhabit buildings. You inhabit apartments. You inhabit spaces your entire life. But how often do you ever leave a mark that is, in fact, an identifying mark?

AG: It's like when you do reconstruction, and you break through a wall and reveal somebody's writing. Even if it's just scratching, like the arithmetic of some sort of construction detail, it's always so fascinating, interesting to make that kind of contact with the past, with a specific instant in time.

KJ: Like the baked paw print of a dog walking over clay tiles in Pompeii.

AG: You see empty blocks all over the school. Because each block has a year sandblasted on the interior face of the glass, you constantly confront, in your visual field, all these points of reference in the future which haven't existed yet. Those years haven't occurred but they are inevitable. Whether or not the school exists or the city exists, the year will exist.

KJ: There is a distinct optimism. It is so mysterious to fathom the senior class of 2034. What will it be like then?

AG: Especially in reference to looking at the block from 1934. Things in the 1934 block are so radically different than what is being seen today.

TF: How did you go about gathering the objects to represent each of the years since 1912?

AG: Most immediately, we rummaged through the school.

KJ: Especially for the early years, where there are not alumni around from the classes.

AG: We found files filled with the index cards from grade reports from 1913.

KJ: I think originally we imagined that each member of the alumni association would take a great deal of time and do it themselves. In fact, that is not what happened. We had a very hard time even getting the mailing list out of the alumni association, because they were sure we were going to sell it. So we kept getting a few more names and a few more names, and we eventually mailed out hundreds of letters.

AG: We got a lot of donations through the alumni telethon that we participated in. We . . .

KJ: . . . hired students, having learned not to rely on volunteers.

AG: So we were actually on the phones, talking to alumni, soliciting materials.

KJ: We'd say, "With your check, go through your drawers and find something, and send it to us."

AG: We put advertisements in the alumni newsletter. We sent out letters.

KJ: Some classes sent us much too much, and other classes were less responsive. The last four months we were calling people all over the country encouraging alumni, describing the project . . .

AG: We also found certain students, or ex-students, who were totally fanatic about the school, who kept every last little memento of their experience.

KJ: So, sometimes if they were there for four years, they would have things from years other than their graduating class. Really gung-ho alumni would be able to help us fill the blocks for four years.

AG: There were many very touching things. For example, we got a little bowl made in shop class from 1913, from someone who had actually become a university president. He had kept it with his personal mementos on his dresser for years. He wrote this wonderful letter. So there were things that were really rather evocative.

TF: Once you had all these objects, you made the decisions about how to assemble them.

AG: We started making files or boxes. We had boxes and boxes and boxes of things. We created collages with these artifacts.

KJ: According to what we got. We went through all the yearbooks and created our own verbal history of the school, so that we knew, for example, that in a particular year there was a new principal. Every time there's a new principal, that was a landmark. We had to create a structure of the history. We knew that

Kristin Jones and Andrew Ginzel, Mnemonics, 1992. Photograph: T. Charles Erickson.

many of the teachers went to war in 1918. We knew that women entered the school in 1969, and there was a lot of controversy. A lot of donations related to the history of the country as a whole . . .

AG: *And since they were moving out of the old building, we got carte blanche to go through and chip off pieces of architecture, and unscrew railings, doorknobs, take numbers off doors, things like that. Many of these objects ended up in the past-year blocks.*

TF: *So, then the third group, around 225 blocks, consisted of objects from all over the world.*

KJ: *We were most interested in this aspect of the project. The whole piece ties together here. We were especially excited about projecting the concept out into the world.*

TF: How many people around the world would you estimate you contacted for these blocks?

AG: About 1,200.

> *For the third group, we were interested in creating this field, almost as if you were in a magnetic field, surrounded by all of the world, fragments compressed down into this school building. So, as you move through the building, you are constantly being referred to other places. For example, think of a student who is assigned a locker, and next to it there is this block with some sort of enigma—like a rock with the geographical coordinates of its origin. We were thinking that perhaps that student would look at it for three years, and then maybe one day he or she would say, "Wait, I'm curious about this. What is it?", and go to the library, look it up, become engaged with it. Because there are so many points in the entire school like that, it creates this whole set of questions.*

KJ: It seemed important to attempt to place the school within the context of the history of New York, but also to place the school and the city in the context of the evolution of the history of the world, because it's so easy to forget.

TF: What were your sources in conceptualizing these blocks?

KJ: In our minds, there were some immediate inspirations. One is this hushed, shadowy room at the Topkapi Palace in Istanbul, where this relic of the whisker of the prophet Mohammed is displayed, and people tiptoe around it. There's that suspension of disbelief. Is that really the whisker from the beard of the prophet? Is it true? Could it be?

AG: We made a point in Stuyvesant that everything that is there is really what it is said to be, except for one thing. There is one block that has this small Inca reproduction figure that was purchased at the Met in the gift shop, and that block is inscribed with the word "false." It serves as a reference point in the whole system . . .

KJ: . . . because people do wonder if everything really is from its stated origin. It would have been a lot easier to turn on the tap and fill up the bottle that says, "Snow, Mt. Fuji."

AG: I want to mention two other important reference points. One is a room in New Jersey at the Edison Laboratories. When Thomas Edison was working on the incandescent light bulb, he and his crew were looking for material to use as filament. There is this one storage room that's filled with different kinds of filaments—from ox hair to coconut fiber. There is a sense of the compression of the entire world within this room . . .

KJ: It is very much of the same time of the old Stuyvesant High School, in the same spirit.

AG: There is a real sense of empirical investigation, that you would actually physically investigate. Instead of relating to the world through a formula or working with a computer model, you are actually bringing something from the rest of the world and using it as a possibility of creating something new. Another important point of reference is the Chicago Tribune Building, which was a result of the famous architectural competition. The building that was eventually built is studded around the perimeter with fragments of other architecture. It is kind of odd.

KJ: These architectural fragments were collected by journalists throughout the world for the Chicago Tribune. So there was this sense of the world in the building, which was very exciting. We thought, "Here we are, this is New York City, this school is going to be a model school. The project is sponsored by the city of New York, by the Board of Education. What are our resources? What can we do here? We have the United Nations. Ahaa!" And so we attempted to tap into all the various consulates that are here in New York. But, in fact, after writing a whole slew of letters to foreign consulates here in New York, we realized that their being here in New York would make the process too indirect to solicit artifacts from beyond the city, from the world.

AG: So we asked the commissioner of Cultural Affairs to write, on our behalf, to every American ambassador abroad, asking them for something that was intrinsic to where they were stationed. The letter indicated some guidelines and suggestions of what sort of donations we were seeking. For a long, long time we'd get these packages in the mail. There was some pretty wonderful participation.

KJ: We called the U.S. Department of State and got their list of ambassadors and consuls throughout the world and their "APO" numbers. It's the interdiplomatic service that requires spending only local postage. I knew about it because I grew up in embassies around the world myself. I also knew that there were cultural affairs officers in every embassy.

The first group of letters that we sent out to ambassadors resulted in some artifacts that we really didn't want, like tourist trinkets. We didn't want a little sculpture of the mermaid in the Copenhagen Harbor, even though it is a tourist artifact that symbolizes the place. And so we wrote a second batch of letters, saying that we wanted something that really could not be bought, that was of the place, either geographically or historically, and saying that we didn't want to become colonial vandals. We wanted to make sure that the artifacts were from the place, but, in fact, that they had no monetary value.

AG: We didn't want things extracted from buildings. We targeted people. For example, we were interested in obtaining leaves from the sacred Bo tree in Sri Lanka. That was one case where a major effort was made on behalf of the Cultural Affairs office from the American Consulate. They actually sent out an employee to wait for one of these leaves to fall from the tree. You have to wait your turn for a leaf to fall outside the walls of the enclosed shrine. The leaves are treasured relics.

KJ: The letter that went out to the ambassadors was quite general. We didn't dictate what we wanted except in a small number of cases. We very much wanted the participation of people's imagination. We said if you have no imagination, just pick up some dirt, or fill a bottle with river water—but send us *something from the place. It was exciting to get things that we just couldn't quite imagine ourselves. We asked the ambassadors themselves for sugges- tions of what relic could be symbolic of the particular country. We felt that it was our responsibility to create a situation for Stuyvesant High School, in which the students could understand that what's accessible to them in a school is the whole world of knowledge, not just the particular lesson of the moment.*

AG: *Another side of this story is that from about 1980, I had been collecting little samples—dust and particles of things from all over the world. I had them in test tubes and little packets. So we did have quite a few relics ourselves.*

KJ: *Andrew already had the fragment from the Great Pyramid of Cheops.*

TF: *You got the commission in '88 and installed it in '92, so collecting all of these artifacts was a four-year process.*

AG: *Yes. And simultaneously, we were working with the plans for the new building, starting to develop a sense of where and how to place the glass blocks. We made the decision that they should all be in public spaces within the build- ing, even though the building is a closed world of sorts. We were also con- scious that the building was going to be used for other kinds of community events, that the pool was going to be open, and that slowly but surely there would be other kinds of interaction with the community within the school.*

KJ: *The blocks were not placed in the classrooms, but in the hallways, the gym, the pool . . .*

AG: *. . . the most public of spaces.*

TF: *There's also a lot of New York City history in there.*

KJ: *I think this was important because the site, the land, had absolutely no history. It is new. It is landfill. We did solicit, or attempt to solicit, artifacts from all the institutions we could dream of that might have some fragments of New York City history, but it was impossible because . . .*

AG: . . . there is no mechanism for deaccessioning things.

KJ: Even if there were 10,000 bricks torn up from a street that were used as ballast in ships coming from Holland, we couldn't have one, because there is no mechanism for a request like that.

TF: So how did you obtain all the relics from New York's past?

KJ: It was a stroke of luck. We called around, starting at NYU . . . Calling various institutions around the city that might teach urban archaeology and New York City history.

AG: We spoke to commercial archaeologists, the ones that get hired by building contractors to search sites.

KJ: We talked to the chief archaeologist at the Landmarks Preservation Commission. She said, "Don't tell him I gave you his name, but call William Asadorian. He is a librarian at Queens College, and he has been, for the last thirty years, going through all the dirt that Con Edison has rummaged through in order to lay pipes in the city."

AG: He goes around and finds sites that are being excavated.

KJ: He is totally passionate about history, about dirt. On nights and weekends, this guy sifts dirt and has gathered together an incredible collection of the history of New York, just by virtue of the fact that the hole is dug. He claims to have gone through 80 percent of the dirt that is the landfill that Stuyvesant is on. He has been searching in all good faith and spirit to find a home for his collection.

AG: But because it's been collected in a . . .

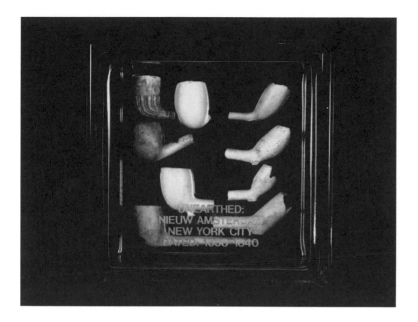

Kristin Jones and Andrew Ginzel, Mnemonics, 1992. Photograph: T. Charles Erickson.

KJ: . . . *totally illegitimate way, archaeologically, without documenting the stratigraphy, so it becomes tainted material in the eyes of so-called legitimate archaeologists. According to some, he's been removing evidence.*

AG: *Of course, when Con Ed digs, they are not about to document the stratigraphy.*

KJ: *The contention is that taking the artifact out removes the reference to site. If Con Edison were just allowed to put the dirt back in the hole, then the site would be relatively intact when archaeologists come around. Asadorian was really hoping to have much more of a historical display of his collection in a cohesive place. I think he would have liked to have had all the history of New York in chronological order on the ground floor. He was very generous, and in the end he was pleased with the project as a whole.*

Kristin Jones and Andrew Ginzel, Mnemonics, 1992. View of students with L. H. Latimer block in lunchroom at Stuyvesant High School. Photograph: T. Charles Erickson.

TF: He gave you, for example, the pipes from New Amsterdam?

KJ: He gave us the 200-year history of planting tobacco in the New World. There is a block with nine pipes from the mid-seventeenth century to the mid-nineteenth century.

AG: The earliest ones, made in Holland, were very small because tobacco was precious at that time. By 1840, the pipes made in the United States were much larger, because . . .

KJ: . . . tobacco was more abundant. The most difficult part was finding anything pre-European in New Amsterdam. He had not found any woodland Indian artifacts in downtown Manhattan or New Amsterdam. The artifacts that he gave us from Woodland culture were found . . .

AG: . . . in Upper Manhattan, or maybe the Bronx.

TF: How would you describe the aesthetics of this piece. Where is the beauty?

AG: Well, I don't know about beauty, but I think that, because of its dispersal, and because of its references, it is about inquiry, and about getting people to think. It's not about our personal egos. There is not much of our hand.

KJ: I hope that the beauty of the work is the collective expansion of the sense of accumulated history—that you exist in a moment in time, and that time continues. I think that providing these relics, these seeds to this whole explosive volume of information reflects the exhilarating side to education.

AG: I think the aesthetic is not quite graspable, that you can't really see it. To experience it, you have to use the building. The work is accumulative. It is a succession of information, of clues. Each segment of it is accessible in a very intimate, immediate way. Looking at a single block you see 1/400th of the whole. You experience one part of it, but it needs to grow.

KJ: There's an intimacy, because each block is the size of your face. Only one person can look at a block at a time.

TF: Public art is normally monumental, meant to be seen by crowds of people, appreciated by "the public" as a group at one time. But here, there could be twenty people looking at different blocks at different parts of the school at the same time.

AG: In a way, so much of the work was the experience of the whole four-year process of making it. That's where we got very intimate, so to speak, handling the artifacts, carefully tailoring and assembling them. As it exists now, it's allowed to be much more "out there" and less personal. The project refers to the person who is looking at it. Our view is not imposed.

KJ: In all of our work we attempt to look at the site and situation. Public art is different. We felt that it was imperative to imagine something that truly could belong and truly could become . . . part of the place, the place itself.

TF: It's interesting that your time for making this piece was the same as a student going to Stuyvesant—four years. It's like you graduated when you finished. Your creative process mirrored the time frame within which people are going to view it. James Joyce said that it took him a lifetime to write Finnegan's Wake . . .

KJ: . . . and it should take someone a lifetime to read it.

TF: Of course, you didn't simply reflect Stuyvesant's reality, but helped to transform it as you reflected it. Stuyvesant has a certain set of ideals. It has a sense of itself that has to do with its history, its future, and its status in the world. What you did was provide an image of its best possible self. It was not critical, in the sense of tearing down an institution, but it certainly encouraged a certain part of the school's tradition.

KJ: Why would you want to tear down this institution? They were building a new school. It's a fascinating notion to take a group of people and give them a name, and give them a sense of purpose. What is a group of people? How do you possibly qualify it? And just the notion of the students graduating and going out into the world is, in a way, symbolic of the work that we did. It's exactly what the school produces, this group of people that venture forth and have entire professional careers that all begin there. It really is the beginning. So each block, in a way, is symbolic of one student, one mind, one person.

AG: There are other subtexts that relate to our sense of the value of all matter. We took objects that are so specific, like a piece of the Great Wall of China, and put them in the same context as this anonymous piece of rock picked up above the Arctic Circle, and displayed them on an equal plane. These things are as precious as the hair of the prophet Mohammed.

KJ: So the red, red earth from Australia . . .

AG: . . . and things that are made by human beings are put on the same plane.

KJ: What is the history of this granule, this handful, this cupful of sand? They are pre-
       sented equally. And there is a perspective on this American phenomena, this
       culture of the accumulated peoples from the world. But where does our his-
       tory begin? It's certainly not just on this continent.

AG: The objects in the project and the population of the school reflect the incredible
       diversity of this city. It is the people of this place that make it so special.

Notes

1. For a catalogue of many of the projects that were installed at New York City's public schools, see *Art for Learning* (New York: Municipal Art Society, New York City Board of Education, 1994), pp. 24–32.

Two Efforts in Public Art for Public Health

In reading about activist public art projects, I have often come across the criticism that the work is "therapeutic" and that therapy is outside the purview of art. At the same time, the word "healing" has a positive ring, and it is used to describe sorts of art that do not necessarily address personal or social issues directly. I think that this is because therapy implies a therapist, which sounds so much more clinical than "healer." Perhaps we sense that the root for the word healing derives from "whole," while therapy conjures ongoing and inconclusive treatment. In any case, the therapeutic value of art that is either hailed or derided tends to be psychological, addressing metaphorical or social "wounds" rather than health in a literal sense. But part IV focuses upon two projects that address public health issues: AIDS and toxic waste sites. The AIDS Ribbon was designed to raise awareness about AIDS, to create a public reminder of the devastation of the disease, and to give people an opportunity to express their ongoing concern. Of course the ribbon itself does not cure or treat anyone, but the hope was that it might help de-stigmatize AIDS and give people an avenue toward compassion and understanding at a time when fear and prejudice characterized many people's response to AIDS. Wearing the ribbon is a symbolic gesture meant to provoke direct action. *Revival Field,* an effort to use plants to clean toxic waste sites, is a more literal attempt to address a public health problem. It is an unusual public art project in that it needed to take place at the least public of places, the toxic waste site. But it addressed public issues, employed public funds, and met with public controversy.

Of course many other art projects have centered on health issues. I will describe only one here because it seems to be so close to both the AIDS Ribbon and *Revival Field*—occupying a position perhaps halfway between the two projects. While the ribbon addresses AIDS, and *Revival Field* uses alternative gardening technology to cleanse a site, in the early 1990s, the Chicago-based collaborative Haha created an alternative garden that produced nontoxic food for people with AIDS. Haha consists of four members, Richard House, Wendy Jacob, Laurie Palmer, and John Ploof, who started working together in the late 1980s after they graduated from the School of The Art Institute of Chicago. In 1992, the group was invited to create a project for "Culture in Action," a citywide series of public art projects organized by Mary Jane Jacob for Sculpture Chicago. After considering a series of ideas, they settled on the notion of creating a hydroponic garden to grow vegetables and greens for AIDS patients. Jacob wrote in the "Culture in Action" catalogue, "Hydroponics has long been used as an experimental, alternative means of food production. Since it utilizes a sterile medium (here rock wool) to support the plant's root system and is nourished by water and minerals under carefully monitored conditions, bacteria present in soil is not transmitted to the plant."[1] The plants grown in the garden were a step beyond the organic food favored by many people with AIDS. Hydroponics eliminates not only the toxins contained in the pesticides employed by farmers, but also the bacteria present in normal soil.

Haha called the project *Flood: A Volunteer Network for Active Participation in Healthcare.* They set up shop in a storefront and began a long series of interactions with AIDS service providers, people with AIDS, and neighborhood residents. *Flood* became more than a garden, more than a small-scale provider of food. Jacob wrote, "Using art in the guise of hydroponics as a vehicle for education and dialogue—about AIDS, about safe sex, about being an AIDS volunteer, about socially responsible caregiving—provided a nonthreatening way to get people to talk about these issues."[2] The site was a storefront garden, but also an intervention in a community's interaction, a new site for dialogue. Demonstrating how essential it is for people with AIDS to eliminate all toxins from their diet taught people about the fragility of living with a compromised immune system, but the garden also gave people with AIDS an active way to participate in their own wellbeing. And anyone who has spent time gardening can understand its therapeutic value. Haha wrote:

Haha's understanding of art in this project, and in our collaborative work as a whole, encompasses an idea of usefulness. The potential usefulness of a garden goes beyond the practical level of production. A garden is a site for cultivation and growth—it demands both active caretaking and a surrender to basic and essential growth processes. (You cannot make something grow—you can only encourage it.) A garden can also be a place for recreation, for contemplation—a place to meet. In choosing the hydroponic garden as our focus, we want to activate its practical benefits as well as its usefulness as a metaphor.[3]

A basic question for *Flood* as well as the AIDS Ribbon and *Revival Field* is to what degree the project must be judged on the basis of practical results. Did *Flood* prolong anyone's life? Did its educational efforts get people to practice safer sex? What is the scientific basis for the assumption that plants grown in normal soil can transmit bacteria dangerous to people with AIDS? These are important questions, but Haha's statement provides a partial answer—that the project aimed not only at practical but also metaphorical usefulness. *Flood* was a healthy environment for interaction, where the process was as important as the product.

The AIDS Ribbon and *Revival Field* are perhaps the least traditionally artistic projects discussed in the book. Where the projects in part I are sculpture and photography, the projects in part II could be characterized as architecture or landscape design, and the projects in part III might be characterized as performance/sculpture, *Revival Field* and the AIDS Ribbon are more elusive. In fact, the status of *Revival Field* as a work of art was questioned by the chairman of the National Endowment for the Arts, and I am certain that few people who wear the AIDS Ribbon think of it as art or recognize that it was designed by artists.

The first interview is with Mel Chin. He discusses his involvement with *Revival Field* and how it relates to his earlier work. Coming off a show at the Hirshhorn Museum, Chin found himself at a bit of a dead end, but took the time to reflect and read, and he came across an article about scientific investigations into "green remediation," specifically the use of plants to cleanse toxic waste sites. His Hirshhorn show had dealt with the theme of alchemy, and Chin determined to try some practical alchemy, to pursue the ecological notions he had read about. He began calling around and soon came upon Dr. Rufus Chaney at the U.S. Department of Agriculture, an expert in green remediation. Chin narrates how he ended up collaborating on the project with Chaney, and how he gained the scientist's trust. At an early stage, a National Endowment for the Arts (NEA) panel recommended a $10,000 grant for *Revival Field,* but Chairman John Frohnmeyer rejected the recommendation, sparking a full-blown controversy. Chin managed to prevail upon Frohnmeyer to reinstate the grant, and the project went forward with increased public awareness. Chin found an appropriate site for the project in St. Paul, Minnesota, and the initial tests were a success—the plants did draw toxins from the soil.

The second interview covers much the same territory, but from the perspective of Dr. Chaney. Chaney discusses how he has been working for years on the idea of "phytoremediation," the use of plants to cleanse toxic sites. However, his work in this area had been shelved. It is interesting to note how Chin and Chaney relate the same story. They agree on the facts, but their style and vocabulary are very different. For example, while Chin calls Chaney his collaborator, Chaney refers to himself as "co-principal investigator." Perhaps the biggest difference in the two interviews is their feelings about the NEA controversy. Where Chin describes a rather harrowing ordeal, Chaney describes with glee how the controversy set the progress of the scientific investigation *ahead* years. What really got things moving was an article in *Science* magazine about the controversy at the NEA. Chaney said that that sort of publicity is almost unheard of at such an early stage of research, but that it jump-started the project to the point that there are now international conferences on the topic.

The third interview is with Frank Moore, one of the creators of the AIDS Ribbon. In the interview, Moore contrasts his work on the ribbon with his work as a painter. He differentiates between the sort of content his paintings address and the simple image of the ribbon. Through an explanation of his painting *Debutantes,* Moore discusses how he came to his current style of painting, a complex allegorical and political realism. The ribbon was conceived in response to the ubiquitous yellow ribbon during the Persian Gulf War, and much to the surprise of Moore and the other creators of the ribbon, it quickly became an international symbol of the AIDS crisis. In fact, it became so mainstream that the United States Postal Service made it into a stamp.

The final interview in the book is with Jackie McLean. In the interview, McLean discusses how she came to be the official manufacturer of the ribbon while she was a resident at the Park Avenue Shelter for Homeless Women. Her participation was the result of the work of the Artist and Homeless Collaborative (A & HC), which was initiated by Hope Sandrow. The introduction to McLean's interview discusses the A & HC, and how it operated within the shelter system. MacLean's work on the ribbon took place at the intersection of two public art projects: the AIDS Ribbon and the A & HC. Now living in her own apartment in the Bronx, McLean credits her involvement with the ribbon with helping her through a very difficult moment in her life, and getting her on her way.

Notes

1. Jane Jacob, Michael Brenson, Eva M. Olson, *Culture in Action* (Seattle: Bay Press, 1995), p. 91.

2. Ibid.

Interview: **Mel Chin** *on* Revival Field

Introduction

Mel Chin was born in Houston, Texas, in 1951.[1] He received a B.A. from Peabody College in Nashville, Tennessee, in 1975 and moved to New York City in 1983. Chin has created a wide range of public artworks across the United States, from permanent Percent for Art projects to temporary self-initiated responses to political events. His work is characterized by a complex, sometimes virtually impenetrable web of meanings. This is particularly true in the smaller portable objects that Chin creates for the museum/gallery context.

Chin received a number of awards starting in the late 1980s including grants from New York State Council on the Arts, Art Matters, the Penny McCall Foundation, the Louis Comfort Tiffany Foundation, the Englehard Award, and, most notably, two grants from the National Endowment for the Arts. These grants were essential in Chin's career because he has never been represented by a commercial gallery. It was an NEA grant that funded *Revival Field,* and a public funding controversy that made the project such big news, as discussed in the following interview.

In *Revival Field,* Chin's goal was to create a solution for the extraction of heavy metals from contaminated soil. In his statement of the nature of *Revival Field,* in a memo to the National Endowment for the Arts, Chin wrote:

Revival Field *is a conceptual artwork with an intent to sculpt a site's ecology. In a traditional sculpture, the artist with an idea approaches a material and fashions it into a concrete reality. Here the idea is the radical transformation of a hazardous site incapable of supporting life. The material will be toxic earth and the tools will be a scientific process utilizing heavy metal leaching plants called "hyperaccumulators." The aesthetic reality will be recreated Nature. The sculpting process starts unseen in the ground below in order to reveal the eventual work, a living, revitalized landscape above.*[2]

Dr. Rufus Chaney of the U.S. Department of Agriculture became Chin's first collaborator on the project. Working together, they found a toxic waste site in St. Paul, Minnesota, and tested the plants, the so-called "hyperaccumulators," that Dr. Chaney thought were the most promising. In the process, Chin was enmeshed in a controversy regarding funding by the National Endowment for the Arts (NEA). When John Frohnmeyer, the NEA chairman, threatened to withhold funding for the project that had been recommended by the panel, Chin responded not by suing but by opening a dialogue that led to the restoration of the grant. *Revival Field* took place in St. Paul, Minnesota, during 1990 to 1993. But the project has continued for a decade: *Revival Field II* was in Palmertown, Pennsylvania, 1992–1998; *Revival Field III* in Soldier Field, Maryland, 1996-ongoing; and *Revival Field IV* is planned for yet unspecified sites in Germany, starting in 2000. In Germany, Chin and Chaney hope to team up with Dr. Robert Richard Brooks from New Zealand, a pioneer in the field.

There are several levels of dialogue in *Revival Field.* First, Chin entered into a dialogue with Dr. Chaney, and they became cocreators of the project. Second, Chin entered into a dialogue with the chairman of the NEA, rather than seeking conflict. Third, the project helped spawn dialogue on the topic of "green remediation" within the scientific field of toxic waste treatment.

Chin has developed an unusual set of strategies for collaboration. Unlike some artists who champion collaboration but seem to have developed a model they can re-use, Chin's collaborations are site-specific, adjusting to the social, political, and aesthetic meaning of the site. This orientation even applies to the catalogue of *Inescapable Histories,* a traveling show of his work, in which Chin arranged to be interviewed by ten people from different fields, including environmental geography, physics, agronomy, social anthropology, and, of course, art. Chin's work addresses all of these disciplines, and engages in dialogue with a much wider range of intellectuals than usually appear in an art publication. In the context of this catalogue, Chin was asked whether it would be possible to call *Revival Field* a success if it turned out that the scientific research was a dead end. He responded, "No, but it can be a successful model of cooperation between disciplines and a guide for navigation through legal, political, and social worlds."[3]

From 1995 to 1997, Chin worked on a very unusual collaborative project called *In the Name of the Place,* which took place at two art schools, a museum, and a network television show simultaneously. *In the Name of the Place* was originally commissioned for an exhibition organized by Julie Lazar and myself called "Uncommon Sense," which appeared at the Museum of Contemporary Art (MOCA) in Los Angeles, in early 1997. In an unpublished interview, Chin describes the impetus to work on network television thus:

The whole world knows L.A. and the U.S. through television and film. After one L.A. visit, flying away, looking out over Los Angeles, I realized that somewhere in those industries

GALA Committee, *In the Name of the Place,* 1997, Museum of Contemporary Art, Los Angeles, California. "Melrose Place" shooting within the installation of GALA Committee objects in "Uncommon Sense" exhibition. (Mel Chin is standing at right.) Photograph: Paula Goldman.

was where I wanted to develop this conceptual public art project. At the same time I was thinking of the virus as a paradigm for this art project. Viruses are self-replicating, but they mutate, and to me, that's like an art idea. I was wondering, how do you jet an idea into a system, and let it replicate within that system? Using the virus as a model, how could I interact with television? I think there were some preliminary notes leading up to these ideas, but it sort of galvanized one evening. Helen [Nagge, Mel Chin's partner and collaborator] was just flipping through the channels on our TV, and I was coming in from a day of teaching. She turned to Melrose Place, and there was Heather Locklear. I had not seen or heard of Heather Locklear in ages, but I knew who she was. There was this face. I just watched a couple more minutes, and when she moved away, there was this background, and then the camera switched to another background, and another. The action moved from an apartment, to an office, to an advertising company, to a bar. It has a large number of sets. And I said, that's the place! *Melrose Place would be the targeted host of a benign infection, or art virus.*[4]

And indeed, Chin did create a public work for network television. Working primarily with students from the University of Georgia and CalArts in Los Angeles, Chin helped form the GALA (Georgia-Los Angeles) Committee. Two factors helped Chin realize *In the Name of the Place*. First, Chin was appointed to the Lamar Dodd Professorial Chair of Fine Arts at the University of Georgia, 1994–1997. This position gave Chin the financial stability to undertake a virtually unpaid, multiyear project. It also gave him access to a large group of students at the University of Georgia, many of whom ended up working with him on the project. Second, Chin won a $50,000 CalArts Alpert Award in the Visual Arts in 1995. Again, this grant gave him financial stability and access to students, because the grant included a requirement that Chin teach for a minimum of two weeks at CalArts. But the GALA committee was not only students. It also included professional artists from across the country, as well as writers and theoreticians. The project became a reality starting when set designers at Melrose Place agreed to let the GALA Committee create hundreds of art props for the television show, many of which were integrated into the permanent sets and appeared repeatedly on the show.

The collaboration climbed the institutional power structure at Fox Television, and by the end, the GALA Committee was able to engineer a scene in which Heather Locklear's character invites a friend to the opening of "Uncommon Sense," because the fictional D&D Advertising firm has taken on the Museum of Contemporary Art as a client. A staged opening was then shot at MOCA prior to the actual opening of "Uncommon Sense" and aired as the show was up. In an ironic twist, Locklear and Melrose Place were in fact publicizing the exhibition; even though D&D Advertising does not exist, it fulfilled its (fictional) obligation to publicize the museum. Chin was an organizer and facilitator for *In the Name of the Place.* While nobody questioned his role as the original impetus behind the project, he insisted that his name *not* be used on the cover or title page of the catalogue, that the project be billed as the work of the GALA Committee. And Chin was not directly responsible for the objects, paintings, and set pieces that were used on the television show. He helped conceptualize some of the pieces, but his role as an artist was focused on the overall "ecology" of the project rather than the individual details. After *In the Name of the Place,* Chin returned to a more free-floating, artistic practice, creating objects in his studio as he continued to work on new incarnations of *Revival Field.*

This interview was conducted in Mel Chin's Lower East Side studio in October 1995. Chin was visiting New York from Athens, Georgia, where he was teaching at the time. It was edited by Chin and Helen Nagge in the fall of 1997.

Tom Finkelpearl: Can you relate the series of events that led up to the creation of Revival Field*?*

Mel Chin: In 1989, I remounted Operation of the Sun through the Cult of the Hand *at the Hirshhorn Museum in Washington, D.C. It was a cryptic, alchemic, mythic, scientific piece in nine parts. The Hirshhorn show also included my first large political pieces, including* The Extraction of Plenty from What Remains: 1823- *(1988–1989), which is a pair of White House columns squeezing a cornucopia. These pieces were combining ideas about political tragedy and ecological tragedy. Politics was starting to show up in my work in a masked, aesthetic form. The pieces lure you into contemplating not only the optic. They're asking you to ascertain the covert message hidden inside. You have to give them time. This is important for me, giving ideas enough time to really click. I need time myself, always being rushed, so I felt that I had to impart that by whatever means necessary.*

My research field for The Operation of the Sun *was the history of alchemy—cultural sources from Greek to Chinese, scientific sources, and the origins of words and forms. For example, where did the first hand ax occur? How did its function relate to its form, and what material was it made of? The usage of material was never arbitrary. I tried not to be arbitrary and (so-called) expressive, but to be compressive, in other words, distill it, cook it, and reduce it, in order to come up with this final thing. I wanted to create works that are like mines. It's okay if the work is cryptic. It's okay if the ideas are embedded. The research was done to put my intuition on trial. I know I can draw. I can make a work that is formally beautiful or ugly, whatever may be necessary. I can be passionate about this construction. But it has to be backed up by something.*

TF: So this examination of alchemy was in how many parts?

MC: *There were nine, as in the nine planets in our solar system. Each one with al-chemic process and mythological reference. For example,* Conjunction and Entrapment *is about Venus—both the myth of the goddess and the science of the planet. The copulation of Venus and Mars and the jealous entrapment by her husband, Vulcan, are represented in various elements. The piece in-cluded Venus and Mars in a net of copper, which also represents the sulfuric acid clouds that cover the planet, woven in the YC bands that were discov-ered by the* Mariner Ten *spaceship, I believe. And it had a left-leaning oyster from the Chinese. So it used myths superimposed on science, on top of the passages of alchemy. I started with a preconceived notion as I normally do, and it was destroyed by process—not only this research, but the making of these objects. This willingness to destroy my preconceived notions was a cen-tral part of the process that led to* Revival Field.

After the Hirshhorn show, things were rough, things were extremely rough. I had gone through this phase where I was so hopeful, but by then I was so broke, and so tired, physically tired. We made the columns for The Ex-traction of Plenty *in my parents' garage in Texas, and there had been set-backs and medical problems. Making those pieces was a tight-knit family affair. It was very passionate and very meaningful to spend that time with them—my mother putting on fans to dry the goat blood, coffee, and mud mixtures, and my father giving great expertise and instruction when things collapsed. And then there was my first major museum show. I had gone through such a process to prepare, and I was basically busted, disgusted, and can't be trusted. And there I was hoping that things would come through and there might be a sale so I could recoup something, and then nothing happened. Good notoriety, a bad review. That's about it, and I was basically exhausted.*

So I came back to New York, and Helen [Nagge, Chin's partner] was here, and I just went into a depression. But somehow I snapped out of it, and said, "That's okay. I can't even buy a hammer or buy a tool anymore, I've spent everything on this, but it's okay, because I quit. What do I love the most? What does everyone talk about? They say Mel can make these things, these art objects, work with materials. Well, if I like this so much, and I could see myself comfortably doing this for the next ten to twenty years, then I quit. I'll have to put myself through another fire, a conceptual fire. This is not enough." So I started free-ranging, roaming through these books, articles, newspapers, without a specific direction. And I discovered something in the Whole Earth Review about Terence McKenna, who is a psilocybin expert. He's into this whole mushroom cult idea, and outer space—great ideas.

His article mentioned something about plants cleaning up waste fields, but he was focusing on Datura stramonium which is known as jimson weed. "Well there it is," I thought, "Jimson weed." So I ran to Helen and said, "I've got it—it's plants. I see it as sculpture." In Texas, before oil drilling, there was agriculture, and before that were these weeds. So maybe the weeds could start it all over again. Here you have it. You have a steady stream of human occupation that eventually reduces the ecological climate, and you bring back the weed in order to get it back into shape. I thought, it's just like a traditional sculpture. The material of the past was marble. In the Carrera marble Michelangelo saw David, and said, "I'm going to carve it." What is modern material today? What is our modern by-product? What has crystallized in our times is in this terrible hazardous waste. The chisel is the plant, and not only myself, but communities, scientists, all these people will be the artists, and we will transform what is potential for death into life. If you can take a place that is basically dead or has a single species growing on it, and make it active or living again, that is a finished sculpture. It's a post-Robert Smithson idea. Let's not just work with ecologists. Let's be active. Let's do something.

Despite all these poetic meanderings, I was in the habit of calling on experts. Like I called Walter LeFeber of Cornell (at breakfast on Sunday morning) and said, "Name the ten worst presidents . . ." ("Who are you?" he interjected) " . . . in terms of their policies in Central America." His responses became the signatures on top of the columns of The Extraction of Plenty. So I thought I'd write to Terence McKenna and see what he said. Well, no feedback, nothing on the jimson weed. I began to learn that jimson weed was not favored for remediation because it would kill cattle and make people sick. It has a lot of drugs in it. It's hallucinogenic.

I started researching and calling scientists and botanists to ask about its cleansing capacity. I wanted to focus on extracting metals from the soil, because that would be a modern metallurgical/alchemic project. That would pull it into the conceptual area that I had started with. Now, I wanted to do real *alchemy*. Well, the more I researched, the worse it became for the jimson weed idea. The Texas boys would say, "Well, don't know about that. It can get your cattle sick." This was not looking good. Finally, I called a Kirk Brown at the University of Texas A & M, who said, "If you are talking about plants and extracting metals, you might want to call Dr. Rufus L. Chaney at the USDA Agricultural Research Service in Beltsville, Maryland." So I called him up and said, "Dr. Chaney, could you talk about the potential of Datura for use as an accumulator of metals or toxins?" He said, "It'll get you high, but it won't pick you up any metal."

TF: You never wrote him a letter or anything?

MC: Yes, I called him cold. He said, "Datura, in its cell culture, reduces to this liquid mass. You can possibly trap some radioactive isotope, but then you have this jelly mass that you have to deal with. But if you want to pick up metals, you've called the right person." I said "Great!"

But Dr. Chaney was skeptical. He said, "I worked with an artist once in the seventies, this guy who wanted to paint with trees. He wanted all the chemistry to make the trees turn yellow and green. Well, I told him how to do it, but nothing came out of that." So I asked him for recommended readings, and he recommended Robert Richard Brooks' Biochemical Methods of Prospecting for Minerals.[5] I started doing the same kind of research I had done for my earlier pieces, and found out there is a long track in alchemic lore and African lore about looking for plants that can indicate metal. So I thought that if it's nothing new, then why isn't this idea being done? In practice, all of the complexities appear: you can't get access to a toxic site, and all the catch-22s start coming up politically.

I asked Dr. Chaney what he needed. "Well, it's just lab now," he said. "It's been shelved. I have no funding." (This is Reagan-Bush time.) "So I'm back to working with sewage sludge." That was his lot. But his passion was this idea. He said, "There is no interest whatsoever in remediation." I said, "No, there must be. We don't need the EPA. We're going to do it through the NEA. We're going to make it art." He didn't know what I was talking about.

When I started to talk to Dr. Chaney about this, he was a bit impatient. He would say, "Mel, it takes me three times over to tell you what it's all about." And I said, "Well I'm just learning." But eventually it got to the point where I was able to understand what he needed. And so I began with the political negotiations to get a site, which was intense. I worked every day on the phone for a couple of hours just to find someone who would admit that they had a toxic waste site. No one wanted to admit it. The EPA said that they would help, but they never did. I would get up the ladder so far, but there was always a wall. And the wall was litigation. If we admit that the waste is toxic, then someone is responsible. The EPA's cleanup methods were either trucking it away, or covering it with a thin layer of asphalt. Every branch would send me to somebody else. I finally got to SITE: Superfund Innovative Technology Evaluation. That sounded good. But they said, "Well, we'd love to help you, but you are not a 'technology.'" I said, "Well how do you get a to be a 'technology?'" Well, you have to have scientific backup. You have to do field tests in order to prove your technique. It was a classic catch-22: they won't let you on the site to test it, to make it a "technology," but only "technologies" can be used. So, in other words, things stay dormant. Nothing really changes. These are things I was confronted with. I kept calling Dr. Chaney, kept trying to find fields.

TF: This is still '89?

MC: We are getting into '90 now. I was waiting for the NEA grant at the same time. We were looking for cadmium and zinc problems, cadmium being even deadlier than lead. There were seeds available for a type of accumulator that would take up tremendous amounts of zinc and cadmium, and that would give us our first test proof.

TF: Who had these seeds?

MC: Dr. Baker in England, and Dr. Chaney had a couple he wanted to try. The race was on. Around this time I identified a potential site outside of St. Paul: Pig's Eye Landfill. This was during my busted, disgusted time. Peter Boswell [Curator] and Martin Freedman [Director] of the Walker Art Center in Minneapolis came to New York, and they were looking at my work. The Corcoran exhibition was down, and I wasn't interested in showing. I was so depressed, I

Mel Chin with Rufus Chaney, Revival Field, Pig's Eye Landfill, St. Paul, Minnesota, 1993 harvest, aerial view. Photograph: David Schneider

guess. They looked at my work, and said if I want to do a show, then let's use this political work and perhaps Revival Field.

TF: Did the Walker help identify the site?

MC: No. I was doing it all solo, though they knew that I was up to something. I felt that I could use the museum to interface with the public. The landfill's a site that you could not go to visit—it's off-limits, hazardous. But I could still present information to stimulate the conceptual drive to implement the Revival Field. *I started seeing this cycle of relationship, the political cycle and the social cycle.*

Then the NEA blew up. I got a call from Lois Bradley, who worked at the NEA Interarts Program. She said, "You know there were forty-seven applicants approved for Interarts grants, but only forty-six got it. Your application was recommended by the panel, and recommended by the National Advisory Counsel, but you didn't get it." I said, "What? I don't understand. It's demo-

cratic, you go through the panel . . ." She said, "It's the chair. [NEA Chairman, John Frohnmeyer] This is highly controversial. It's the first time in NEA history that a chair has said no. This is not good." I said, "Yeah, It's not good at all."

I thought, I will fight this, but I'll do it quietly and I will not do any TV interviews. I got a call from NBC. They said, "It'll be a good giggle piece, about your plants." I said, "Giggle piece? Forget it. I just won't do it." My idea was to say as little as possible in public, because at the same time, I continued negotiations for the test field.

This intense struggle for the funding ensued. People called me saying that they would give me $10,000 for the project to replace the NEA money. I said, "No, it's a public problem, and it should be public funds. We should show that arts can be important for public service. I don't want private funding. An idea like Revival Field is for the public domain." So it went, step by step. I was quiet in the press, but I called the National Association of Artists Organizations (NAAO) and started working with Penelope Boyer and Charlotte Murphy. They were with me, and they started writing letters. Then I called Martin Freedman, who was preparing my show at the Walker, and he started working on the American Museum Directors, also writing letters. As it happens, he was on the NEA's National Council, and he talked to all his friends. Ned Rifkin at the Hirshhorn was working on it, too, and [De Menil Collection curator] Walter Hopps. And I had my Texas sponsor, who is an ecology person.

So, I heard that Frohnmeyer was livid. All he had wanted to do was to make a political statement for John Sununu and President Bush. He thought it would be simple. He found my piece questionable enough from his perspective, and he hated the words "invisible aesthetics" that I used to describe my work. According to the NEA bylaws, Frohnmeyer did not need to meet with anybody. But, because of all the letter-writing from powerful people, we were getting to him, and finally he agreed to have a meeting.

TF: You know, if you spend time in government, you will find that there is a lot of hidden un-democracy within democratic processes.

MC: I know that. I'm totally aware of that, but you've got to believe in the principle, and you have to speak out when it's being abused. Everything was at a boil-

ing point, but I just had to keep it quiet. Also, keep in mind that I was at the most sensitive level of negotiations with the site, and then this came up. It was very tense because I saw this amazing project just going down. So anyway, a museum director and my sponsor decided to go to the meeting with Frohnmeyer on my behalf. I was vacillating because there was so much pressure. I decided not to go. And then I decided to go. I had to go. I stayed up all night and just questioned whether or not . . . and, finally, I decided that in principle I must go, because, in principle, this is about the voice, and if I don't have my voice available, then we've lost. So I tried to reach these sponsors, and they would not return my calls. I felt this was wrong. I kept calling, saying "I've changed my mind." I finally got through to the offices and they said, "Well, the museum director and your sponsor have just flown to Washington, and they are going to meet John Frohnmeyer tomorrow." I felt this was not right. We were supposed to be working together on this project. So I called Walter Hopps, who was playing this political game, talking to Richard Andrews [former director of the Art in Public Places Program for the NEA] on the other line. Walter said, "Mel, you've been listening too much to the Walker, Peter Boswell, and all those guys. They don't know anything about politics." I said, "Walter, just get this straight. If I don't go, then we've all lost already. It's not about the money and winning the $10,000. We have lost if we don't get beyond that." And he said, "Hold on a minute." When he got back on the phone, he said, "Richard Andrews agrees with you." So Walter turned on a dime and said, "You're right, you have to go, I've been telling them that you shouldn't." And he was the one who had told them not to call me back, to let me wait it out. So I made an appointment with the NEA, and got on a train to D.C.

When I got there, my sponsors were angry at me. They were playing a political game, and they made me wait, they treated me horribly. They wouldn't even talk to me—I was going to ruin everything. I said, "Look, it's my project, and I really appreciate your being here." I was nice to everyone. But they gave me this sense that: "You don't know politics, and this ecology sponsor knows George Bush and his family." They were going to play that card. They said, "She will lead the discussion." I said, "Fine, you've come here to help." It was an awful dynamic. I was so beaten, in a way, not even hopeful. I told them, "I only ask one thing, if we win or lose, it's no problem, I'll get this project done, but it's got to be done with some integrity." Before the meeting, when they gave their presentation to me, I said, "I know what his response will be to your presentation. He'll say, 'Why don't you take this up with the EPA instead of the NEA?'"

So we went to the meeting, and they were not even looking at me. We sat down, and Frohnmeyer came in (a Washington situation) and they started giving their presentation in a really official style, "Chairman Frohnmeyer, I represent such-and-such, this museum director represents the art community, oh, and there's the artist." I was just listening and watching Frohnmeyer, and he's getting angrier and angrier. Finally, when they were done, he (as I had predicted) said, "Why don't you take this to the EPA instead of the NEA?" So I pushed my chair back, stood up, and said, "I think I have to respond." I slowly began to explain, "First, you should understand what these plants do, and then understand how I see Revival Field as an artwork. And I also want to explain the words that you hate: 'invisible aesthetic.' There are some things you cannot see in the social world, others on the molecular scale, but they can be the foundation for amazing transformations. To me, that change, that escape from sameness, is beautiful." I talked for quite a while about that and he seemed more interested. He said, "You mean plants are so loaded with metals that you can mine them, sell them as ore, and pay for the process?" I said "Yeah, it's a revolution. You sculpt an environment from one state of being to another. To me that is a modern sculpture. Sculpting away social problems. You have to work with other people to do that. It's not just me. It's all the scientists, the agencies. And the NEA is part of it." He started coming around in some way.

Finally, I asked him if I could say one more thing. At that time, I was using Elaine Scarry's book The Body in Pain [6] *to think more conceptually. She divides the world into pain and imagination. The final incarnation of pain is war and torture. It's the unmaking of the world, because it removes the capacity of the human being to use language. If you are being tortured, you can cry out, but you cannot formulate thoughts under intense pain. Death also silences. And then there is imagination. Not the frivolous imagination, but a very objective definition of this word. It's fundamental to the invention of language. Through the imagination is the remaking of the world. I said, "Now, ideas of art come from the imagination, and they can be about sexu-*

Mel Chin with Rufus Chaney, Revival Field, Pig's Eye Landfill, St. Paul, Minnesota, aerial view with St Paul in the background. Photograph: David Schneider.

ality, homosexuality, politics, ecology. They can be about aesthetics, about anything, but they come from that source. And my only question to you, John, is which camp are you in? That's all I have to say." I thanked him, and he walked out.

Fifteen minutes later he came back in, he's smiling, and says, "Well, I've decided to reverse my decision." We were shocked. We agreed that he got to write his own press release, which made me look like I did not have my act together, so that he would look better.

TF: Because you had not explained yourself fully before?

MC: Yeah, yeah, but it was a formality that he wanted. I feel that what I had told him changed his mind. I felt he finally understood it, and he liked the idea about this camp that he would now be part of. You're either going to be for the artist or for the politician—you can decide. So it was a major breakthrough.

During this same period, I was calling people involved with the Min-
nesota Waste Control Commission. I heard they owned the Pig's Eye Landfill,
a state superfund site in St. Paul. On the first call, I told the guy all the good
stuff about Revival Field—*how no one else in the world was doing anything*
like this. He kept getting angrier and angrier. Finally he said, "You know, you
are opening a can of worms, and even if I wanted to hear you, I couldn't.
Goodbye." He slammed the phone down. So, I kept pestering them. I was
getting somewhere, finally, after eight months of solid work. Dr. Chaney ex-
pected it would take seven years to get a site, and he wasn't even going to
budge forward until something real was in sight.

One of the people whom I talked to said, "If you are an artist, all you
want is publicity. You don't want anything real—especially if you are a per-
formance artist." I said, "No, it could be totally confidential, and I'll work
with you, because I know that these issues are so sensitive. The main thing is
to get something done for the people who have to live around this site." But
because I was involved in the NEA mess, there it was in the New York Times,
and so this guy who was saying that I was going after publicity was nervous.
Word was out.

During this period, also, I had done a piece at the Corcoran School of Art
related to three student uprisings: Tiananmen Square, Kent State, Mexico
City. It was called Forgetting Tiananmen, Kent State, Tlatelolco *[1989].*
Though the piece was not directly related, it's a funny story about how things
work, politically. One of our fundamental arguments in Forgetting Tiananmen *was that one person called the shots, and then the students suffered*
because of that decision. There was a woman involved with the piece at the
Corcoran, Mary Vento. She called me and said, "I normally don't mention my
husband, but he's in the House of Representatives. His name is Bruce Vento.
He is very much into ecology, and I think he understands your project. You
can call him in D.C."

TF: *She worked at the Corcoran?*

MC: *No, she was one of the students working on the piece at the school. We had*
many discussions about relationships of power at that time. Mary Vento saw
the NEA controversy and Revival Field *as another issue of power. She said,*

"What you taught was about the same thing. I will tell Bruce to give you a call, and you all can have a one-on-one, to talk about Revival Field." So he [Bruce Vento] said, "Sounds great. Are you having trouble with the Minnesota Waste Control Mining Commission? Well, I know so and so, he's the head." A couple of days later, my answering machine had a message from the head of the Metropolitan Waste Control Commission. He kept calling and leaving messages for me to call him back. Of course, it's because of the state relationship. It's political. We finally talked, and I told him I knew the history of the Pig's Eye site. This company dumped highly loaded cadmium ash mix there in the seventies, which closed the whole landfill down. I just wanted to do a simple experiment there. He said, "Well, it's not for me to say. It belongs to the city." In other words, his team had been playing a cat-and-mouse game with me to get me farther away from the source. I called the person who is in charge of the solid waste management for the city of St. Paul, and he said, "You are going to do something to clean it? Great, it's just sitting there. And it's hundreds of thousands of dollars to remove it, maybe millions." Of course, this "yes" was premature. So we had a meeting with the Mayor's Office, the Waste Control Commission, Minnesota Pollution Control Agency (which is their EPA). Everybody was finally around a table. The lawyer for the Metropolitan Waste Commission, a Ms. Flood, said, "We're just going to stop you." We start talking, and I said, "Let's not say that, let's just start discussing the issues. I'll tell you honestly what this piece is about, and we can go from there." I had gotten a lot of training on how to negotiate at the NEA.

Finally, they said I could proceed if I changed the language of the project description, put on a press block, and shot no photographs to identify the site. I agreed to that. That's why the earliest photographs of Revival Field are below the horizon line, looking down at it. Only the later ones show St. Paul in the background.

TF: They relaxed a little bit later?

MC: Yes. Later they felt it was a success and good publicity for them. Of course there was one more obstacle. Tim Diamond, the city councilman who ran that district, said, "No. I'm not gonna let no goddamn taxpayer money go to some flaky art project." I went up to his office (here's this guy at a desk covered with yellow post-it tabs everywhere), and I said, "Look, it's government sponsored, the mayor wants it, and you will be the only one who rejected this. After all this effort, against the wishes of the Waste Control Commission and a member of the House of Representatives—you will have the ultimate distinction of being the stellar one who will say no. You will tell your constituents that this guy wanted to try this solution at the landfill and you said no because you don't want art." He just looked at me and said, "Mr. Chin, I admire your dedication and perseverance. I'll let you do it."

So we went out immediately to plant the field. Tam Miller, my assistant was the first "scientific safety officer" on the site. We had to go through all the EPA training. Barron Brown, my other assistant was there as well.

TF: So you designed and built the structure around the planting area?

MC: We treated the field, built around it. We used the funding to pay for the fencing. And we structured it with the look of a hazardous containment compound. Finally, there was our test site, and there were ninety-six different plots. I organized the whole site with Dr. Chaney. Helen and I went and transplanted plants in Beltsville, Maryland.

TF: On the site, did you need to wear a special gear?

[Tam Miller, Chin's assistant, had entered a few minutes earlier.]

Tam Miller: The main danger at that site was ingestion. So we just wore jumpsuits, dust masks, and gloves. We wore equipment for a "Level A" site, the lowest level. Some things were important: Washing every time we left, not eating or smoking at the site.

MC: We learned about everything up to the self-contained breathing apparatus (SCBA) during our "Hazardous Materials Incidence Response Training" at the EPA. Minnesota Pollution Control made us do that. It was another of these last minute things.

TF: *Your show at the Walker Art Center was up at the same time. Did it include documentation of the* Revival Field?

MC: *Yeah, the maquette was in the show. That was the irony. The piece was showing at the Walker while the NEA was saying it was not art.*

The first year, vandals tore the fences down, and I had to borrow money from the Walker to fix it. Animals got in and ate the test plants. But we put it back up, and we added extra groundhog control fencing. We did it again, and the second year yielded the first confirmation, that, yes, the plants suck it up.

TF: *Dr. Chaney took the plants and analyzed them?*

MC: *We planted it in the spring, harvested it in the fall, and sent the samples to him.*

TM: *And, according to his instructions, we had to carefully wash each sample and bag it specially. We had ninety-six different, specially labeled samples. That was quite a process in itself, just keeping track of everything.*

MC: *With almost no funding. No one wanted to sponsor us. So, [laughs] Tam suffered severely.*

TM: *I even had to dry worms from the site.*

TF: *Dry them out and send them to him?*

MC: *So he could grind them up and see what's in there.*

TM: *That's one of the first indications of soil contamination, because they ingest so much dirt.*

MC: *Initially, when we were digging, we noticed that there were very few worms. It was not good soil. It had a monoculture on top—but this plant was not accumulating anything. It had just adapted to this hostile climate.*

Mel Chin with Rufus Chaney, Revival Field, soil sampling, 1992, Pig's Eye Landfill, St. Paul, Minnesota. Photograph courtesy of the Walker Art Center.

TM: *During the second year, it was amazing how many insects we saw, compared with the first year. It was incredible.*

MC: *The second year, the test results proved that the scientific process can now move forward.*

TF: *Did you tell Frohnmeyer?*

MC: *Yes, and later on I heard he got a* Revival Field *T-shirt.*
Then we started the Palmerton, Pennsylvania, field. That's a National Priority Superfund site. These two sites have yielded information for Dr. Chaney to enable him to move forward. That's where I learned about the giveaway principle: Right now the people of Palmerton basically own and

operate the site. The local Zinc Information Center plants it and works with Dr. Chaney and gives him the results. Without funding, we laid it out and did the preliminary work with them. This idea now is alive and well in Palmerton, and as far as I'm concerned, I don't care if they know who I am. I've learned that it's necessary to have a sustainable relationship with an idea, in order to let the idea go. Now it is part of the picture at the Department of Energy, where they have finally accepted "green remediation," as it's called.

TF: So what is Chaney's relationship with it now?

MC: He's the lead person in the United States. I feel that our suffering through the process allowed for it now to proceed.

We started an ecological art project, but used it as the seed for another idea about education. To recontextualize public art we had to deal with this tremendous wall of psychological space. That is the big sculpture, socially. The barriers were psychological—people's feelings and apprehensions of where art fits within Revival Field, from the scientists, to the funders, to the public. Where does responsibility fit? How do you interface? I've had successful and unsuccessful relationships with the public, but I feel that over time, I also have to maintain this self-critical discourse. Right now, I'm more like the quiet PR man for Revival Field. It's going into privatization, opening up this whole field of technology. A lot of people are going for plant patents, trying to make the money. I think fifty scientists claim that they did it first. My response to that is, "Great!" If it's alive and well, that means Revival Field will be done some day. It's in progress in a good way, as opposed to a oneshot demonstration. Well, that's real-world dynamics, and I just want to see the field. I want to see 4 square miles transformed. Our industrial past can have one more possibility for regrowth through these managed systems. It's a piece that will be, because of this beginning.

TF: One consistent element in your work has been its enigmatic or cryptic nature. You really ask your audiences to work hard. The work in the Hirshhorn show had a set of meanings imbedded within them that you wanted the audience to "mine." Of course, the wall labels were a series of hints about the meanings, because sometimes the meanings are so deeply encoded.

MC: Yes, though in some exhibitions, like the show at the De Menil Collection in Houston, I asked that there be no labels. I love unauthorized readings. That's invention, and that is imagination. And if you could stir that up, that is as powerful a tool as anything else that public art could do. It means you are doing your job. I think of the case of Vincent van Allen, a security guard at the Hirshhorn show, and how he looked at the Helmet of Pluto. He began giving unauthorized tours of The Operation of the Sun through the Cult of the Hand. He knew about some of the pieces because we talked about them. But when he got to Pluto, I had never discussed it with him. It was this head-dress of coal, and an inner layer of ceramic, and then alchemic gold held by great arsenical copper underneath. Vincent would tell people, "This was the headdress of an African king," and that was that. My assistant, Barron, was disturbed when he overheard this because he really got into all these intense levels of meaning after a year of research at the Library of Congress. But I was very happy Vincent said what he said. I called him to thank him. Looking crit-ically, he exposed my rip-off—the cult of the hand being out of Africa, basi-cally, and metallurgy is still alive in Africa. I borrowed it from that source, and he exposed my theft. It happened because something truly propelled his imagination to come to that conclusion. I feel that that's important.

I have made work less "clear" to increase curiosity, to get people to say, "Now what is that?" I think that is where restraint comes to play. If you say everything, then it's all set. It is nice to let word spread as opposed to saying, "Okay, this is what this is about, here's the interpretation, that's it, good-bye." I try to give people more credit. I do not want to always reintroduce the most direct approach to living in a consumer-oriented, market-driven world. I am embarrassed that that is the culture that I live in. I am delusional most of the time as an artist. I have great problems even with myself, because I know that my desires are manufactured toward another end, beyond my control. Normally I feel that we head toward stasis when we talk about sur-vival, or ecology, or evolution, because it's such a narrow bandwidth that is broadcast. Because it's more comfortable, and it does not create aberrations for individual exploration.

TF: I've always thought that one of public art's primary roles could be to confuse people a little bit, because people are too comfortable with a certain level of under-

standing of their environment. If you put in little question marks throughout the space somehow, that could be a positive role. On the other hand, something like Tilted Arc, *was confusing without any access. There can be positive levels of confusion created by a piece.*

MC: *I feel that certain artworks have to be invented that function in the in-between levels of neither/nor. And sometimes if I say too much then I'm pushing it back into the art that is expected or art that is* known, *and therefore reinforcing the everyday politics of division. So that's why my restraint is not to make it more cryptic, but to give the benefit of the doubt . . . so that reasonable doubt of the artwork is okay. If you doubt it, then there may be a possibility for human discovery. When I am given that leeway to discover something on my own, I think I have a more profound reaction to any kind of information.*

There is no solid ground to talk about the political and aesthetic dimension of what public art should be, because we don't know. This whole field of exploration is necessary now, because, after a lifetime spent in art, I'm moving away from art. I'm more interested in these in-betweens, like working at a drive-in, or behind the scenes. Projects can evolve in these sorts of sites over time and without the mantle or the psychological threat that art has accumulated. There's a psychological threat in art's elitism that has been used effectively in a political sense. We have to find new methods of combating it.

Notes

1. The biographical information in this introduction is drawn from: Lucy Lippard and Ben Huerta, *Inescapable Histories: Mel Chin* (Kansas City, MO.: ExhibitsUSA, 1996).

2. From a "Position Paper Draft, December 26, 1990. To: NEA Interarts: New Forms. Re: Reconsideration—*Revival Field* Application." (Unpublished, courtesy of the artist.) As discussed in the interview, Chin's NEA grant for *Revival Field* was an on-again, off-again affair. This memo was Chin's argument in favor of the notion that the project was art as well as science.

3. Ibid., p. 31.

4. From an unpublished interview I conducted with Mel Chin, 1997.

5. Robert Richard Brooks, *Biochemical Methods of Prospecting for Minerals* (New York: John Wiley & Sons, Inc., 1983).

6. Elaine Scarry, *The Body in Pain* (New York: Oxford University Press, 1985).

Interview: **Dr. Rufus L. Chaney**
on Revival Field

Introduction

Dr. Rufus L. Chaney is a research scientist at the United States Department of Agriculture. The following interview took place over the telephone in 1997. Since that time, Chaney has been active in the technology discussed in the interview. In 1999, ten years after the initiation of *Revival Field,* Chaney and Chin were actively investigating the possibility of working with a company in Germany to apply some of Dr. Chaney's findings.

Tom Finkelpearl: What sort of work do you do at the United States Department of Agriculture?

Rufus Chaney: I do research on soil-plant relationships and the safety of heavy metals in the food chain. I study heavy metals' toxicity to plants or the dangerous transfer of metals to the food. Over the last twenty-five years, I've developed lots of the rules of thumb that people rely on today. Because I am an expert in heavy metal uptake and tolerance by plants, I was familiar with the development of knowledge that led up to this whole idea of "phytoremediation," which is used in the Revival Field. *I wrote about it around 1980. Mel Chin heard about it in 1990, and the rest is history.*

TF: Mel had been calling around to different people trying to figure out an approach to remediation of toxic sites.

RC: Yes. He read about it in Whole Earth Catalog *or something like that. The specific ideas he had read about were hardly relevant at all, but they gave him the idea. That's the beauty of a spark that allows your mind to form a different combination of thoughts and—zappo, you have a new idea. I think it's fair to say that at least twenty to thirty people have independently come upon this idea over the last thirty years (and only later found out that I had written about it). It's implicit in the writing of several other people as well.*

TF: How did Chin first contact you?

RC: He was hunting for a site to do a study in Texas. I always joke that if you have hard enough problems, or ask long enough, you get referred to me, and that's what happened. I get a lot of calls that are, let's say, curious. They are always interesting, because they have a new problem or way of seeing that I had not considered before. But I was amused when he called. This guy Kirk Brown referred him to me. Kirk's an old friend in heavy metals, who knew that I had done work in this area but had to lay it aside because of Reagan administration policies. When Mel called, it revived a pleasant memory of that period back in the early 1980s when we started this work. I was wondering what an artist was going to be like. What does he really want? In our first conversation I told him that he had a good idea, but the specific approach he was thinking about was a dead end. I told him about some of the plants that are really hyperaccumulators rather than just tolerant cell cultures. I don't know if you understand that the first thing that he'd read about was actually a cell culture, a slurry of cells, and you aren't going to remediate a lot of soils with a slurry of cells. He didn't understand contaminated soils enough yet to understand how he could be as creative as he wanted to be in the art aspect of this science. And so we had a long talk; I sent him papers, and he started to learn more.

The first conversation was only an identification that we really did have an overlap of interest and that he had to learn some more. Now, the second and third conversations were the important ones. He showed his sincerity by actually reading the materials, showing that this wasn't just some little silly, momentary interest. He read and tried to understand and asked good questions. Then he started thinking about actually submitting a grant to the National Endowment for the Arts, and I helped develop his ideas so that he could be technically correct in what he was trying to do. I think the thing that worries a scientist in this kind of collaboration is that the artist won't understand the science and will embarrass the scientist. It's a legitimate concern. There is this matter of trust. It takes a while to work it out in any collaboration, between scientists, between artists. You have to believe the other guy is going to share responsibly and treat your information in a fair and valid way. Well, Mel showed me that. I showed him that if he was interested in doing this, it really was the kind of idea that deserved the break that his making it into art would give it. As he learned more and more about it, he

Mel Chin with Rufus Chaney, Revival Field, Pig's Eye Landfill, St. Paul, Minnesota, detail of thalaspi caerescens, a hyperaccumulating plant. Photograph courtesy of the Walker Art Center.

became increasingly convinced that it had the promise that he conceived himself.

The important outcome for me was to bring attention to the idea. We wanted to illustrate with art a possible solution that would help citizens. That's Mel's view of the world, and it's mine, too. If you met me you'd wonder. I put off some people because of my size and my flattop haircut. They worry, boy, this guy must be so straight. Instead, I'm a classic humanist trying to do good with a public career. So, Mel and I were soul brothers, as it were, and in many ways, we had the same idea of public service. Only he could do something that I wouldn't be able to do by myself.

TF: *Once you established this trust, after the first three or four calls, then you submitted the NEA grant?*

RC: *He did, and I just helped him with the science. It was his grant. I was not a co-principal investigator (to use the terminology from the science world).*

TF: So the grant proposal blew up into a public controversy.

RC: It was beautiful. The Reagan people just made it as easy as pie for us.

TF: How so?

RC: They did a stupid thing for political reasons that brought great attention to this idea. It got into newspapers across the country. There was an article in Science *magazine about this blowup at the NEA, which, incidentally, described the scientific idea of phytoremediation. That journal is international. It was much more successful as a communication of the idea than one could ever have hoped for. It spread the idea probably four years before I could have gotten similar attention for the success of the experiments that we've done. The idea stands alone after it's brought to your attention.*

TF: Had you and Mel already devised the experiment at the time of the controversy?

RC: We'd laid out the idea, and I'd gotten the seeds, and we started learning. I had a graduate student, Sally Brown. She was so enamored with the idea that she decided to do it for her master's degree. So she started learning how to grow the plants. When you start with a plant that nobody has ever really studied scientifically before and try to make it into a "technology," it's a hard job. Creating a technology from the roots up, that's a tough one. Well, I had a colleague in England who was also trying to follow up this idea: Alan Baker, the guy that collects germ plasm. So we were confirming each other's successes all during this early period. We were two cooperating but competing groups. Meanwhile, Mel and the art community went out and told their green friends, "Did you hear about this?" And then regulators started asking, well, how good is this?

Because of what all this raised, the Department of Energy sponsored an international work group to evaluate the idea for solving their contaminated soil problems. We met in August of 1994, and we prepared a report, which was published, that summarizes the promise and what experimental areas have to be explored to address different kinds of environmental problems. Just think about what it takes to get an idea mature enough that a ma-

Mel Chin with Rufus Chaney, Revival Field, 1991 harvest, Pig's Eye Landfill, St. Paul, Minnesota (with St. Paul skyline in background). Photograph courtesy Walker Art Center.

jor agency would fund a conference, bringing people from around the world to sit and argue for three days and come up with a written report. This is one of the steps in converting it from a good idea to the stage of "technology development," and that's where we are at now. We've had proof of concept from Revival Field, and complementary work. We've had review and extension of the idea. We have people doing DNA transfers on some of these ideas. But now we have to convert the idea into a day-to-day technology. And it takes time and money.

TF: And this is all moving forward? Are there other people working on this now?

RC: Yeah. You heard about the Missouri Conference? That was held last April [1995]. Nearly 300 people showed up. I think there were twenty or thirty countries represented. For anything to make that kind of progress from a standing start five years ago, when it was published in Science, *is remarkable!*

TF: What do you think about the art aspect of it? How do you see that?

RC: Mel and I have talked about the art aspect. I think he views it as an artist trying to communicate a promising idea to receptive audiences. The art needs to il-lustrate the range of the idea, but it needs to do it in a way that draws people's attention. The original Revival Field *was a bull's-eye form. It did what an art piece is supposed to do. It was beautiful just to look at, in its own way, especially if you like plants. Its form had beauty, but the idea was big-ger than the form. Although there is art that is only beauty, there is art that is conveying an idea in an infectious way, and this certainly had that power.*

TF: Do you have any complaints about the art community?

RC: Well, I went to a showing at a gallery in D.C. of Revival Field *and three or four of Mel's other pieces. He's done some very interesting work. But they don't give you a one-page summary of all the things that are in it. When you talk to him, you find out how incredibly complicated and beautiful the thinking is behind some of his art pieces. For example, he got a block of Jerusalem limestone, carved a shape of Israel out of it, had it attached to a center axle with a cord made of something from the Holy Land, and it was essentially dragged like a boat on a tether through plaster of paris to make several circles around, leaving a wake. There were subtleties within subtleties within subtleties. And I guess if you have access to the art community's record, you find a write-up about it in a magazine, or you talk to Mel. Then you say, "Oh, my God!" After seeing the show, I went home and prepared a one-page summary of* Revival Field, *just so that if somebody wanted to know what it was, they could actually find out. In a sense, that is my biggest complaint with the art: that so much is not shared unless you're an insider.*

TF: Do you see possibilities for artists and scientists to work together in the future, or do you think this was sort of a one-shot deal that happened to be the right scientist and the right artist at the right time?

RC: I think that the opportunity is always there. But it does take a collaboration be-tween people who are open-minded and who are creative. I think that Mel has been very effective at his end of this idea. I think he's very pleased that the circumstances allowed it to have such powerful effects so soon.

TF: *What is going on now with* Revival Field?

RC: *Well, Mel and I were talking about what would be the next thing we could do to help promote this idea. We felt that we needed to get* Revival Field *on a really hazardous soil. Palmerton, Pennsylvania, is a barren area with only a few volunteer weeds. It's an environmentally serious mess.*

TF: *This is a site that you knew about already?*

RC: *Yeah, I had been working there since 1979. I approached them and they said that they would replicate our idea according to what we thought ought to be done next. Right now we are testing different genotypes. We have genotypes from many countries around the world. We're trying to find bigger plants that we can find the genes in more easily, and so on. This is a truly hazardous site, where we would expect to be able to achieve full demonstration of the capability of the plants to decontaminate zinc and cadmium, because it is a zinc-cadmium contaminated site predominantly.*

And I am trying something new in the art piece that we are doing in Palmerton. I used it not just for the hyperaccumulator, phytoremediation idea, but also what I've called the in situ remediation. That's when you add something that changes the risk without actually removing the metals. Honestly, we don't have a plant that will strip lead out of a soil. I can strip out a bunch of metals, and I can clean up a lot of sites, but I can't strip the lead out of soil with phytoremediation yet. And lead is one of the big ones. Well, I had done work with sewage sludges, some of which were high in iron, and iron is very important in changing the way that soil binds metals. Sludges are also high in phosphorus, and this combination of high iron and high phosphorus can cause a precipitation and binding of lead that reduces the absorption by children or by animals that eat soil.

Palmerton, Pennsylvania, is a zinc smelter town, with some lead in the community as well, and nobody had been able to grow grass on their lawns for maybe fifty years! I mean, it's a nightmare. We had to help them grow

Mel Chin with Rufus Chaney, Revival Field II, 1994, Palmertown, Pennsylvania, reviewing growth of hyperaccumulator and metal tolerance species. Photograph courtesy of the Agriculture Research Service, USDA.

some grass. When you drag mud and dirt in the house, you worry about lead exposure from that. Grasses have a different mechanism of taking up iron than other species, and because of how they take up iron, they are more susceptible to zinc toxicity in alkaline soils. You make soils alkaline so the zinc is not taken up, but that makes the iron less available and the plant tries to get more iron but it gets more zinc and poisons itself. Bluegrass, in particular, dies. Our experiments had indicated at the laboratory level that if we used one of these high-iron-sludge composts, we ought to be able to establish ordinary grasses, or at least reasonably zinc-tolerant grasses that would thrive on the amended soil.

I added the sludge compost treatment rather than just limestone or sulfur that we used at the Revival Field *in St. Paul. And by using sludge compost that had limestone in it, we showed that if you use a high-iron compost biosolid, you can achieve thorough revegetation with lawn grasses in one treatment. This was particularly important for Palmerton. So I snuck one in on*

Mel! Palmerton is more than the Revival Field *the way that he saw it. Of course, the heart is still phytoremediation, because stripping the metals out, giving yourself a site equivalent to the uncontaminated site, is still a better goal than fixing it in place so that it's not an environmental hazard. But we have some urban areas where we need an immediate, one-shot fix.*

TF: *When do you think that it will be complete?*

RC: *Mel and I agree that* Revival Field *is not done until it has become a technology. Mel would say it's finished when the first full site has been decontaminated. When we have companies doing this commercially, it's going to be a great moment. We'll make sure Mel is there. He deserves it. It will be done when it's part of the normal way society solves problems. Wouldn't that be a re-markable, effective art project?*

Interview: **Frank Moore** *on the AIDS Ribbon*

Introduction

Beginning in the late 1980s, AIDS hit the world of the arts very hard. While political and social issues from the civil rights movement to the war in Vietnam had tremendous impact on artists of their time, AIDS was an *immediate* issue within the mainstream art world, as artists, curators, collectors, trustees, and their partners fell to the disease. For some people, grief, mourning, and anger became constant facts of life at that time. Attending AIDS memorial services every month created a relentless sense of urgency. Therefore, there was opposition from many in the "AIDS community" against spending scarce resources on anything aside from research and prevention, and art related to AIDS was often put to a very practical test: Will it help save lives?

Almost nothing is acceptable to everyone when it comes to AIDS and its representation. A well-organized, four-year effort in San Diego in the early 1990s failed to produce an AIDS memorial because of an unusual alliance of opposition from the right and the left. But a memorial does not need to be the sort of traditional public artwork that was envisioned in San Diego. As Americans are reminded each May, a memorial can also be a day. In this spirit, "Day Without Art" (started in 1989) was conceived by Visual AIDS, a group of artists and curators in New York, as a "day of mourning and call to action in response to the AIDS crisis." Although originally intended to be an art moratorium, this open-ended invitation to artists and arts institutions has resulted in a wide range of activities at thousands of sites, from closing museums to presenting special AIDS-related programs.

One of the more influential works created in response to the epidemic was by the New York City-based collective Group Material. It was *AIDS TIMELINE,* (1989). In the gallery context, the timeline took the from of a number of other Group Material projects: information and quotations interspersed with contemporary art that addressed the issue of AIDS in one way or another.

Group Material has a long history of finding unusual sites for their work, and they did so with the AIDS TIMELINE. For Day Without Art in December 1990, with the help of Visual AIDS (board member Tom Sokolowski and Director Patrick O'Connell, in particular), they published sections of the timeline in eleven art magazines in the United States and Canada, including *Afterimage, Art in America, Arts, Artforum, October, Parkett,* and *Shift.* At one level, this was the ultimate insider artworld site; to see the entire timeline, you needed to get all eleven magazines. On another level,

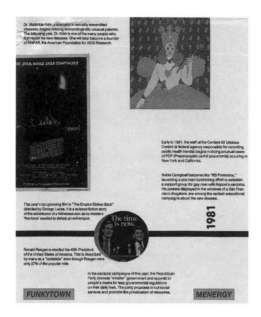

Dr. Mathilde Krim, a specialist in sexually transmitted diseases, begins noticing immunologically unusual patients. The following year, Dr. Krim is one of the many people who first report the new diseases. She will later become a founder of AmFAR, the American Foundation for AIDS Research.

THE STAR WARS SAGA CONTINUES

Early in 1981, the staff at the Centers for Disease Control (a federal agency responsible for recording public health trends) begins noticing unusual cases of PCP (Pneumocystis carinii pneumonia) occuring in New York and California.

Bobbi Campbell becomes the "KS Posterboy," launching a one-man fundraising effort to establish a support group for gay men with Kaposi's sarcoma. His posters displayed in the windows of a San Francisco drugstore, are among the earliest educational campaigns about the new disease.

This year's top grossing film is "The Empire Strikes Back" directed by George Lucas. It is a science fiction story of the adventure of a fatherless son as he masters 'the force' needed to defeat an evil empire.

The time is now.

1981

Ronald Reagan is elected the 40th President of the United States of America. This is described by many as a "landslide" even though Reagan wins only 27% of the popular vote.

In the electoral campaigns of this year, the Republican Party stresses "smaller" government and appeals to people's desire for less governmental regulations on their daily lives. The party proposes to cut social services and promote the privatization of resources.

FUNKYTOWN   MENERGY

Group Material, the AIDS TIMELINE as it appeared in
Arts magazine, December 1990, pp. 162–163.

though, it demonstrated how AIDS had rearranged the artworld. For a moment, all of these magazines put aside their differences to produce a collective project.

Aside from the AIDS Ribbon, perhaps the best-known AIDS related project is *The NAMES Project AIDS Memorial Quilt,* which started in San Francisco in 1987. A growing patchwork of tens of thousands of 3-foot by 6-foot panels, each piece is a memorial created to commemorate the death (and life) of a specific person, usually a family member, lover, or friend. A project open to anyone who wished to contribute, the *Quilt* is the result of creative effort by tens of thousands of people—artists and nonartists alike. Cleve Jones originated the Quilt when he heard that the death toll from AIDS in San Francisco had reached 1,000 people. With the silence that surrounded AIDS in some communities in 1985, Jones thought, "We could all die without anyone really knowing."[2] For an AIDS rally, Jones asked participants to create placards naming friends who had died. When he saw the results of this effort hung on the front of the federal building in San Francisco, it reminded him of a patchwork quilt his family had used to comfort people who were ill. Jones made the first panel of the *Quilt* in early 1987, and later that year invited forty other people to create panels for the Lesbian and Gay Freedom Day Parade, and by August there were

400 panels. Word spread, and national media attention followed. By 1988, there were 8,000 panels, 20,000 by 1992, 32,000 in 1995.[3] The enormity of the quilt gives scale to the AIDS crisis; viewing the *Quilt* is cathartic because it gives a human face to the numbers—both the numbers of those who have died and the numbers of those who are living and grieving. It is a memorial constructed through a mass effort by the grieving. In his essay on the *Quilt,* Peter Hawkins describes it thus:

The range of panel designs as well as the materials used in construction vary as widely as the makers' skill and sophistication. Shirts and ties, teddy bears, crushed beer cans, merit badges and credit cards, photographs and computer-generated images, leather and lamé, wedding rings, cremation ashes—anything goes. Unlike the paraphernalia of memory that mourners bring each day to the Vietnam Veterans Memorial, *and each day is taken away, the personal souvenirs incorporated in the quilt are not extraneous to its formal act of memory. They are intrinsic to it, "snapshots of the soul" that one touches up, censors, edits.*[4]

There has been some criticism of the *Quilt* that the makers of the panels have engaged in self-censorship—Where is the leather? —but Jones says that from the beginning, the notion was to create a memorial that would be widely acceptable. "We very deliberately adopted a symbol and a vocabulary that would not be threatening to nongay people . . . We mobilize heterosexuals; we mobilize the families that have been afflicted."[5]

The AIDS Ribbon is a memorial and reminder that functions as an opportunity for interaction. The ribbon was conceived by artist members of Visual AIDS during the Persian Gulf War, as described in the following interview with Frank Moore. At the time, yellow ribbons were everywhere, the constant reminder to "support our troops." By appropriating this tactic, the artists wished for an omnipresent symbol. The intent was to create a portable symbol that could be made from three cents' worth of ribbon. The ruby-encrusted models came out later as a fund-raising device for AIDS organizations (and opportunists).

The upper-right-hand corner of an envelope has long been a site for public art. In fact, postage stamps continue to fill the roles of traditional public art: commemorating heads of state, memorializing heroes and events, or simply decorating the envelope. On December 1, 1993, the United States Post Office announced that it would issue a red ribbon stamp, an announcement that met with the sort of controversy common to government-sponsored public art. The AIDS Coalition to Unleash

Power (ACT UP) staged a protest at the unveiling of the red ribbon stamp at New York City's General Post Office, chanting, "A stamp is not enough. A stamp is not a cure." Perhaps because of the political pressure, in months following the release of the stamp, the United States Post Office began to place advertisements in newspapers and magazines using the stamp to urge the public to seek HIV/AIDS information by calling the National AIDS Hotline. The Post Office's public relations budget was being used to educate the public on a health issue.

On November 30, 1997, the day before Day Without Art, the *New York Times's* Arts and Leisure section sported an AIDS Ribbon 15 inches tall, under the headline, "An Emblem of Crisis Made the World See the Body Anew."[6] Aaron Betsky, the author of the article, argued that the ribbon, along with other AIDS graphics, was instrumental in a reemergence of the body in art, and represented a Postmodern hybrid of art and advertising:

Few other emblems in our society are as succinct and as recognizable as the AIDS Ribbon. It has all the power of a good advertising gimmick and all the immediacy of a cry in the streets. Wrapped in a little curl attached to the body. It shows us how good artists and designers have become at honing a message and how versatile signs have become in our society. The ribbon is art as advertising and as political statement. [7]

Betsky's notion that the ribbon reflects Postmodern artistic practice—particularly the appropriation of advertising strategies—disregards the degree to which AIDS changed the art world. It is not so much that AIDS activist artists have felt free to appropriate advertising techniques. Rather, they feel obliged to convey their message by whatever means necessary. Attacks on the ribbon have not criticized its use of popular culture techniques as much as they have questioned its effectiveness in fighting AIDS.

In the following interview, Frank Moore discusses two aspects of his artistic practice: his painting as well as his AIDS activism, particularly his role in the initiation of the AIDS Ribbon. The specific authorship of the AIDS Ribbon has been somewhat debated among members of the Visual AIDS Artists' Caucus. It should be clear from this interview that Moore does not claim to be the sole originator of the ribbon. In the first press release from Visual AIDS in May 1991, announcing the launching of the ribbon at the Tony Awards, it says clearly that "the Artists' Caucus, a component of Visual AIDS, is the organizer of this grassroots project."[8]

In recent years, Moore's work has consistently addressed issues of environmentalism, homosexuality, and AIDS. His paintings have been well received in both
the museum and gallery context. He was included in the 1995 Whitney Biennial and
is represented by Sperone Westwater Gallery in New York. At the same time, Moore
has created activist/public art projects, including posters and broadsides for Visual
AIDS. The *New Yorker* described the paintings in an early 1990s show thus:

*Frank Moore's crisply drawn and color-saturated paintings, with their updated Adiron-
dack-style frames and various trompe-l'oeil effects, suggest the combined influences of
the Hudson River School and American artists like Harnett and Peto, and Europeans like
Magritte and Ernst, with perhaps Jared French thrown in for good measure. But his picto-
rial themes address contemporary ecological and biological crises with such relentless intensity as to seem truly millenarian.*[9]

While there might seem to be a split between his gallery/museum work and his activist art, the following interview reveals a sensibility that unites the two.
　　This interview was conducted at Frank Moore's Soho loft, where he lives and
works, June 1995.

*Tom Finkelpearl:　You have created work that is public or political in a number of different
　　　　　ways. It would be interesting to talk through the meaning of one of your paint-
　　　　　ings, and then compare it with some of the work you have done to raise public
　　　　　awareness about AIDS, particularly the red ribbon project that you were inti-
　　　　　mately involved in developing.*

Frank Moore:　Fine, although there is not necessarily such a neat distinction.

*TF:　Okay. How did you evolve into the artist that you are now? How did you get from the
　　　　more nature-oriented work you were doing in the early 1980s, to your current hy-
　　　　brid style with more overtly political content?*

*FM:　First of all, I am a child of the sixties. I was politically active then—marched on
　　　　Washington, blocked the streets in New Haven when Nixon bombed Cam-
　　　　bodia, joined Greenpeace when it first began. But I was trained as an abstract
　　　　painter. When I went to Yale, that was considered the direct lineage of mod-*

ern art. I tried, but I could not project myself into that lineage. It just didn't take (although I think you can still see some of those influences, particularly in my attention to the frames in my work). The problem was to find a voice as a painter that I could identify with, open enough to include all of these other languages and interests that I have. I think the painting I was trained to emulate was based on a single language—a single conceptual framework. But I was interested in Hudson River School painting, advertising, folk art, Surrealism, Mexican mural painting. It took ten or fifteen years out of school sorting through all of these things. There was a long hiatus in the middle, where I started to do theater and film work to earn a living: I'd work for three weeks, go on unemployment for two weeks, work for five weeks, go on unemployment for a week. I was working, but I had time to paint because of the unemployment. And the theater work itself was having an influence.

TF: This is getting to be the mid-1980s?

FM: Yes. And finally there was a nexus of circumstances. My lover and I found out that we were HIV positive in 1987. I had been tracking the AIDS story very attentively since 1979, when I first saw an article about Kaposi's Sarcoma (KS). I had a growing unease, and then anger about the situation. This began to branch off into research that I was doing into the history of gay and lesbian people. A major impact on me was John Boswell's book Christianity, Social Intolerance, and Homosexuality. It was the first time I had seen a persuasive history of homosexuality from before Christ to the thirteenth century. I could begin to see things in a historical framework.

Now, I had a long-standing concern about the environment. From the Adirondacks to Long Island, I had seen environments become degraded. Over the period of ten years, it seemed like everything died in the lake that I grew up near. And then there was this health care crisis, where I could see clear instances of social injustice everywhere. This was immediate because some of the cases involved friends of mine—not like just reading it in a newspaper. I began to connect it to traditions of homophobia.

And there were all sorts of instances where the environmental problems and the AIDS crisis began to overlap. One of the first instances in my work was a painting called Safe Fantasy. Robert and I had bought a little house up *in the country—which was a crazy thing to do because we were both HIV positive—and I began this garden. Immediately, I was up against problems with insects, and I began to use pesticides. The gypsy moth caterpillars were stripping trees bare. You can't simply stand there and pick them off. So I sprayed. At the same time I had begun taking prophylactic medications for HIV. I was putting these toxic chemicals into my body and toxic chemicals into my garden. I was having a lot of the same qualms about both of them, and I made a painting about that. And there were many other instances, like the widely published photographs of the New Jersey coastline, when all of this medical waste washed up on the shore.*

TF: *And, of course a lot of the hysteria related to medical waste centered on hypodermic needles that were thought to hold AIDS-infected blood.*

FM: *Yes. In the most literal sense it was a pollution problem. But, as an artist, you also think of the idea that the sea is the cradle of life, the bloodstream of the planet. Our blood is salty because we came out of the sea. Our inner environment, our inner ecosystem is a model for the world as a whole.*

The more that you study it, the more interconnections you begin to see. And finally you realize what John Muir said: that you can't pull anything out of its context in the universe. Everything is stitched onto everything else somehow. It is like pulling a thread out of a garment. By the time you finish pulling out the thread, the garment is in pieces on the floor, disintegrated. Certainly this is true with environmental issues and health care issues. As I saw these connections in my life, I began to put them in my paintings.

[There were several paintings in Moore's loft at the time of the interview, from his recent exhibition. I asked him to walk the viewer through Debutantes.*]*

FM: *The two boys are a friend of mine, Hilton Als, as a child, with my self-portrait as a young child as well. We are walking in this park. There are some private references that nobody could ever get, but they are there for personal reasons. For example, this Scotty, the dog that I am walking: my godmother, who was a dyke, always had a Scotty. The two boys are walking in this park. There are a series of monuments, three of which are on pedestals, which are shaped like pills. On these pedestals are photo reproductions, silkscreens. On the left is a rectal pear. In the other two cases, I used photo silkscreens of woodcuts that show judicial punishments used against passive homosexuals at various points in history, and in various points in the world—Turkey, Germany. All of these were taken from an Amnesty International catalogue about instruments of torture and death. The amazing thing to me was how many of the punishments in the publication were targeted against homosexuals. It was published a full ten years before Amnesty International recognized that people who are in prison because of their sexual orientation could be deemed prisoners of conscience. In every instance, you see that the punishment for a sodomite is to turn the site of sexual pleasure into the site of their death.*

On the upper left, there is a concrete block bunkhouse with an inquisition scene from the 1300s. It is the type of torture, described in Boswell's book, that a man named Jean de Molay underwent. Here he is being dropped onto this pyramid. You have the actual torturer who is raising and dropping him on the point. You have the scribe who is taking down all of the information. Someone here is offering him money, almost as if to bribe him into a confession. You have a priest presiding, and then there is the person asking the questions, the inquisitor.

This relates to another painting that I did called Clinical Trial. *In the early days of the epidemic—less so now because of the efforts of some doctors and ACT UP—there were cases where effective treatments were withheld for lengthy trials. A common ailment for people with HIV or AIDS is cytomegalovirus (CMV) retinitis. In the early days doctors discovered that Gancyclovir is a drug that could halt the progress of this disease and save people's eyesight. Well, the FDA demanded that they conduct a placebo-controlled, double-blind trial to prove that the drug works. One of my doctors, Dan Williams, was quoted on the front page of the* New York Times *saying something like, "Look, we can see the lesions on the person's eye. We give them Gancyclovir and the lesions go away. We take them off of the drug and they come back. We can do this any number of times, but this is not enough for the FDA. They insist that eighty people go blind so that they can satisfy their rules and regulations about testing. This is obscene." This was particularly*

Frank Moore, Debutantes, 1992, oil on canvas with wood attachments, 51" x 69".
Photograph courtesy of Sperone Westwater, New York, New York.

obscene to me because during this period I had a friend who went blind be-
cause Gancyclovir hadn't been approved.

So, I thought that the situation was like this scene of torture. You have
drug companies offering financial incentives. You have inquisitors—the doc-
tors responsible for running the trial. There are the people who are dealing
with the data. There are the nurses and technicians who are administering
placebos and watching the person go blind.

TF: The tragic irony of the "double-blind test."

FM: Yes, and then there are the ethics committees. It is so insane to me that you can
have these ethics committees presiding over a trial that allows people to go
blind when there is a drug that they know works. So every figure in the etch-
ing has a contemporary counterpart.

All of the flowers around the monuments and the bunkhouse are blooming, really pretty. One critic said they looked like Florine Stettheimer's work, which they do. But they all have different representations of the AIDS virus in the center. The enzymes, the genetic structure.

TF: Those are also photo silkscreens?

FM: Yes. From scientific textbooks. I silkscreen stuff to make sure people know I did not simply invent it. It is clearly coming from another source.

Above, there are two lesbian girls on a tricycle. On the fence in the background is the pink triangle, presented in the form it was in the Nazi concentration camps, pointing down. This is the limp form. There is the erect form, which was used for ACT UP's SILENCE = DEATH logo, with the triangle pointing up. There is barbed wire on the fence. You know, some people have thought that this is a park outside of a concentration camp.

TF: That's strange. It certainly seems to me that you are being kept in by the fence.

FM: Yeah, that was the intention originally. This park presents a social history of gay people. It is the kind of park where these kinds of flowers thrive. All of the details are peripheral to the core issue for me, which is the question of what a young child is taught. If you talk to gay people, many will say that they first became aware of the fact that they were gay when they were five years old. I, myself, was aware of that difference early on, and also became aware of a repressive response that I met whenever my difference became obvious, when people noticed it. The core question is, What do kids think, What goes through their minds? How does it affect them when they experience this? There is a homage to Paul Cadmus that you can see here.

TF: The erect penis visible in your shorts?

FM: Yes. One reason for the hard-on is that gay people have traditionally eroticized the oppressor. You go into gay bars, and you see cops, and you see leather men, Nazis. You see all of the personages that have oppressed or murdered gay people, turned into erotic icons. That is very real. It tells you that repression, the punishment of gay sex, is a part of the sexuality of the culture as a whole. The torturers are expressing their own sexuality in a destructive way.

TF: You're drawing on a bunch of realist traditions, but there is certainly an appeal. It's brightly colored . . .

FM: It's perky. Finally, there is a core element of hope. If you look at these children, they are not in bad shape. They are both very nicely dressed, out for a Sunday stroll. He's walking his dog. The critical thing is that they are being educated. There is a double meaning. On the one hand, you could think that this represents what gay kids went through, because that is me, right? You see all of the seeds of fear and self-loathing, the motivation for the double personality—the surface persona that many gay people develop to present to the world, that conceals their real desires and needs. You can see where all of this comes from. In the fifties and sixties, "faggot" was a common taunt on the playground. Or our parents would tell us to "act like a man and don't be a sissy."

But you can also look at the painting as being a statement about the present. For the first time, some kids are beginning to get an education about homophobia and gay people, about the kind of discrimination that they have faced. That is a very helpful thing. If they are educated, they are in a position to make a change.

TF: So, let's shift gears and talk about the ribbon project. Where did the idea originate?

FM: During the Gulf War in 1991, up in Deposit, New York, where I have this little house, there were all of these yellow ribbons. Mark Happel and I were talking about it. It was just insane. For example, there was this huge cube on top of a factory with its logo on it. They had this yellow ribbon tied around the cube that must have been seven feet wide. We kept looking at it and seeing in our mind's eye what it would be like if it were about AIDS rather than about this war. Mark told me that he would be willing to donate ribbon from his costume shop to make this happen.

Around that time, Alan Frame called me up and said that he thought Visual AIDS's Artists' Caucus should get together and talk about ideas for the

Day Without Art that was coming up. I said I had a couple of ideas that I wanted to propose. We set up a small meeting at P.S. 122 Gallery. One idea was to do a ribbon for AIDS, and the other one was to create a character for the Gay Pride March that would be the AIDS virus. That idea sort of fell by the wayside, but a lot of people grabbed onto the idea of the ribbon. We began thinking of ways to alter or modify the design. There were a whole slew of ideas about colors or texts to go with each ribbon to help people understand.

We made a little subcommittee that met two times and then brought the ideas back to the Artists' Caucus. Everybody got behind it, and we brought it to a general Visual AIDS meeting at the Clocktower Gallery, where we presented it to the group as a whole. A few individuals objected, but basically everyone approved. I remember that you said that you had such loathing for the yellow ribbon that you could not feel comfortable with this idea of an AIDS Ribbon.

TF: *That's right. I was definitely against it. The problem that I had at the time related to my problems with the yellow ribbon, of course. Anything that used that conceptual vocabulary, that type of communication, seemed oppressive. But the simplicity of it allowed for it to open up and expand. I did start to wear the ribbon, and began to understand what it could generate in terms of conversations, direct personal interactions, millions of them, all over the world.*

FM: **You know the strategy was not too different from that of the pink triangle [used in ACT UP's symbol]: taking the oppressive symbol and subverting it. In fact, my first idea for the ribbon was to use the yellow ribbon, but print text on it that would compare casualties in the war in Iraq with the war on AIDS, and compare the resources mobilized for each war.**

TF: *Using the yellow ribbon might have been confusing. But you used the same site for public expression that was created by the yellow ribbon. And, of course, the site, as reconfigured by the red ribbon, has now been employed for several other causes. So how did the ribbon get from a small meeting at the Clocktower with twenty people to international recognition?*

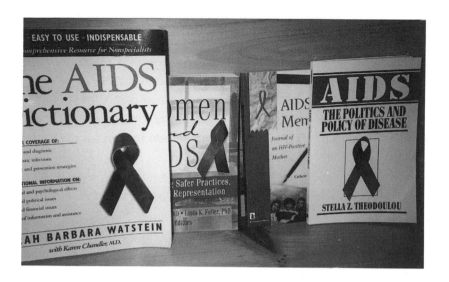

AIDS books featuring the ribbon.

FM: There is only one way for me to explain it: there was this vacuum waiting to be filled. It is like when you see how a wildfire starts in a dry Midwestern forest. It just took that spark and took off. It became quickly apparent that Visual AIDS could not direct this effort. We were spurring it on, but it had a life of its own. If we had not made the symbol, someone else would have. What interested me was that, unlike most other symbols or logos, it was quickly adopted by just about every major AIDS group: Broadway Cares, Funders Concerned About AIDS, American Foundation for AIDS Research, Gay Men's Health Crisis, the World Health Organization, Classical Action. This is because we made no attempt to retain proprietary rights or control over it. In the end, that was probably the most useful thing that we could have done. By leaving it in the public domain, it became more available, which led to the red ribbon postage stamp, and so on.

[At this point Moore brought out a cardboard box full of press clippings and mail order catalogues, a wide range of images of the ribbon.]

Here is the first press release that I wrote about the ribbon. Here is the Eiffel Tower with the ribbon in red lights. The French now have a ribbon postage stamp. These are statements made by the homeless women at the shelter who actually made the ribbon. This [photo on the front page of the San Francisco Chronicle] is from a San Francisco Giants game at Candlestick Park. All of these people are forming the ribbon with the Giants in the middle. Here is a picture of the Palazzo Vecchio, where they put a ribbon up above Michelangelo's David. It is amazing the freedom that people feel in relation to this symbol.

The first efforts were to distribute the ribbons on the street. But the first major manifestation was on the [nationally televised] 1991 Tony Awards, hosted by Julie Andrews, who did not wear a ribbon, and by Jeremy Irons, who wore a big ribbon. I would say that about a third of the people on the show wore the ribbon.

TF: And did they talk about the ribbon?

FM: No, they were told explicitly by the network that they could not say what the ribbon meant or say the word "AIDS."

TF: Ironically, I'll bet that helped. People watching the show on TV knew that there was something going on, but they were not sure just what it was. I remember that when I was wearing the ribbon on the street at that time, everybody had seen it, but many people did not know what it meant, and they'd ask. It had a mystique about it. You know, Madison Avenue could not design a campaign to make an image this famous.

FM: There was another important battle that occurred at the beginning. Initially, we fought the sale of the ribbon. In the long run that was really beneficial because in a lot of the early press they made a point that it was not being done to raise money, but specifically to enable people to show how they felt about this issue. It was a symbol of concern, not of a cash donation. This helped establish the credibility of the symbol. For example, we fought off an attempt by Conrans to create a whole boutique where there would be pens, and letter openers, and mugs, and everything with the ribbon on it. I also feel that some of the early items produced for sale were influenced by our efforts to prevent the commercialization of the ribbon. For example, 100 percent of the proceeds from the sale of the cups and the plates that Swid Powell produced went to the Design Industry Foundation for AIDS (DIFFA). People were not making money off of it then. But by now it is pretty much open. Many new red ribbon items are produced without any money going directly to AIDS causes.

TF: At Percent for Art, we were very proud of the diversity of the artists we work with. However, when we have really analyzed the process, we have found that the bulk of the money in our commissions goes to the fabricators—foundries, sand-blasters, stonecutters, etc.—and they all turn out to be white-male-owned businesses. So I am interested to hear how it came about that homeless women in the Park Avenue Shelter were hired by Visual AIDS to actually make the ribbon for distribution early on.

FM: For the first six to eight months of the project, when we got a request, the Artists' Caucus made the ribbon. We had ribbon bees all over the city, at different locations.

TF: I always thought that these ribbon bees were a great aspect of the project: a design so easy to fabricate that thousands of people all over the country participated.

FM: Sure, and we would give people instructions on how to do a bee. But it got to the point where the demand for the ribbon was outstripping our ability to produce them. Many institutions wanted to buy the ribbon and to give them away. We were burning out on it. I was friendly with Hope Sandrow, who was working on a long-term project in the shelter [the Artist and Homeless Collaborative]. It occurred to me that the ribbon could be made there, especially since so many women in the shelters are HIV positive. Hope was totally gung-ho. I was a bit apprehensive since I did not know how it would affect the women's benefits, whether it would be possible to run something like this in a shelter without running afoul of some bureaucratic rules. But the shelter was pretty loose. They didn't object as long as we did not ask for anything.

At any rate, I went to the shelter, explained the project to the women, and asked if people wanted to sign up, and the response was great. We went about trying to find a strong woman to run the project. The point was to set up an entrepreneurial effort run by the women themselves. It would be their business that they were running. It ran pretty smoothly, although there was a lot of turnover, and personal problems. Ultimately the manager changed to Jackie McLean, who is still running it, and it is completely independent now.

We were getting orders from museums, from other health and AIDS-related groups. In a couple of cases, the orders were too large, like 100,000 ribbons, which we could not handle. But we took orders for between 500 and 10,000 ribbons, at ten cents each. The material costs were around 3 cents per ribbon, and the rest went to the women for their labor. [See interview with Jackie McLean and Edith Wallace.]

TF: *The ribbon has certainly become mainstream. This is anathema to many people in the art world and the activist community. But the question is, who are you speaking to? In a way, that is the essential question of public art. The ribbon is able to speak across a lot of different lines. Certainly AIDS crosses a lot of different lines of class, race, gender. The ribbon was able to reach across the lines that everyone said they wanted to reach across. The ACT UP symbol has great power, but it is most powerful within the gay community. Its meaning could be translated, "If we, the members of the gay community remain silent, we will die." The pink triangle makes it a community-specific symbol.*

FM: *Exactly. And we were really conscious of that. We were trying to identify a broad constituency that would support the sort of action that we felt was necessary in terms of research, education, treatment. We had the idea that there were many people across the country who were ready to express concern, but they did not have the right vehicle. We saw that many people were coming from a point of view of concern and compassion rather than rage or anger at the government. So we wanted to enable those people to stand up and be identified. I feel that the activist community wrote off that constituency early on. They got so polarized, so paranoid, so bitter about society at large that they were actually repelling people who were prepared to support action con-*

cerning AIDS. I have watched the genesis of the AIDS crisis in France and Italy, and I feel that the ribbon has been a helpful vehicle in opening up discussion about AIDS there as well.

TF: Having discussed the ribbon and a painting, perhaps we could compare the two. It seems that, to some extent, you are trying to do similar things with both: to raise awareness, to promote tolerance. But you are expressing yourself in totally different languages. One is a language of allegory, the other is a public icon. So, is it possible for you to compare them, or are they simply apples and oranges?

FM: Well, there is a time differential. The ribbon is meant to be seen in a second. A poster is meant to take a bit longer. Someone might put it up in their office for a couple of months, so it can afford to be a little more complex. Paintings have a much longer time curve. Sometimes they don't even "happen" until a couple of centuries after they were painted, like Vermeer.

But it is not such a simple division. For example, I designed a poster for Day Without Art, and images from the poster ended up in my paintings, and

The United States Post Office AIDS Awareness Stamp, 1993.

The AIDS Ribbon on the Eiffel Tower, Paris, France.

I have used the ribbon in paintings as well. I see these various things on a graded scale. To have an immediate impact we have to strip away ambiguity. It is interesting to me to see that the ribbon has a different kind of ambiguity than the painting does. In a painting, I often create deliberate ambiguity, deliberate paradoxes, deliberate mysteries. These are all things to promote thought and reflection. There is also the ambition that, as culturally specific as this picture is, that one hundred years from now, when the social landscape is transformed, and this moment does not have immediate relevance to the life people are living, that there will still be enough substance in the painting on other levels to retain interest.

TF: *Whereas it is absurd to think of someone wearing a ribbon one hundred years after the AIDS crisis is over.*

FM: *Precisely.*

TF: But I would argue that it would be great, a hundred years from now, to hang a red ribbon next to Debutantes *in a museum, to talk about your creativity, the environment within which you painted, and this cultural moment.*

FM: I sort of agree with you. I feel that the objections that people have to museums are based upon curatorial timidity rather than to the works of art themselves, or their supposed lack of relevance. Earlier I mentioned the notion of the thread that holds together the fabric. Well, artworks can be like the stitching in our cultural fabric. If you look at a painting by Nicholas Poussin, he is depicting a classical scene that happened a couple of thousand years earlier, and now we are looking at that depiction a couple of centuries later. Or, look at the woodcut in Debutantes *from 1300; that is in a picture that is talking about the 1990s. All of these historic moments are woven together. Each reference is like a stitch that is connecting events and images across time. That is what makes a fabric.*

Notes

1. *Art in America,* December 1990, pp. 162–163.

2. Quoted in Peter S. Hawkins, "Naming Names," in Reesa Greenberg, Bruce Ferguson, and Sandy Nairne, editors, *Thinking About Exhibitions* (London and New York: Routledge, 1996), p. 135.

3. Ibid., p. 136.

4. Ibid., p. 140.

5. Ibid., p. 148.

6. Aaron Betsky, "An Emblem of Crisis Made the World see the Body Anew." *New York Times,* November 30, 1997, Section 2, Arts and Leisure, p. 1.

7. Ibid.

8. Press release written by Patrick O'Connell, released by Visual Aids for the Arts, New York, New York, May 30, 1991.

9. "Taking a Hard Look," *New Yorker.*

Interview: **Jackie McLean** *on Making the AIDS Ribbon at the Artist and Homeless Collaborative*

Introduction

This interview was conducted in September 1995 with Jackie McLean and her partner, Edith Wallace (known as "Peaches"), at the Visual AIDS offices. As the official manufacturers of the AIDS Ribbon, they had come to pick up supplies for an order received by Visual AIDS. They were getting ready to bring spools of red ribbon and boxes of safety pins to their apartment in the Bronx, make them into AIDS Ribbons, and deliver them to the organization that had placed the order. On a very basic level, this work by Wallace and McLean took place at the intersection of two public art projects: the AIDS Ribbon and the Artist and Homeless Collaborative, a dialogue-based project very much in the spirit of those discussed in part 2 of this book.

When Frank Moore and Visual AIDS decided to seek an alternative for the fabrication of the ribbon (they had been using a novelty concern in Queens), they turned to the A & HC. All involved thought that it might be a modest source of income for the women and that the shelter, with the high incidence of AIDS among homeless people, was a perfect setting for the creation of the AIDS awareness symbol. After women in the shelter had been involved in making the ribbon for some time, it was determined that one should lead the group, and McLean was hired to direct the effort.

Hope Sandrow, a photographer and activist based in New York City, founded the Artist and Homeless Collaborative (A & HC).[1] After working at the Catherine Street Family Shelter in 1987–1988, Sandrow moved her efforts to the Park Avenue Shelter for Homeless Women in 1989, and formalized A & HC in 1990. The Park Avenue Shelter, which housed women from forty-five to eighty years old, was the site of intense juxtapositions of wealth and poverty. Situated in the center of Manhattan's affluent Upper East Side, the shelter was located in an armory that also houses a tennis club, and periodically hosts high-end antiques shows. While the women staying in the shelter entered through the less-than-glamorous rear door, the sense of the surroundings was strong and ever-present.

Almost without exception, the projects at A & HC were collaborative and interactive in nature. They ran the gamut from posters, to installations, to life-drawing sessions, to sculptural self-portraiture, to lectures and discussions. Artists who created projects in collaboration with the women at the shelter included Kiki Smith, Robert Kushner, Ida Applebroog, the Guerilla Girls, Whitfield Lovell, Judith Shea, Pepón Osorio, and many more. The A & HC expanded to encompass projects with residents at the Sixty-ninth Regiment Armory on Twenty-fifth Street (home of the famous Armory Show in 1913), as well as the Regent Family Residence, a facility that housed homeless children. The children's program spawned a relationship with the Whitney Museum of American Art's Education Department that is still in operation at the time of this writing (fall 1998).

Sandrow said that A & HC was "the culmination of what I learned as a volunteer creating art projects with the homeless for two years and my focus on creating art inspired by personal experience. The A & HC is a public art project where the concepts and concerns for social issues are translated by artists into activism that gains shelter residents experiences and skills to redefine their lives by cultivating self expression. The relevancy of art to life is exhibited in collaborative art works where the homeless are co-authors of their representation, while the artists' experiences of art making from 'within' and 'with' the public alters perceptions drawn by myths and fears."[2]

The A & HC came to an end in 1995. There was a complex set of reasons for the demise of the A & HC, including the relocation of most of the women from the Park Avenue Shelter (fought by Sandrow and many of the women), the closing of the recreation room in the Sixty-ninth Regiment Armory (fought by Sandrow and the residents of the shelter), scuttled plans for the city to take over operations of the A & HC, and difficult problems in the organization itself. Sandrow ended the project exhausted and dispirited, although she has kept her nonprofit corporation intact. Three years later, she feels she is almost ready to reenter the field of activist art, although she feels that one must enter such a project "with total and unbridled enthusiasm." Despite her intense disappointment in the dissolution of the A & HC, Sandrow takes pleasure in some of the ongoing benefits of the program. For example, the Whitney Museum still conducts workshops with the Regent Family residence, and a young women from the shelter still works on these projects. It was gratifying for Sandrow when several of the women from the collaborative showed up at the opening of her fall 1998 exhibition at the Whitney/Philip Morris and told her that they are still making art. Also, some time after Sandrow and the A & HC left the Park Avenue Shelter, it was privatized. Administration of the facility was turned over to a neighborhood group that has made vast improvements in the quality of care, including psychological counseling for the women. Sandrow says, "They do not really need me there now since the conditions are so good."[3] Sandrow worked in the shelters for seven years.

Her long-term commitment to the program was rewarding and enriching for her as well as for her collaborators, but it left her somewhat disillusioned—a realistic assessment of many such projects.

Jackie McLean declined to provide biographical information outside of what is discussed in this interview.

Tom Finkelpearl: Can you tell me how you first heard about the ribbon project, and how you got involved?

Jackie McLean: When I went to live at the Women's Shelter on Park Avenue, I was very depressed about just being there. I had never been in a position like that before. It happened that I knew a few people who was in there, people that I had seen for years, and then I met them in the shelter. I came downstairs one day on a Monday night, and I noticed that Hope [Sandrow] and everybody was doing arts and crafts and everything. I was just looking to see what was going on, and it so happened that somebody who was involved with the ribbon project had left, and my friend Tony said, "Well Jackie is here, maybe she could do it." I thought that I'd try it, and that is how I got involved. This was in 1992.

TF: Peaches, when did you get involved?

Edith Wallace: When I got to the shelter, I met Jackie, and she invited me to do it. We had nothing to do all day. I did not like to stay in there. As soon as I'd wake up, I would get out of there. After we hooked up, I enjoyed doing it.

TF: Were you making ribbons in large quantity at the shelter?

JM: Yes, there were six women working on the ribbon at that time. Some of them were mess-ups, just doing it to make a dollar or whatever, but their hearts weren't really in it. Gradually, I do not know exactly how it happened, I got promoted, more or less, to manager. I brought the number of women working down a little bit to make it manageable. We had a lot of work, but we did not need that many people, and there was a lot of bickering in the group.

Woman wearing several AIDS ribbons, 1996.

Women wanted to do what they wanted to do, when they wanted to do it. But if we wanted to have something serious going, we just couldn't do it like that. I felt that it was good of Hope, Patrick [O'Connell, the director of Visual AIDS], and them to give us the work, because they could have gone anywhere. I had decided that this was something I really wanted to do. You have to realize that while we were there in the shelter, we were only getting $22.50 every two weeks. We was provided meals and a bed, but that money was for everything else—coffee, cigarettes—and I was on a low-salt diet, so I couldn't eat the meals that they gave us. I don't know what I would have done without the extra money. So the ribbon was a way of income, but also the feeling that you were doing something that was right. I was trying to keep it organized so that we wouldn't lose it. I got it down to four women, though it was sometimes three because maybe somebody had to go to the hospital or whatever.

TF: How did you feel when you saw the ribbons out in public or on TV?

JM: That was *great*. It was a good feeling. I remember one time when Patrick called us up at the shelter and said, "You see your ribbons?" It was broadcast from California, the Academy Awards.

TF: Something like a billion people watched that.

JM: Yeah, and right after that it seemed like everybody else was coming in on the ribbon. They started making it mechanically, and it wasn't the same. Of course they could produce more than we could, but it seemed artificial. It's harder now. But it's like everything else: when the competition comes in, the mom-and-pop stores go out (laughs).

TF: Your ribbons are handmade.

JM: Yeah, and the people that's doin' are doin' it because they knew people who died from AIDS—especially us. There was friends of ours that had died—people we knew from childhood, coming up. I remember the first time I heard about AIDS. I saw a friend of mine with her husband, but she was walking so slow. She looked terrible, but this was before we knew about AIDS, the seventies. A month earlier, she looked healthy—she'd lost a little weight, but it wasn't nothing to really comment on. Two days later, I heard she was dead. It struck so fast.

TF: Did the ribbon help the women learn about AIDS?

JM: Yes. Well, for some it was purely monetary, but even that's okay as long as once they are doing it, they start to feel something. I can't blame anybody for wanting to make a dollar, but it is even better if they really get involved.

TF: I found, especially in the early years, that the ribbon got people on the streets and on the subway talking.

JM: Yeah. I have found that people are afraid to ask questions among their peers because people would think that they had AIDS. They would keep quiet. The ribbon got people asking questions.

TF: Was there a lot of AIDS in the shelter?

EW: Not really. This was a shelter for older women, so there wasn't that much.

JM: We had a few cases, but it wasn't so much AIDS as it was HIV positive, I think. In the shelter system as a whole, there were a lot of cases, though.

TF: You are out of the shelter now. For how long?

Both together: Two years (with sighs of relief).

TF: And you have moved the ribbon-making operation to your house?

JM: Yeah, and we are living in the Bronx.

TF: You know, in my job, I am all over the city, in all the boroughs. I have noticed that the ribbon does not show up nearly as much outside of Manhattan.

JM: Yes, yes. And you know it is more downtown Manhattan than it is uptown in Harlem. You know we have tried to get it started up in the Bronx with the churches and all. But it is hard.

TF: Why do you think that is so?

JM: I think it is because for people from our background, these things are just natural for them. They have been through so many things that it is just another thing coming. It is not like a surprise. I don't know if you understand what I am trying to say. They don't feel no difference about this than they do about cancer, or TB, guns on the streets. They feel that this is just another thing coming in: "So what?"

TF: While for some people downtown this could be the first great disaster in their life.

JM: Yeah, it could be. Up there they have had plenty of disasters. But it is a shame. It shouldn't be like that. That's why I'm always talking. I was surprised to see that there are a lot of people who are interested, but they just go along with the program. This is the same thing that I say about voting. It is the same thing for us. They'll say, "What's the sense in voting anyway?" What do you mean what's the sense? It is your God-given right. Use it. You've got to start speaking out more. But I can't stop speaking out or I'll be just like everyone else.

TF: *So how do you think that the ribbon affected your life?*

JM: *It gave us something to really think about. And it made us want to learn more about AIDS itself. A lot of people are still ignorant. I was just reading in the paper today about the Masons. They promised these kids with AIDS a summer camp for two weeks after the regular camp let out. These were kids that had never been to camp or nothing. The kids' parents had bought them new clothes and they were tagging them up, getting ready to go, and the Masons pulled the whole project because they were afraid that their regular campers wouldn't come back in the following years, knowing that people with AIDS had been there, okay? I just can not understand that. It is not fair to anybody. That is ignorant. Very ignorant.*

Notes

1. For a good discussion of the Artist and Homeless Collaborative, read, "Making Art, Reclaiming Lives: The Artist and Homeless Collaborative" in *But is it Art?: The Spirit of Art as Activism,* ed. Nina Felshin (Seattle: Bay Press, 1995), pp. 251–282.

2. From an unpublished text on the project by Hope Sandrow.

3. Quotations are from discussions with Sandrow, November 1998.

Index